SYSTEMATIC POLITICS

Charles E. Merriam

UNIVERSITY OF CHICAGO PRESS · CHICAGO

SYSTEMATIC
POLITICS

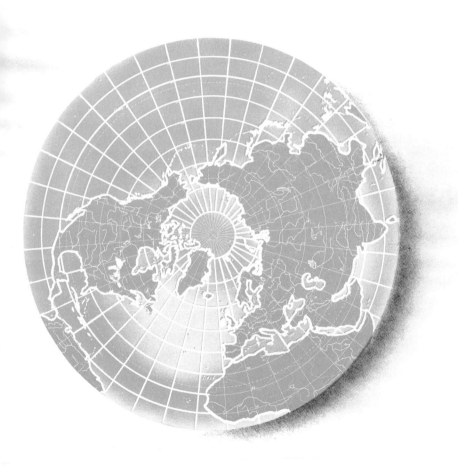

THE UNIVERSITY OF CHICAGO PRESS, CHICAGO & LONDON
The University of Toronto Press, Toronto 5, Canada

PREFACE

OVER long periods of time mankind has been moving forward in the work of constructing a stupendous and complicated organization which makes it possible for human beings to live and work together. With the emergence of the human personality on the higher levels of life, the task became far more complex and difficult than before. The earlier primitive order had to be replaced by associations of a different and higher type in which human reason, human emotions, and human will are fused in new patterns of action, in institutional and philosophical inventions and conventions.

A continuing and fundamental problem of human association is the integration of the human personality, on the one hand, and his relationship to the group of which he is a part, on the other. The struggling personality is torn between the need to trust and the need to distrust his fellows, between the logical demands of his own private world and the logical demands of the public world about him. Very slowly, indeed, we observe men emerging from the dominance of custom and force, to intermingled types of explanation, interpretation, rationalization, and justification of the world in which they live. In the end, authority to act must combine both right and might, while liberty must unite personal and social responsibility.

Government (I use the word interchangeably with "politics," upgrading the latter term with its lower implications in many quarters) is a special form of association, but there is much private government alongside of public government. The line between them is not so sharp as is generally supposed. There are many rule-making agencies in social affairs; there are many types of subordination, superordination, and co-ordination; there are many types of leadership, of consent and assent of the governed. There are many forms of adjudication, of common counsel, of management; many problems of liberty and authority, of morale and discipline, of adaptation, adjustment, and co-operation, outside of government. The family, the church, the union, the corporation, the profession, the cultural society—these all have their special forms of governance, not by any means entirely unlike the governmental.

Unless, indeed, the practices of government were closely akin to the practices of the social group in which they are found, successful political action would be impossible. The basic fact is not that government is entirely different from other forms of association but that it is so much like them. Government is set in a series of associations, all concerned with the development of the human personality in the frame of reference of the group—economic, cultural, familial,

v

political. Government may be the archetype of co-operation and control, but it does not stand alone.

The needs which government can satisfy are only a cross-section of the larger body of needs which are satisfied in social living on a broader scale. All governments are set in social patterns and cultural patterns, in which the aspirations and interests of men are expressed and developed. Knowledge of the functions of association in general and the special conditions in which a particular government is placed is essential to a clear understanding of the political process. The family, the church, the occupational groupings, the social groupings—all condition closely the nature and forms of governmental activity and in turn are influenced by the governmental. To the consideration of these reciprocal impacts and influences attention will be directed later.

The proposition that the distinctive characteristics of a government (the word "state" is usually employed at this stage) are a fixed territory and a legal monopoly of violence has value, if it is not pushed too far as indicia of government. But there have been nomadic states and many states with very flexible boundaries. If there were a world state and no threat of violence from any external group, there would still be government.

A sounder line of distinction between public and private is found in the consideration of the typical ends of government, including security, order, justice, welfare, freedom; of the tools of government, including custom, violence, symbolism, persuasion, strategy; of the special problems and services with which government is concerned; of the special skills, forms, and organs of government, such as headship, adjudication, management, and counseling as they have developed historically and now appear. Fixed territorial basis and monopoly of legality may be added as a further means of identification. These ends, tools, problems, skills, and organs overlap those of other associations; but, when the whole pattern is considered, the special nature of the government appears, as distinguished from social control in more generalized form. If we examine the specific contribution of the family, for example, or the church, or the economic organization, or the cultural, or the professional, it then appears that, while there is much interchangeability of function, the specific role of each component element may be established.

In simplest form the task of government is the satisfaction of a broad range of human needs. What are the needs from which government arises? This is a basic question at the threshold of the political. The problem of human needs goes down to the roots of human nature and up again to the heights of the physical, the intellectual, the spiritual character of man. What it is that man wants or needs, consciously or otherwise, has long been a subject of profound speculation, which probes the problem from every possible point of view; and the quest is still on. Discussion of the wishes, drives, dynamisms, ideals, destiny, and values of men has led to minute and searching analysis by many competent inquirers, although without complete agreement in classification or priorities.

I am not undertaking an inquiry into the nature of nature, the nature of human nature or of the supernatural. I am not solving the meaning of man in the universe, nor am I assuming that life has no meaning. Government deals with the traits, aptitudes, characteristics, and values of men in various stages and forms of culture and with the development of the human personality in the framework of the commonweal. I am focusing upon a linked series characterized as political and identified in the manner above described. I am assuming the indefinite perfectibility of men. I am assuming the validity of continuing creative evolution of mankind in the direction of higher levels of the physical, intellectual, and spiritual.

Broadly speaking, the special needs of men which government satisfies or helps to satisfy are (1) external security, (2) internal order, (3) justice, (4) welfare, and (5) freedom in varying forms and proportions, interpreted, justified, and elaborated in a variety of ways, in different times and places.

These ends we may establish by observation, experience, and reflection from which the type forms of governmental action emerge. This type is not merely an average of observations ranging from Nero to Roosevelt, but a consensus of judgment, indicating what the type government tends to become. He would be a poor observer who did not perceive many forms of political associations in which the above were not the ends in view. Injustice, disorder, private welfare, slavery, and insecurity have appeared again and again in human affairs. But to characterize any or all of these as the real ends of government would indicate a view of human political relationships meeting with disavowal even by those who perverted the true ends of government. Few will repudiate the desire to serve the common good, to promote the security and welfare of the group, to establish order and justice as they see them, to provide liberty for those who could utilize it. Governments, like human beings, may be sick, or mad, or vicious, but these qualities are not set down as characteristics of mankind in comparison with other animals. The ends of government are those which are identified with its operation in its developed and developing estate, as in the case of other species; and these are the characteristic aspects and action of the political society in its typical form.

A long-time student of political power, I repudiate the conclusion that government is merely a struggle for power or a means of exploitation of the weak by the strong. It is not realistic or naturalistic, while observing the many personal and group battles for the power, to lose sight of the main end of the whole process, namely, the progressive development of associations in which human personalities may best live together. The pangs of birth and the agonies of battle have another meaning than that of an action pattern alone. Birth has a definite function; wars have significance other than mere physical killing and destruction; struggles for power lead to other than personal glory. At this point some observers of government have lost the way, forgetting human evolution in the noise and tumult of its advancing phases. The origin of species may be grim and dirty and bloody. The dinosaurs devoured each other, it is true, but all this need not obscure the fact of origins, or the later facts leading to other and higher types of life. The characteristic of the struggle for survival is not alone the struggle as such but the survival and the evolution of survivors to loftier forms of human life.

This study is an analysis of the experience, observation, and reflection of men on the problems of politics, filtered through my own experience, observation, and reflection. Obviously such a study is subject to many corrections for lack of comprehensiveness and for inaccuracy and error in interpretation and conclusion. Access to and analysis of all the data of political reflection and behavior in all times and places would be an enormous task, and I have done no more than sample here and there. Institutions are action patterns reaching into psychology, biology, sociology, philosophy, ethics, anthropology, economics, geography, science, and technology, always in terms of reason, reflection, experiment. The underlying processes and relations are more significant than the specific formal institutions themselves and reveal more intimately the inner nature of the political. Types of personality, social and economic forces and groupings, cultural patterns of many lands, scientific changes, modes of reflection, moral and religious ideals, are the material of political action.

I propose to analyze political behavior in the light of the factors that surround institutional forms, ideologies, political patterns, or clusters of patterns in particular political societies. I shall use both the naturalistic and the rationalistic approach. Far from being incompatible, they are inseparable in the understanding of politics.

I shall show how far we have come governmentally and how we might advance farther in the light of what we now know. Politics, if it does not reach precision, is at least useful in the task of relating known precisions. This is one of the most important tasks that confront mankind. Weal and woe lie in these relations more than in any other complex of human affairs. Information, sophistication, and understanding in political relations are the basis of political behavior and mark the level on which political life rests, with all the immense social responsibilities it carries. Our chief problem is how to utilize most effectively the data we collect, the analyses we formulate, the conclusions we draw, the forecasts we make from stage to stage of historical development, to the end that we may insure the progressive use of intelligence in political decisions and political action and the continuing advance toward a fuller meaning of life, liberty, and the pursuit of happiness. This is, indeed, the task of civilization itself, but it is in important part the special task of the political thinkers and practitioners.

Both the microscope and the telescope are useful instruments, but they are not to be used without regard to generalizations drawn from observation, experiment, and reflection. Nor need politics ignore any of the hierarchy of human values in the pursuit of its appointed ends or fail in rating the hierarchies and the scale of values. History, logic, experiment, insight, intuition, invention—none of these is foreign to the search for truth in the study of government. There is no one royal road to political wisdom, to be followed implicitly and exclusively. In a world of political phenomena there is broad room for hypothesis and testing, for experimenting in recurring situations, for philosophical analysis, and for their combination with insight and understanding. The cumulative values of observation, experience, and reason are seen in the growth of governmental systems and values.

To the question of whether men are rational or emotional, we may readily answer that they are both in part and at times, as proved both by St. Paul and by Dr. Dewey. The rational control of man and his aspirations for betterment and elevation are not refuted by the astonishing (to some) discovery that a part of man's nature is emotional and animal. The struggle for civilization is the battle for the better ordering of factors in humanity, with the continuing but not unbroken victory of the higher side of man's nature over the lower. Government is only a phase of this continuing battle for advancement.

A type of study of government might be based upon an observation and analysis of current manipulations of various sorts, but a deeper study requires attention to the evolutionary quality of political effort and achievement, of rise from lower to higher forms, both material and other. It may be assumed or concluded that such a struggle is fatalistic and blind, emerging and returning to a vast void, and hence interpreted in terms of determinisms and fatalism of various sorts, materialistic, historical, economic, psychophysical, or other.

But another and sounder assumption and conclusion is that the whole life-process is one of creative evolution in which the type and values of the species continually rise in the scale. Governmental processes are not merely wormlike squirmings, in which men are enslimed without gains or goals, but are parts of the process of transition from darkness to light, from slavery to freedom, from drift to mastery.

Many ancient ways of life have been shattered by the new forces of democracy and science, challenging as they do the evils of past and present at many points. The dignity of man and the consent of the governed hold no terrors for the scientific study of government, with its indifference to privilege, its trend away from the thralldom of force, fear, and want. The finest reasoning and the most decisive experiments point in the direction of the goals which humanity hopes to attain.

It was a long step forward from politics as custom, symbolism, violence, and superstition, interpreted somewhat by wise sayings, maxims, and proverbs, to the formulation of abstractions, of theories of government, however crude or however obviously the rationalizations of power.

It is a still longer step from politics as abstract speculation or intuition to systematic investigation of political intelligence in the context of the total physical, economic, and social scene. It has proved almost equally difficult to escape from the formal, legal, structural approach to the intimate study of the political process, dealing with interest groups and power relations, with skills and understandings, forms of communication, and personalities as revealed by modern penetrating understanding—all this shot through and through with the struggle for the realization of human ideals and aspirations.

This volume develops a systematization of the methods and materials of politics—a stage in integration. Old material and new material are brought together under new classifications and lines of arrangement. This has been done before in the history of political science, but from time to time it must be done again in the light of new materials and methods. Much of this material I have developed more fully elsewhere in other writings, individual and with others.[1]

In recent years the social sciences have made available great masses of data in psychology, anthropology, economics, sociology, history, jurisprudence, and psychology, while the natural sciences have made contributions of far-reaching significance, notably in the closely related fields of biology, geography, and the basic data regarding land and people. In order to compass this area, I have been obliged to deal with wide ranges of material in these areas, using the best analyses available. These studies have a meaning all their own, but they also have indispensable meaning for government and cannot be omitted from an adequate appraisal and analysis of political problems. An integrated study of government cannot exclude consideration of their contributions to the common life of man, however imperfect the synthesis may be at a given time.

The approach of the study of government is not confined artificially either to science or to reason. For my part I have learned something in the precinct, something in philosophy, and something in the effort to synthesize the earthy knowledge of the field with the stratospheric understanding from above.

My father was postmaster in a country town in Iowa. I went to New York

[1] See my *New Aspects of Politics* (2d ed., 1931); *Political Power: Its Composition and Incidence* (1934), chap. x; *Prologue to Politics* (1939), esp. Appendix; and *The New Democracy and the New Despotism* (1939).

and studied Tammany Hall. For some years following that I served in the city council of Chicago and was adviser to several mayors. I was a Bull Mooser with Theodore Roosevelt. Presidents Taft and Wilson offered me positions which I declined because of my preoccupation with Chicago governmental affairs. During the first World War I was in charge of American propaganda in Italy. I was a member of President Hoover's Committee on Recent Social Trends (1929-32); of the Public Service Personnel Commission (1935); of the Commission on the Social Studies (1932-35); of President Roosevelt's National Resources Planning Board (1933-43) and of his Committee on Administrative Management (1935-37). I was associated with the beginnings and developments of the Chicago Bureau of Municipal Research, the American Political Science Association, the Social Science Research Council, the Public Administration Clearing House, and the agencies of public administration centering at 1313 East Sixtieth Street, Chicago.

With wide-open-eyed wonder I sat at the feet of Gamaliel studying politics, economics, sociology, and jurisprudence in the accepted schools of Iowa, Columbia, Berlin, and Paris, emerging with my credentials in the form of *The History of the Theory of Sovereignty* in 1900. My education was continued by my colleagues in Chicago, Washington, and New York on down to the present day and in many wanderings overseas. I cannot forget my natural science brother, John C. Merriam. I was never out of debt to him.

It would doubtless be unorthodox to say that I learned more from men than from books—and perhaps not true. But it is true that I have had numerous opportunities during a long period of time to interrelate practical and theoretical knowledge of government.

My study falls under several main heads. It begins with the foundations of politics, including the developing social and material bases. The ends or purposes of government then follow and the typical governmental problems and services. Then comes the consideration of the tools and skills of politics, both in general form and in specific enumeration. After this comes a discussion of the organs of government, dealing with the general theory of organization, with headship, with conciliar organs, organs of adjudication, and organs of management. Informal government is next considered, including here custom, revolution, public opinion, suffrage, elections, and parties. Next I consider politics with reference to stability, on the one hand, and change, on the other, dealing with conservatism and radicalism, with invention and change, and with the relationship of government to scientific advance. Then follows an examination of the types of the interrelationship between political societies leading us to the emerging jural order of the world. From there I turn to a consideration of the historic trends of politics, following the categories already set up. And, finally, I deal with what the future of government might be—the next stages in the evolution of political society.

I am deeply indebted to more of my colleagues than I can count during the long time this work has been in progress. Without their scholarly co-operation and encouragement in faltering moments it would not have been possible to carry through this undertaking; but I hasten to absolve them from any of my errors of omission or commission—or of professional heresy either.

I am under obligation to the McGraw-Hill Book Company for their generous permission to reproduce various materials from *Political Power* (1934) and from *The New Democracy and the New Despotism* (1939).

CHARLES E. MERRIAM

UNIVERSITY OF CHICAGO
May 1945

TABLE OF CONTENTS

CHAPTER I

THE ROOTS OF GOVERNMENT

WHAT are the situations which lead to government as a social institution? It is possible to have a clearer understanding of the basic necessities which government satisfies by examining both the typical complexes which call for political action and the conditioning elements in which it lives and moves. The tangled maze of human relations is so wide-ranging and intricate that it is easy to lose the way. Many there are who have mistaken some one of the factors here discussed—land, resources, races, classes—for the whole explanation and have never found their way out of the allurements of master-race, the fascinations of geopolitics, or the materialistic determinisms of many shapes to a unified view of the political society in its true light. The patterns and types of political behavior will be clarified best by analyzing the factors involved.

We shall start by noting that government arises from the necessity of adjusting the needs and desires of human beings struggling for forms of association through which human personalities may be adjusted, aided, or advanced toward higher levels of attainment. Instinctive organizations are found among subhuman groupings such as ants and apes, but political association begins with the emergence of conscious and purposeful personalities. Rudimentary as primitive forms of association may be, they point the way toward higher levels of intelligent co-operation and control.

In analyzing the types and patterns of political behavior, we may consider the important factors in the forms, processes, and directives of government by examining the adjustments of human personalities, and then the modes in which these adjustments are conditioned by habitat and resources, population, and ethnic, social, and cultural groupings.

I. PERSONALITY ADJUSTMENTS

The adjustments of personalities to enable men to live and work together in the framework of the general good are fundamental in meaning. Looking objectively at government, whether in my precinct or in the League of Nations in Geneva, I have always been struck by the personalities who must somehow be reconciled to the general set of understandings, experiences, institutions, and ideals which make up the group. The biological and social heritage brings forward a broad variety of different types of individuals who must in one way

1

or another be set in the enmeshing web of social and political relations without tearing themselves to pieces.

Underneath the social interests and ideologies of democracy, fascism, communism, and absolutism there is an underlying governmental problem quite different from that of the historic and traditional group struggles for power. The aristocrat, the democrat, the communist, the autocrat, each finds that, after the noise and shouting of the battle die away and victory makes possible responsible direction, the problems of personal claims, values, and modes of life await solution. These problems remain after every crisis to be considered and balanced in an unending series of adjustments arising out of the differing personality patterns and demands of the citizenry. The special form of social interest or the special type of rule will supply the general directions to various forms of action, but there will remain the perennial problems of millions of varying personalities struggling for expression and recognition, for the realization of the special values in life which they cherish and adore.

Types of personalities must be adapted and adjusted under all systems by whatever means are available—by force, custom, persuasion, social pressure, individual reorientation; otherwise the group will not go forward, will not function. And this adaptation of energies, interests, and value systems constitutes one of the great tasks of social control in general and of political organization and association specifically. This lies at the heart of the governmental problem under all forms of political and other social types—the staple of their activities, after the argument over the ideologies and the group interests has been for the moment disposed of.

What, then, are the main types and needs of personality from the point of view of government?[1] In the older terminology there were good men and bad men; there were just and unjust; there were docile and insubordinate; patriots and traitors; dreamers and doers; there were power-hungry and power-indifferent persons; masters and slaves. In later terms there are introverts and extroverts; there are those with high and low and medium I.Q.'s; there are differentials determined by long "batteries" of tests technically administered by psychologists, biochemists, gland specialists, physiologists, constitutionalists; there are those with father and mother complexes; there are those with superiority and inferiority complexes, aggressor and timid; there are sadists and masochists; there are narcists and exhibitionists; there are obsessives and hystericals; paranoiacs, manic-depressives; acid and alkali types; psychotics and neurotics. Some of these types become or tend to become mild deviates; others, criminals; others, patriots, martyrs, slackers, traitors, with high or low

[1] T. N. Whitehead, *Leadership in a Free Society* (1936); Paul Pigors, *Leadership or Domination* (1935); Elton Mayo, *The Human Problems of an Industrial Civilization* (1933).

civic morale.[2] These multifarious types of personalities, centers of their little worlds, whirling among millions of others, carry infinite possibilities of collision, confusion, destruction, and co-operation.

Psychology and psychiatry are producing an increased sureness of insight, if not of scientific measurability, into the factors of human psychology which are operating to produce the present stage of man's inhumanity to man. We can no longer rest content with attributing social disorganization and pathology to the instrument of personal devils. It is not merely that good will is lacking among power-holders but rather that they grope for comprehension in an unintegrated world and, groping, are beset by an insecurity that accounts for their overreaction to the challenge of change, demagogic or scientific. An increase in social *anomie* may lead to an overreaction in the direction of overhierarchization, too great rigidity in the social and political structure, and eventually to a thunderous explosion in the society. To advocate merely a change of heart and of outlook is not enough; good will without a sound program is futile.

But not only are there many widely varying types of men among whom the conduct and objectives of the government must be adjusted, but the attitudes of the same persons change from day to day and still more from one mode of experience to other modes and shades of social contact. There are those who cling to life as if shipwrecked in some great storm, anxious only about clinging to a thin rope of existence which may at any moment break. Others are full of the *joie de vivre,* with every step and every breath a thrill radiating throughout their being and questioning nothing in a world of sheer delight in existence.

There are great groups entirely indifferent to affairs of state; not consciously irresponsible, but blind and deaf to the affairs of such a world or almost so. They wake from time to time to challenge the great outside forces with which they do not usually concern themselves. There are those who resist and rebel

[2] On the topics of social disorganization and insecurity see Franz Alexander, "Psychoanalysis and Social Disorganization," *American Journal of Sociology,* XLII (1937), 781-813; Elton Mayo, "Psychiatry and Sociology in Relation to Social Disorganization," *American Journal of Sociology,* XLII (1937), 825–31; Paul Schilder, "The Relation between Social and Personal Disorganization," *American Journal of Sociology,* XLII (1937), 832–39; David Slight, "Disorganization in the Individual and in Society," *American Journal of Sociology,* XLII (1937), 840–47. A different point of view appears in G. W. Allport, *Personality* (1937).

On the more specifically political aspects see H. D. Lasswell, *Psychopathology and Politics* (1930), *Politics: Who Gets What, When, How* (1936), and (with Dorothy Blumenstock) *World Revolutionary Propaganda* (1939); R. Michels, "Psychologie der antikapitalistischen Massenbewegungen," *Grundriss der Sozialökonomik,* IX (1926), Part I; F. H. Allport, "Psychology in Relation to Social and Political Problems," in P. S. Achilles (ed.), *Psychology at Work* (1932); H. F. Gosnell, "Some Practical Applications of Psychology in Government," *American Journal of Sociology,* XXVIII (1923), 735–43; Karl Birnbaum, *Grundzüge der Kulturpsychopathologie* (1924); Edward Glover, *The Dangers of Being Human* (1936); F. L. Schuman, *The Nazi Dictatorship* (1935); and Franz Alexander, "Peace Aims," *American Journal of Orthopsychiatry,* XIII (1943), 571–81.

with and without reason; some in one form and others in another mood. There are the rivals—the outs—unrecognized by authority, the "unconsulted." There are the temperamentals who may be radical or conservative as far as economic class is concerned but who are fundamentally difficult of adjustment in any case—the ultras, plus or minus. There are those who fear all power and those who bow and scrape to leaders.

Much of the adjustment of the emerging and developed personality is, indeed, effected without the aid of government, some through the family, the church, the union, the gang; others through less organized forms of orderly association. But many adjustments require the assistance of the government to effect the reconciliation of competing claims and interests. The values of the producers as against those of the consumer, of seniority and youth, of ins and outs, the secure and the insecure—these are balanced by a variety of methods. One of the methods is the political, in which are imbedded many of the main elements in adjustment, as in the case of inheritance, property, contract, currency, trade regulation, taxes, minimum standards of existence, boundary lines not only of land but of reputation, privacy, rewards of invention and enterprise, and interchange of values in a wide-ranging series of instances. The standards of personal-social responsibility, the limits of permitted deviation from the mores, the care for a wide group of defectives, dependents, delinquents, without special regard to the group from which they hail—these are tasks often devolved upon the government; and this whether it is bourgeois, proletarian, tribal, theocratic, or otherwise.

The government views the situation as a whole, having in mind all the interests involved. The citizen views the situation from the side of his personal interest and advantage as modified by that of his group and by that of the state as a whole. Between the extremes of docility and criticism, men oscillate as social experience, social tensions, advantages, and the impact of power determine.

Every government is adjusted, delicately or roughly as the case may be, to the situations which require the co-operative control of the community. If this cannot be done, then the group cannot be defended, the law cannot be enforced, the taxes cannot be collected, both order and justice sicken and fade, the morale of the community wanes, and the governing group dissolves or gives way to another.

To this the apparatus of governmental lures and threats must be adapted. Rule of thumb has answered the purpose of control for centuries. Now with deeper understanding of human nature there comes a new stage in the ordering of authority. In a rough way, results have been achieved through such devices as the appeals of military necessity, the regard for the maturity of the elders in the state or community, the sundry provisions for seniority in rank and command, the efforts to conciliate the discontented, on the one hand, and

4

vested rights, on the other, by the interest appeals to various groups, and, more than all, by the steady reliance upon fear, upon desire for recognition and security, and upon hope, as great driving impulses of human organization. (See chap. iii.)

But more than this is possible through the study and application of the recent knowledge in the field of human personality, as yet imperfectly developed, and still more in the not distant future with the further progress of social science. The deeper understanding of these types waits upon fuller knowledge of the developing studies of human personality, upon further advances in the undertanding of orientation of personalities in their private worlds.[3] We may look forward confidently to much more complete and systematic knowledge of the "constitutional" bases of human behavior, including the biological and the psychological, in the interrelations which yet defy the inquiring eye of the scientific observer and baffle the student of behavior.[4]

Not only is this true, but the government must further take account of the development of the personality through various periods of growth and change, the varying age groupings, and the changes that take place as the individual advances from one stage to another of the great life-drama. There is the problem of the child in relation to association and authority as seen in judicial procedures; the shift to adolescence and its vital implications for social adjustment or maladjustment, to maturity, and on to senescence, reflected in old age security measures. These times represent important variations of the personality with direct bearings upon the problem of adjustment and adaptation in a political and social framework. Each stage and group must be carefully considered with reference to the position of the governmental situation and the growth of subordination, superordination, and co-ordination in the political association. The genetics and the dynamics of personality must be considered to make possible the finer adjustments of the governing function in a community.

In the field of personality, however, we encounter overemphasis upon its emergence in the earlier stages. Overemphasis upon origins and underemphasis upon possibilities of later growth and development may lead to forms of determinism of behavior and character from which the personality has no way of escape. There is involved here not merely the relation between heredity and environment but the bearing of early stages of growth and early experience upon the whole of subsequent life. A way out may perhaps be found through

[3] L. K. Frank, "The Emergence of Personality," *Transactions of the New York Academy of Sciences*, VI (Ser. II, 1944), 149–56.

[4] A summary of the significant literature in this field may be found in American Psychiatric Association, Committee on Relations with the Social Sciences, *Proceedings of the Second Colloquium on Personality Investigation* (1930), Appen. C, pp. 170–206.

the prescribed forms of cure or social experience. But in many instances fatalistic acceptance of early origins and retardations may seriously affect the whole range of later experience and effectiveness.

Here we find one of the roots of politics. Another is to be sought in the world of ideologies and interest. The two are inseparably united, for all these factors are parts of one indivisible problem, however they may be differentiated in ordinary observation and thinking. Economic, religious, and racial issues come and go, but the personality types and problems of common living recur and linger far beyond the life of an ordinary social issue, however revolutionary its implications may be. The struggles and wars which are the outcome of the clash of group interests, the efforts of the power-hungry, are only episodes in the long struggle for the development and association of the conflicting types of human personalities. These ends are the eternal stuff of which government is constructed, the continuing factors in a world of changing forms, leaders, groups, and processes political.

These adjustments rest, however, upon a wide variety of conditioning factors, determining the metes and bounds of what may be done. The land and its resources, the nature of the people, the types of social and cultural groupings in and around the given political society are of far-reaching importance in any state.

II. SOCIAL AND CULTURAL GROUPINGS

In examining the roots of government, it is essential to explore the nature of the associations or groups with which government is concerned. A government deals not alone with individual persons but with clusters of persons associating in many other forms for other activities than governmental. These clusters of persons and clusters of groups and their complicated interpersonal and intergroup and intergroup-personal relations provide situations which call for the help of some agency of co-operation.

Here the roots of government may be observed, and some of its essential characteristics and processes discovered. Government is a phenomenon of group cohesion and aggregation, a child of group necessity, a function of the social relations of men.[5]

The social situation constantly involves the maintenance of equilibrium between groups, classes, and factions. These groups are held in combination by custom, by living interests, by symbols and associations of diverse colors, by

[5] Valuable contributions have been made at just this point by Gustav Ratzenhofer, *Wesen und Zweck der Politik* (1893), and Rudolf von Ihering, *Der Zweck im Recht* (1877–83), and by Durkheim, Spencer, Simmel, Sombart, Max Weber, and Wallas—in general, however, without knowledge of the more recent developments in the fields either of personality or of social control or the most recent manifestations of mass phenomena. Interesting doctrines have been advanced by Freud but without a sure touch in the field of governmental or social relations. Lasswell has developed important aspects of this subject in his *Psychopathology and Politics.*

6

physical proximity and familiarity, by violence, by all the bonds that may draw men together in communities of interest. In broad terms these groups may be ethnic, religious, economic, regional, cultural.[6]

The problem of cohesion in the state often involves the relationships between several ethnic groups, religions, economic classes, regions, and a mass of cultural groups of innumerable types. Even in simple homogeneous communities there are still distinct areas. There are sharp clashes of interest among producers and consumers regarding the equitable intervaluation of their skills and services. There is the possibility of further internal differentiation into many minor groups which break up into yet more minute splinters. And if there were no groups there would still be individuals, as aggressive and difficult as groups themselves.

The accommodation of these groups (and of the individuals within them) produces a need from which political authority emerges, either in dire distress as a last resort or as a constructive adjustment of a co-operative type. Out of these combinations comes association for some common purposes, the emergence of the government and the rulers, equipped now with power in various forms that cuts across class lines and individual dispositions.

Once the need or advantage of governance is generally recognized, whether through consent, duress, prestige, or other elements of cohesion, the governmental power comes into being, and its personnel and its functions eventually are regularized and accepted. The group struggle may be continued with vigor, but within the boundaries of the legal order. If the type of cohesion is not sufficiently developed, there remain the roads of war and violence, until either separate states are set up or some common authority wins its way to the generally accepted status of government.

It may also prove true that the profession of general interest and responsibility is merely a verbalism to cover selfish exploitation. But, in any case, deference to the "common interest" is a tribute to the basis of authority. It will be paid by the tyrant as well as by the demagogue, by the patrimonial ruler who must care for his people as for his cattle as well as by the popular courtier who flatters and fawns as a part of a play for prestige and domination.

A dominant class will often think of itself in a vague way as a trustee for the community over which its scepter extends. It will be a guardian of family, clan, or tribe of inferior peoples, of backward regions, of undeveloped classes, of groups who require some form of tutelage for their own best and highest interests. Every other group will receive the justice to which it is entitled in the judgment of those who hold the power. In point of fact the dominant group may from any objective point of view be correct in principle and in practical

---

[6] For fuller treatment of this subject see my discussion in *The Making of Citizens* (1931), chap. i, and the various volumes in that series of studies of civic education in various countries.

plans, but it may also be sadly wrong, as many bitter experiences of subject peoples attest. From every century there rise the cries of those who fell victims to the ruthlessness and ignorance of a dominating group.

In searching for the origin of the political situation, we find that actually there arises a series of intergroup relations, calling for a balance and ordering of some type, preferable to the distress caused by lack of common arrangements and understandings. There are also, however, the relations of a group of external political groups; and by this road we come into the field of interstate or international arrangements and understandings, seriously complicating the symmetry of the simpler local situations. This becomes all the more intricate when we observe that many of the local intrastate groups have extensions outside the boundaries of the political association (e.g., nationalities, linguistic groups, religions, etc.) and the web is correspondingly more involved as the number of possible interrelations increases. The task of political association is thus a manifold one of reconciling the interests of the internal groups and at the same time of the external groups, and simultaneously of the internal projected into the external interrelationship. This may be illustrated by observing the difficulties of a multi-ethnic or other group state, such as Switzerland, when it undertakes to deal with other powers as represented, let us say, in the days of the League of Nations.

The bearers of governmental power are mediators in many ways between social groups of various forms. Among these are the religious groups, the economic classes, the ethnic groups, the regional groups, and a variety of cultural groups of widely ranging power and importance. The similarity between these groups and formal government is in reality much more marked than is perhaps generally perceived, for in common parlance and thought the government is often set apart as a thing by itself, as different from other organizations as the state of peace is from that of war. In point of fact these groups in great measure govern themselves, maintain a system of organization, discipline, and morale within their own ranks, with problems of social service and leadership, subordination, superordination, and co-ordination, and dictate to or resist the bearers of political authority.

Two of these organizations have sat at the table with government for many centuries, namely, the family and the church, constant companions of the political brokers. Even more than this, both of these groups over long periods of time have been able to assume the major part or a material share of the functions often performed by governments. The family still continues to be in all parts of the world a center of authority. Sometimes, as in China, the family is so closely interwoven with the political group as to be almost indistinguishable in personnel and powers.[7] The power of the father, or the mother, has been the focal point in the life-organization of millions of human

[7] See on this point L. S. Hsü, *The Politicial Philosophy of Confucianism* (1932).

beings, especially in more primitive surroundings. It was the great agency for power transmission by heredity and remains an important element in the formulation and application of social rules. The family, in spite of many alterations in form, is down to this day an important member of the circle of social organization. It is the channel of property transmission in great numbers of instances, a school of social training often more important than the formal school system itself, a unit of consumption and often of production, and the vital center of human affection. In the family may be observed some of the happiest illustrations of the projection of prestige through the growth of practical sagacity and acumen and, on the other hand, some of the saddest examples of the survival in senescence and senility of faded ability ornamented with colors borrowed from other days.[8]

The social education of children has been in large part and still is, although in less degree than before, in the hands of the mother; through the mother-father complexes emerges the conception of authority, command, obedience, discipline, co-operation, which plays so large a role in the associated life. Types of personalities are shaped in familial relations which are relatively fundamental in shaping the behavior of those who have been so influenced. The rebel and the authoritarian may appear, as a result of these situations, in forms that never change through life or are modified very slowly with age, social experience, and training. The suppression, the sublimations, the aggressiveness, the fears and feelings of guilt, and the insecurities that accompany these years leave deep traces in the lives of rulers and ruled and are a great part of the stuff from which political association is actually made. These patterns endure even through changing forms of class, caste, and government, for they are deeper than all these and survive the most revolutionary changes either in political or in social organization.

The part played by sex antagonisms and affinities in the formation of the opinions of men and women is of vast importance in the field of social and political control and, while little recognized in the tomes of government, is fully appreciated in the manuals of practical earthy power, demonstrated by all those who survive the rude storms of political life.[9] This influence may appear in the domain of the family or in the extrafamilial relations recognized or unrecognized by the law: we find examples in Helen of Troy, the Queen of Sheba, Mme Pompadour, Deborah and Barak, Cleopatra and Antony, Beatrice and Titus, and General and Mme Chiang Kai-shek.

[8] Aristotle pointed out centuries ago many interesting analogies between family and other forms of power. Studies in the law of the family may be found in great profusion, but from the juristic point of view rather than the governmental and chiefly with reference to property and personal rights (see Institut für Sozialforschung, *Studien über Autorität und Familie* [1936]).

[9] See Lasswell, *Psychopathology and Politics.*

It is commonly assumed that the monopoly of political power has been enjoyed by one sex to the exclusion of the other; but this is based upon a fundamental misapprehension of the nature of political authority. In point of fact vast power has been wielded by women not only in matriarchies of early days but elsewhere without regard to laws or constitutions.

That the earliest sex tendencies evident may not be those of the more mature period of direct participation in political activities is evident. With the socialization of many earlier familial functions such as education, food supply, clothing, etc., with the rise of industrialism and the decline of militarism, it may well be that the distinctively male and female contributions to political patterns may differ far less widely than in historic times.

Another social group of importance in government is the ecclesiastical, in its many forms, and in relations including union with, subservience to, and domination over the bearers of political authority. From the beginning, religion has gone hand in hand with government. Later the church became an association with many members, much property, elaborate rules and regulations, personnel skilled in the politics and administration of religious affairs, with conceded jurisdiction over great ranges of human behavior, and a voice in other ranges. The church has not hesitated to rebuke rulers or to assist in their deposition or to aid in the spiritual and mental preparation necessary for revolution as well as conformity. In any case it provides a moral basis for government in general and the particular governors in charge of the political association.

The church may have its own law, and the canon law has been the analogue and even the precursor of the civil for generations in Western Europe. Churches organize councils and conferences, lay down rules, pronounce the appropriate penalties, set up administration on a magnificent scale, and provide for adjudication of disputed cases through the agency of ecclesiastical courts. At different times this ecclesiastical government has been democratic, aristocratic, autocratic, or theocratic.

Not only does the church lay down the rules of life for its own citizens but it may also suggest, aid, or even dictate to the political group the enforcement of these regulations. It is precisely at this point that the church governors may develop an attitude almost indistinguishable from that of political power hunger; in short, the church may become "politically minded"; and here may begin bitter struggles between the church and state for the right to determine the metes and bounds of human conduct.[10]

---

[10] See my *The Making of Citizens* (1931); A. N. Holcombe, *The Foundations of the Modern Commonwealth* (1923), with special comment on the church in leading modern states, with reference also to the attitudes of the Catholic, the Jewish, and the Protestant denominations. See also R. M. MacIver (ed.), *Group Relations and Group Antagonisms* (1944), and F. E. Johnson (ed.), *Religion and the World Order* (1944).

We shall not discuss the complicated relations between church and state in times present or historical, except as an aid in illuminating the underlying principles of the process of government. But it happens that nowhere in the great mass of political-social phenomena is there richer material to illustrate the inner quality of the political than in the interrelations between these two types of social organizations. The parallel organizations of these two groups, the competing loyalties which they present, often in tragic and dramatic fashion, the jagged border line between them—all these serve to illustrate the nature of government in social relations and the intimacy of social inter-dependence. And this is equally marked whether we look at the institutional side of their parallel development or fix our attention upon the life of a per-sonality. For the struggles of the rival institutions are equaled by the deadly battles within the penetralia of the human personality which may find its own private world torn by the competition of vital loyalties that split the very soul.

It might be supposed that the mystical element in religion would prevent conflict with the realism of the politicos. But mysticism may point in more than one direction. It may lead toward retirement, seclusion, hermitage; or it may assume an attitude of earnest responsibility for the direction of human conduct, a proprietary duty in the name of unquestionably high purpose. In order to save the souls of men or to insure their moral welfare, in whatever terms this end is couched, it may become indispensable to regiment and direct the lines of human conduct, immediately through the political agencies. The validity of this ultimate (moral) purpose will not be submitted by religion to the determination of any other group in society but will be established by the technicians of morality themselves. The ways and means of establishing the implications of spiritual principles in actual behavior will also be asserted by the ecclesiastical experts, but may be challenged by the laymen in government or elsewhere, when the aid or the tolerance of the other groups is required for the execution of a policy. And the allegation of a spiritual and therefore un-reviewable purpose, or the appeal to the agencies of ritualism and ceremonial-ism, will not be sufficient to prevent a check on these ecclesiastical positions and pronouncements by other groups, including the political.[11]

In last analysis both religious and secular agencies appeal—though this is not commonly recognized—to the ultimate sense of "right," which is deeper than the "legality" of one or the external "morality" of the other, and which is not expressed fully in the institutionalization of either. Whether the church or the state is "right" is a question which cannot be answered either by the authentic interpretation of divinity, on the one side, or by the supreme inter-pretation of the law, on the other. Both proceed with outward dogmatism, corresponding perhaps to an inner uncertainty, as to what the judgment of layman, political and religious, may be. The outcome may well be determined

[11] Cf. Edwin E. Aubrey, *Present Theological Tendencies* (1936).

by the comparative proficiency of the parties in the art of propaganda and promotion; in earlier times by magic and superstition, or by anathema, excommunication, confiscation, exile, fire, and sword.

If we look in the depths of the human personality for light upon this troubled question of the priority of the religious and the political demands, we find that the disturbing and varying factor is the different facets upon which these lights are playing. The feelings of guilt and inferiority which so often prove the prison walls from which the tortured human soul would escape may be primarily neither religious in nature nor moral but constitutional or experiential. At times one may find satisfaction and release in the beautiful symbolism of the church,[12] constantly presented by the ecclesiastical propaganda of the faith, or in the thrilling community exaltations provided by the politicists, as in war, or in participation in great events and identification with great leaders and companions. In one mood the confessional may meet his need; in another it may be the *jubel* of the vast throng of which he is a part, or the leadership of the great man, civil or sacred, who reflects a thousand reveries written large in great days and great deeds. In the dark hours of suffering and sorrow we may become pious or patriotic or both; and if piety and nationalism do not agree, then there is distress until decision cuts the cord. It is in such inquiries as these, as well as in the citation of the historic narratives of the struggle between church and state, that a more intimate understanding of the conflict between these two forms of association may be found in great measure.

Although the family and the church have been historically important members of the family of authority, they do not exhaust the long list of those later born but increasingly important. Conspicuous among these are the economic classes, as they are loosely termed. The agrarians, the oldest of them all, business or the bourgeois, the labor group, assuming that only laborers labor; these groups are themselves made up of many different and discordant elements and contain many types of personalities, often with more in common across the group lines than within them. Each of these groups possesses an organization and a form of inner government of its own and a disposition to dictate to government—at times becomes the government. From time to time the line between the special group organization and the holders of political authority may become a most precarious one, if one assumes that in the tangled skein of social control these factors need be kept rigorously apart.

The oldest of these groups, since the days of the nomads, is the agrarian. Land, patrimony, and political power have been woven into a close fabric of control for long periods of time. The ownership of the land carried with it the control of the people on the land and attached to the soil. The great lords were

---

[12] Henri Hubert and Marcel Mauss, "Le Sacrifice," in *Mélanges d'histoire des religions* (1909).

the landlords. They were not merely related in some manner to the govern ment; they were the government—or the governors, perhaps more accurately speaking. By common consent the political community accepted them as the rightful rulers and their rules as the natural course of life and accepted also the transmission of their authority through a biological line of succession. It was even difficult to distinguish between private law and public law; between the rights of the individual as a landowner and the rights inhering in the community itself. Likewise the landlords were warriors, and the occupants of the land might owe them service on the field of battle as well as on the field of agriculture.

In later times the smaller farmers had a different status, but they were for a long time still the dominant factor in the determination of political tendencies and personnel; and still later the organization of farmers became a powerful agency in the affairs of the modern state. Their independence and isolation have made perfect organization difficult, but not impossible, to achieve. Frequently their most effective line of influence has been exerted through political parties in which their numbers may be very important. In the more recent stages of political development, however, the farmer has found a way to action through occupational associations, of the type of the Farm Bureau in the United States,[13] and like organizations elsewhere, even to the "Green International."

These groups have been able to accomplish the defeat of measures in parliamentary or other bodies, to carry through their special projects, and to obtain wide recognition at many points through effective lobbying and other political pressure. The tariff on food or on machinery, the tax on land, or the support of agricultural research, the organization of farm credits or the subsidy of farm economics, or even the redistribution of population and the decentralization of industry—these are affected by such organized agencies of social and political pressure.

The urban-industrial movement in all Western lands and the rise of capitalism and communism have greatly weakened the earlier authority of the agricultural group, at one time uncontested, but have by no means destroyed it. The farmer's power and prestige may be diminished, and the trend may lead still further in this direction, but substantial weight still remains; and the government must still recognize the very great strategic importance of the agrarian element in the process of social and political control.

Collaterally, with the rise of industry and the development of the system which has come to be known, loosely, as capitalism, the group of business has come to hold an important place in the power situation, in many ways comparable to that of the agrarian group in earlier times.[14] The traders, producers,

[13] See *Fortune,* June, 1944.
[14] Beardsley Ruml, *Tomorrow's Business* (1945).

13

profit-makers, distributors, and financiers, however, did not desire to become the actual and personal government of the land. They remained in great part outside the formal government. Business might dictate to the government without becoming the personal proprietor of political management. At the outset of the industrial revolution, industry wished to be freed from outgrown restrictions and was satisfied in the main with a policy of laissez faire. From within, business began to be ruthlessly competitive but later integrated its force in large and often monopolistic units.

In the highly industrialized countries the business group, although loosely organized, was intimately related to the political management group, which was regarded as in great measure corrupt, tardy, or incompetent from the point of view of swiftly changing industrial enterprise. Trade regulation, banking and currency, and foreign policy began to fall into the hands of the industrial group, and their will was likely to find its way into governmental action, except at points where they encountered the resistance of the older agrarians or of labor or the protest of the masses. Their concentrated economic power began to make them influential in the new techniques of political campaigning, in the control of the political press, and in the cruder forms of outright personal corruption of the official staff.

In the course of time, business became still more highly concentrated and began to develop more fully its own internal government. Corporations, trusts, holding companies, and powerful trade associations developed, both special and general, and built up smaller governments and administrations of their own, as in the case of the United States Chamber of Commerce,[15] or, on a larger scale, the International Chamber of Commerce. In cities, states, and provinces smaller units of like associations sprang up, reaching higher up into the large areas, national and international.

A wide range of activities fell within the compass of these newly forming groups, including production control, fixing of prices, trade practices, and attitudes toward labor, foreign relations, taxation, and finance. The paternal aspects of industry were also reflected in the benevolent organization of government within the confines of a single enterprise, in which various forms of politicization sprang up at widely different points.[16] Company unions, organizations of shop government, and works councils in many different experimental forms became the commonplace of industrial life, and in these undertakings were seen many of the characteristics of ordinary political government.

Indeed, as the units of industrial enterprise became larger and larger, with

[15] See H. L. Childs, *Labor and Capital in National Politics* (1930), a special study of the United States Chamber of Commerce and the American Federation of Labor as quasi-governmental agencies.

[16] See James Myers, *Representative Government in Industry* (1924); H. S. Dennison, *Organization Engineering* (1931); R. A. Brady, *Business as a System of Power* (1943).

14

a scale of operations involving now many thousands of men, large revenues and properties, and broad plans for further development, the whole business enterprise took more and more the characteristics of the state itself. Railways, chemicals, steel, oil, sugar, and liquor became kingdoms in themselves. To make the situation still more complex, these units extended beyond the boundaries of particular states, and "cartels" became international in many of their activities and institutions.[17]

But these new industrial empires, with their kings and czars and grand dukes, find the state on the one side and labor on the other and are obliged to conduct their affairs within the limits set by these two counterorganizations, likewise with men and money and some knowledge of the technique of social welfare. The church and the family, of course, are likewise a part of the play.

It is now important to examine the latest member of the family of government, under the name of labor. This newest comer obtained a position only as the result of a long struggle for recognition as more than a bastard child, at first placed under the bar sinister, and only slowly admitted into the fellowship of his elder brothers at the table. From slavery to serfdom, serfdom to status, status to organization and recognition, recognition to responsibility and control; such is the progress of the organized labor movement into which so many millions of the humankind have been drawn and to which they now acknowledge an allegiance second only to that of loyalty to the nation and the church.

Here also is a form of private government,[18] with personnel, program, social tactics, disposition either to command the government or to dictate terms to it, and with many notable successes in its archives. The number of trade-union members in the world is difficult to measure exactly but may roughly be placed at forty-four million. Furthermore, this group of organizations is rounded out in the internationals. Of striking significance is the International Labor Office, surviving the League of Nations and concerning itself with living and working conditions the world over.[19] The trade-union groups constitute a formidable world of quasi-political management in themselves and tend to become centers of authority of the most important nature, with economic, political, social, and cultural implications of vital significance. Whereas the business group may employ the agencies of corruption, social influence, or the army, the labor groups may make use of the strike, of picketing, of various forms of sabotage, of political action through political parties, and, indeed, of corruption. They enter the halls of state in person, take an active part in the

[17] Francis Delaisi, *Political Myths and Economic Realities* (1925).

[18] William M. Leiserson, formerly a member of the National Labor Relations Board, has in preparation, at Johns Hopkins University, a manuscript on the government of trade-unions.

[19] See the *Record of Proceedings* of the International Labor Conference held at Philadelphia in 1944 and the program there adopted.

15

affairs of the government, and obtain in this manner not only personal social prestige but important results for their movement as well.

The communistic branch of the labor movement cultivated an international or supranational basis, in that all workers were included in the fraternity of the proletariat, and the economic class became theoretically the basis of the new order of things. In Soviet Russia the proletarian group has assumed the actual political direction of the community. But, while the proletarian group has taken possession of the reins of power in Russia, the political government has not disappeared; on the contrary it has been endowed with far greater powers than ever before under a regime of collectivism. Thus the apotheosis of the group of toil climaxes in the activity of the state, for while the three factors of (1) the party, (2) the trade-unions, and (3) the all-Soviet parliament each possesses great power, the dominant figure is that of the political party, itself a political agency, overshadowing parliamentary authority.

In all the great industrial countries of the world the labor group has acquired a seat in government and, however unwelcome a guest from the point of view of the older brethren, is widely influential in determining the course of the state, in addition to the ordering of a great variety of activities local to its own organizations. It sits now alongside the family, the church, the agrarians, and business.

But these questions may properly be raised at this point: "Are not these new organizations of labor and business tending toward the elimination of the political and the substitution of the purely economic directive factors in human society? Should these pressure groups be made the government even?"[20] The substitution of an economic council or government for the political council or government would signify nothing more than the employment of one name for another, an exercise in verbalism of little importance to the hard realities of power. Whether government is called an economic organization or something else matters little.

In addition to the economic, family, national, religious, racial, and cultural patterns of many kinds are all determining factors in human behavior. We may call all these "economic," but, if so, this extends "economics" to include all social relations and makes the term quite a different one from that with which we started the discussion. "Social control" would be substituted for "political" management, and we should begin again the advance toward division of labor, with the prospect that the name of the new division would read suspiciously like that of government again, however it might be pronounced. The workers, however, might play a better-recognized part in the association in such a regime.

While we are speaking of cultural groupings, we must not overlook the fact

[20] See Karl Mannheim, *Ideologie und Utopie* (1929); Hans Freyer, *Soziologie als Wirklichkeitswissenschaft* (1930).

16

that there are also professional elements—techniques and technologies important to social organization and engineering. At one period the custodians of science are represented through the church; at other times they whisper in the ear of government as consultants, or advise industry, labor, and agriculture. In more modern times, with the vast growth of science and the immense projection of education and of research, it may be said that science is accorded a seat at the table of government, almost, although perhaps not quite, recognized as one of the family. These groups cut across the lines of the church, of economic classes, of racial and cultural cohesions, and are indeed occupied in the service of all groups. They are busy weaving the cultural heritage of the race into the new discoveries and inventions of the day and projecting them on into the morrow. And science may be and is integrated into and a tool of the government itself, as well as magic and force.

Science is not ambitious for government and does not threaten the position of the political power. Theories of the rule of the philosophers may be evolved from time to time, as in Plato's "guardians" or the modern picture of the technocrat's state; but, on the whole, these do not seem a serious menace to the sovereign state. In recent times it must be observed, however, that science occupies a far more important position than in other periods of history. The immense proliferation of the public schools; the universality of education, its range of years; the growth of adult education; further, the vast expansion of natural science and of machine technology; the rise of social science and engineering—these have contributed to the growth of research as a factor not only in the state but in all the other integrations of social authority.[21]

In individual states the position of technology is increasingly important, and various forms of technicians become increasingly significant in the affairs of society. Further, in the larger field of international relations the technical groups tend to stretch across other boundary lines. The Committee on Intellectual Co-operation of the League of Nations was a rudimentary form of organization. The international organizations of many scientific societies more specialized in nature are highly important today.

Governments often look a little askance at science. They rejoice in its powerful aid in production, in war, in education, and in its support of the various claims advanced by different groups from time to time. But, on the other hand, they look with fear upon its fundamental disregard for established authority in any field, even its own. Rulers can never be sure that the basis of their command may not have disappeared even as the order is issued, and they cannot reckon the assured support of their position. Thus there arises a feeling of rivalry between the power groups built upon what has been, and science, which looks forward as well as back and may dispel the illusion upon which authority rests. Neither business, nor agriculture, nor labor, nor racial groups,

[21] See E. A. Mowrer, *Sinon, or the Future of Politics* (1930).

17

nor the church, nor the state itself feels entirely at ease with the restless curiosity of science and its constant logical and experimental challenges and tests of their comfortable assumptions. They may attack it from the front but endeavor to utilize its forces none the less. It is hard to close the eyes and ears at all times to technical advice, unwelcome though it may be, if advice comes from those who sometimes know the truth and the better way. This, too, is one of the persistent problems confronting the politicos. Under the name of technology the role of science and reason is more readily acceptable—indeed, is sought for diligently, alike in peace and in war by all types of groups and beliefs. Social philosophy as such or political or economic doctrines may be feared or assailed, but the practical techniques of science, natural and social, are welcomed as supporters of authority.

In a broader sense the conditioning factor of government is the whole complex of customs, institutions, ideas, and ideals, acting and reacting upon each other and upon the going concern of government. The political association must adapt its policies and programs to these networks of social custom and thought. Idea systems, inventions, and contrivances of all types, some helpful to authority and some revolutionary and subversive in character, arise on every hand and tax the ingenuity and resourcefulness of those in power. Repression and suppression may be attempted, but here again comes another set of serious problems of rights and wrongs in the community, of maintenance of both discipline and morale in one and the same formula. Moral and religious codes, social and political ideals, attitudes and predispositions are basic in the process of governance.

Back of all is the culture pattern of the time in which government and other institutions are set. More important than land, resources, and groups of various sorts is the basic group of traditions and understandings upon which the whole society is built. In the end it is seen that government is a cross-section of the culture pattern of the society in which it exists, set up not for itself alone but to serve the culture from which it springs. Great and powerful governments, it is true, may overcome and even obliterate small cultures, but the battle is never an easy one when the struggle is with local language, local ways, and the customs of the group which condition modes of thought and action.

If every culture pattern was bounded precisely by the boundaries of a special state, there might then ensue a conflict of separate and special cultures each defended by an individual government. And there have been such struggles for survival in many areas. But the problem is usually more complex, for the culture pattern may be broader than the political state, or the state may include several conflicting types of patterns within its own borders.[22] The striking power, the productive power, the staying power of governments is conditioned

---

[22] See Arnold J. Toynbee, *A Study of History* (1934), for an interpretation of conflicting cultures and governments.

in large measure by the possibility of unifying and energizing these various patterns, either in crisis moments, such as war, or in long-time periods of peaceful development.

One of the continuing needs of the social groupings and governments just considered is the maintenance of an accepted order of relationships between them, between them and the common good of the larger community of which they are a part, and at times between these groups and their own members. Coercion and co-operation may both be involved in the development of these intergroup relationships, or other agencies at the command of the political society may be utilized.

To the extent that these societies and groups are autonomous and self-sufficient, the political organization has little to do with or for them, in either the form of co-operative devices or the compulsions of force. But the family, the occupations, and the church require a common denominator, a representative of the common good, and this the influences and agencies of political society provide. This is one of the roots of government.

III. POPULATION

The character of population, its number, density, distribution, ethnic composition, age and sex grouping, and its migration or stability of settlement, are of basic significance in government. The movements of populations from one place to another are full of political problems. Nations, races, regions, classes, even religions, may draw such lines as to precipitate governmental problems. Population problems lie at the roots of all governments and become the object of anxious concern in all political societies from the primitive to the most highly developed. In modern times formal and exhaustive inquiries into the problems of populations are projected in many states.[23]

These involve not alone the adjustments of racial groupings but birth rate and death rate, immigration and emigration, analysis of population composition, trends and tendencies, conservation of population on the highest levels, and a wide range of problems many of which the governmental agency is called to consider and act upon as a part of governmental policy in the large.[24]

Many of these questions have imposed the severest tests upon the political community—as, for example, exogamy and endogamy as policies, the burning of widows, infant exposure, treatment of the aged; and in other times population incentives and birth control, ways and means of health conservation, relation of size of population to military exigencies, on the one hand, and to subsistence, on the other; amalgamation of populations or the opposite, or various compromise adjustments as seen in India, South Africa, the United States, and Brazil, for example.

[23] See National Resources Planning Board's reports on population especially that of 1938.

[24] See N.R.P.B.'s report on *Human Conservation* (1943).

The biological facts of population shade over into the characteristic of what are called ethnic or racial groups. The literature of politics is filled with the celebration of the distinctive qualities of these groups. If the group is numerically small, it is qualitatively great; if it is young, it is full of vitality and promise; if it is old, it may revel in a wealth of tradition of great days. An array of story, song, memorials, ceremonials, greatness past, present, or millennial, weaves a pattern of loyalty which becomes one of the most closely meshed and tenacious in the social world.

These ethnic cultural groups are conspicuous factors in government. They are not to be elbowed out or shouted down by raucous voices or stared out of countenance by a scowl. Their problems are perhaps the most difficult of all in the political situation, for prestige is of primary importance in their world—recognition, toleration, domination if possible. This pattern is persistent beyond most others. It cannot be readily or quickly modified by economic advantages, although not indifferent to such considerations; it cannot be suddenly converted to religious attitudes, for these may be reinforced by the tribal pattern itself. It is not readily suppressed by superior force, as many a conquering host has discovered. From crushing military defeat "races" may rise triumphant, dominant in culture—even when subdued in battle. Romans, Chinese, Poles, Norwegians, Hollanders, may win or lose, but still stand like a rock as a group, waiting an hour when the flag may be again unfurled.

The racial minorities and the racial majorities alike demand and command as the occasion offers, are insistent and persistent perhaps beyond all other groups, with the exception of the ecclesiastical. How these beautiful and powerful groups of symbolic synthesis come into being is one of the most fascinating studies in human relations, and one to which much more objective study should be given. Under what conditions does political recognition become an indispensable part of the "race" urge, and, on the other hand, what are the conditions under which this fades away, merged in another unity of emotion or interest appeal?

The history and tactics of racial minorities and majorities are close to the problem of government, and the racial composition of the political community is of vital importance in its interpretation.[25] These groups are culture bearers, and under their banner come also economic claims and religious interests and other social demands which may be appropriate. Along with language come the gods and gold as well; and the combinations often test to the extreme the elasticity of the political community as well as the toughness of the "racial" group.

The racial sets do not develop uniformly an inner government of their own

[25] See studies in my series on civic education, especially those of R. C. Brooks, *Civic Training in Switzerland* (1930), and Oscar Jászi, *The Dissolution of the Habsburg Monarchy* (1929), for brilliant illustrations of the problems of multiracial governments.

but may hope for a flag proper and a political order of the usual sort. When all else fails, they may prefer their ghettos or their courts, or their own special tribunals or committees in exile. But their association is not commonly a highly organized, disciplined government such as one may see in the church or in industry or labor. Behind the singing society or the *Verein* or the school, there may be, it is true, some form of government; but ordinarily this is more loosely developed than in some of the other types of the family we consider. The race may confer immortality and fame on those it favors, enshrine them in song, sculpture, memorial days and observances, confer the degree of hero or martyr on those who have served the race. No special mechanism need exist for this purpose, but out of the folkways of the group there may shine this special form of exceptional distinction. The racial group may, on the other hand, inflict the severest penalties upon those who deceive or betray it. The hell of the church and the prison of the state and the poverty of the economic group may be surpassed perhaps by the bitterness of the scorn and exile to which the renegade or the traitor may be condemned. No group can more thoroughly punish offenders than the apparently powerless culture center.

These groups are not wholly without organization and government, however. There are racial societies in all lands, both in their political milieu and outside. All nationalities are full of associations for the promotion of the special form of culture of the particular group, French, German, American, British, Chinese, Russian; and their auxiliaries are found stretched around the globe in many cases of larger or more mobile groups. Poles, Hungarians, Irish, and Greeks may seek refuge under another flag when their own has fallen and wait a favorable moment for revival of their political prestige. Thus modern Czechoslovakia was made by a treaty between Czechs and Slovaks negotiated in Pittsburgh, Pennsylvania, in 1918. True, the sun may not always rise again, but hope does not easily die. In the darkest hour the enthusiast holds fast to his expectancy of a better day.

These patterns may fade, but their colors are fairly fast. Yet in the long run they may be caught up in another scheme of life. England, Scotland, and Wales may furl their local flags, the regions of France may come together under a larger banner, and the older flags adorn the museums. Genoa and Venice and Rome, Bavaria and Saxony and Prussia, cease to war upon each other and assemble under a common symbol of larger unity, in which all the older cultures find their niche.

Summarizing, many or most of the wide-ranging problems of population devolve upon the family, the church, and voluntary associations of many types; but inevitably many of them can be solved only with the aid of the political association. Hence population is indeed one of the important roots of the governmental, and its problems are likely to be of even greater and greater importance in the not distant future. There may not be a special department of population as some have urged, but there will be many agencies dealing with various aspects of the population problem, ranging from eugenics to international order, and somewhere these threads will be brought together.

IV. THE PHYSICAL HABITAT

The roots of government run down into the physical bases of social life. The geographical element in politics is of continuing significance as a conditioning factor, from the point of view of government in general and of any particular state. The true line of appraisal has been confused by those who relied too heavily upon geographic, environmental, or economic determinism and who endeavored to work out complete explanations of political behavior upon such data alone.[26]

The early interpretations of geographical environment by Bodin in the seventeenth century and Montesquieu in the eighteenth century were somewhat grotesque, but they pointed the way to a closer analysis of neglected data of very great importance in the categories of the political. The growth of freedom in England may not be attributable to irritability caused by climate, and liberty may not always love the mountain tops, but nonetheless these basic factors are in the final reckoning. In our own day the elaborate pretensions of Haushofer's geopolitics, developed in propaganda form as the tool of German militarists seeking expansion, have somewhat discredited the authenticity of such material, but this should not lead to the abandonment of important points of view relating to the geographical basis of political society.

So fascinating is this area of world and national resources such as soil and minerals that some not only have found them the useful tool of statecraft but have discovered the determining factors in political direction—"true power" as distinguished from ideas or ideals. "Power politics" may thus make natural resources plus population perhaps as the ultimates in political behavior of groups. While this doctrine is useful in that it calls attention to elements of political reality sometimes neglected, it does not explain the historical relations of resources, except as human resources are added to the argument, so that the relative positions of England and China may be better understood. Over and again despised peoples have risen to seize the material possessions of the power-

---

[26] See Ellsworth Huntington, *Civilization and Climate* (1915). Cf. C. E. Merriam and H. E. Barnes (eds.), *A History of Political Theories: Recent Times* (1924), chap. xii: "Some Representative Contributions of Anthropogeography to Modern Political Theory" by Franklin Thomas. See also the following titles: N. J. Spykman, *America's Strategy in World Politics* (1942); Isaiah Bowman, "Commanding Our Wealth," *Science*, C (1944), 229–41.

On "territorialism" among simian societies see C. R. Carpenter, "Societies of Monkeys and Apes," *Biological Symposia*, VIII, 190; cf. also discussion of federation and combining of groups and the lack of abstract symbols to facilitate federation of groups. See also Wilson D. Wallis, "Environmentalism," in *Encyclopaedia of the Social Sciences*, V, 561–66.

ful or have discovered new ways and means of utilizing resources in revolutionary fashion.

Physical geography, economic geography and geology, and social geography developed in the form of ecology are of fundamental meaning in determining the ranges within which governments may operate. It is no more possible to make bricks without straw, figuratively speaking, than it was centuries ago. When linked with developed studies of demography and anthropology, these data are of even greater importance as guides to political action. But the structure of "real politics" and of "power politics" sometimes attempted on these foundations alone, at the expense of systematic ideas, institutions, and culture, may produce very disastrous results.

No one can challenge the immense value of minute and accurate information and analysis of topography and of economic and social geography, especially in their relation to industrial, military, or cultural developments; but, on the other hand, the transparent devices for transforming geography alone into moral or scientific claims for political control are not to be taken seriously.[27] But for the intelligent development of national and world resources the data of genuine geography are of the very highest value. They supply data for statecraft rather than the directive of ideals.

But however important material resources and population may be and are, it is a fundamental error to conclude that a vast wealth of land and minerals necessarily produces a powerful state. The society must know how to utilize its resources, to organize and develop them, to shape them into patterns of strength and utility. The Indians roamed over the resources of North America for generations; Japan and China slumbered for centuries; almost all modern states have greatly increased their output within the last hundred years by new means of utilizing what was already in their possession. Holland, Sweden, Switzerland, and Denmark are conspicuous illustrations of the facility with which small nations may improve their position and enhance their prestige. Spain discovered a new world only to lose it little by little. England expanded from an island to world empire, not without regard to the physical and economic factors underlying states, but by understanding and utilizing them through institutions and ideas.

Furthermore, the effect of regions upon the composition of the state and upon the sense of state allegiance is of wide-ranging importance. A region may be outlined in terms of physical geography or the old-time barrier boundaries, indicated as lines of military demarcation. But many of the older criteria of political geography are inapplicable to boundary lines under modern conditions. Rivers may unite rather than divide populations. Mountain ranges are not an effective barrier against the invaders of the air. Oceans may more easily be

[27] See, on geopolitics, Robert Strausz-Hupé, *Geopolitics* (1942); J. F. Horrabin, *An Outline of Political Geography* (1942).

spanned by a bridge of ships. In many instances distances are not measured in miles but in minutes, in time of transportation which may be a jagged line depending on selected routes for rapid transit. Distance and physical obstacles are still, to be sure, factors of very great importance in relation to political boundaries but not as in the days when man's control over nature was less than now. Furthermore, the great improvement in means of transportation has made territories and populations relatively independent of the local food supply, of raw materials for industrial purposes, and has thus again transformed the conditions of political and social existence. Under present conditions it may easily happen that parts of different nations are in closer touch than parts of the same nation. England is the classic case of the development of a state in violation of the earlier canons of political geography. While, therefore, we must constantly reckon with regionalism as an element in the structure of the state, the role of territorial isolation is on the decline and of less importance than ever before in the making of political patterns. Economic geography and modern means of communication may become more important than imposing natural barriers, which a century ago might have been decisive of national boundaries.

Yet under certain conditions geography may be a factor of prime meaning in organizing or disorganizing the elements of state unity and strength. This is of special importance when the particular region happens to be the seat of some economic, ethnic, or religious grouping, and the strength of each component element is reinforced by another or by a series of others. Religion plus a region, or race plus a region, or a race plus region and religion makes a combination of no little influence on the stucture of state authority and prestige.

To the region, also, there attach many subtle values of high utility in the formation of political sentiment. Around the immovable territory cluster many attachments in a moving world. All the lure of the familiar is at its command. Thus the ancient mountains, the old plains, the majestic rivers, the lakes, the seas, the color of the seasons—all these enter into the picture of the native land.[28] The childhood scenes, the places of recreation, the memories of battle with the foe or with the still more stubborn soil, local sunshine and storms, are factors in the weaving of a texture of the common and familiar, to which the personality inevitably attaches itself. The moods of reminiscence sweep along these channels from time to time in the life of every individual, and, as they go, they taken on the color of a political attraction which may surpass all others.

"Breathes there a man with soul so dead who never to himself has said, 'This is my own, my native land'?" expresses the organization of the familiar in terms of the soil and of the state also. For soil and state, patrimony and patriarch, land and people, have come down together from time immemorial.

[28] For admirable illustrations of this see J. M. Gaus, *Great Britain: A Study of Civic Loyalty* (1929).

Of course, it is possible that this sentiment may attach itself primarily to the city or the local community or to the world at large or to the county or the local ward; but, in point of fact, under the modern political order the tendency is to bring them together under the symbolism of the state, which for the time at least has overshadowed the others in its superior attractiveness. In another period the attachment might be otherwise made. The psalmist spoke of his worship of Jerusalem, a city; likewise the Roman, of Rome. In the medieval period the city again emerged, and Florence or Venice was the object of the poet's song.

Since the days of the nomad state and the adoption of the sessile form, the soil and political power have possessed a strong affinity. With the break-up of the system under which the inheritance of land carried with it the inheritance of political power over the people on the land, and with the further tendency to nullify the agricultural economy as the chief way of life, the whole basis of the modern state seems to crumble at this point. But the poetical and sentimental tendencies have not yet caught up with the changes in the economic and political world and still utilize the older imagery, which, of course, still has wide application in great ranges of the world's area and population. The newer imagery of the city and the factory just begins to emerge in writings like those of Sandburg and Hudnut[29] and has not yet woven itself into a political form. Furthermore, the high rate of mobility in the economic and political structure of later days will make this a difficult task for some time to come, although in the end it will doubtless be achieved.

In the political process, of course, methods of holding together far-flung regions of different natural interests have been found. The outstanding example is Britain, whose widespread territorial lines seem an invitation to the development of sectional interests and sentiments antagonistic to central control. India, Egypt, South Africa, Australia, Canada, New Zealand, and the islands of the sea, scattered all over the globe—this might seem the very description of rampant regionalism. In many of these instances there are also racial and religious differences, emphasizing the geographical separation.

Lord Milner, however, once said: "I am a British race patriot..... It is not the soil of England, dear as it is to me, which is essential to arouse my patriotism, but the speech, the tradition, the spiritual heritage, the principles, the aspirations of the British race..... I feel myself a citizen of the Empire. I feel that Canada is my country, Australia my country, New Zealand my country, South Africa my country, just as much as Surrey or Yorkshire."[30]

The British navy, British trade, and British diplomacy have been able to bind these scattered fragments of empire together in a working political

[29] "The Political Art of Planning," *Architectural Record*, XCIV (1943), 44–48.

[30] See Gaus, *op. cit.*, chap. v: "The Citizen and the Empire," p. 75; Robert Michels, *Der Patriotismus* (1929).

unity and to develop and maintain an effective form of solidarity and morale. The severe test to which British allegiance was subjected during two world wars left no doubt as to the vitality and tenacity of the sentiment and the strength of the central pattern of loyalty. The picture of the nation as a whole has been superimposed upon the picture of the individual regions, and another territorial allegiance has been generated. This whole policy is, of course, radically different from the classical or modern autarchistic idea of a self-sufficient state, as nearly as possible isolated from the rest of the world.

On the other hand, the sharply broken contour of Switzerland, small as its superficial area is, produced many isolated regions in which there developed a strong local consciousness and a keen interest precisely in independence in local governing affairs. In few if any other states has there developed so powerful and tenacious a local pride as in the Swiss cantons, which, although close together in terms of miles, were often separated by physical obstacles of most formidable proportions. The very mountain ranges which made it possible to defend Switzerland as a whole made possible at the same time the development of separatism and localism of an intense character.[31]

"The Swiss federal citizen," says Brooks, "is always in first instance a Bernese, Basler, Zürcher, Glarner, or Appenzeller. In that which he names his liberty a bit of his native heath is inviolably preserved." Or again, "The Swiss are fond of likening their country to a rambling old chalet with twenty-two rooms, all strikingly peculiar, but all under the same broad and sheltering roof."

Both in Germany and in the United States territorial regions were the centers of powerful resistance to unionizing tendencies, and in both these cases the solution was not reached without the instrumentality of war.

From the point of view of physical geography, the various regions of the United States might, under European conditions, be the material from which nations were shaped. The East, the Middle West, the South, the Southeast, the Southwest, the Rocky Mountain area, the Coast—any of these and minor subdivisions within them are large enough and isolated enough geographically to constitute an old-time empire. The force of economic and social conditions, however, and the rapid development of transportation have been sufficient to counteract local tendencies and to bring about a solid national unity. These regions inevitably develop differences in economic and social interest, which are often the occasion of sharp political conflict and conceivably might become still more intense and bitter; but within recent times the geographical sections have not menaced the central pattern of allegiance to the national group.

In Germany, likewise, regionalism was an important factor in the creation of the national political pattern. In Catholic South Germany were centered religious differences widely apart from the Protestant tendencies of North

[31] See Brooks, *op. cit.*, p. 407.

Germany, and this was accentuated by a slight differential in culture pattern between Prussian and South German. The ethnic and industrial differences were not of primary importance, but they were of some significance and, in combination with the regional isolation and the religious differences, were sufficient to cause a long struggle preceding the full establishment of the Reich in its later form. Since that dramatic struggle from which emerged the triumph of the nation, the industrial forces and the growth of transportation have aided materially in the unification of the several states into a central whole.

The Russian state, covering about one-sixth of the globe in a fairly compact physical organization, presented relatively few acute regional problems, under either the old regime or the new. In the main, the several geographical divisions of Russia adhered uniformly to the central state, even when there were ethnic bases for regionalism, as on the Chinese or other borders, as in the Ukraine or in the Turkish borderlands of the larger state. The range of Russian territory was so far flung that it seemed to make relatively little difference whether any particular areas were devotedly attached to the parent-center. In addition to this, there was always, either by law or by custom, more commonly the latter, a wide degree of autonomy for the separate sections of the great geographical expanse. These local areas developed a sense of region, but this did not lead them to attack the larger empire or soviet as the case might be. On the contrary, they seemed to be willing to accept the general protection and supervision of the central power, provided it were not too meddlesome in the affairs of the province or locality.

None of these areas coincided either with a differentiating economic class interest, with a widely divergent ethnic group interest, or with a religious interest; and in consequence the territorial position alone was not sufficient to develop any counternationalistic sentiment or dogma. Regional disintegration, therefore, was not a serious problem in the formation of the Russian state pattern of allegiance. Under the Soviet government in particular there was developed a loose sort of federalism in which ethnic regional elements were allowed full play for their local language and culture on condition of the recognition of the general supremacy of the soviets and general acquiescence in the policy of the communist state.[32] Nevertheless the Soviet government created sixteen different areas and invested them with a broad measure of independence not unlike that of the British Commonwealth of Nations.

The roots of government, however, are found not alone in physical geography or in neighborhoods and regions, important as they may be, but also in the spheres of military and naval operation and in economic geography. Sea power, land power, and air power each brings its own special set of governmental problems, with technical changes overturning etablished policies from time to time. "The Rhine is henceforth the boundary of England's interest,"

[32] See S. N. Harper, *Civic Training in Soviet Russia* (1929).

27

said one statesman—but "England is no longer an island," said another inter-preter of modern air warfare. The airplane and the new guns outdate all boundaries and make futilitarian any statecraft based upon relative isolation. The generalizations from military experience of governments show the im-portance of constantly broadening the range of observation to keep pace with the advances of technology affecting these conclusions. Otherwise, defenses such as mountains, rivers, and seas become useless.

A related root of government is also seen in natural resources and particular-ly the strategic materials essential for peace or for war: the soil and its possibil-ities of development. Raw materials are of vital importance to populations, whether required for nutrition or for industrial production. From time to time these materials have varied from hunting grounds to grazing lands, rich soils, fishing rights, staples of modern industry such as iron, coal, oil, rubber, tin, copper, and aluminum among many others. Italy, for illustration, now finds itself without the essentials of coal, oil, or iron in an industrial age.

The terms and conditions of access to and exchange of materials involve tariffs, subsidies, modes of exchange, operating through treaties, conventions, understandings, misunderstandings, and often wars. Within the state these negotiations take the form of sectional struggles which may open the gates of discord and eventuate in wars with conquest or separation as the outcome. The opposite sides of a state, a city, or a unit, however small, may find the same basic problems. One side of the river may be against the other or one side of the town against another. The valley and the hill, the east side, west side, or north side, may encounter economic, social, or other rivalries which call for adjudication by some of the numerous ways and means of government. In one city, divided by a river, the rivalry over the site of the Y.M.C.A. became so acute that the building was located in the river on an island.

It is regrettable that the high values of land, resources, and population, as a basis of governmental activity, have often been turned to certain generaliza-tions of value less than zero; the false doctrine of geographical determinism, developed from materialistic determinism; the doctrine of economic deter-minism; and the doctrine of master-races and master-peoples in the area of population.

In each of these instances an important consideration in the formation of state policy has been twisted into a pernicious principle of action. While geog-raphy is of very high significance in the life of a state, it is not the chief determinant, and its importance is easily pulled out of proportion. The military and economic value of geography is, of course, of very substantial importance but not the sole determinant in the life of political associations. The same may be said of the determinism of social geography.

That economic conditions are of deep meaning to a government is unques-tioned but that the policy and life of the government are the creatures of economic conditions is not tenable as a form of generalization. Only if the word "economic" is stretched so far as to include practically all human values can it become a "determinant." If economics means all useful human activities, then it is perhaps true that all human activities condition all human activities— but there is little advance in such a conclusion.[33]

Another fallacy is that of the master-races, predetermined to rule their fellows. This is a generalization from race differentials but without any substantial basis in observation. It is rather the conclusion of group chauvinism and imperialistic ambition. The expansive efforts of states are easily understandable, but they do not require the addition of twisted rationalizations such as the destiny or necessity of the rule of some special branch of humanity.

V. CONCLUSION

Our expanded knowledge of the nature of human personality, of the habitat of man, the characteristics of population, of economic, social, and cultural groupings is far more extensive and intensive than that available in the days when Aristotle, Bodin, and Montesquieu commented on these conditioning factors in governmental relations. Psychologists, geographers, biologists, economists, sociologists, and anthropologists have brought together and analyzed monumental masses of data regarding these fundamentals of social and political living and have uncovered new techniques and devices. We are now in far better position intelligently to appraise and utilize the personal, the geographic, the ethnic, the economic, and the social factors establishing the needs and conditions of political association and human progress. We may make them our servants rather than our masters, either in practice or in theory.

We know far more today about ourselves, about the situations to which we must intelligently adapt ourselves, and about the situations which we are able to modify and control through intelligent action. We know, for instance, that pestilence, war, and famine are not necessary in human living. We know that fire, flood, and drought may be effectively controlled; that under certain conditions the productivity of the soil may be increased a thousand fold; that the use of national resources may be greatly expanded in relatively short periods of time. We know the possibilities of basic population improvements through well-established methods. We know that ignorance, malnutrition, insanitary conditions, bad housing, undeveloped minds and bodies and souls as well, are not the necessary outcome of fixed and immutable conditions imposed upon us from without.

We understand far better than ever before the roles of medicine, engineering, and education in the promotion of civilization, in the modification of what seemed insuperable difficulties. We know the possibilities of personal and group adjustment.

[33] See my *The Role of Politics in Social Change* (1936).

We know more about the dangers and possibilities of an unbalanced economy, of limping development and conservation, of unbalance of population and economy with government, social order, and progress. We know more about the nature and control alike of material and of social erosion.

In short, we understand far better the limits and possibilities of the modification of nature and the training of human nature by man and are in a position to apply this knowledge progressively to the betterment of human conditions, both material and on the higher level. We need not use ignorance, superstition, and fear as the guides of life but may utilize the reason of men as the tool of advance to higher levels of attainment. We know that there are nonrational factors in the human composition, and we know increasingly more about the adjustments to be made between the various sides of complex human nature.

More intimately and effectively than before we are able to relate political theory and practice to the conditioning factors of geography, of economic structure and process, of ethnic elements, to the broad culture patterns in which the government must be set. While we learn more and more precisely about the nature of nature and the nature of man, we make use of this knowledge for formulating purposes and plans to advance the development of the human personality and the common good of man.

We know the falsity of the claims of the innate political inequality of men.

We know the fallacy of superior and dominating races.

We know the fallacy of geographical determinism of political destinies of peoples.

We know the fallacy of economic and material determinism of personal and social action.

Much of our new knowledge in these important fields has been appropriated to the use of false philosophies and cunning propagandas, but we are at last in a position to cast them aside in theory and in fact as instruments of power and, through a better understanding of the political, to utilize resources not as instruments for enslavement or intimidation but for the benefit of mankind, for the improvement of human personalities.

It is clear that the roots of government are found in the need for establishing conditions under which human personalities may flower in association with others. They run through the many diverse human personalities struggling for expression in the framework of the common good. They reach into the ambitions and aggression of the power-hungry and into the aspirations of the many. They run through the associations that make up a society. Land, population, resources—natural and human—establish in large measure the possibilities and policies of particular political associations. Through all these tangled and often bloody situations, the role of government is that of facilitating the co-operation of men, the expansion of the human personality within the purview of the common weal.

In the misunderstanding and perversions of these needs may be found the key to much of the woe of the world. In our own day we have seen the devastating effects of the doctrines of master-races, of geopolitics and *Lebensraum*, of submission to economic determinism as the guide of life. But we also observe the growing genius for human co-operation in satisfying the genuine needs of man, through means adapted to his nature and ends appropriate to his high destiny.

The ends of government discussed in the following chapters are the rational answer to the needs of mankind depicted in the foregoing analysis of groups and personalities in their material surroundings.

CHAPTER II

THE ENDS OF GOVERNMENT

IN VIEW of all the complexities confronting mankind for many centuries in many parts of the globe, some have concluded that human nature is either wholly bad or wholly good and that, consequently, nothing can or need be done, since action is either hopeless if we are wholly bad or superfluous if we are wholly good. We may concede that this is a world of freedom of thought and expression, yet neither anarchy nor pessimism is a solution. The anarchists fall back upon "spontaneous mass action" when the evildoers become too annoying. The pessimist, unless he wishes to accept Schopenhauer's suggestion of universal suicide, comes to violence. But, since continuing and uninterrupted violence is impossible, he emerges finally with some form of government based on some other principle. Even violence and atrocities finally form a pattern— a configuration of violence in which precedent leads to a type of order.

A clearer view of the growth and evolution of mankind observes the weaknesses of man but also his strength, his failures, and his triumphs. Alternately and with equal good will we may curse and cheer the government of the day. We recite its frailties, and they are many; but we rejoice in its constructive achievements from time to time in the establishment of security, order, justice, welfare, freedom. Men are willing to die for the cause of the nation or carry the scars of battle to the grave. The agencies of government have not the custody of the good, the true, or the beautiful but other ends which likewise call for human effort and sacrifice. What are these ends?

The ends and purposes of government, much discussed by men of all ages, may be simply stated as follows: (i) external security, (ii) internal order, (iii) justice, (iv) general welfare, and (v) freedom. They may be summed up under the term the "commonweal," or the common good. This assumes that there is a community, made up of human personalities; that they have pur-

31

poses, values, and interests in common; and that there is a commonly accepted organization for carrying out these common purposes.

It cannot be said that these functions are the exclusive property or responsibility of the state alone. They are shared by other members of the family of groups, and without their co-operation the political society can do little. The state provides a broad framework within which other societies and persons may operate more effectively and undertakes common functions which it can more conveniently carry on than other associations. At every step along the way there is room for wide and sharp differences of interest and opinion regarding the proper course of conduct, but there is general and effective agreement upon the main principles of action, the persons in charge, and the main lines of action. Otherwise the state is sick—and perhaps unto death.

The postulate of political society is that there is a common good and that there are agreed ways and means of achieving it in practice for the community. If this fails, all else fails in the long run, however impressive the triumphs of rulers who avow different ends. This is the secret in the soul of state which brings to its defense the "last full measure of devotion."

We may, of course, inquire whether security, order, justice, welfare, and freedom are in reality what the rulers think they are or what the community thinks they are or what some outside or later group may think they are. What if insecurity, disorder, injustice, private welfare, and slavery appear in political action rather than the opposites? What if there are, and surely there will be, conflicting interpretations of freedom, welfare, order, and the other ends of the political society?

In all these cases both the feeling and the fact may be drawn into consideration, as well as the idea or ideal of freedom, justice, order, welfare, security. Indeed, the interplay among these elements is one of the most subtle and difficult phases of the political, testing to the utmost the cunning, the insight, the judgment, the intelligence, and the skills of the rulers as well as of the ruled.

Government rests upon basic understandings, sometimes of the whole community and sometimes of special groups, and these understandings must be woven into the action pattern and policy of the state. Even among outlaws there are understandings about basic purposes and conventions which cannot be violated without imperiling the life of the group, whatever it may be, within or without the formal law.[1]

I. EXTERNAL SECURITY

The traditional task of the political association has been the protection of the group against other groups, or attack upon other groups, as the case may be. Again the state is not the only agency through which interstate relations are

[1] See "Law among the Outlaws" in my *Political Power* (1934).

conducted. Commercial and cultural relations of many varying forms and types are found flourishing across state lines. Trading companies and modern cartels are sometimes more powerful than the smaller states, while "internationals" of many colors stretch through the network of politics.[2] Modern communication and transportation have enormously increased the number of interpersonal contacts throughout the whole world and correspondingly the complexity of political relationships.

The studies of war and of peace are so numerous as to challenge condensation. Militarism and pacifism have hosts of theoretical defenders, while the history and science of warfare fill many ponderous tomes.

The fundamental differences turn upon basic differences as to the quality and possibilities of human nature. Few writers remain who now characterize war as desirable, although they may find warlike impulses inevitable and unavoidable even if undesirable. But the inevitability of war is no longer generally conceded as a fundamental fact in social relations. Violence is increasingly recognized as a lower form of organization, serving only as a substitute for the higher and possible types of organization in which other modes of action are substituted. With the increasing spread of intelligence in social affairs and with the rise of respect for the dignity of man, the resort to violence tends to lose its hold upon social adjustment.

There are incidental advantages derived from war, such as discipline, alertness, and attention to organization and sacrifice; but, on the other hand, the vast losses of war are an incalculable burden on the human race. Suffering and anguish, loss of manpower, destruction of human assets of every type—all these and others constitute an intolerable load for struggling mankind to carry. Both the material standards of living and the higher values of life are torn down ruthlessly in the midst of war.

The compensations of war are, like the compensations of disease, pestilence, and poverty, interesting to chronicle but unconvincing in the march of humanity toward higher levels of living and enjoyment.

In time we approach a closer-knit system of international jural order; and ultimately there may well be a single society, whatever it may be called. In that day physical security will no longer be a prime function of the state, but there will remain the effort of particular regions or interests to preserve their relative position in the larger commonwealth of the world without discrimination.

Even if war is at last ended, there remain external relations of great im-

---

[2] For discussion of international relations see below. On war see Quincy Wright's massive volumes, *A Study of War* (2 vols., 1942); Alfred Vagts's *A History of Militarism* (1937); Edward Mead Earle's *Makers of Modern Strategy; Military Thought from Machiavelli to Hitler* (1943); and "The Organization of Violence," in my *Prologue to Politics* (1939), pp. 1-22.

portance to the political society, until such time, if ever, as the number of associations is reduced to one. The status of nationals abroad, the relations of trade and of culture, a thousand streams of in-and-out influence require the interest and activity of the state. Diplomacy, strategy, and forms of co-operativeness present problems of the first order to the governors. Treaties, conventions, and understandings are the basis of a great network of international relations in which the role of the political is of prime importance. The state is the agent of its citizens. Even without an army and without striking a blow much may be won and lost.

Special arrangements and special groupings affecting labor or agriculture, finances, industry, the arts and sciences, may be built up within and without the fabric of the political. Group security looms largest in all these relations, but in time the effective group or groups become larger and larger as the range and the intensity of groups increase.

In the course of time a vast apparatus of international relations has grown up, with intricate establishments of international diplomats and a whole body of international law, with many widely varied experiments in international institutions, from tenuous alliances to closely integrated associations, tightly knit in their arrangements and purposes. (See chap. viii.)

The development of forms of autonomy and independence becomes the task of the agencies accepted as political. To be sure, the governmental is not the only instrument for this purpose, for there are cultural, religious, and industrial forces and forms of great significance in this connection; but it assumes the leading role in such groups.

Out of this situation emerges a great variety of theoretical and practical problems—the rules of war, the laws of nations, the procedures and protocols of diplomacy, the nature of nations or other associations and of sovereignty and independence, and the elaborate paraphernalia of armies and navies, with their intricate rules of procedure. Custom, precedent, ideals and ideologies, might and right, all the conventions and artifacts of intergovernmental association, legitimacy, neutrality, belligerency, come into play. These and other considerations must be developed and applied in relation to the other ends of government, in relation to lively individual and group interests, to general considerations of morality and philosophy.

On the lower levels might means might for might's sake, the raw power of persons and groups, the shrill and savage application of fire and sword, torture and death, slavery and imprisonment, chiefly for the attainment of personal ends of power-hungry persons. On the higher levels might becomes the agent of right, the instrument of the higher purposes of men, the mode of survival against violence and brutality. The end of government at this point is to make possible the union of might and right in the same broad sweep of human purpose. But, alike in war and in diplomacy, there is a powerful tendency for both or either to become ends in themselves rather than means of common purposes of political groups.

The armed force may become the great end of life. Mars may become the outstanding god, the diplomats may become cynical and selfish—Machiavellis and Metternichs. Aristocracies caring chiefly for themselves may monopolize personnel and dictate the policies of warriors and diplomats, so that these forces may be used against the commonweal rather than in its ultimate interest. Might and strategy may become ends in themselves and betray the common good in the name of the commonweal. In the long reaches of time through which the rulers were conceded to own the people and to be the state themselves, this was normal rather than exceptional practice. Slaves could not lawfully criticize their masters nor could underdogs quarrel with the share of the common product thrown them by their overlords. But owners, of course, could not be consistently indifferent to the value and care of what they owned, nor could paternalism be wholly unmindful of its children and dependents.

Endowed as they must be with powers over life, liberty, and property, the tools of external security have been at all times a central problem of politics. What should be the size of the armed forces, their type and composition, and for what purposes employed and for how long? What should be the forms of common control over the common tools and what the relations of religion, education, science, industry, and labor to these special agencies of the government? What kinds of tensions and conflicts demand the use of force and under what conditions? What lines shall be drawn between the civilian and the military share of national production and share of human life and values?

On the outer and sometimes the inner rim of armed authority spring up the unwelcome but ever recurring questions: Under what circumstances is it lawful or moral to resist by violence? When does treason to the old become loyalty to the new?

Beyond these questions come forms of pacifism challenging the utility of the armed forces and their methods. These may take the shape of religious scruples and of conscientious objection in many different types. What are the forms and limits of toleration under such conditions? In the same connection arise the problems of civil disobedience so adroitly and successfully cultivated by Gandhi and his followers in India.

II. ORDER

The second function of the state is the maintenance of order. But what is order?

Order refers to a system in which there are reasonable expectancies as to what is to be done and by whom in the field of social behavior. In a condition of disorder no one knows what is to be done or who is to say what shall be done. There are no expectancies as to what is required or intended. In an orderly system there is a well-understood division of labor and of responsibility; there are rules, regulations, officials, agencies, procedures, and expectancies which are understood and accepted and which are held to promote the common good.

Expectancies and understandings are the essence of orderly living, of orderly arrangements. In well-ordered traffic there is a definite understanding as to what is to be done and how and when. Even if the system adopted is open to criticism, it may be better than no system at all. We may leave a building in an orderly manner, or the opposite. There may be order in the schoolroom or there may be the opposite. The house may be in order or in disorder. A system may be regarded as unjust by many or a few, and than we come upon a conflict between order and justice—one of the oldest in the history of mankind.

Other associations also have the duty of maintaining order in their respective systems and in their special forms of order, as in the church, the union, the trade association. The political society maintains public order, directed toward the commonweal, in the category of the political. But, when all else fails, the state may be called upon to establish order in the special society, as the church, the political meeting, even the family, in extraordinary instances. Or when disorder arises because of struggles between conflicting associations of a type which cannot otherwise be resolved readily, whether these societies are racial, religious, social, political, or what not, they are not permitted to make war upon each other within the confines of the state. And their property rights are also subject to adjudication by the political society in case of inability to agree. The state does not undertake to say what religious doctrines are orthodox, but it may be called upon to decide what persons are, indeed, the owners of church property.

In short, when no one else can establish order, the political order must be called upon to settle the unrest into some form of calm. Nothing is more dangerous to the state than to be unable to establish order. This, in fact, may lead to intervention by some neighboring state, assuming the function and perhaps holding the role for a long time, or to revolution from within.

Many of these situations present the very greatest difficulties, and, indeed, many a state has been overthrown by failure to deal effectively with the clashing interests of its constituent groupings. A catalogue of these conflicting interests would fill many heavy volumes, running through recorded time, as races, religions, classes, and regions struggled for mastery or for recognition from place to place and from time to time.

If we ask for a definition of order, it is not easy to set down in precise terms, although it may be identified. There are many types of order and many forms of order situations, seeming to defy accurate generalization regarding them. Nor can order be considered outside the context of the other functions of the political society into which pattern it must fit. Curiously enough, disorder is more clearly and definitely identified than is order itself on the positive side. The essence of order is a recognized and enforced pattern of behavior of a durable type. The archetype of order is seen in the military way of life, in which there is a division of labor, accompanied by sharp distinctions in authority and responsibility, with fully established rules of action, covering a wide variety of situations, although not all. A court likewise is a symbol of orderly behavior, operating in accordance with established procedures, and with someone in complete charge at all times. But as we approach policy-determining bodies such as legislative assemblies, or popular discussion groups, the symbols of order are less conspicuously displayed. There is a wider latitude in proceedings up to a point of disorder. However, the maintenance of a scheme of order is essential to successful operation, even in these assemblies. Robert's rules of order have their place and "fair play" even in a tumultous election campaign. "You are out of order" is a compelling phrase at many if not all times. It may be said that the greater the degree of political sophistication in the group, the higher the form of external order which prevails, whatever may be the internal situation. In sports like wrestling and boxing there are rules to be obeyed, and even in war there are conventions that cannot be transgressed even in the extremity of conflict, such as the flag of truce, the red cross (usually), the treatment of prisoners (usually), and other agreed rules of warfare.

The undoing of order may arise from inaccurate measurement of existing forces and of failure to respond to the necessities of change, and these two considerations are often intimately related to the balance of power in the given community. A change in the personnel of the rulers, or a change in the political system itself, follows close on the heels of misjudgment of forces and their stability or instability. There may come a time when orders are no longer obeyed and when the symbols of the old order are dragged in the dust, a notice of weakness, not of strength.

The nature and meaning of organization are of great significance, but they are reserved for later sections of this work dealing with the organs of the state in more detail (chap. iv). Sovereignty, however, presents a generalized aspect of order which may well be presented at this stage of consideration of the ends of the state.

Sovereignty is an attribute of the state, although not an end of the state, except as a phase of order, as here considered. Sovereignty is the high point in the political hierarchy. It is a concept adapted to ultimate decisions as to order and organization—a symbol of intent to decide as well as to deliberate.

Sovereignty does not imply omnipotence in all affairs; not even in the narrower field of the political, for sovereignty cannot be more than the given political order contemplates. Political society exists for the commonweal; sovereignty exists to make effective the common will regarding the commonweal. Rightly understood, sovereignty is not hostile to or incompatible with either internal public law or external public relations.

Sovereignty, in short, is not a distinguishing end of the political society; for the aim of the society is, after all, the common good, and sovereignty is only a means to that end. We cannot, of course, deny that states have not always acted in the common interest or that sovereignty has not been used to defeat the purpose of the common good through legal channels.

The emerging sovereigns of nations came out of their bloody struggle with feudal lords, whom they overwhelmed, not only masters in fact but with a new sovereignty in law. This meant that for the vanquished little feudal lords there was no longer any appeal from violence to reason. I am not unmindful of the fact that Jean Bodin left some exceptions, such as the common custom, the law of nature, and the law of God—but the catch in this was the question of who should interpret these laws, the vanquished or the victor? In later days the philosopher across the Channel, Thomas Hobbes, closed up even these limited and difficult ways of escape in his famous work on the *Leviathan*. There was nothing left but absolute and unrestricted sovereignty without recourse.

It has been seriously proposed to delete the word "sovereignty" from our lexicons. But the question of what should be substituted always arises. Preuss's proffer of the term *Herrschaft* and Cole's "democratic supreme court of functional equity" are not very helpful. "Leadership," "authority," and "supremacy" do not carry us much further. What shall we call the substitute for the thing we have thrown out? What is it that takes the place of sovereignty in a world of nonsovereign states? After all, is it the word we wish to throw out, or the concept, or the implications of the concept or the word?

The truth is that the old-time "sovereign" has disappeared, although, of course, there are still kings and queens and shadows of the potentates of the past. But we are not overawed by them. Crowns are no longer gold but tinsel. We pay the tribute of social pre-eminence, but our knees no longer tremble at the sight of royalty nor do our voices stick in our throats when we address them.

But is not sovereignty absolute and irresistible in its very nature? No, the essence of sovereignty is not in these attributes. Sovereignty lies in the concentration of recognized authority for the purposes of the common good; in the concentration of power necessary for community action. The lack of understanding regarding power and its locus of action and its realm of decision may be and at times is extremely dangerous. Absolutism is an evil we seek to avoid; but so is anarchy an evil we seek to avoid; so is indecision and so is unending vacillation. The dangers of one are as terrible as the dangers of the other. Of course, if there is no common understanding regarding what is the common good, or if there is no common understanding regarding the ways and means and forms for exercising authority, then we do nothing but oscillate between anarchy and absolutism, or run from one absolutism into another, a different color perhaps but of like kind. Sovereignty is self-interpreting and self-determining within the borders of what is recognized as the current legal or political order; but there are other orders and values. Authority may define its own rules and regulations with precision and finality, but this decisionism is not final or precise socially unless it is acceptable to the society.[3]

The growth of modern society and modern civilization has made it possible to avoid painful and costly extremes in political behavior. It is in the light of these gains of civilization that we must measure the concept of sovereignty. What are, we may ask, the specific recent developments which affect the centralization of political authority? They are as follows:

1. The growth of the consent of the governed, of forms of constitutional government and civil rights, the idea and practice of representative government, the responsibility of the government to the governed. In short, the evolution of free political society with its ideas and institutions has fundamentally changed the social order in which political leadership must operate. This is why the British Parliament may possess complete legal sovereignty but serve free people. It was none other than the great authority on the British constitution, Professor Dicey, who once declared that if the British Parliament should order that all blue-eyed babies be put to death, that would be the law. The British Parliament, he went on to say, can do anything except make a man a woman. But the commonly accepted understandings regarding the nature and operations of constitutional government make such behavior impossible and unthinkable. The legal power is there, but the system and the practice are based upon consent. All this rests upon the basic fact that political power can operate only within the radius of its own political and social system—whatever that system may be. Woe be to him who misunderstands the common understandings and overthrows his own reason for existence. And this is something the jurists cannot always tell him.

2. Outside the world of juristic positivism and the symbolism of political preeminence there has developed in recent times a body of scientific certitudes of profound importance. Appeal to these scientific and rational verities may be made from the conclusions of the political as well as those of any other social authority. These verities do not have political power as such, but they have social reality as such, and they influence the patterns of social economy and political behavior. True, the final legal judgment cannot be illegal; but if these judgments are unscientific, their force is weakened or nullified. Strangely enough, it may seem to some, the cumulative growth of science, learning, and reason have become checks upon the arbitrariness of political power or any other social power. The doctors, the engineers, the scientists, physical and social, do not possess a veto, but they can set up red lights and warnings. Any

[3] For a discussion of legitimacy, cf. Guglielmo Ferrero, *The Principles of Power* (1942).

one of these warnings may be ignored and often is, but the general body of warnings can be ignored only by destroying the basis of science, technology, and reason upon which power, military or civil power, really rests. Rulers who do not believe in thinking cannot long control the process of thought. Reason and science are expansive, creative, and incapable of continued repression.

3. Systems of moral, religious, and social values serve more than ever as checks and balances against arbitrary political authority or other social authority. If religious and moral values are less formally organized than during the Middle Ages, they are not less but more powerful. It is never wealth and arms that make religion powerful but an inner force more cogent. Seek ye first the kingdom of God. Value systems are stronger now than ever before, and they constitute nonlegal courts of appeal and centers of resistance against the absolutism of political authority. These checks are not powers of veto but of protest, of remonstrance, of legal resistance. The civil disobedience of Gandhi is a striking illustration of the possibilities in this particular direction.

It is within this newly emerging framework of libertarian political institutions, of scientific certitudes, of moral and religious values, that emerging sovereignty must operate if it is to function usefully in a political society. Reason, not force, is to be its milieu.

But, it may be said, does not sovereignty stand in the way of a jural order of the world? Are not unlimited sovereignties inconsistent with the reign of world justice and order? Are they not in conflict with the unlimited rights and sovereignties of others? The briefest answer is that there never were unlimited sovereignties in any world of justice and rational order, nor can there ever be. No state can justly demand omnipotence, but only co-ordination, integration, unity.

The truth is that nations never were omnipotent either in fact or in law in their relations with other nations. Whether or not international law is real law, as Kelsen forcefully maintains, justice has actual power among men.

That nations have not had full freedom of aggression against their neighbors has never been regarded as a limit upon sovereignty. In a world of order which forbids aggression and outlaws war, nations are not permitted to attack at will. Yet this is not in reality a restriction on the sovereignty of fifty-odd states but a reinforcement of it. Without security against aggression, liberty is not possible for the bulk of mankind. The person who does not consent to some established order becomes an outlaw. He cannot claim a right without conceding the counterright. A nation within a jural order of the world no more loses its personality than does an individual in a democratic society. The nation which will not participate in a world order becomes an outlaw. It cannot claim a right without admitting a rule of law. Neither outlaw individuals nor outlaw nations can complain if the treatment of outlaws is visited upon them.

Nations do not lose by action in concert with other nations in the pursuit of the aims of common humanity. On the contrary, they are gainers. The exchange of piracy for the security of world organization was a good trade. We do not know, of course, how far the Four Freedoms may be taken under general protection or in what manner, but many hope for practical agreement which will bring freedom from fear and want to all men everywhere. A jural order of the world must have behind it a reserve of economic, social, and cultural advantages and values. A plank in the platform of the United Peoples might be the development of the national resources of all peoples and a positive common effort toward the elevation of human standards of living. The authority of the United Peoples will not be directed to imperialism, either old-fashioned or new, but toward the increasing recognition of the dignity of man and of the right of men everywhere to fair participation in the gains of our civilization—gains the full meaning of which we have hardly begun to realize.

The United Peoples can have no authority except as to the functions deputed by common consent. The framework of sovereignty as the legal apex of a hierachy will remain where it is. Sovereign states can exist and operate in the larger framework of a legal order of the world and only in such a framework can they be secure. World organization of law will not impair the rights and values of states scattered around the globe; on the contrary, these groups will be insured against aggression, oppression, and annihilation. Nations will still be nations. But there will not be fifty omnipotent and irresistible sovereigns, nor were there ever. There will be nations whose peaceful and prosperous existence is insured by a world order of law.

Sovereignty need not and will not be allowed to serve as a screen for arbitrary personal power. Nor can violence and brutality or special privilege be allowed to protect themselves against the common good by appealing to a mistaken concept of sovereignty. The special privileges and the special interests which are in conflict with the common good, whether these interests are regional or economic or cultural, cannot be permitted to stand in the way of the realization of the ideals and purposes of common humanity. The gold in these interests will remain, but the dross must be burned away. Internal sovereignty never was really complete. It was always limited by considerations arising from justice, liberty, general welfare. There might be juristic finality, but there remain effective limits. If the parliament declares that all blue-eyed babies shall be put to death, that is the law; but it is not the fact. At this point psychiatrists would be needed rather than jurists. External sovereignty in relation to other states was never absolute and unrestricted, except as a matter of force and not of law—and it was contrary to international law at that. If a state is omnipotent internationally, it need not invoke the law at all.

Three hundred years ago the emergence of the concept of sovereignty aided greatly, along with communication, industry, and science, in the transition from outgrown feudalism to the ampler boundaries of the national state. The result of this change was an enormous gain for mankind. A broader field of justice, of communication, and of administration made possible the adjustment of the political order to new conditions in technology, to new forms of industry and trade, to new areas of freedom. It would not be possible to go back to the old system now, and who would suggest it?

Sovereignty as the rational defense of irrational deeds, as the jurist's plea for what the despot's power could not achieve, is dead. But sovereignty as a symbol of the unity of the state, the dignity of the common good, the apex in the hierarchy of order, the determination to decide as well as to deliberate—in this sense sovereignty still lives, an animating spirit in the government of men. If sovereignty speaks as one having authority, it will be because it speaks as one having reason, justice, liberty, and human dignity, as the authors of its authority.

It must always be noted that political order is one of many forms. Family, school, church, industry, labor, professions, and groups of all sorts have their own systems of order, developed in their own fashion and implemented in their special ways. Governmental order is a large tent under which many other forms of order are covered, but it does not operate all of them.

The nature and limits and implementation of governmental order is an outstanding problem in all times, determined by long-standing custom (with interpretation as time goes on) or by newly enacted law. What are the kinds of behavior orderable in given times and places? And who shall make and carry out these orders?

In military establishments alertness and instant obedience to orders is assiduously cultivated, but even here there are ways and means of appeal in many instances. Police are also instruments of public order and may operate by force or intimidation. Or, again, order may be most successfully obtained by means of persuasion and appeal. I once saw a crowding mass of citizens, struggling toward the tomb of Lenin, called to order by one who cried out, "Comrades, we must be orderly and show that we can be in good order." They responded to the exhortation.

In many instances we observe almost automatic forms of order developed, as in the traffic on a crowded street and in the lining-up for various purposes. In times of crisis we may be surprised at the emergence of unexpected order, as in fire, flood, or bombing, where the established forms have been overthrown. The opposite is seen in panic, where disorder has taken over. But generalized disorder is so difficult to maintain that even in stampedes semblances of direction and common momentum may be observed. So difficult it is for chaos to perpetuate itself with consistent inconsistency. The demolition of a pattern of order requires as much skill and persistence as its construction.

In internal as distinguished from external affairs governments may deal with group disorder on a considerable scale, regional or groupistic, or with individuals widely scattered. The problem of the central authority may be that of suppressing what amounts to or is civil war, out of which, indeed, separate governments may emerge—with the near revolts of special groups such as races, religions, regions. The occupation of conquered territories provides unending problems in the relation of central authority to separatistic influences.

The problem of the minorities is therefore one of the prime questions of political association. How to deal successfully with dissident groups is an abiding problem, reaching alike into theory and practice, running through the whole fabric of the culture pattern of the time and place. What is the common good under such circumstances? How shall it be determined and how put into practice?

For thousands of years this has been a continuing query of the harassed politicos. And with widely varying techniques the effort has been made, ranging from brutality and terror to the most refined methods of reconciliation, appeasement, adjustment, co-operation, and integration.[4] The successful development of Switzerland is an outstanding example of brilliant success, though not without a bloody civil war; and the United States is another, with like costly violence on the way.

In the long history of mankind many cultural patterns possessing the qualities and attributes of political society have been completely crushed out and their names forgotten or discovered only by diligent workers delving in antiquities. But the stubborn resistance in later times of the Jews, the Poles, and the Czechs illustrates the difficulties of overpowering a well-knit group with demands for political expression and autonomy. The resisting power of the small nation is an unending surprise to those who reckon upon force as the last argument in government.

In any case, order as an end of government cannot be wholly isolated from justice, welfare, freedom, and security, all of which must be taken together in the state constellation. Thus far no recognized and generally accepted techniques have been developed through which the awful sufferings of adaptation to some system of order might be avoided; indeed, in some ways the existing hatreds and rivalries seem as great as ever or even greater, as the standards of hope for better life are everywhere raised and as disfranchised and disaffected groups rally around them. Negroes in America, Jews in Germany and elsewhere, Hindus in India, illustrate problems of order.

Intelligent analysis, the spirit of moderation, administrative aptitude in dealing with specific instances, due regard for the common good and the ends of the political society—all these are possible ways and means of realizing more effective forms of order among dissidents. But it must be conceded that the spirit of toleration, the appeal to moderation, may fall far short of effecting

[4] See my *The Making of Citizens* (1931).

43

the improvement sought, as many dreadful debacles testify.[5] It is easier to be good neighbors when there is enough to go around and when cultural equality is not overshadowed by the fear of economic hardship and peril.

In dealing with individual cases of disorder rather than with groups, order becomes more largely a problem of dealing with types of personalities in their special setting. Here we enter the field of crime, offense against the dignity and order of the state. Government is expected to mark the patterns of deviation not permitted and to act for their protection and preservation. Immorality, treason, crimes of violence against persons and property, variations from physical and mental standards of conduct or status, "dangerous thoughts" even—all these and others enter into the problem of order.

The state must identify the deviations that are not permissible. But the eternal question is: What are the boundaries of the permissible and how and by whom shall they be determined? Slavery, imprisonment for debt, prostitution, and prohibition are modern forms of problems in which the temper of the government and the community has been sorely tried. What pronouncements shall be made in the name of the state, and by whom? Who orders order? What is fraud and what is fair? What is gambling and what is speculation? What is obscene and what is entertaining? What is vested right in property? What is profit and what is exploitation? What is legitimate criticism of government and what is treason?

But such problems are more readily understood if we recall that the state does not stand alone in all these decisions. For the family, the trades, the professions, and the church are joint formulators of what shall be banned in a society at a given time and what part of the deviation shall be noticed by the government. All utilize their special sanctions.

A typically political problem is that of determining what the role of the government shall be in these instances in relation to the role of other value and organizational systems, of asserting its own ends stemming from the common good, and, further, of providing the means of application and administration and of adjudication.

In primitive societies the government is so closely entwined with magic, religion, and custom that its lines of action seem relatively simple. The "inside" interpretations of custom are perhaps not even consciously followed by the governors themselves. At other times *rex* is *lex* and might is right; and at times *rex* identifies with the Most High. Later, systems of conscious law as well as customary emerge, in practice or in theory, or both intermingle as in the Roman law. Later come the formal legislative systems of modern times, still dependent, however, upon application and adjudication in large measure and, of course, upon other considerations of justice, welfare, and freedom as well as those of order.

[5] Mortimer Adler, *What Man Has Made of Man* (1938).

The recurring problem is that of refining in the light of modern intelligence and advances the instruments for ascertaining what situations require action to secure order, what is the relative effectiveness of sanctions applied, and what shall be the personnel of the doctors, so to speak.

Otherwise prisons may become schools of crime; order the road to personal exploitation; fraud and contempt may stain the whole fabric of so-called "order" with corruption and slime.[6] After all, the measure of public order is not the number and variety of laws and penalties or the punishments thereunder, important as these may all be, but a state of relations within which human enterprise may find its way.

Order is an end, but it cannot stand alone. For by itself order may be slavery; order may be the prison or the concentration camp; order may mean the orderly exploitation of the many by the few or of the weak by the strong; order may be the apotheosis of might and the shame of right. It is only as order becomes the implement of the common good that it is respected and followed.

Order is not heaven's first law, but only one of its useful servants, helpful at best and like Lucifer at the worst.

III. JUSTICE

One of the major ends of the political association is that of justice. Looking at the long array of injustices parading in political garb, it might be said that this is not an accurate or adequate description of the actual functions of the state, whatever they may be in theory or in hope. Certainly the catalogue of human injustice could be piled up in terrifying masses of iniquity.[7] But deeds of evil may also be piled high, and yet we do not say that there is no good in the world.

Justice consists in a system of understandings and procedures through which each is accorded what is agreed upon as fair. It assumes the existence of value systems in which each person finds a value rating and value recognition upon that basis. Justice implies the existence of institutions and procedures through which these understandings may be identified and applied. It also assumes standards of justice outside the governors or the political society or all political societies, rights and claims which are not exhausted by the formal declarations of organized agencies. Either natural law and justice are asserted or other criteria of justice outside the strictly legal justice. Social justice in the broader sense is often developed outside the courts through other channels.

If there is not such a system in the culture of the community or if the gaps in agreement are too wide, justice will not be found in anything like general form. Such gaps are always opening up between races, classes, religions, areas,

---

[6] See René Belbenoit, *Dry Guillotine: Fifteen Years among the Living Dead* (1938).

[7] See my *Political Power*, chap iv: "The Shame of Power."

and individuals, and cries of injustice will then arise. If there are too many who find themselves unjustly treated, then the morale of the state is shaken; and if this process goes far enough, it may be shattered and broken. Even the consciously unjust will appeal to the sacred name of justice, and those who are not conscious of their own injustice will make the same appeal to a justice which does not in fact exist in their own behavior.

Nor can it be forgotten that the meaning of justice is not confined to the realm of the political alone but reaches out through the range of human institutions. The family, the school, the market place, the church, all play their part in shaping the dominant view of what is justice. The observation and reflection of scholarship outside the field of jurisprudence and politics is also significant. When formal justice strays outside its social basis, there is certain to be acute discontent and readjustment following, particularly if it becomes true or seems to be true that formal justice is moved in the direction of special rather than general interests, through prejudice or something more sinister in human relations.

If it is assumed that the person has certain characteristics peculiar to his special pattern of personality and that this individual pattern possesses a certain relation to the community around him, then it may be said that justice would be the recognition of this special status of the person or, in case of interpersonal relations, as between those affected and adjudged.

In one sense justice may be deemed the equivalent of equality in that each is given that to which he is entitled on an equal basis of consideration and in relation to other claims upon the community by other men or groups. Justice from this point of view is the old "equality before the law," which was a great gain over inequality before the law but lagged far behind full fairness of personal treatment. Proportional justice, however, leaves the way open for broad inequalities, which in turn may be tempered by other considerations, involving the common good and the dignity of man. Equality is not identity but equitable treatment upon a level of humane and social interest.

The feeling of justice is as important as the fact of justice, and common understanding is the basis of morale in this field as in others in the social realm. To this end the symbolism and the tradition of the court are eminently adapted in all lands and times. Agreement to adjudicate is one of the earliest political institutions to emerge and one of the last to disappear in the organization of a social structure. In the midst of arms there still stand the laws of war, military and martial law and justice.

It is at this point that justice is seen to be intimately related to order, freedom, welfare, and other ends of the state. It is a great gain to have justice which is blind as distinguished from justice that looks to see who is who and favors the stronger. But what is justice as between master and slave, looking ahead to their respective cultural advancements? Justice of one kind might freeze the pattern against the slave or the inferior, or tend to freeze it; or justice might tend to free the possibilities of the inferior, assuming that he possessed them.

The priorities of justice, order, and welfare present some of the most puzzling and difficult problems in the whole range of politics, while the factor of freedom is also drawn necessarily into consideration. The rivalry between military and civil government, between justice and equity, between social welfare and national or group security—these are recurring examples of pressure and counterpressure in the field of the political.

The needs of justice have led to the establishment of special machinery for its authentic declaration and application. The creation of courts and the elaborate apparatus of adjudication deal with this special form of state purpose, while the body of learning called jurisprudence has been elaborated far and wide.

In the wealth of facts and philosophy developed in comparative jurisprudence may be found the full story of the ramifications of institutionalized justice—legal justice. Filtering through myriads of special cases and through many systems of legal philosophy may be traced the underlying purposes of the state in different places and periods. These great monuments of learning and masterpieces of analysis are testimony to the struggle of men through political associations to arrive at a state of justice, differently understood, it is true, by different men in different situations.

Of course, it cannot be concluded that formal justice was always substantial justice or that the element of power and domination did not enter into the decisions reached by the judges. The justice involved in broad questions of public policy is primarily the responsibility of the political leadership of the time, wherever this may be placed, and not that of the courts. The focus of conflicting interests and wide divergencies in policy are the burden of the executive or the legislative branch of the government specially equipped for this purpose. Yet one would be blind to the majesty of the Roman law or the common law or unmindful of the stream of current interpretation of public and private law if he did not observe the important role played by the courts in this process.

Formalized justice arises from the inconvenience of men judging their own cause. They may give themselves the benefit of any doubt with right good conscience. The rise of organized justice, however crude, is one of the great triumphs of human intelligence. It is true, of course, that the judges may not be wholly impartial in view of their group affiliations, and indeed there may be openly recognized differential systems of justice for various sections of the community according to castes and classes. The rapid change in circumstances often makes old rules out of date under the new conditions. Then the application of the old rule may, indeed, work severe injustice, not contemplated at the time the rule was made.[8] Equity in legal systems has been invented and intervenes to remedy many of these injustices through a more liberal interpretation of the rigid and outdated rule.

The problems of justice have absorbed much of the attention paid to government. The concept of justice has always challenged the attention of philosophers, on the theoretical side, while the practice of justice has been professionalized on a wide scale, comparable from early times only with that of the armed forces. Acute intelligences have wrestled with justice for centuries under various systems and, from time to time, realized a high state of advancement. The techniques of adjudication, after escaping from magic and mumbo jumbo, adopted the method of the oral dialectic, with assumed principles of law and with professional personnel for its operation. The basic and perennial problems here are: What are the underlying principles of justice? What is justiciable? Who shall administer and elucidate justice? How shall we insure the neutrality or objectivity of justice? How shall we reconcile the purposes and demands of justice with those of the other ends of government—with order, freedom, welfare, when they conflict? How shall we apply these principles to particular instances arising under rapidly changing conditions of human life, occasioned particularly by modern technology?

Here, once more, the caution must be given that government does not stand alone. There is justice or injustice in private as well as in public government, in family, church, group, gang, and profession, in all the walks and ways of life. Governmental justice is a cross-section of total justice as it confronts the personality along the way.

We cannot avoid noticing that justice, like order, has often been the captive of private rather than of genuine public interest; of power rather than of genuine devotion to the common good. Justice was often unfair, sometimes corrupt, often unconsciously blinded by coloration of class or other social factor; often suffered from the occupational disease of bureaucracy in its most virulent form. But the struggle for neutrality, for objectivity, and for rational judgment went on even under the most discouraging circumstances. The logic of justice, whatever the intentions of those who for the moment control it, cannot be wholly irrational. There is not imagination enough to originate a new device in principle for every arbitrary whim of power; the older forms recur again and again, even in the midst of saturnalias of greed and violence.

But governmental justice reaches beyond the boundaries of legal justice inevitably. What are the demands and possibilities of social justice? The court may, of course, interpret an ancient law or custom. The court may "project" an interpretation of its own and in effect make a new rule of social justice. But the open determination of a new social policy is more commonly the task of

[8] See the exposition of justice by Plato in his *Republic* and by Aristotle in his *Politics*.

48

the lawmaker in recent times or of the administrator who also applies the law to unforeseen situations.

Here modern government approaches one of its very greatest problems. What is justice in sharing the gains of civilization? What is justice in wages, working conditions, prices, taxes, rules and regulations for social justice at a thousand points? How far shall the state go in this direction and where shall it call a halt, and upon what principles and what reasonable conditions? What is equality among equals and among unequals. How far shall justice be interpreted as identity of conditions and how far as complete equality of advantages? "From each according to his ability; to each according to his need"? And who shall make the decisions at these difficult points? And what techniques shall be utilized in perfecting the reasonableness of these decisions as we go along? Here justice becomes no longer the monopoly of the profession of justice or its formal instruments but the property of the community in the broader sense, but without the long-established rules and procedures and the trained personnel of the law.

Again, what is justice as between conflicting groups, in a given society, racial, religious, or regional? Feelings of injustice may at any moment flame out into discontent and even revolution. The forms of order may be shattered and the life of the state itself threatened or destroyed. The sense of injustice and the slogan of injustice are far-reaching in their influence upon the course of political events, while, on the other hand, the sense of substantial justice in governmental policies and administration provides the securest basis for effective co-operation.

But justice between white and black, between farmer and manufacturer, between Hindu and Mohammedan, is not readily resolved by a general formula. Long-established custom, mutual interest, suavity in the higher strategy, the feeling that a sincere and practical effort is being made in the direction of justice—these are factors in the equilibrium of social forces difficult to reconcile. The Dominion of Canada and the nation of Switzerland are striking illustrations of successful rapport, while Austria-Hungary and India point to other less successful efforts.

On the broader field of the relations between independent units or nations the problem becomes increasingly complex, and the principles and agencies of adjustment less perfectly organized or less generally accepted. International law is less clearly defined than the general bodies of law, such as the Roman, the Anglo-American, the Germanic, or the Slavic, and at the same time the organs of administration and adjudication are far less developed and with less of force, material, and morale behind them.

The great problem here is to find a frame of reference within which justice may be developed and received. Notable progress has been made in this direction, but not enough. International conferences are still personal, but the persons no longer rule and speak in their own personal and hereditary right. Truman, Churchill, and Stalin speak for many. Experts and expert data are now assembled in great strength and play a significant part in the deliberations and conclusions, while social events are less conspicuous and influential.

The role of armed force remains vastly important, but it is no longer the only or always the dominant factor. In many kinds of conferences—commercial, industrial, social of various kinds—the military element in the problem is far in the background. The concerns of production, labor, agriculture, and sanitation come into the foreground. In any event might must endeavor to identify itself with right, however strained the interpretation; and this appeal goes beyond the conferees to the masses of people represented by the negotiators, not too obviously in all instances, however.

In the wide range of questions centering around justice, the role of government is not merely the arbitrament of the sword, the arbitrary decision of irresistible force. It is the problem of government to find a principle of action, to appraise the various value systems involved, to construct acceptable agencies of responsible and definitive consideration and decision, to bring to bear upon proceedings the best analysis of relevant data, to raise the level of issues constantly higher and higher. In private law, in public law, in group relations, in international conference, ignorance, partiality, fraud, and special interest may often hand down the decision to be ratified and confirmed by the hand of violence; but there are splendid examples of successful operation.

IV. WELFARE

The fourth end of the state is the welfare of the group as a whole and of its constituent members. Under the broad term "welfare" many different elements are found. Security, order, justice, and freedom are parts of the general program of welfare from time to time. But in a broader sense welfare affects the citizen and the group in many ways other than these. On the negative side, pestilence, flood, fire, and famine demand the action of the political society either in crisis moments or in the long-range programs of prevention of these evils. Education is seen as a part of the work of the state. Protection against the hazards of the business cycle, against depression and especially against unemployment, is now a part of the business of the state.[9]

In general, the state provides a framework within which, or services through which, the welfare of the individual and the group are fostered as far as possible. But it becomes the duty of the state to aid in the fullest possible development of the material and other resources of the community it represents, guarding against waste and loss, on the one hand, and encouraging enterprise and invention on the other. Thus the political society encourages in one way

[9] A. H. Pekelis, "The Case for a Jurisprudence of Welfare," *Social Research*, XI (1944), 312–53.

and another agriculture, industry, and trade, productive enterprise in every field, whatever tends to promote the national income and national gain. The government protects property and contracts, on the one hand, and the working conditions of workers, on the other, and both for the same common purpose of promoting the general welfare in the given state. The types and range of these activities are too wide to describe, for they cover many sections of human activity, now and in earlier times.

In broad terms, the state may be said to have a residual function, a duty of undertaking what no one else is prepared to do, but which, it is recognized, must be done by someone for the general good of the society.

It may seem, however, that over great periods of time the purpose of the state was not the general welfare but that of the small group in actual authority. This may well be and, indeed, has been at many times the case, where the bulk of the community were slaves, or serfs, or excluded from the centers of power; yet even here the state was always a symbol of community of one sort or other and a bond of unity which inspired men to allegiance and even to battle. Slaves and underdogs may be concerned with the protection of that state, or its expansion, even if their personal share of the gains is a small one, perhaps only an additional increment of prestige or glory as member of a conquering community, as distinguished from a defeated society. Without this loyalty on the part of the bulk of the community, the triumph of the leaders would have been out of the question; hence the need for a sense of participation on the part of those removed from the immediate centers of power. Small groups exploiting the masses for the benefit of a few justified themselves on the ground that the many were being given all that their qualities required for satisfaction.

The welfare function of government derives from the common good as the over-all interest of the political society. Beyond external security, order, and justice there is the "general welfare," the protection of the health, safety, morals, comfort, and convenience of the public, once called the police power. Looking back over the broad sweep of history, it is clear that the government at one time or another has done almost everything in crisis or in the pursuit of its welfare aims. Pestilence, war, famine, fire, flood, business depressions, mass unemployment—all these and many other situations have challenged the activities of the government to improve the situation and avert the evil, not otherwise readily restrained.

These welfare functions of government are not, as is often asserted, new activities of the political agencies. From the beginning political authorities were responsible for many aspects of the general good. The head was as paternalistic as a father. Early government dealt with many phases of life, some of which we now call social security and production of utilities.

Much later the feudal lord functioned as the owner of the people and the owner of the land, and fine was the distinction—if any—between public and private law, for the lord was the author of both. Under the patrimonial absolutistic state there was no question of governmental interference, the head of the state being himself the law again. *Rex* was *lex* once more, and by the grace of God as well.

On the other hand, great ranges of activity were taken over by the church and by the guild somewhat later. The caritative functions were the responsibility of the church for a long period of time, while the guilds performed many of the types of regulation later assumed by governments. In another period trading companies like the Hudson Bay Company and the East India Company were given wide powers, semigovernmental in nature.

With the rise of industry in importance and influence, the patrimonial function of the government fell back in significance, although the instruments of force, order, and justice continued their surveillance and protection of private activities. This form of governmental action was often characterized as the police state—interested primarily in policing rather than in the promotion of the general welfare. But what are sometimes called the caritative functions, including care for the helpless, in various forms, and education, are developed often alongside the more limited police activities of government; and more elaborate forms of social security also begin to be adopted and applied.

Likewise social legislation for the protection of working and living conditions, for wages and hours of work, for protection against accident and disease, developed; and the tragedies of the business cycle and the terrors of mass unemployment brought about numerous measures developed as preventives against them.

Freedom from fear and want became new guide lines of governmental action in this sector of the common welfare. Welfare was thus extended to include health, education, social security, recreational and cultural activities, and concern for the productivity of the society and the protection of many of the incidents of the productive process, from worker to owner, to consumer to manager. In the middle of the nineteenth century came the formula of collective ownership of the means of production, linked strangely enough with the demand for abolition of the state. This gained momentum and by the twentieth century had been put in practice on a large scale by the Soviet authorities in Russia.

Under all these circumstances, accompanied by sharp conflict sometimes on the field of dialectics and again on the field of battle, what are the specific tasks and responsibilities of the political society in the area of welfare?

The task of government as one of the responsible agents in these affairs is that of determining as sharply as possible the principle of public welfare in the given situation, the meaning of the value systems and interests at stake; of determining the areas of state activity, the ways and means of action, the agencies and instruments of policy, and the relation of all these to the other ends of government, order, justice, and freedom.

This responsibility is, of course, shared by the governmental instruments with other social groupings, with economic groupings, with social and cultural agencies, and with the directives of philosophy and ethics, for the problem is not merely one of state action but of social principle and social action, in which industry, labor, church, the professions, and a great variety of individuals and associations are concerned. The governmental machinery for these purposes is found scattered through legislative, administrative, and judicial agencies, variously set up in different states.

The general types of agencies seen in Soviet Russia, in Sweden—the middle way—and in England and the United States illustrate differing possibilities. That bitter controversy develops, even reaching to revolution and war, is nothing new in the long history of the political agencies.

Given the task of establishing order, justice, welfare, and freedom in the midst of whirling ideologies, interests, organizational devices and forces, the governments cannot be said to have brought about the stabilization required under the given conditions. Nor was success obtained in the rivalries and clashing interests of separate nations of the globe, which in two great world wars shook the foundations of the modern world to their depths.

General agreement could not be found regarding the basic principles of political and social action, regarding the competing value systems involved, regarding the tools and instrumentalities of action, or the organs and mechanisms desirable under the conditions. Order and justice were often in conflict, and justice and welfare, while freedom might clash with all of them, and national security be threatened by or threaten all the other ends of government. What was the common good and how common and how good were questions constantly flung at the apostles of order and justice who pleaded for unity and order. The rhetoric of policy-determining bodies, the oral dialectic of the courts, and the neutrality of public administration were all drawn into the arena of conflict, which might turn into revolution or war at any moment.

In considering the meaning of welfare functions of government, it is essential to look at the whole picture and the whole story. For from time to time various elements have undertaken to utilize the ideas and mechanisms of government for their own primary purpose. The patriarchs in their day, the warriors, the landlords, the clericals, the guilds, the corporations, and cartels, the agricultural and labor organizations, all have their day in the shaping of state policy and its management in practice. The modern industrialists, whether employers, managers, or workers, are newcomers in name only, since like claims and like struggles have been known for thousands of years. The areas of state action come and go, and will again, as technology and philosophy do their work. With the change to the factory from slavery and serfdom comes the problem of the recognition of the dignity of every man. The government progressively learns what it can do and also how to do it technically. The active principle of the general welfare remains the same, while its application changes with the culture patterns of the time.

It may be said that all this leaves the idea of "welfare" very vague. What is "welfare" and how shall we know it when we see it? The answer is not so difficult if we bear in mind that the state is not the only human association dealing with and promoting human welfare; there is also the family, the church, and a multitude of other associations concerned with welfare in one form and another. They may, and often do, and should indeed, overlap the activities of the political society at times. But the state's interpretation of welfare is set in the constellation of security, order, justice, and freedom in a manner differing from the other societies of which men are part, just as the state itself is set in a group of other societies as an institution.

What the state does chiefly is (1) to make sure that other institutions are functioning in their own fields of welfare; (2) to promote welfare where other institutions cannot well function; (3) to press forward the welfare of the whole group, as distinguished from special groups, and the welfare of all persons in the society as distinguished from the welfare of persons as members of special groupings; and (4) to aid neglected persons and groups of various kinds.

This will not provide a precise demarcation of what is or is not welfare in all particular instances, but it will give a general standard or guide. The understandings and the institutions which implement welfare in the several societies are of paramount importance in practical determination of specific courses of action. But of greater meaning is the spirit, the general direction, of welfare in a time or place.

The welfare function of the state, old and new, does not consist solely or even principally in the aggregation of a wide variety of special "services" but rather in (1) increasing the productive power of the state, the total national income; (2) establishing minimum standards of living for all, based upon productive possibilities; (3) utilizing the advances made by modern technology, physical and social, in education, medicine, personality adjustment, a broad range of possibilities in the field of invention; and (4) making possible the fullest and highest development of the human personality in the framework of social relations.

V. FREEDOM

Freedom is an essential end or purpose of the state. Looking around on the panorama of time, some must find this a senseless statement on the ground that it might be true in the ideal state but not in the practical state. In what sense did the long line of human tyrants strive to develop freedom? But the answer lies deeper down than that. Let us look first at the meaning of freedom and its implementation in societies.[10]

The doctrine of freedom is essentially that of opportunity for free development of personal desires for expression, with the possibilities of the personality related, of course, in the pattern of the common good. Who says liberty says life. Liberty is an end in itself, but it is more than that. It is also a means of arriving at other ends, a method of expression of personality, a mode of obtaining recognition and possibly of rising in the hierarchy of values in the society.

The world's literature is rich with erudite discussions of the nature and implications of liberty. The philosophers have emphasized unendingly the struggle between determinism and voluntarism, the theologians, the status of liberty in the relation between the personality and God; the social psychologists have dwelt upon the relation between personality and the surrounding culture; others on the relationship between inheritance and environment or between total environment and man; and the students of government have dwelt upon the conflict between the citizen and the state.[11]

In democratic theory and practice liberty has had a negative and a positive side. On the negative side, mechanisms have been set up with the design of protecting the citizen against arbitrary and oppressive conduct. The apparatus of civil rights was devised for this purpose. In earlier days emphasis was laid upon small-size states, upon decentralization, and upon the separation and balance of powers, following Montesquieu, as guaranties of the liberty of citizens. Positive mechanisms were also set up, providing for participation in the affairs of the state, as in suffrage and in representation, giving to the electors control over the general direction of the policy of the state.

But the terms "liberty" and "individualism" were taken captive by the economic world at times, even under democratic or semidemocratic forms of association. The techniques of government were turned to the fostering of a special type of "economic" freedom—one among many—even at the expense of the civil or political liberties of the citizen, who might be and was oppressed by the very machinery he set up to emancipate himself. It was Anatole France who referred to "the majestic equality of the laws, which forbid rich and

---

[10] See Dorothy Fosdick, *What Is Liberty?* (1939).

[11] Among the outstanding studies in the field of the relation of the state to the freedom of the individual are John Stuart Mill, *On Liberty* (1859); De Tocqueville, *La Démocratie en Amérique* (2 vols., 1835–40); T. H. Green, *Lectures on the Principles of Political Obligation* (1895); J. E. Acton, *The History of Freedom and Other Essays* (1907); F. C. Montague, *The Limits of Individual Liberty* (1885); J. W. Burgess, *The Reconciliation of Government with Liberty* (1915); Harold J. Laski, *Liberty in the Modern State* (1930); Léon Duguit, *Souveraineté et liberté* (1922); H. M. Kallen (ed.), *Freedom in the Modern World* (1928); G. B. Logan, *Liberty in the Modern World* (1928); T. V. Smith, *The Democratic Way of Life* (1926); Jacques Maritain, *Freedom in the Modern World* (1936); Erich Fromm, *The Fear of Freedom* (1942).

poor alike to sleep under the bridges, to beg in the streets, and to steal their bread."

Liberty, however, is not merely negative but is also positive in its nature. Liberty connotes the fullest and richest possible development of the possibilities of the personality of the citizens. In a sense liberty is life, the "good life" of the Greeks, the "spiritual life," the "more abundant life" of our time. But the personality is set in a framework of social and spiritual interests and values. Even anarchism in its later phases as developed by Kropotkin recognized the values of association and co-operation.[12]

Liberty involves a wide range of alternative choices in which autonomy is possible—choices that are not confined to industry but reach far beyond. "Individualism" and "enterprise" are not limited to an economic area but run through the whole gamut of human living. "Individualism," "individuality," and "personality" have many facets, including the economic but not ending there. It is the function of a democratic association to give the widest possible play to the widest possible range of choices by its citizens—to encourage intellectual and creative enterprise. There are producers' choices, there are also consumers' choices, and workers' choices, and leisure-time choices, and cultural choices of a wide variety.

Much confusion has been caused by the struggle for priorities in liberty—or perhaps more accurately by the failure to recognize the many competing human-value systems in each of which there is an area of alternative libertarian choices. This area expands and contracts with the time and the tension of the social situation—external and internal.

Political liberty, economic liberty, religious liberty, social liberty, artistic liberty—liberties of many modes and tenses—are all involved in the whirling social equilibrium. And we must reckon further, not only with personal liberties, but also with group liberties of endless types in the given society. Racial, regional, occupational, and cultural associations of widely varying forms and purposes are intertwined in the complex movement of the period, whatever it may be. These liberties are not necessarily exclusive, one of the other. The state provides the setting for all of them, balancing their impact upon each other and adjusting and adapting otherwise more severe collisions and conflicts.

If all these competing types of life could agree upon the field and priorities of their "liberty" or "liberties," there would be no need for the political association. They might pursue their peaceful ways, revolving in their own orbits without clash or conflict. But it is precisely one of the functions of the state to balance these ways of life and to prevent an anarchy of liberties, rudely crashing against each other and leading to an intolerable chaos.

Any of these systems of liberty may assert itself against the others, drawing

[12] P. Kropotkin, *Mutual Aid, a Factor of Evolution* (1902).

in, as it were, all liberty to itself, as in religion, economics, art, science, culture. And each, of course, tends to give itself at least a high rank in the scale. From time to time one or another attains such a position of trust or preponderance that it may in effect direct the action of the state and, without assuming technical responsibility, determine the lines of governmental function.

In most discussions the problem of liberty is oversimplified. In reality there are many liberties balanced against each other or revolving around each other in plural fashion. The personality lives in a complicated, ever changing system of choices, not always related to each other in the realm of conscious personality. Furthermore, there are many other factors in the social equilibrium and movement. Liberty must be balanced against order; against justice; against equality; against the rate, type, and direction of social change or social tension; against internal, international, racial, religious, and regional interests and demands.

Even in his own personality the citizen must himself balance his own liberty against his own sense of justice, his own sense of order, his own sense of social interrelations, and his own responsibility to them. If "my mind to me a kingdom is," it presents all the problems of a kingdom, from which the personality cannot escape even by abdication. He cannot flee himself, his own inner constituency and constitution. The personality itself contains a cross-section of anarchism, another of despotism, one of tolerance, another of intolerance. Hence, the statesmanship of personality is also a perennial problem of life. In the larger society the problem is much the same on a vaster scale, but with much the same elements struggling for position.

In the political sense this liberty is attained in the framework of mechanisms, procedures, and understandings we call "government." It is not primarily negative, although there is an element of negativism in it, but primarily positive. It is not "No," but "Yes," in the main—not prohibition, but release.

Free choices may be blocked not merely by law but by custom. Not only do the power-holders themselves unduly magnify the importance of their office, or seek to prolong their brief authority, but the bulk of the community bears down heavily upon variations from established habits and customs.[13] An invention of intelligence such as the school may itself be used to repress the spontaneous development of other ideas from other intelligences. Tendencies toward stability and conformity, which possess important elements of value in the functioning of a community, may operate against the life and vitality of the nation by becoming an obstacle to adaptation to new conditions. The

[13] See Mill's admirable analysis of this tendency toward mass oppression, not governmental in nature, but social in its characteristics (*op. cit.*, chap. iii). See also J. C. Merriam, "Conservation and Evolution in a Changing Social Program," *Proceedings of the American Philosophical Society*, LXXIII (1934), 351–70, and *The Inquiring Mind in a Changing World* ("Rice Institute Pamphlets," Vol. XXI, No. 3 [1934]); Adolf Löwe, *The Price of Liberty* ("Day-to-Day Pamphlets," No. 36 [1937]); Nicolas Berdyaev, *Slavery and Freedom* (1944).

graves of ancestors may block not only the building of railways in China but also the reorganization of international relations in the interest of human happiness. Education itself may be used to stifle free thought. Mass pressure for conformity may crush down freedom of thought, of behavior, of creative initiative.

The chief difficulties centering around the discussion of liberty, then, arise from the failure to realize the pluralistic nature of liberties and the widely varying types of situations under which they are operating. Competing forms of liberty must be brought together and reconciled not only in the general framework of the state—always a difficult problem—but also under widely varying kinds of crises in the life of the state itself and in the life of the various constituent citizens and groupings operating within the state, or partly within the state. How to reconcile order, justice, liberty, stability, variation—these are continuing tasks of the state; and the allocation or recognition of wide-ranging areas of free choice is a perennial problem of democratic statesmen from which they cannot escape.

The problem of liberty is not absolute but relative, not merely negative but also positive in character. It is not merely political, or merely economic, or merely ethical or religious, or merely racial, regional, or occupational; not merely artistic or scientific. It is a general task which calls for the general view of the total situation, requiring insight, judgment, and sense of balance and proportion in a dynamic, moving situation.

Democracy protects its citizen against arbitrary governmental intervention and against encroachments upon his personality by the small or the great, whether individuals or group. It strives to foster the optimum conditions for the unfolding of all human personalities positively and aggressively. The very mechanisms of democracy are designed to be constant reminders of what human association means, of the importance of an expanding range of free life. Its popular forms and procedures refer to the understandings and objectives of fraternal association and co-operation as a way of life. Frames and forms of government are essentially psychological in nature. They rest upon and induce understandings, reactions, conditionings, operating with enough regularity to make possible the forecasting of behavior and counterbehavior. The symbols of democracy are the symbols of liberty, of free life, of wide choice, of the expansion and expression of the personality of its citizens.

There are two sides of freedom—freedom *from* and freedom *for* something. Liberty is, on the one hand, absence of restraint, as when we are free from shackles, from prison, from a concentration camp, and no longer bound to submit to the commands of custodians. A soldier feels free in a sense when he obtains his discharge, or a mother when she is released from a hospital. But, on the other hand, freedom carries with it the idea of freedom for something:

58

to run, to fly, to create, to construct, to enjoy, to work, to expand, to improve, to make the best that is in us blossom out, to have a share in the good things of life, on the level the state of the economy will permit.

Freedom to become a slave, however, is not freedom at all; freedom to make a contract to work sixteen hours a day is not true freedom, although it may be enforced by necessity. Freedom to work if there is not a job available is hardly true liberty. Freedom may become and does become a mockery for men and women who are free to do what they should be able to do but cannot do. This was not the freedom in mind in earlier days when the Declaration of Independence was adopted, for then equality was coupled with liberty and liberty with the pursuit of happiness.

It has been understood for centuries that the soundest statecraft would provide for the widest range of liberty consistent with the common good. But why was so little done about it for so long a time? The early leaders did not have the idea of the equality of men but proceeded on the theory that men were essentially unequal and that systems of law and economics and ethics too should be built accordingly, on caste and slavery systems. Liberty was essentially for the few, to whom was committed the right to rule and to possess and to enjoy the fruits of the civilization of the time, whatever it might be. They even convinced the slave that his chains were good for him and that he should be happy to be alive under competent masters. To quarrel with custom or with the will of authority was evidence of a disordered mind—subversive, we say in our day—and those who hatched such foolish ideas as liberty were flouted and clouted by those who were on the inside. The lawyers, the warriors, and sometimes the priests closed in on them and cried shame.

It was a great day for the human race—the new day of Creation—when the idea dawned that every man is a human being, an end in himself, with a claim for the development of his own personality, and that human beings had a dignity and a worth, respect for which is the firm basis of human association. This was not the doctrine of the caste system; it was not in the magnificent passages of the great Plato, but it was found in Stoic philosophy, in the Roman law, in the New Testament, in the natural law philosophy, where there emerged the ideas of equality, of human rights for human beings. The early assertion of rights and claims was translated little by little into legal rights and claims, into political rights and claims, and, finally, into actualities as well as claims—all with the progressive support of ethics and religion, of law and government, of science and organization. Slavery, serfdom, and institutional inequality in turn fell before the advance of reason, religion, and science, ushering in with discovery and creation a new world in new form.

This is the pedigree of liberty in the modern day. This is why the liberty of the present day which it is the function of the state to protect and preserve is not alone liberty from chains but liberty for the fullest use of human faculties and abilities consistent with the general welfare.

One of the most subtle of all the many questions regarding the inner nature of liberty is the distinction drawn at times between freedom as an inner feeling and freedom as a fact. A slave may feel that he is free and rejoice even in his chains. Or he may be free and not know it. Or a free man may in reality be confined without realizing his limitation. He has not felt the tug of his chains, as he might if he went a little further. The prisoner may go back to his prison, happier within than without. A determinist may conclude that man is never really free but always obeys some set of dominant forces shaping his judgment for him—physical, economic, cultural—forces beyond his control and beyond his knowledge even. This may be economic determinism, or mass pressure of the crowd or group, or some set of emotional characteristics personal to him.

A voluntarist, however, will maintain that alternative courses are open to a personality and that in reality a wide range of free choices is spread before him. He may, indeed, prefer spiritual freedom to any other, or mental freedom to any other; in short, his desire for freedom may take other than legal, political, or social forms as commonly understood.

How far human actions may be predetermined, I leave to theology, philosophy, geography, and economics. For my part, I find less difficulty in assuming that there is freedom of choice in social relations than to assume there is none. Hence we may postulate choice as the basis of systems of government and society. I would go further and declare that, with the progress of the race, the human personality obtains a wider and wider range of free choices within which he may construct his personal world. His own creative powers expand in the world which he develops as he goes and which the society and state progressively and increasingly help him to construct on higher and finer levels.

This is in fact, then, one of the great ends of the state, one of the state functions which becomes increasingly important with the growth of science and civilization. We need not fear slavery to the state which seeks to emancipate us from shackling conditions; nor need the state fear the revolt of its citizens—the free men whose consent is itself the cohesive element in the political society.

The purpose of authority, it is clear, is not authority as such, but freedom; not merely might, but might and right in one. Authority may be abused, turned away from its true purpose, and may then in fact promote nonfreedom. We cannot assume that power will not be turned into personal or selfish channels. On the other hand, the unrestrained and unorganized relations of individuals to individuals, or groups to groups, and of groups to individuals would not of themselves and by themselves produce a resultant of complete liberty for all. Freedom is really possible only within the general framework of common understandings and procedures, some of which are set in the framework of the political society and others outside in other frameworks of social organization.

The development of human personality depends in large measure upon the types and forms of assistance and encouragement provided in the political setting. It is not the purpose of the state to repress liberty but to encourage, foster, and promote it on the largest possible scale. In providing security against external aggression, in organizing systems of order, in promoting justice, in encouraging the general welfare, the state advances the growth of liberty in the true sense of the term.

Freedom is a genuine end of government, obscured as this end may be at times by the greed and brutality of rulers. The government provides a framework of relations within which men may develop the best that is in them, consistently with the common good. Order, justice, security, and welfare all contribute to this end, twisted though the forms may be in practice. Much of the time freedom has seemed to be only that of the one or the very few, who were free to do their will at the expense of the others.

Most men have been slaves or serfs or low-ranking underlings, living on the fringe of recognition. But it is true that often their masters or lords were slaves also—slaves to custom, slaves to ignorance, slaves to uncontrolled emotions—limited in outlook and in opportunities of achievement. Custom, magic, religion, or superstition; these were the chains that were forged around the slave; sometimes force also.

Aristotle's assertion that a slave could be identified by looking at him was not a scientific observation worthy of a great scholar. Rousseau's comment is still true: that if there are slaves by nature, it is because there have been slaves against nature. There are natures more aggressive than others, or less resistant than others, as modern psychological research reveals. But all the variations in ability taken together do not add up to complete lack of legal or moral status.

The early forms of freedom as an end of the government took the shape of freedom of the state as a unit, or freedom of the rulers and those who were technically called "free." Those outside the circle were given, it was held, all the freedom that they could absorb or utilize; in other respects they were kept as wards of the masters, protected from situations they could not face alone. Such, indeed, was the argument down to the verge of the American Civil War.

The role of government in the furtherance of human freedom has been a varied one, ranging widely over noble heights and deep dark sloughs and depressions. A cynic might say that the trend of government has been to give as little rather than as much freedom as could be granted. The shame of power has often covered the deeds of selfish rulers, who found luxury, ease, and prestige in the possession and exploitation of fellow-humans and defended their cruelty in terms of necessity of one sort or another. The work of government in the development of human liberty is, nevertheless, most important and impressive.

The line of advance is from legal freedom to political freedom, from political freedom to genuine economic and social freedom. At every step of this long way there has been struggle over the ideologies involved, the frames of procedure and forms of protection of liberty, and the meaning of liberty in the constantly changing value systems of the time. The moral and ethical bases of liberty were in evidence at every stage of freedom's advance.

In the growth of legal freedom the governmental problem was that of building a series of guaranties or protections against arbitrary interferences either by government itself or by private individuals with the person. Out of this came the well-known body of civil liberties, in which legal status was assured to many citizens. They became legal persons with the rights and privileges of person and property surrounded by established procedures and personnel. In the nineteenth century many of these rights were also granted to corporations who also became legal persons in the meaning of the law.

The governmental problem has been in great measure that of reconciling the capacity of men for legal rights and duties with the status quo. Thus women obtained elementary civil rights with great difficulty and after long argumentation and struggles. Negroes in the United States had to await the outcome of the Civil War and an amendment to the basic law before they could enter these rights and then wait further upon their adequate enforcement—still in the future. In the earlier phases of the controversy the relation of private rights to the authority of the absolute head of the state was much discussed, but in later years this has played a minor part in the discussion. Opposition has latterly centered upon prejudice against the improved status of the grantees and the dangers to other segments of social life if such rights were conferred upon stated groups of whatever color or background. Social relations have constituted one of the chief barriers to the emancipation of many groups of persons, otherwise looked upon as harmless and tolerable. Millions of the human race still do not possess these rights in the systems under which they live and imperfectly even in the freest.

The struggle for political freedom as an end of the government was carried on with equal acrimony and for long periods of time; indeed, it still remains outside the capacity of most of the human race as far as any effective use of it is concerned. The right to vote and to hold office long remained the perquisite of the relatively few and long depended upon property considerations, dating from the times of the Greeks and Romans and in later times extending to the jealousy between racial groups. Nonpropertied persons were traditionally barred; women and workingmen long were held outside the area of voting.

Religious barriers were also raised at this point to protect, it was said, the security of the state against the church.

The arguments on suffrage pro and con were not on the whole carried on upon a very high level of discourse or social sophistication. In many places there was frankly an unwillingness in the propertied group to share the privileges of political control with those who were outside the circle of custom and of property—especially real property.[14] Sex qualifications precipitated battles in many lands, and the issue was finally determined by the rise of industrialism and the improved economic and cultural position of women.

In brief, the type of problem here submitted is that of determining, by the categories of governmental institutions, who the political people are, and to what extent and how they shall participate in the decisions made by government. On the whole, it cannot be said that the ways and means of arriving at decisions have been characterized more by reason and intelligence than by social force of interests struggling for recognition or against it. With respect to holding of office, however, the controversy often reached a higher level of discussion, since the qualifications and disqualifications were more readily subjected to careful analysis and reasoned conclusions.[15]

Freedom of speech and press, freedom of association, and freedom of worship fall in the same category of essential freedoms in political society and have all been burning problems for centuries, in one form and another. How far these freedoms may impinge on the common good, and how this shall be determined, has been one of the central points in governmental controversy and still is. Very often, however, the decisions have been judicial or administrative as well as legislative in nature. In like manner the freedom of science, research, and thought has been a basic problem for centuries, with decisions reached by force, argument, and strategy. Government as a guild has never been fully reconciled either to science or to religion, looking askance at them and not fully trusting either, although relying upon both in times of stress and in times of calm as well.

In recent times, too, emphasis has been placed upon freedom from fear and want. In a sense these have been the ends of government from very early times, in connection with fear that the enemy might enslave the people, fear from within that the tyrant might abuse them, or want of the basic essentials of life, as determined by each particular culture group.

These fundamentals have been universal in their range, but their application was confused and delayed by the identification of the interests of the ruling

[14] See my *A History of American Political Theories* (1931).

[15] See Macaulay's famous memorandum on civil service in England in 1854 and *Better Government Personnel: Report of the Commission of Inquiry on Public Service Personnel* (1935).

few with those of the whole community and the government. From time to time over seemingly endless stretches of time, war awakened one and famine and poverty the other. With the best of will, governments might be unable to obtain permanent peace or to arrive at adequate production of commodities, on whatever the level of the economy from the most rudimentary to the most advanced in type.

If, then, we look at the ends of government and run back over the types of problems that have come up under each of these heads, we may form a picture of the central problems of government from period to period. We may look at the questions arising, at the ways of approach to them, the kinds of techniques and tools employed, and at the cumulative value of these social inventions and configurations. We may examine more in detail the various tools of governments, the main forms of political aggregations, the principal forms of governments, and the organs of government. We may look at the unending struggle between the forms and the functions of government from time to time, between ideas and interests, customs and inventions. We may look at the outstanding trends of government and take a look forward at what government might be under optimum conditions.

Government is not a newcomer among human institutions. It is one of the very oldest, and its successes are as notable as its many failures. Only when anarchy comes, do we appreciate what the government is doing as a matter of course in the elementary maintenance of order, justice, security, and welfare.

VI. PRIORITIES AMONG ENDS

The struggle for priority among the ends of the state is one of the central points of the history of politics. What are the relative priorities of justice and order if they come in conflict? Theodore Roosevelt once said to me, "Merriam, in case of a choice between order and justice, I will always be on the side of order, wouldn't you?"

"Perhaps not," I replied. "I belong to the Sons of the American Revolution."

What if there is a clash between freedom and welfare or between security and freedom? In the long run these ends will be balanced against each other, but, in the short run, precedence will be given to one or another, following the lines of the common good as determined by those who have the responsibility of deciding. These decisions, we know from both history and reflection, will be colored by the interest and by the social attitudes of the rulers and the ruled as well. Both external security and internal order are closely dependent upon general morale for their functioning and cannot go too far afield in defying or disregarding or misinterpreting the common good as it appears to the generality of the community. Otherwise armies cannot win battles or wars, and internal order breaks down in disorder and disturbance approaching revolution.

To make the most useful appraisal or evaluation of the functions of the state, it is necessary to consider them in their relationship one to another. The state does not exist for any one of these functions such as order, or justice, or welfare alone but for the group of functions taken together and in their relations to one another. The political pattern is found in this weaving-together of various social duties and opportunities in varying ways and forms from time to time.

Historically observed, the different political associations have not always performed all these functions or in balanced systems. Sparta was a warrior state; Athens a welfare state; Rome a justice and order state. Many states have been welfare states in the imperialistic sense that they plundered and exploited their enemies from time immemorial. In the last century and a half some of the western European states combined all the functions of the state except freedom, and some everything but welfare; and some of the smaller states, like Switzerland and Holland among others, everything but security, provided in large measure for them by others.

All these states were set in the culture pattern of their time, which the political association in part reflected and in part created. Prevalent ideas and practices in religion, in familial relations, in agriculture, in industry, and in science and technology colored the policy and philosophy, however obscurely formulated, of the various governmental associations. In the narrower political field war cast its shadow over the whole range of governmental activities, darkening the days of men, through their failure to rise above the lower levels of violence as a means of aggregation. Failure to appreciate the dignity and moral equality of men bred doctrines and structures of caste and class, of slavery, serfdom, and domination by small groups of power-hungry persons, who only too often employed their trusteeship for cruelties and oppressions of unspeakable brutality. Only late in the history of the race was there intellectual and moral room for human equality, human freedom, welfare for all, and a fair share of the gains of human advancement.

It is small wonder that men have drawn the conclusion that the state has been nothing but an instrument of exploitation and have demanded its elimination from human forms of association. Or that others have cynically concluded that the political is typically and inevitably the picture of exploitation of the many by the few and that all calculations based upon any other assumptions are misleading and futile. Or that the essence of the state is military organization exerted for conquest or even for the forcible development of peoples by means of the warrior state. Nor is it strange that industrialists might fear the heavy hand of government habituated to deeds of blood and schemes of personal aggrandizement through violence or fraud.

If we were to close the books of observation too early, such conclusions might well be drawn, so slowly did justice and freedom break through the crust of custom and selfish interest, so tardily did general welfare find its way into modern state policy, so persistently were ideas of order interpreted in the light of special interest, and so frequently were wars precipitated at the behest not of general security but at the instance of exploiters seeking prestige or material plunder through conquest.

With the dawn of human dignity, the faint precursors of equality, justice, and freedom find their way through the gloom, moving toward the light of better life—but even then with unending limitations, restrictions, equivocations, and ambiguities that broke the pledges given. Scientific invention and technology, a jural order of the world, the rational defense of human rights and dignity—these made possible states with high purposes, achieved as well as acclaimed, made it possible in these latter days to carry out more fully than before the expression of the aims of the state in daily life and practice. The greatest foe of the developing state, moving toward the fulfilment of its highest purposes, has been the misconception of the nature and meaning of power. Political power as an agency of violence, fraud, corruption, ignorance, and intrigue has been the poison running through the life of genuine association. This has had the effect, first, of attracting personalities to whom such power appealed and, at the same time, arousing the fears of those to whom power had become a menace. There are those who fear all power as there are those who fear life itself, who dread organization and even association in any form; perhaps from temperament, perhaps from lack of aptitude in interrelations or practice, perhaps from some sad personal experience with governmental agencies.

But government may also be regarded not as a foe, a tyrant, an oppressor, a brutal hand upon the shoulder, a prison cell, the lash, but as a friend and guide, a companion, a special service, an instrumentation of personality.

Government of the creative and constructive type is slowly being ground out with infinite pains and with vast and widespread accompaniment of effort, often with temporary disillusionment. Government may be positive as well as negative, creative rather than destructive. Maladjusted powers in nature and in social organization may devastate life and happiness; and it has been found convenient, and, for all I know, useful, to have a demonology to which these wilder and less restrained powers may be consigned, as devils, evil principles, wicked spirits, until such time as the intelligence of mankind has found ways to tame and utilize them in social relations. The mighty advance in mechanization aided in this process of the maligning (diabolizing) of power, and thus there came to be unusual forms of resistance to authority per se, quite without precedent in the historical development of government.

But just as the subordination of the mechanism and its application to the finer purposes of life become dimly evident in modern organization, so adaptation to the presence of vast authority and the recognition of its broad social purposes may be expected to unfold gradually in the consciousness and in the institutions and in the ideology of men. Authority may then appear as an instrument of mankind, not as its master, as a means of enlarging the capacities of the group rather than as a brutal limitation. It would, of course, be fatuous to conclude that such a condition had already been reached in our day, or is to be expected in the very near future, but the slow development of the power process tends to advance in this direction, notwithstanding the many opposite evidences of momentary movement in another course.[16]

In this sense the so-called "struggle for power," which is cynically held up as the mark of the political, may in reality become a struggle for rendering service. Power may not be obtained through violence and fraud but earned as prestige and preferment arising from genuine contribution to the happiness and well-being of mankind. This is a hard doctrine for some to comprehend or accept, but it lies at the basis of emerging political association. "Whosoever will be chief among you, let him be your servant."

VII. CONCLUSION

Inevitably discussion over the true or proper functions of the political society has developed from time to time in many different forms. What the state "ought" to do has been declared with great dogmatism by many thinkers, past and present. On one occasion or another all the social groups within the boundaries of the political society have concentrated their attack upon activities of the state. The family, the church, the guild, the army, the union, the corporation, the farmer, and the professional society have all contested at times the jurisdiction of the state in special lines of action, and sometimes the controversy has raged with great bitterness—with more heat than light. Most of the time these struggles have been seen in group pressures, in resistances, riotings, and revolutions, as slaves, peasants, minorities of various descriptions, churches, business, and labor came to grips with the political society or its momentary rulers. But many of these were thinly disguised power struggles in which reason played a relatively small part. In time, however, elaborate rationalizations began to appear.

Looking back, we observe that the controversy between the ecclesiastical society and the political society occupied the center of the stage in western Europe for many generations. Church and state presented elaborate justifications of their claims for responsible direction, both in general and in particular. The whole field of philosophy, morality, organization, and economics was traversed in the course of this historic controversy between the Holy Roman

[16] Reinhold Niebuhr, *Moral Man and Immoral Society* (1932) and *The Nature and Destiny of Man* (1941). See E. E. Aubrey, *Present Theological Tendencies* (1936), for a review of the theology and the crisis of culture.

Empire and the Roman church. While the church did not claim temporal power as such, or the Empire assert its control over spiritual power as such, the boundaries and overlapping lines afforded ample room for theoretical and practical differences of policy and practice and for sometimes overt and sometimes veiled policies of action. The Empire was in no sense the ancient Roman Empire, and its practical position in the feudal political society of the day was full of political uncertainty, especially as the rising country states or nations began to assume their new forms of jurisdiction.

The position of the church was also weakened by internal dissension and ultimately by the rise of the Reformation movement. Nationalism presented quite a different front from feudalism and the Holy Roman Empire; and the answer was the union of church and state in the national state. But, of course, the boundary lines between law and morality are a perennial problem, recurring from time to time in one form and another.

In more recent times there has been sharp division as to the functions of the state centering around the best relations between industry and government.[17] Yet close observation helps us to see that the problems of government and of economics are not widely different from other problems arising in our daily lives at many different points of the compass. The fact that government has force, the power of life and death, is deceiving; for it wields such weapons only as the trustee of the community, whether the rulers admit this or not at particular times or even for long periods of human history. Modern economic organization also has at its command the staff of life, in the sense of material commodities exchangeable for human needs. But man does not live by bread alone, and human services are interchanged for other things than coin of the realm—and many services have no price or no market, whether too few or too many. Differential rewards for differential services are found in many ways and walks of life as well as in commerce.

Thus it seems that the worlds of government and industry both have many limitations upon them. Their rivalries may be characterized as struggles, but more accurately they are only the impact of forces in a moving equilibrium; they are not properly checks but balances, supplementing each other rather than trying to destroy each other.

Liberty is not a plea for no government; nor is government a plea for no enterprise—nor are liberty and security foes on the field of social struggle. In recent times, however, the conflict between the government or state and industry has set the world in flames more than once and might well do so

[17] See my *The Role of Politics in Social Change* (1936) and *Public and Private Government* (1944); Beardsley Ruml, *Government, Business and Values* (1943) and *Tomorrow's Business* (1945); L. S. Lyon *et al.*, *Government and Economic Life*, Vol. I (1939); Wesley C. Mitchell, "Economic Research and the Needs of the Times," in National Bureau of Economic Research, *Twenty-fourth Annual Report* (April, 1944).

again, if we do not adapt our thinking to the new conditions under which we now live. We must think how this situation has arisen and then think our way out of it.

The worst traits of government have been reinforced by various factors. The oldest and the latest of these is war. In war the government emerges as an arm of force aimed at destruction of the enemy. Here government becomes an organization for the security of the society, but an organization of force rather than an organization of consent. Although the state is in reality an organization for the promotion of the good life, emphasis is shifted to and fixed upon violence as the supreme test of the success of the state. This makes its mark on all the ways of the state, both in peace and in war, and operates against the finer qualities of association. Necessary though it may be for the life of the state, war stamps upon its qualities that operate against the peacetime ideals of the state.

A number of other factors have also affected the life of government in recent times. One of these is the large-scale nature of activities and another is complexity of activities. The modern nation emerged as a large-scale state, in contrast to the smaller and petty feudal lords and lordlets. Justice and order were cast upon a far larger stage than ever before, made possible by modern transportation and communication in France, Spain, England, and, finally, Germany and Italy.[18]

Next the modern state encountered the swift changes of modern science and technology that made the world over again. Changes in ways of life, changes in forms of association such as those of labor and capital, the growth of great urban centers—all these factors were a sharp challenge to the competence and ability of the political association. They required more rules, regulations, laws, and decisions than had ever been known before. They taxed the ingenuity, the honesty, and the judgment of officialdom as never before—and often overtaxed them. Both liberty and security were endangered at many points in the wild rush of change.

But the industrial world likewise met the challenge of new conditions much the same as the challenge to government. Such was the tremendous onward push of change, unparalleled in the history of mankind, increasing production beyond the wildest dreams of men a half-century ago and upsetting ancient landmarks.

Large-scale industry, like large-scale national politics, called for new capacities, and there were not only large industries and large-scale corporations and cartels but labor combinations of various types. So it happened that the state and industry had much the same general type of problem to solve: (1) large-scale and complex operations and (2) the flood of modern scientific and

[18] See my *The Making of Citizens.*

69

rational change. No one anticipated or was prepared for these new demands upon organization and leadership in a world of science, on the one hand, and mass control, on the other.

It should have been clear to the average man, but it was not, that the New World was to be dependent in large measure for its justice and order upon the types of political and industrial associations which would now come to the fore, with the war lords and the landlords in the background. It should also have been clear that these new forces must make their peace with science, with reason, and with the higher values of religious aspiration including its many institutionalized forms.

Unfortunately, the new nineteenth-century philosophies and their twentieth-century echoes were one-sided and inadequate. Both placed their whole weight upon the new economics without saying very plainly what they meant by "economic." But they agreed, both Marx and Mill, that economic considerations should furnish the guide of life. One held that the state should come to an end, the Marxian doctrine, and the other that the state should do next to nothing, laissez faire.

With a do-nothing government "the fittest would survive," some said, and with no state at all, said others, under economic collectivism the world would belong to everyone without interference either from government or from capitalists. These doctrines lead to class struggle, revolutionary uprisings, and widespread bitterness, raging through Western society, both political and industrial, and threatening the equilibrium and advance of interests and ideals alike.

But neither large-scale government nor large-scale business was an end in itself; they were both among the means by which the new-found talents of man were moving toward higher productivity, wider prosperity, higher standards of living, and a truer development of the principles of consent, equality, human dignity, and the pursuit of happiness. Communism, capitalism, and anarchism were all interpreting human life in terms of economic forces alone and were unable to provide the broader basis necessary for the good life. It was not that associations were large, that they were complex, or that "enterprise" was involved, but that a new world was opening to the mass of mankind.

It was inevitable that men feared the loss of liberty in the midst of many new regulations to which they were unaccustomed and that they feared for their security in the midst of vast industrial movements of boom and collapse. Such fears were often based upon sound observation and conclusion from the clumsiness of government, on the one hand, and the clumsiness of industry, on the other. Nor was it strange that in the gathering gloom men failed to find the beam of faith and leadership and confidence on which they might make their perilous advances into the unknown.

It is precisely at this point that the need for rethinking our present situation is urgent. Indeed, at this special point the immediate future of our modern civilization may well be decided. No civilization has a permanent lease upon life and growth, and over and over again the "guiding principle" may fade and die. Toynbee's *Study of History* is an impressive portrayal of the tragedy of past civilizations that ceased to grow, faded, and went back.

The Fascists and the Nazis have proposed a cure for all the ills of our time, but this has already been proved false. If this error had not been discovered and cured, however, it might well have wrecked the civilization of our times. Nor can it be presumed or concluded that collectivism in its various forms is a specific for our ills. Some of its values are useful and may be interchanged, but the same preoccupation with economic causes which produced laissez faire produced communism; and, unless the root error is cured, nothing permanent can emerge.

It may be said roughly that the prestige of government has suffered most from the tradition of violence and from hereditary transmission of authority. Impatience and incompetence were encouraged by these factors. Business, on the other hand, has been relatively free from violence but often has been able to employ government as its agent at home and abroad. Heredity has played and plays its role in industry but has its difficulties, and the immortality of the corporation has taken the place once held by heredity. Custom and magic have not been able to enforce their restrictions upon business in the main, in modern times, whatever may have been their vogue in earlier days. And, of course, trade is cast in the matrix of prevailing customs, of buying and selling and otherwise.

The art of salesmanship may center on the very point of adaptation to the special practices of a group, class, or nation—to the consumers. This, indeed, has been conducive to a form of toleration in industry, toleration of the customs of others within the framework of industrial relationships of mutual advantage, regardless of race or creed. If the missionaries carried creeds, the traders carried new ways with their new goods, and the scientists and technologists were not far behind in their special forms of enterprise. The trader might try to sell his own goods, but he must prepare them after a measure of adjustment to local custom. The trader must not be baffled by what is new, for this very newness may be the means of enlarging the radius of his trading operations.

What I am trying to say, then, is that industry long retained much of its rule-making, constitutive power without surrendering the capacity for quick adaptation and adjustment to new factors, and this without being charged with immorality or violation of immemorial custom, always of course, within a broad framework of legal regulation and common consent, which must not be too boldly or rashly transgressed, on penalty of either the law or the market.

71

Thus interest, for a long time outlawed and immoral, could gradually become respectable, but with difficulty; and necessitous bargaining, long outlawed, might find its way back through one form of monopoly or other, direct or indirect. In all this process, as already shown, violence, heredity, and magic played relatively unimportant roles, although not wholly out of the picture, so to speak.

The chief competitor of competition has been competition itself and its own ruthless destruction of itself—devouring its own children like Chronos of old.[19] Governments once created monopolies, but free enterprise also produced monopoly and crippled competition on a great scale.

Through all these considerations, it is by this time apparent that "enterprise" is an accompaniment of the activity of a group which is least bound by traditions, customs, and conventions.[20] It must be equally clear that "enterprise" may flourish on the same basis in science and technology, for much the same general body of reasons—namely, conditions favorable to the proliferation of adventuresome lines of inquiry and of organization.

Government and industry alike in our time, and indeed all forms of institutions, are faced by the major problem of complexity of organization and size of organization; by the hardening of success with vested forms resisting change. The diseases known as bureaucracy and obsolescence—which spring up in all institutions, familial, religious, professional, but for the moment center in industry and government—are the freezing of what should be fluid capital or power, which works against the forces that made it.

The question of how to deal with this politico-industrial set of problems is challenging the whole world of organization.[21] Industrialists who contributed liberally to the organization of Mussolini in Italy or of Hitler in Germany in the hope of ridding themselves of one or another form of organization such as trade-unions, the socialist or communistic partisans, were quickly disillusioned. They found themselves in the grip of other forces, military, on the one hand, and party, on the other, uniting in common cause against whatever industrial element stood out against them.

A circumstance which has escaped general observation, however, upsets almost all the calculations of those who philosophize or emotionalize on the "proper" extent of regulation as a social phenomenon, and especially of government regulation. The modern way of life, based as it is upon an entirely new form of scientific and rational apparatus, has enormously and incredibly

[19] Arthur R. Burns, *The Decline of Competition* (1936).

[20] Cf. Richard H. Tawney, *The Acquisitive Society* (1920).

[21] See my *Public and Private Government;* James Burnham, *The Managerial Revolution* (1941); R. A. Brady, *Business as a System of Power* (1943); Beardsley Ruml, *Tomorrow's Business;* Oscar Lange, *The American Way of Business* (1942).

expanded the range of human activity. It is not easy to set down a precise figure, but it is well within the limits of moderation to say that the average man has increased the range of his activities, his possibilities, by a hundred fold, and this may be expanded many many times more by pending discoveries and inventions.

This increase in the range and variety of activities also brings with it an increase in the range and variety of regulations of activities. If the number of human activities is ten and the number of governmental regulations is one, the percentage is 10. But if the number of activities is a thousand and the number of regulations is ten, the percentage is only 1.

Two situations must be observed: first, one in which the variety of regulations is really far less proportionately and, second, one in which new regulations are in a way absorbed, that is, they become automatic, unconscious, as in driving, so that they are no more restraints in the repressive or oppressive sense of the term.

On this basis there is much ground for believing that the continuing extension of governmental regulation as such is really an illusion. It is just as possible to assert that what is in store is the diminution of governmental regulation. The controls which government requires to carry out its community functions are of a strategic nature only and do not call for continuing enlargement in the sense of collective actions indefinitely expanded.[22] A sounder knowledge of human nature, a better type of organization, and a more effective manner of evaluating rapid change, on the part both of government and of the community, will go far to stabilize the futile struggle over "more" or "less" government as such.

This should not be interpreted to mean, however, that there are not from time to time significant expansions of governmental activity in crises or periods of transition. War and unemployment are the two great unsolved problems of our time, and the strategic controls essential for their restraint are not easy to find. All the ends of government are here involved—security, order, justice, welfare, freedom. The development of broad understandings, institutional inventions, and acceptable practices and procedures is not the task of a day. But when agreements have been reached on a sufficiently wide basis, and strategic forms of co-operation and control established and accepted, the degree of governmental controls and sanctions tends back again to situations where there is far less tension and far more tolerance; where both armed forces and governmental directives play a less significant role.[23]

[22] See my *The Role of Politics in Social Change*, chap. v: "Strategic Controls."

[23] See the program of future government outlined below in chap. x.

CHAPTER III

THE TOOLS OF GOVERNMENT

THE tools of the political society are the means commonly employed to make its policies and plans effective. Of course, the whole range of human motivation, interests, ideas, emotions—anything that moves human beings in one way or another—may be utilized by the political society. We shall take up, first, the broad forms of inducement and restraint, and once again the caution must be sounded that they are also employed by agencies other than the governmental. These general methods must also be read in the context of the special methods and instruments of the state to be considered later: (i) custom, (ii) violence, (iii) symbolism and ceremonialism, (iv) rational consent and participation, (v) strategy, and (vi) leadership.[1]

I. CUSTOM

The vast and persuasive influence of custom acts as one of the agencies of politics. Authority may be a recognition or an enlargement of custom, but, when authority is once established, custom is utilized to support it. In primitive societies this is, indeed, the main support of the political society, as of other associations. What has been is accepted as given, except as time and special occasions modify the mores of the group. The form of government, the persons vested with governmental authority, and the special rules and regulations proposed by the authority are all covered by the great cloak of the customary, the traditional, the habitual. And this is true down to the present day.[2]

Custom, magic, religion, and authority are mingled together in a web of authority, which is adequate for social living. To defy the system of group cohesion in which they are imbedded marks the objector as an outsider—unless he is strong enough to carry through what then becomes a revolution, personal or otherwise.

Primitive codes are compilations of understandings which spring out of common custom, tradition, and habit. Later on, from time to time, they are brought together in more formal manner, as in the Code of Hammurabi. Wide-ranging systems of law and justice spring up without special enactment or specific sanction, as has the common law of our own land. But, beyond all

---

[1] See my *The Making of Citizens* (1931), chaps. ii and iii, on the social composition of civic cohesion, and also summary and conclusions in chap. ix. Cf. H. D. Lasswell, *Politics: Who Gets What, When, How* (1931).

[2] See Robert H. Lowie, *The Origin of the State* (1927).

this, custom stands as a tower of strength for the political authority, as in fact for any and all authorities. The weight of custom, the immense balance wheel of social relations, as it has been variously characterized, reinforces *what is* with all the economy of effort which customary action involves. No hesitation in decision here, no wasted moments wondering whether or no, but instant and automatic action. We need not stop to aim with custom; we know the range. If help is needed, magic and religion are at hand to give the necessary force; and violence is not far away.

It is as difficult to argue with custom as it is to argue about the steps in the midst of the dance. In fact, when custom becomes an object of serious discussion, it is greatly weakened if not on its way out. For skepticism destroys its automatic quality. By the same logic, however, custom may resist change which is urgent in some national crisis and thus imperil the life of the state. The fugitive from justice in Berlin who would not violate the mandate "keep off the grass" was caught, when he might have escaped. And nations have met the same fate when superstition stood in the way of important action.

On a somewhat different level traditions are also significant in strengthening the tenacity of the political society. Traditions have a higher rational basis than custom, for they are often founded on reflection and generalization at some moment in the history of the group. All enduring forms of political society have incorporated in their list of implements of survival a body of traditions which are deemed to be characteristic of the group. These traditions are passed on from generation to generation and become slogans of unified actions in moments of necessity for solidarity.[3] To be able to say, "This is in the best tradition of the group," is an unquestionable element of strength in any group and not least in the political society.

Here again, however, the tradition, like the custom, may stand in the way of essential change and thus block the purpose of the group itself. Armies and navies may cling to outgrown methods of equipment and strategy—to their downfall. Judges and political leaders may do likewise, appealing to traditions or interpretations of traditions which have become obsolete or obsolescent. Yet in the main the great traditions are powerful supports of the political group, powerful implements for the performance of the functions of the state—supports without which, indeed, none of the great ends of the state could be realized.

We might conclude, of course, that custom is not a tool of government but a maker of government; that government is in reverse a tool of custom. But custom is never entirely automatic. From time to time the customs must be interpreted and authentically interpreted by someone who is accepted as a recognized and competent interpreter. If there is no change, there is little to

---

[3] See my *The Making of Citizens* for traditions of leading states.

interpret, but in any community there is likely to be war, pestilence, famine, flood, and drought, along with inventions and contrivances which compel alterations in the ways of life. The government is in a position to interpret and apply many of the old customs to the new situation, even without the appearance of any change in the old. Not all the interpretation and applications are governmental, for most are religious, familial, or other; but many of the changes are quietly adjudicated by the governing officials, and at such points government employs the customary as the tool of the political.

II. VIOLENCE

Force is one of the tools of state authority.[4] In the early theories of despotism and in the Nazi theory, violence is a central factor in political association, both in external and in internal relations. The Fascists and the Nazis have repeatedly proclaimed the significance of might as the basis of right and eulogized violence and war as crowning glories of mankind.

In international relations war is by no means the only implement of authority, but it remains as one down to the present hour. Diplomacy, trade, and cultural relations of various kinds are also a great part of the intercourse between nations. Yet war still continues, in spite of its outlawry as an instrument of national policy, as a powerful factor.

A major problem in the organization of violence is presented by international relations. Until a jural order of the world is established, nations will maintain armed forces for their national defense—forces more or less elaborate according to the strategic situation or the temper of the particular state. But how shall the nation protect itself against its own protectors, if there arises a difference of judgment between them?[5] Evidently the effective restraint upon the power-hunger of any army will not be that of superior physical force; it must be a form of control arising from custom and wont, resting, perhaps, upon a rational basis.

Perhaps the general who might take political power does not want it for personal reasons, preferring military command under direction. Perhaps he recognizes the system of civil-military relations and accepts it as sound. Perhaps the soldiers who make up his army recognize the principles of policy determination by civil authorities and are not willing to embark upon a countercourse. Guns are important in military organization, but so is the willingness to obey. The Russians had an army of some eight million at the close of World War I, but one fine day it melted away. The will to obey disappeared, leaving commands but no response.

[4] See my *Prologue to Politics* (1939), chap. i: "The Organization of Violence," and Edmund Taylor's *The Strategy of Terror* (1940).

[5] See my *The New Democracy and the New Despotism* (1939), pp. 132 ff., and citations there.

76

If the head of the army is also the head of the state and is, at one and the same time, a general and a statesman, the solution is relatively easy—just as easy as the idea of the philosopher-king of classic renown. There are, of course, Caesars and Napoleons and Washingtons, but more commonly the virtue of the military leader and the virtue of the political leader are not found in the same man. Mussolini had a military pose, but in the war he rated a corporal. Hitler's language was sanguinary, but he, too, was ranked a corporal. Hindenburg and Ludendorff would be given about the same relative rating as such political leaders as ward committeemen. General Grant will always be admired as a soldier, but he did not add to his distinction in the field of politics.

The truth is that the most neglected of subjects in the whole domain of political science is that of the organization of military violence in relation to political government. Our courses in government were, for a long time, called "Civil Government" and are sometimes so called even today. Even the wide vogue of public administration leaves military administration as dry as a desert, with hardly an oasis. Neither, with few exceptions, have the students of parties and public opinion done any better. The reason for this, in the main, is the assumption that there should be no violence in the rational state and that in a democratic state especially organized violence is a shameful thing that may best be ignored, outside the ranks of the career military officials. Modern democracy has neglected the role of armies in the modern state because it was absorbed in the contemplation of the ideal state—without war. At the same time, many liberals have recoiled from the collective security which would guarantee a world of peace.

Nationalism put an end to the endless feuds of petty lords, but it did not put an end to the greater wars of the greater units emerging in the place of the older little principalities and feudalities. An English historian has well described the ways and means by which the early English liberals starved the army because they feared—and, indeed, experience with Cromwell showed—it might be used against them. On the other hand, the relations between the military and the civil authorities, once war broke out, were ill prepared and sadly defective.[6] Similar accounts of German experience have recently been developed by Huber and by Höhn in comprehensive works showing the long struggle between military administration and efficiency and the democratic movement in the German state.[7]

But is this a subject with which democratic states may concern themselves? Or is it not a topic for the professional students of military administration? What have we to do with brute force?

[6] J. S. Omond, *Parliament and the Army, 1642–1904* (1933).

[7] Ernst R. Huber, *Heer und Staat in der deutschen Geschichte* (1938); Reinhard Höhn, *Verfassungskampf und Heereseid* (1938); Sir Ian Hamilton, *The Soul and Body of an Army* (1921).

By way of reply, the following conclusions are pertinent.

1. We must concern ourselves with force in order that we may be able to reason—in order that we may carry on the pursuits in which we wish to engage. We must set up a world in which the values we cherish may live and grow and come to their special forms of perfection.

In the modern world, with its modes of communication and transportation, we cannot lose ourselves "in the vast woods where flows the Oregon." There is no longer any space for the hermit. An expedition, organized by some anthropologist, would find us out and take movies of our hermitage. The scientists are at the door, applying anthropological methods to contemporary society.

2. What we call "violence" is, indeed, an inferior form of organization itself. It is the task of reason to examine this organization, to understand it, to invent forms of reorganization which are superior in type and which may come into general acceptance as we go along. Violence is really the inferior organization of vital life-forces. We do not seek to abolish energies: we aim at their reasonable control.

In modern times the weapons of warfare are the product of very high intelligence. Where do high explosives come from? Who invents airplanes and tanks? Who are the authorities in ballistics? In wartime one group of scientists is summoned to work on submarine detectors; another group on ballistics and trajectories, on rocket bombs; still another to decipher codes; doctors are drafted for surgery and care; specialists are recruited for propaganda; administrators are called upon for administration; etc.

The difficulty is not with the high explosive per se but with the purposes to which it is devoted in a given situation. The organization of violence is a technical question, to answer which men of reason will be called. But there is no reason why bandits and gangsters and gorillas should be given the secrets of the laboratory, of management, of psychology, of medicine, for their bandit purposes alone.

Science is properly modest and tentative in its conclusions where data are not complete; yet in situations where action is imminent, urgent, and unavoidable, it is not scientific to do nothing because all cannot be done. We aim even if the aim is imperfect. We save the drowning man with a smash on the jaw perhaps; we lose a limb to save a life; we chance an operation sometimes when death is the grim alternative.

It is one of the tasks of political science to undertake the solution of the critical problem of the organization of violence—military violence—in its relationship to the political controls and guiding points of the occasion. Before the storm breaks, we may consider what the storm will be like, what it will do, and how we shall meet these new situations. This is the way that ships are sailed and the way that ships of state may be navigated by their commanders and their crew.

If you learn how to breathe while swimming, you do not fall into a panic on swallowing a little water. If you know what the incidents of war and emergency are, you do not collapse, paralyzed with unreasoning fear, but adjust yourself to the known, even if unpleasant. The passengers keep quiet during the storm, but afterward they may be heard—*in extenso* perhaps.

There are three principal aspects of this problem as far as politics is concerned: (1) the organization of violence in relation to the treatment of ordinary social deviations in the category of crime; (2) the organization of violence in relation to dissident groups on the edge of legality; and (3) the organization of violence in military form (see chap. iv). They are all the same problem, but the central question is seen from different points of view.

1. In dealing with ordinary crime, more progress has been made than elsewhere. The state has largely taken over the "monopoly of violence." Private wars are banned, in the main, in modern times; also private vengeance by force. Even the duel is on the decline. Casual hooliganism, accompanied by violence, is still with us from time to time, but it tends to disappear. The organized underworld blossoms out here and there with banditry and murder but is increasingly beset with obstacles by the state, as communication and transportation integrate central control. Lynchings and private justice are on the way out.

The treatment of crime has changed, in the main, from repression to prevention. Beatings and brandings and mutilations—diabolical torture—are on the decline. Capital punishment is restricted in its application, and slowly—very slowly, too slowly—the prison looks in the direction of the hospital. Education, medicine, recreation—the whole apparatus of social and economic organization—are being utilized in an effort to control in advance, to prevent the conditions out of which social deviations of a distressing type arise.

This process is a long way from completion at the present time, but there is every reason to believe that in the not-too-distant future the goal will be reached. True, Butler's *Erewhon* in 1872 predicted the time when those who carelessly became sick would be punished rather than those whose natures drove them to crime. Nevertheless, the process of prevention, the rule of management without force, is on its way. The general principle of prevention has been accepted, and the details of management are in course of development. A shot in the arm even takes the place of a strait jacket. When Al Smith demands a jury of psychiatrists to aid the court, we may read the writing on the wall; or when the Sing Sing football team (according to the movies) begs the governor not to pardon its star halfback, we know that something is happening in crime treatment.

2. The problem of violence and its application becomes more difficult as we

deal with dissident groups of persons instead of individuals; with races, religions, regions, and interest groupings of various types; with special forms of ideology and propaganda.

Let it be said at the outset that this is not, as some suppose, a problem peculiar to democratic states but a general problem of all organized governments of whatever type, for this goes down to the roots of morale in the political association. It is very simple to say that whoever disagrees with the ruling powers shall die or be imprisoned, but this is not done under any government and could not be enforced. All governments find some *raison d'état* for action, however transparent they may seem at home or abroad.

How far may we go, it may be asked, in tolerance or oppression of the special practices of various races, or of various religious beliefs, or of special neighborhoods, or of special classes of occupations, of interests, or of special groups interested in particular types of propaganda or of education?

Many factors enter into the calculations here—confusing, perhaps. What if the ought of the state conflicts with the ought of other groups—let us say the church? Or of a special racial group or of a class? And who shall say what is the relative oughtness of the respective oughts? At this point conflicting answers may be returned. At a given moment the state authorities decide; but there is an appeal from their verdict to reason, experience, and judgment, authentic though the decision may be in its special framework.

The religious problem has flamed out for centuries. Industrial groupings are often hot fields of controversy. Colonial expansion has brought about the sharpest clashes. Racial minorities have been the magnetic center of disturbance from time immemorial and are not ended, alas, in our day.

Now racial-nationality propagandas—pro and con—become disturbers of the peace of the community. Let us look at the latter problem just for a moment. May the state permit the organization of private armies, with uniforms, barracks, drillings, parades, and mimic warfare? May the state permit the operations of associations aiming at its overthrow by violence? May the state exercise violence to prevent free discussion of the fundamental principles of governmental associations?

To these queries two replies may be given—one very general and the other special in nature. (*a*) In general, the state permits all forms of discussion and association not substantially threatening its existence and operation. (*b*) The state represses all organization and action constituting a substantial disturbance of the peace and a menace to the safety of the state.

Beyond this the field is one of management and administration of public order, subject, first, to judicial appeal and protection and, second, to legislative review and reversal of administrative management. I do not take "administrative management" to mean the decision of the officer on the beat alone but to include also the mature judgment of administrative officials charged with the maintenance of the public safety and order. This judgment might well be supplemented by the advice of citizens consulted for this special purpose, contributing their special knowledge of local situations and their relation to the commonweal. In the case of instructional problems these are obviously the primary responsibility of the professional and technical group in charge of education at the given time, with ultimate review in the light of state policy.

The real difficulty often lies in one of these factors: a lack of good will to reach the right results; a lack of intelligence regarding the basic situations out of which the clash comes; indecision or panicky and hysterical attitudes in decision; a lack of imagination and inventiveness in contriving wise ways of meeting emergencies. In general, these sum up the lack of administrative *savoir-faire* in dealing with minorities and in understanding the methods of morale maintenance in a society.

If ill will, indecision, ignorance, narrowness, hysteria, and insensitivity dominate the scene, they are met by the deep-seated capacity of underground groups for devising ways and means of legal resistance. Gandhi's ingenuity in keeping usually within the letter of the law, while breaking its spirit, is a modern illustration of a practice that is as old as human association. Any school child can furnish information as to how to tease the teacher within the law. In all such cases there is an equity that softens the strictness of the law to good advantage, but there is also an equity that tightens up the law a little, also to good advantage at times—as Shylock discovered.

In dealing with ingenious dissidents, seeking to break the spirit of the law while keeping within its letter, it is also useful to observe what Bagehot once called "illogical moderation." In such cases I should prefer one who is not a logician by profession but an expert administrator—for though a logician would undoubtedly outtalk the dissidents, a man convinced against his will is of the same opinion still. The skilled adjudicator would outmaneuver the dissenters so that they would seem to be opposing themselves rather than the administration—blaming themselves and not the agent of the law.

III. SYMBOLISM

A significant tool of government is that of ceremonialism and symbolism in their myriad forms. In all states there is found a cult of authority, expressed in a wide variety of ceremonials and symbolisms.[8] These symbols of the group are appropriated by governors and those who hope to govern. They may, of course, be weapons of revolution and revolt as well as authority. These are

[8] See A. N. Whitehead, *Symbolism* (1927); John Dewey, *The Quest for Certainty* (1929), chap. vi, "The Play of Ideas"; Robert Michels, *Der Patriotismus* (1929); Thurman Arnold, *The Symbols of Government* (1935); James Marshall, *Swords and Symbols* (1939).

found in early stages of primitive life, and they appear in the highest forms of civilized association. By no means peculiar to the political type, they character-ize the life-process of all groups—economic, religious, cultural, and otherwise. Impressive situations, either historical or hoped for, are presented in a desirable light, with life, warmth, and color; and vigor and vitality are developed in the otherwise abstract sentiment of group unity. Flags, music, festivals, and holi-days, initiations, coronations, funerals, weddings, and christenings, demonstra-tions, monuments, buildings, and public ways—all play their part in the ritual-ism which envelops social life in a network of observances, intimately associ-ated with tension moments in the lives of great masses of individuals. When an old group goes under, its symbolisms often survive its life, as the Roman eagle still stands as a symbol of power; and, when a new society emerges, it proceeds with all possible dispatch to develop symbols of its own.

Powerful devices have been produced by all groups. Mighty among them are the Cross and the Crown, historic symbols of church and state, sainthood and knighthood, with their ceremonial background. Flags have been from time immemorial the emblems of cohesive groups, especially the political, while music has preserved for the group symbolic unity in peace and war. Holidays and festivals serve the purposes of the group or cult, impressing their symbolism deep on the participants. If the state has the tremendous and savage symbolism of human conflict expressed in war, the church has the symbols of birth, wedding, death. If the state has the prison and the scaffold, the church has excommunication, confession, penance, the pains of hell, and the dreams of heaven. Kings and princes, rival saints, archangels and kings of kings, cardinals and bishops and popes, compete with generals, statesmen, emperors, with great savants, great artists of every race, region, and religion.

Which of these groups has the most impressive flags? Which of them has captured the most appealing songs and poems? Which of them the larger and more impressive array of holidays and festivals? In the service of which is found the most impressive and majestic architecture? Which of them stages the most colorful demonstrations and mass movements?

To answer these questions it would be necessary to carry through a long series of studies in political symbolism, and in the end, perhaps, there would remain no impartial judge competent to render a decision. Each group has its own symbolisms, which, shot through and through as they are with experience and emotion, seem the dearest, and surely are the most powerful in their appeal. The important point is that the students consider these symbolisms in the light of their relation to groups and situations with which they are insep-arably allied, and consider further the relation of these various symbolisms, one to the other. For life lies in their totality rather than in their separate and individual treatment. It is when all these symbols are adjusted and reinforce each other that the complex appears in its most vivid light.

In the domain of music the political symbol is highly developed. It is impossible to undertake any comparison in a field where judgments differ so widely, but certainly all would agree on the vitality of the French "Marseillaise" and the Russian "Internationale," which have gone around the world. The impressive "Star-spangled Banner," "God Save the King," and "The Watch on the Rhine" are surcharged with symbolic significance not only in their own territories but on a wider field. The songs of Switzerland and Austria-Hungary each had a value locally but are less generally familiar. It may be said that these songs are all fighting music, the outgrowth of military situations, and in a sense this is true. Many of them embody a certain idealism, however, in addition to the ferocity of a fighting song and are forward-looking as well as backward-looking in their appeal. This is notably true of the "Battle Hymn of the Republic" and the "Internationale," while the spirit of the "Marseillaise" is that of emancipation and the downfall of tyranny.

The real value of these musical symbolisms, however, is in their appeal to a rich body of associations, called up in the individual out of his own experience and those around him. They have a distinct survival value, in that they summon from the depths of ancestral experience the group coherence and tenacity without which it cannot maintain its independent existence. Their real tests come when the song of one group impinges upon the song of another—the local upon the national, or the religious group song upon the political, or the ethnic upon either. Which will stir the heart most deeply in the border-line cases—the musical appeal of the church, the patriotic song of the state, the haunting melody of the race, the folk song of the family and community, or the war cry of the class? In many a person this test is made, searching some of the deepest emotions of his nature. But, of course, the final decision is affected by many other factors than the rhythmic alone, although the musical may be one and in a number of marginal cases may be the decisive one.

Undoubtedly the most condensed symbol of political unity is the flag, which from centuries back has been a token of the group, and most commonly, although not exclusively, of the political community. There are, of course, ecclesiastical flags and cultural group flags and economic class flags and all manner of social group flags, but by common consent the political flag is the most distinctive and its connotations most clearly understood. The flag is primarily a military symbol, serving its main purpose in times of battle as a means of identification in the earlier times and still to some extent. One of the first tasks of a revolutionary political order is to devise a new flag, such as the swastika, to wave as the symbol of the new regime, showing its colors in the literal sense of the term. The symbolism of the flag is maintained, however, in times of peace as well as war, and many other high values are read into it.

The symbolism of the state uniform is also of importance in an appraisal of these appeals to color and form as supports of civic tradition. Originally the uniform was cultivated by the hereditary group for distinctive purposes. The decline of class distinctions, however, and the disappearance of the nobility as a separate order has very greatly reduced the importance of the differentiating meaning of the state livery. Only in the army does the wearing of the uniform survive in its original value, and here it is, of course, of very practical importance. Red, blue, gray, green, and their variations are intimately associated with the military fortunes of the states, and the color scheme cannot be separated from the fate of the British army, or the French, or the German.

Diplomats still wear on state occasions their distinctive garb and orders or decorations, but otherwise the statesmen have come to wear ordinary costume, or, at the most, are classed among the frocks and the top hats. The modern world is not, however, without its colorful survivals of the compelling power of the uniform, as is evident at coronations and inaugurations, or in England in the deliberations in Guild Hall of the City of London.

Architectural symbolism has also been called upon to support the claims of the body politic. Towering edifices proclaim the majesty and dignity of the state and impress even the casual with their social meaning. Capital buildings, town and city halls, palaces of justice, monuments, and monumental figures, adorn conspicuous places in every commonwealth. The houses of Parliament in London, the Hôtel de Ville in Paris, the Reichstagsgebäude in Berlin, the Kremlin in Moscow, and the Capitol in Washington are among the most impressive pieces of architectural display anywhere to be found, while palaces and halls are scattered everywhere.

The figures of great political heroes are likewise important in the visualization of the state. Westminster Abbey and Trafalgar Square in London, the Washington and Lincoln monuments in Washington, the Place de la Bastile, the Place de la Concorde, and the Tomb of Napoleon in Paris, the Red Square in Moscow, and the Siegesallee in Berlin—these are notable illustrations of the general use of the monumental in perpetuation of the purposes of the political group. They are continuing object-lessons in civic training, the objective of innumerable pilgrimages to these civic shrines. War memorials are, of course, scattered over every land, commemorating the sacrifices or victories perhaps in great national struggles. The most notable of these in modern times is the Tomb of the Unknown Soldier.

The most aggressive symbolism is that of the Soviets, who have covered Russia with the images of Lenin and have established thousands of Lenin Corners, visible reminders of the meaning of the revolutionary cause. The Red Square, red under the *ancien régime* and still red with quite another connotation, affords an interesting example of the facility with which symbolisms may be transferred from one order to another. Pulling down the memorials, especially the personal ones, of an earlier group, is an impressive opening for the new symbolism, but the conversion of the old is equally possible and frequently occurs.

The streets and public places have been largely appropriated by the political group, and one-fourth of the superficial area of most cities is taken up by public ways. An analysis of the street names in any of the great capitals, or in the smaller cities for that matter, shows an overwhelming preponderance of political names. Religious, cultural, and class figures are represented, but only in a relatively small percentage of cases. An uninitiated observer, seeing for the first time a modern city from the air, might be struck with the competing types of architecture. He would see the spires of churches on every hand; he would see the smokestacks of modern manufacturing as well; he would observe the spread of impressive educational structures; and he would notice the massive town hall and other political buildings. He would perhaps find the ecclesiastical group with the most impressive structural monuments, but he would find the political community fully represented in the picture; and if a moving picture were unfolded before him, covering a century or so, he would observe the gradual decline of the ecclesiastical and the rise of the commercial, the educational, and the cultural, and, likewise, although not in the same advancing ratio, the political.

Many of the state activities would be represented by buildings and places less spectacular in appearance and less impressive to the eye. Examples of this are the institutions for the care of the defective and dependent, for medical care, for recreation, for education, prosaic types perhaps of public works, like the T.V.A., whose symbolic value on the traditional side at least have not been so well developed as that of the more magnificent and ornate structures. Yet they represent, on the whole, a continuing series of specific and useful services rendered to the citizen by his group, less impressive than the more warlike memorials traditionally constructed by the political group.

Always a powerful stimulator of civic interest is the great spectacle or show organized by various groups for the celebration of some group rite or ceremony. The size, splendor, and impressiveness of these exhibitions are some of the indices of group solidarity and vitality. In these moments the group may be said to live its fullest and highest life and the member of the group to be lifted up with it to its heights. What, then, are the great sights which might be exhibited to one who sought for political demonstrations? Military and naval reviews are among the most impressive exhibitions of organized political life, and their color and movement are inspiring even to those who hate war. Great mass meetings, either of parties and factions or of the whole citizenry assembled on some occasion of state, are likewise impressive to any observer and still more to the actual participants. The swaying of the multitude under the inspiration of some popular orator is full of life and power, while the unled action of an ungovernable mob is even more so. Or the sweep of a great parade with bands and music and marching feet is heartening to friends and disquieting to foes. In more highly organized form the great parliamentary discussions are often impressive to the last degree, when conducted upon a high plane of political ability. The great actors in the great drama of state have a compelling power upon the political community, of which few are fully conscious, but which is felt long after the echoes have died away. The radio broadcast to many millions, widely separated, is also deeply impressive. Television and other new devices will add to this.

Coronations under the hereditary regime and inaugurations under the new order are impressive moments in the life of the state, and their pomp and solemnity dignify the political group in its own eyes and in those of observers, friendly or unfriendly. In a hereditary scheme all the domestic events of the nobility become a matter of public concern, although sometimes with questionable advantage where there is too great a gap between the dignity of the ritual and the personality of the participants. "One disadvantage of the monarch as a symbol is that he may behave as a human being as well as a symbol; he may be insane like George III, or self-willed like Victoria."[9]

The funerals of great state personalities are useful moments for civic training and are so employed in all groups political or otherwise. They provide the framework for the repetition of the virtues of the deceased and also the virtues of the group of which he has been a part. All the maxims and sayings of the tribe or nation may on such occasions be taught at a moment when the hearers are unusually susceptible to impressions of a civic nature and when the words of the teacher are reinforced by the solemnity and the sadness of the occasion. A sense of common loss pervades the group and intensifies the solidarity of the citizens, as well as the feeling of the importance of their society.

Thus the funeral rites of Lenin were vastly impressive to the thousands who assembled in the Red Square in the dead of winter to take part in the final tribute to the departed hero. The interment of Edward VII was uncanny in the impression made by the gorgeous spectacle that wound its way through the streets of the capital city. The funeral passage of Lincoln was one of the most impressive events in American history. The last rites of Roosevelt were profoundly impressive and compelled the rehearsal of his statesman-like services for the whole world.

The greatest and most impressive spectacle of the political group is, of course, war, foreign or civil. The impact of armed forces, the outstanding battles, with victory or defeat, as may be, the tragic losses in persons and property, the scenes of danger, death, sacrifice, struggle—these surpass all others in dramatic quality and, in fact, have supplied much of the imagery of other groups. Unquestionably the civic value of these scenes is very great and their influence of abiding quality. But there lurks a danger in the cup of

[9] Quoted by J. M. Gaus, *Great Britain* (1929), p. 51.

86

war, to war itself, for from it may come war weariness, war exhaustion, and lack of confidence in the ruling group; and this in turn may spell the disintegration of allegiance and the melting of the power either of the order or of the state. The Russian monarchy was dissolved in the midst of a great war, and another political group sprang up almost by magic; likewise the Kaiser in Germany and his military entourage were as if by miracle overthrown and sent tottering to their ruin. Of like quality was the Austrian participation in a losing venture, and with like result. The end of Mussolini and Hitler was tragic; in this case, not only disaster to the personal holders of the highest power in the state, but the dissolution of the political group itself came as a sequel.

These, then, are types of symbolisms employed, consciously or unconsciously, in the promotion of civic morale in the various states here canvassed. If one were so far master of the material world that he might command moving and talking pictures of these events and group the cases in appropriate fashion, he would be able to give a much more intimate knowledge of the political process than is usually the possession even of those who pass as politically sophisticated. For in this civic ritualism lies the secret of the state, or, more accurately, one of them; since these ceremonialisms, devoid of a live interest and sound advantage content, will not long endure. When their vital core is gone, they are promptly cast away and others are sought and found without much delay.

It is the great fallacy of the ritualists that in the form alone lies the power, whereas the power really lies in the intimate relation of the symbol and the vital force it seeks to stimulate, release, express. Nothing is more tragic than the sight of holders of dead symbols invoking obedience in their lifeless names from those whose eyes are fixed upon the more vivid symbolisms of a new political or other order. The fleeing Kaiser might storm impotently; the pitiful shadow of the emperor of all the Russias in captivity at Ekaterinburg looked in vain for a salute from the soldiers. Mussolini reached a moment when his scowl no longer terrified king or people. The symbols of power in these cases become inciting irritations, and their only power is to inflame and arouse opposition. As with the political, so with other types of group symbols. They are not immortal, and their power holds as long as they serve vital interests and ideas.

Running through the whole body of symbolism is the influence of religion and magic, especially in primitive societies, and lingering down to the present day. Some form of the supernatural emerges early in organization and lends its sanction to the operations of the society. The political head may be both human and superhuman in his origins and authority, both king and priest, with intermingled authorities in one person. Likewise magic in another sense enters into social relations, political as well as others. Sometimes black magic and sometimes white magic. Anthropologists distinguish between the later secular era and the earlier era of magic, custom, and religion intermingled in the fabric of authority, and of social control in general. The family, magic, religion, custom, and authority are often practically one, and only slowly are they separated as time goes on; indeed, they are never wholly separated. The threads are more clearly distinguishable in the later days of specialization. The concurrent action of agencies of control is, of course, of the essence of substantial authority and of social equilibrium as well as political.

The whole apparatus of ceremonialism and symbolism just discussed is closely connected with that of custom and tradition.[10] But, of course, there may be a symbolism of the future as well as of the past. Custom and tradition glorify what has been, but there is in revolutionary appeal the symbolism of the new, the yet unattained—the utopian in social organization and result. The symbolism of those in authority tends to rely upon days that are gone, but the symbolism of the underdog, the oppressed, looks to the future. In slavery, degradation, and oppression they look forward to a new day of revelation and revolution. This new day may, of course, be pictured also as the old and original day when all men were free—in the garden of Eden, the golden age.

The "Marseillaise," the "Internationale," songs of hope for this world or the next, lift up the hearts of men and inspire them to endurance and devotion for the sake of the cause. For centuries the songs of oppressed nationalities have nerved men to stand together in the pursuit of the aim of the political group for the time being driven from the face of the political earth, as in Poland, Greece, Hungary, Bohemia.

On the other side symbolism is related to education and propaganda, to psychological warfare on a somewhat different level of behavior and technique. It would be a serious error to conclude that symbolism has no place under modern conditions.[11] On the contrary, it possesses distinct values in any educational system and may contribute important elements of strength to any plan of control in a political community. While a system placing principal emphasis on symbolism may be ineffective under modern conditions, the opposite extreme of complete neglect of ceremonial values falls equally short of attaining the full strength of civic educational possibilities. Symbolism may be either an abdication of intelligence, a tribute to the unknown, or a form of totem or taboo, adding emotion to attitude, or it may contain an element of reason in the background. It may substitute automatism for reason either because there is no reason or in reinforcement of a valid function.

Historically, it has been chiefly the former; but technically there is no reason why this should be true. Especially in the political community where the hered-

[10] See my *Political Power* (1934) on credenda, pp. 113-32.

[11] See Whitehead, *op. cit.*; Dewey, *op. cit.*; Michels, *op. cit.*; Arnold, *op. cit.*; and Marshall, *op. cit.*

itary system prevailed, the prevailing symbolism was employed as one of the chief supports of the dynastic principle and the personalities who were its beneficiaries. "The boast of heraldry, the pomp of power" were assets of the ruling class, and their meaning was not merely that of artistic expression but was definitely related to economic and social privilege in the shape of land-holding, taxation, and an array of perquisites, privileges, and forms of prestige. The cult of the court and the elaborate ceremonialism of the crown were symbolic methods by which the will of the ruler was imposed upon the subject.

When the fury of revolution burst upon the ruling group, and a new set of governors emerged through the storm, the emblems of the aristocratic and monarchical lords were thrown down. Statues, memorials, and names intimate-ly associated with the ancient regime were likely to be ruthlessly destroyed, even at the expense of artistic values they might contain. But this is not the end of ceremonies and symbols. The revolution, too, has its dramatic scenes, personalities, places; and these reappear in a new form of vivid representations of the new order. New monuments, new statuary, new uniforms, new heroes: and these are the property of the rising forces of the community.

In more recent times many of the older symbols have been appropriated by the nation and have become an adjunct of nationalism in the abstract or the country in the concrete rather than of persons and families as under the old order. The succession of prestige follows the line of the national state rather than that of biology. The nation in turn has employed these symbols for the same purposes as the rulers in the earlier period—that is, chiefly for their prestige value, a short cut to the imposition of an ideology or a sentiment. National heroes, monuments, memorials, holidays, art, and culture have been woven together in the ceremonialism of the modern political society. What has been lost in the transition from the easy incarnation of the political idea in a set of hereditary personalities has been regained in the far broader popular basis everywhere given to the new nationalism, even in the nominally mo-narchical states. The holiday in celebration of "us" is as significant as the holi-day for "them," and the monument to the people as effective as the memorial to the reigning house.

Even a leader of the type of Napoleon, little interested in the general theory of democracy, was an instrument for the creation of a new symbolism replacing the old. The Legion of Honor in a way took the place of the older decorations and yet almost immediately became vastly effective in its influence. He opened lines of recognition to the unrecognized (and under the ancient regime unrec-ognizable) and thus uncovered wide sources of support never touched by the older rulers in the aristocratic system. A comparable case is the symbolism of the Soviets, likewise tapping a new source of strength in the "Group of Toil" practically unrecognized under the Romanovs, but now suddenly confronted with great possibilities of prestige and recognition. The Red flag and the

"Internationale" are symbols of great specific value in enlivening the general theory of the social order. The distribution of titles by the Labor group in England is another illustration of the new uses of ceremonialism; and the new "Order of Lenin" is equally notable.

On the whole, there has unquestionably been a simplification of symbolisms during the last hundred years, owing partly to the Puritan and partly to the democratic movement. But there still remains a wide range of symbolic devices, and many of these tend to assume, as time goes on, the character of protective devices for the past rather than control devices for the present or myth devices for the future. Prestige earned in one situation is likely to be translated into unearned prestige in another. This is not possible as in the case of individuals holding hereditary political power, but the transmission may be made in the case of groups or classes claiming privilege under ancient systems and fortifying their claims with the taboos of symbolic sanctity. This is particularly important in states where hereditary rule still survives in nominal form only and where a constant effort is made to employ this modicum of survival power for defense of special situations. The power of the House of Lords, for example, was long consistently utilized for the purpose of protecting the landlords and the vested interests from the advance of the new heirs to economic power— business and later labor. In America the symbolism of the changeless Constitution has been invoked to protect corporations against regulation of their enterprise in the general interest. In the larger states the national symbolism is employed in defense of the imperialistic or expansionist movements now characterizing their development.

It is, of course, inevitable that the dominant group should endeavor to use the current symbolism for the protection of its special interests and capitalize the experience of the whole group for its particular advantage. This struggle is unceasing. The tendency is, however, for the symbol to lose the essence of its meaning and to become formalism alone or chiefly so. In modern systems of civic education it is clear that the symbolic often loses its essential survival value for the group as a whole and becomes either an appeal to unreason or a defense of a special interest group. At this point it is intimately related to the inflexible type of training which has just been discussed in the preceding paragraphs in connection with the subject of invention and tradition and may become one of the most effective supports of the routine, traditional unadaptable form of civic education. This situation might lead in turn to a reaction against ceremonialism, ritualism, and all forms of political symbolism, not merely on the earlier puritanical ground that they were the defenses of ancient privilege, but that they tended to inhibit constructive thought on actual problems of state and aided in the development of an inflexible type of political mind.

There are, however, distinct values in symbolism, and it is not necessary to abandon them because of the possible or actual misuse of this important agency of social control. There are emotional values in symbolism that reach below the levels of ideology and tap basic sources of human enèrgy profoundly important in the organization of human behavior. Whether in stimulating emergency action, or in the slower development of long-time mores, or in the learning process of civic education, the symbolic relationships are indispensable. "There has been no great people without processions," wrote George Eliot in *Romola*, "and the man who thinks himself too wise to be moved by them to anything but contempt is like the puddle that was proud of standing alone while the river rushed by." Unorganized and untrained emotions are likely to be the servants of prejudice and impulse, and these impulses may become the masters of conduct, as in panic and rout, or may be exploited by designing interests and by demagogues. That the children of darkness are wiser in their day and generation than the children of light is a saying applicable here. The technically untrained but practical specialists have often given this subject more attention than the more highly trained students, devoted exclusively to ideologies. In this sense the unscientific have sometimes been more intelligent than the presumably scientific, for there is no reason why the functional values of symbolism should not be employed in the service of modern systems.

The visual appeal through color, the rhythms of music, the form appeal of sculpture and monument—these as such have nothing to do either with action or with inaction. They may be used in defense of either. The symbolism of political behavior as distinguished from that of the special political order or the special form of a national state may, in the future as well as in the past, be essentially forward-looking, fixing its eyes on a state of human relations not yet attained, one in which the crudities of the existing order are progressively eliminated and finer forms of adjustment constantly made.

Art may serve the present and the future as well as the past. If symbols point back, this is not the fault of the symbols but of the way in which they are employed by a special order or of a special territorial state. Perhaps the Romanovs or the Hohenzollerns may resist this; and unquestionably vested interests will endeavor to use symbols to aid them in their struggle for retention of power or prestige. But the emerging interests and patterns will develop their competing symbolism, and the contest is on. The German struggle over the flags of the old and the new order is a present-day example of a vivid sort, indicating clearly the features of this struggle constantly going on.

Given adaptability or flexibility as an objective of training, the task is then that of the artistic invention of adequate symbolism corresponding to the new aim. Much of religious symbolism and of cultural symbolism is of the prophetic type, looking forward to higher worlds or finer types of grace and beauty. A richer and more glorious life is indicated and suggested as within the range of possibilities. Religion, it is true, may teach resignation and passivity, and

91

during a great part of the world's history has done so, but this is not the only mission of religion or of its accompanying symbolic features. The symbolisms of heaven and hell are powerful reminders. The whole range of artistic and aesthetic beauty is as ready to serve the possibilities of mankind as its limitations, pains, and penalties.

Hence it is wholly unnecessary to abandon the great treasures of the symbolic to the uses of the stereotyped and set forms of the historic past. The reaction against elaborate ceremonialism has made this inevitable in the transition period, but for the future there are striking possibilities in the cultivation of more skilful use of the symbolic and the ceremonial in the process of civic education. We may see in the future the more scientific study of political symbolism and more extensive use of its possibilities in civic training, not only of the formal but also of the informal type.

This important field is so wholly unexplored that it is not possible to anticipate the developments which might ensue from its careful examination by experts, but a few possibilities have been suggested. For example, the formal entrance into mature citizenship is at present signalized by no meaningful ceremony. On the contrary, the citizen approaches the first exercise of his franchise in the modern state under circumstances which are wholly uninspiring. In the United States he will probably approach the ballot box in some barber shop or the basement of some unattractive building. In other countries the initiation into the suffrage is almost equally drab and unattractive. From the psychological point of view, the political community loses a moment of great importance in the life of the initiate—a moment when he might be impressed with his entrance into a new world of opportunity and of corresponding responsibility. Primitive groups were more effective at this point.[12]

Various forms of introduction might be devised for this moment, and of the possibility of improvement over the present gray and unattractive situation there can be no doubt in the mind of any person endowed with ordinary imagination. An interested community would readily devise the ways and means of dealing more gracefully and beautifully with this civic crisis, now so sadly wasted. The symbolism of change and adaptation might be developed much more effectively than at present. Comment has already been made upon the fact that much of political symbolism of the New World has been based upon the hypothesis that change is undesirable; that some fixed and perfect state of political society is the ideal form; or that particular systems must ponderously protect themselves against the disintegrating influence of change.

In a world of great mobility in social organization and relations this old form of symbolism does not correspond to the needs of the time and might readily

[12] See Elizabeth Anne Weber, *The Duk-Duks: Primitive and Historic Types of Citizenship* (1929).

be replaced by another, more nearly related to the evolutionary tendency of the times. Politics does not involve the permanence but a relativity of relations in some form of working equilibrium, which is no sooner born than it begins to die. The relations shift, and the center of gravity shifts with them if it is to remain the center of power. The emphasis on permanence was the result of a situation now changed by the logic of political progress and the newer types of conscious social control and direction.

What this symbolism should be, I do not undertake to say, nor could anyone say. We may merely indicate the possibility of other forms of symbolic interpretation of changing political relationships and point out the possibility that new forms of symbolism may replace the older and outgrown. When once the doctrine of conscious control over social and political evolution is conceded, then it becomes possible for types of builders, creators, inventors, and apostles of change to emerge as figures in the world of political art and symbolism. The sensitiveness of the economic and nationalistic order may delay this development, but in the long run it is certain to appear and to compete with other symbolisms.

IV. RATIONAL CONSENT

Another important tool of governments is that of rational consent—the test of participation on the part of the community, the foundation of intelligent interest and enduring morale. "Governments derive their just powers from the consent of the governed" is an axiom that lies at the basis not only of modern democratic government but of all forms of association. It may, of course, be said that there are and have been governments exercising unjust powers—and how is this to be reconciled with the consent of the governed as the tool of the state? We must first look more carefully at the nature of consent.

What is consent, and what is violence; and how are they to be distinguished? In the extreme cases it is not difficult to distinguish between robbery with a gun and a free market for exchange. But between these extremes there are many shades of color that blend into each other when we look more closely. Centuries of human experience have dealt with phases of this subject under the three general heads of private law and consent, natural law, and sovereignty.

Private lawyers and jurisprudents have dealt with the problem of consent for centuries and with many wavering nuances between consent and non-consent.[13] A contract may look simple, but it contains many possibilities of misinterpretation or invalidation. Was there contractual capacity? Was there

---

[13] On the growth and development of "the" common law see Sir Frederick Pollock's *The Genius of the Common Law* (1912) (still very suggestive); see also Roscoe Pound, *The Spirit of the Common Law* (1921).

a meeting of the minds? On what did they meet? Such problems have filled case records and fattened textbooks and pocket-books[14]

The natural-law philosophers dealt with the intricate refinements of the social contract in many imposing and illuminating tomes. It was Rousseau who once remarked that apparently a man had to be a philosopher before he could become a man, so complex were the engagements upon which he entered when he joined up with society and so elaborately entwined were the implications of these engagements.

With the rise of modern nations came the modern sovereign in person and sovereignty in theory. But sovereignty, sooner or later, raised the double problem of supreme violence, on the one side, and mass consent on the other. This challenged the construction of forms of government, or responsibility, and of public law for generations. It raised the problem of the scope and method of consent in myriad forms.

Bentham and the Utilitarians turned their attention away from the formal terms of the contracts to the motives and interests which prompted and sustained such relationships in society.[15] In general, however, we may say that emphasis continued upon the machinery by which, rather than the social situations or social psychology through which, command and obedience, coercion and co-operation, are conditioned.

In more recent times we turn again to the human material with which we deal, to social and individual psychology, and to a reanalysis of political behavior in terms broad enough to include both men and machinery. Between coercion and consent there are many intermediate stages that run into each other so subtly as to make distinctions difficult. There is the continuum including intimidation, threat, and fear. There is information, suggestion, persuasion, and duress.

There is consent on the rational level and on the nonrational level; there is consent that is legal and consent that is illegal; there is voluntary consent and involuntary consent; there is often consent without command—by imitation of another's behavior. A true picture of the process of consent would show the necessity of viewing coercion and consent from several different angles or dimensions, the combination of which indicated the point of action. There

---

[14] On the *naturrecht* theories see W. A. Dunning, *A History of Political Theories from Luther to Montesquieu* (1905), and standard writers in this field. Recent developments are dissected in G. E. G. Catlin, *A Study of the Principles of Politics* (1930), chaps. v–vi. A careful, rigorous body of normative theory of law has stemmed from the school of which Kelsen is perhaps the ablest representative. See Hans Kelsen, "The Pure Theory of Law," *Law Quarterly Review*, L (1934), 474–98, and *ibid.*, LI (1935), 517–35. See also William Ebenstein, *Die Rechtsphilosophische Schule der reinen Rechtslehre* (1938).

[15] Leslie Stephen, *The English Utilitarians* (1900), and Élie Halévy, *La Formation du radicalisme philosophique* (1901–4; trans. Morris, 1938).

are configurations often of a very complex nature. There are wide ranges of varying capacity for, or concern with, consent in the field of government.

What is involved in these situations goes far deeper than surface phenomena of consent or nonconsent, so flatly stated as that. What we come upon is the whole philosophy of obedience, the nature and area of voluntarism and determinism, the inner essence of social cohesion, basic principles of social psychology, leadership problems of the most complex character.[16] Some of this material is old and well worn in discussion, but much of it is just emerging from the toils of observation and discussion, yet too immature for confident application.

What actually goes on in a command-obedience situation is not so simple as a relationship between A and B. There is a third party, in the shape of the society in which their interrelationship is set. Or again, while there is will involved, there is also reason; there is interest calculated and uncalculated perhaps; there is symbolism and value judgment; there is faith, and there is fear. The decision may really be made by an event in ancient history, by a forgotten experience in childhood, by a spasticity of the colon, by heart or stomach trouble, by an overwhelming hope, by a sacrificial surrender.[17]

In our time the whole doctrine of consent has been challenged by important groups of theorists and activists. Authoritarians are declaring that organized consent is unnecessary in any formal setting or form. Interpretation of the public interest by the leaders is a more adequate way of insuring the protection of the commonweal, they allege, and a more effective guaranty than the electoral machinery. Masses, it is held, are incapable of understanding what they want or need. This must be developed for them by authority. Much may be done *for* them, it is declared, but not *by* them.

The superiority of force is openly proclaimed as the alternative to the organization of consent. Acquiescence is demanded. Assent is measured by the size or enthusiasm of crowds gathering to greet the lords of earth and by the general alacrity of obedience. The rulers are responsible, each to one higher; and the highest is responsible only to the spirit of the race, as he sees it.[18]

Consent involves a wide variety of ways and means in different societies with widely different culture patterns. Among these devices are the development of a body of doctrine to be believed—credenda—inculcated and generally accepted

[16] For a recent discussion of the problem from the standpoint of the making of constitutional consensus see C. J. Friedrich, *Constitutional Government and Politics* (1937), chaps. viii–x.

[17] See H. F. Dunbar, *Emotions and Bodily Changes* (1935); see also K. S. Lashley (ed.), *Studies in the Dynamics of Behavior* (1932); Kurt Goldstein, *Human Nature in the Light of Psychopathology* (1940).

[18] I have discussed this more fully in my *The New Democracy and the New Despotism*. See also A. B. White, *Self-government at the King's Command* (1933), for the ultimate possibilities.

propaganda, on the border line between education and symbolism, forms of participation and co-operation in political society.

The political society thus has at its command and fully uses the political education of the community in various forms of beliefs which lie at the foundation of the system of the nation. All the agencies of the social order contribute to this end result—the school, the church, the classes—and groups of all types act concurrently.

Governments utilize what may be termed the credenda of power. These are things to be believed—on the "must" list. They contain the reasons which oblige the intellect to give assent to the continuance of authority. And this assent may be due to government in general, to particular holders of the power, or to the special system of authority in vogue at any given moment in a particular unit of power. The club and the mass movement are not enough even in the early stages of human development, and hence systematic explanations of authority have been devised for more than two thousand years, as a means of reinforcing the other aids of the power group.

Traditionally the most common basis of obedience is no reason at all—not to raise the awkward question: to assume obedience, as the parent, associating obedience with affection and protection, superiority, and perhaps a little pressure of force. So the fatherhood of power was simple, and the rule of the elders almost as simple. Magic and the club were at hand to quicken the sluggish imagination or silence the querulous tongue, raised like that of Thersites. But in time the ideologies of power appeared and began their century-long struggle for survival.

It is not my purpose to write a history of political ideas, but it is important to recall again the chief types of credenda. Broadly speaking, the principal forms of inculcated belief have been as follows, with due apologies to the numerous variations and overlapping forms: (1) government is ordained of God or the gods; (2) government is the highest expression of leadership; and (3) government is the will of the community expressed through some form of consent.

These are the more important systems of competing credenda. They are all related to the tools which have already been described. One may say very broadly and with oversimplification that the first two systems have proved strongest in the symbolism centering around personalia, while the latter, the democratic contained deeper elements of appeal to the mass sentiment underlying political action. If power is personal leadership, the king and the king's court are the figures upon which the robes of authority may be most gracefully hung, but if power lies in fraternity, in the essential dignity of human nature, in the community feeling, the stronger impression may be made by the dramatization of the mass itself as the source of authority and the object of adoration and belief.

Beyond these general forms of belief, there are basic principles of "consent" to be accepted as reasonable in all systems. They may be grouped as follows: (1) respect for government—deferential attitudes; (2) obedience; (3) sacrifice; and (4) monopoly of legality.

1. Respect for government is a cardinal principle underlying all systems of government of every type. Whatever may be the difference in the derivation of authority, whether divine or human, the outcome is the same—namely, deference to the institution of government and respect for its administrators, regardless of their personal qualifications. The family, the church, business, and labor may from time to time sneer at the state, or at some particular form or phase of it, but the basic attitude remains the same throughout, whether the government be paternal or fraternal, centralized or decentralized, of the many or of the few. The degree and form of respect for government may vary widely from place to place and from time to time and through widely different types of external expressions of presumed inner attitude, but the inner spirit remains much the same, as far as the government per se is concerned.

There is the widest range of variation in attitudes toward the bearers of authority and the degree and type of submission to be displayed before them. The army has developed a standard form of external respect in the form of the salute, which is a continuous reminder of the visible presence of authority—institutionalized deference. "Attention" is likewise a pose of deference. But there are innumerable other forms of prescribed submissiveness, bowings, genuflections, risings, prostrations, bootlickings, crawlings, acclaimings, applaudings, and other external evidences of the internal approval of authority. The feebleness or cessation of these manifestations is an important index of trouble for existing power.

2. A second canon of the credenda is that of obedience to the authority established, without special regard to the method in which it was set up. Obedience, indeed, is the *sine qua non* of authority, and all governments are built on the presumption that conformity is accorded by the bulk of the community to most acts of authority. It is indispensable, therefore, that the importance of obedience be instilled in each generation from the earliest to the latest moment of life. Every system of ideology and of symbolism contains this principle as one of its chief precepts. This idea may be inculcated as a duty, as the result of a contract, as a matter of expediency, as a pleasure even, by fear or force; but it is essential that in the end result it appear as an accompaniment of power, as a vital part of political behavior.[19]

The implications of obedience and the degree of its implicitness may vary widely with peoples and circumstances. All systems contain safety valves against too complete an obedience, under circumstances where church, or wise men, or some group or other may stand in the way of the madman who may

---

[19] James Bryce, *Studies in History and Jurisprudence* (1901), chapter entitled "Obedience."

have stepped into authority; but in the main they all arrive at the same point, the generality of obedience by the bulk of the community. The generality of this tendency to obey is the basis of military discipline and the foundation of civil order as well and underlies the whole fighting and building power of the group.

The inevitable exceptions are only the proof of the rule. It is not that every law is always obeyed but that, generally speaking, the bulk of the laws are obeyed by the bulk of the community. Some governments have indeed recognized the right of revolution in the fundamental instruments of their establishment, as in France and the United States, but these declarations have been unusual. The right of revolution, too, lurks in the background of authority.

That the government must be obeyed is, then, one of the important credenda of all power groups and is usually imposed with success upon all communities.

Why do men obey? Some from theory of one sort or another; some without thought; some from fear; some from expediency. Others are caught up in a sense of enjoyment of the process of surrendering themselves to a higher power which thereupon assumes the responsibility of their ordering. Others are swept on with joy in the sense of following a leader who may embody on a larger scale their own aspirations and ambitions. The consciously and the unconsciously inferior may follow with a feeling of exaltation, not unlike that which is found in religion, finding peace of mind and security from the quest for certainty and authority.

3. A third canon of the credenda is that of willingness to sacrifice for the general good of the group. This is perhaps implicit in obedience, but it carries obedience forward beyond mere sullen conformity. The citizen or subject must be willing to obey even at the loss of property, liberty, life; but, more than that, he must be on the alert for the common good without being expressly commanded to do a specific thing. He must possess the continuing willingness to care for the good of the power group of which he is a member. The most dramatic expression of this willingness is seen in the unlimited sacrifices required by war, both for combatant and for noncombatant as well. But in times of peace the maintenance of the spirit of sacrifice is equally important as a means of bridging over otherwise intolerable and impossible situations, through "public spirit," "good will," "patriotism."[20]

On the whole, the community presumably serves the generality of interests, allowing for forms of exploitation by minorities and their failure to appraise correctly the value of their own services. The citizen is trained to believe this and that it is his duty to sacrifice himself if deemed necessary by those who interpret and administer the common good.

Why should he do this? The political explanations of this process have been

[20] See chap. viii, "Abnegation and the Road to Power," in my *Political Power*.

98

many, varicolored through many centuries of experience. But at this point all the other members of the family of power come to the aid of the political group to reinforce the claim of sacrifice. The family and the church in particular, but likewise the race, the class, and the region add their voices to the general chorus of insistence upon sacrifice as an essential of group life and advancement. The whole mores of the associated life bear down upon the citizen to compel him to give up his apparent advantage for the larger interest of the whole. They wind around him a chain from which it is well-nigh impossible to escape.

But it is a chain from which he does not wish to disentangle himself in many instances, for nature has provided the basic compensations and satisfactions which make sacrifice itself a pleasure, or, if that is not perhaps the word, a fulfilment of his personality. No element in the whole credenda, not even that of obedience, in itself a discomforting and barren precept to many, has the wide vogue attained by the doctrine of the importance and necessity of sacrifice in the interest of the group. None is more beautifully and constantly interwoven in the culture of the group than this same doctrine or more harmoniously intertwined with the whole network of social organization and allegiance.

4. Another canon of the credenda is that of the "monopoly of legality." It is one of the articles of belief constantly inculcated in the political community that the government enjoys the exclusive right to a special type of social authority called the "political." Along with this goes the doctrine that every attempt of every other group to infringe upon the government's monopoly will be punishable by the community in such manner as may seem appropriate.

The generally conceded possession of such a prestige position is of very great value to any contending group, and in cases where the outcome is otherwise doubtful such a belief may swing thousands one way or the other. In crises it may determine the attitude of smaller numbers in strategic positions, such as the army or those in leading places. The group carrying this banner appears as the trustee of the social and political order, as the representative of the basic function of the association, and as the special custodian of the great treasures of the political world.

The dominant group, of course, persistently spreads the doctrine that no other and rival group possesses similar rights and moves vigorously against any claimants of equal authority. All others are rebels, outlaws, pretenders, Absaloms organizing their revolts in their caves of Adullam, or Lucifers plotting against the Most High. In recent times this exclusive right of the political group has been contested by Duguit and some of the Pluralists, who, of course, maintain the equal right of all other associations and deny the superior validity of the commands of the state.[21] From this point of view every association has

---

[21] C. E. Merriam and H. E. Barnes (eds.), *A History of Political Theories: Recent Times* (1924), chap. iii; F. W. Coker, *Recent Political Thought* (1934).

power and right in proportion to its contribution to the social welfare or social solidarity, and no one is entitled to claim legalistic priority as over against any or all of the others. The laws of one group are as good and valid as those of any other group. Whatever may be the sounder position in political theory, in actual practice, in the mustering of power, the symbolic value of "legality" is of far-reaching importance, and it is never neglected by any realistic dealer in political power.

These lists do not by any means exhaust the credenda of politics. A long series of beliefs must be added to cover the special virtues of special political systems. Each political system presents a body of credenda regarding the qualities of that particular state, England, America, Russia, China, Germany, France, Italy, Japan, and so on through the list of the fifty-odd units of the present world. It is to be believed that each of these nations is in possession of qualities and skills that mark it out as a chosen people. These enumerations of characteristics take on the form of jingoism at times and again are somewhat careful analyses of the supposed special faculties of a people,[22] resting on a psychology or perhaps on even a biology of the people, and finding inevitable expression in their government. These often naïve assertions of national or group priority began in fine form with the discovery of the superiority of the Greeks over the barbarians and have continued down to this day in the Germans' pure Aryan doctrine. Much of this enumeration to be sure, is inclusive of cultural traits in general, but a special section is devoted to political national gifts and to the very special advantages of the governmental system in question.

In modern times these credenda are developed systematically in far-reaching systems of civic education, which build from the ground up. Beginning with the early years of childhood, the process of instruction extends over a long period of years, directed with great ingenuity and unflagging persistence toward the goal of producing what are called, in modern parlance, "100 per cent citizens" of whatever nation or political group. The modern system of mass education has basically altered the earlier situations in which the subjects were not educated and obtained their line of belief largely from the family, group imitation, and religion. Now, however, the struggle for the schools is almost as significant as that for the control of the army, perhaps more important in the long run, and becomes the basis for broad campaigns of morale-building effort.

In these systems the credenda and symbolism are blended, the eye and ear are trained along with the emotions and the intelligence, and the subject is pointed toward an end result—the absorption of the special beliefs and ceremonies of the state. In the newer political associations such as Soviet Russia

[22] Cf. F. H. Hankins' devastating characterization of these analyses in Merriam and Barnes, *op. cit.*, chap. xiii.

and Germany these plans of political education are especially developed and range over a wide area of life. The Soviet system has the triple task of replacing religion, capitalism, and democracy with a new idea scheme and of filling this with vitality and interest. The remarkable methods by which this basic plan has been carried through are well described in the analysis of Harper, which developed in detail the intricacies of this complex method of inculcating doctrinal conformity.[23] But the Japanese[24] and Chinese have not omitted this important factor in the fixation of the national political pattern and have made great strides recently in the direction of comprehensive organization of the national ideology and symbolisms.

There is no need to undertake here a fuller discussion of these vast systems of civic education which have become so essential a part of the tools of the modern nation or to consider the many problems arising in the most effective construction of these pedagogical propaganda forms. We may merely note that some of the most vital of the power problems center in processes often only remotely associated with the grimmer realities of conventionalized authority.[25]

In comparatively recent times there have developed new forms of consent, partly rational in form and partly nonrational. Originally a mode of inculcating a religious faith, propaganda became a method of mingling tradition, ceremonialism, and symbolism with reasonable arguments regarding policy through organized mass drive. It became a means of raising public morale and a weapon of warfare employed for weakening the will of the enemy or, at any rate, of disturbing his sleep. Thus propaganda may at one time be wholly true and at other times wholly false, depending on the end pursued; but it must be plausible and palatable for the consumer.

On its rational side propaganda is an effort to persuade through processes of instruction in facts and principles; but on the other side it may be looked upon as an attempt to manipulate mass opinion by whatever means are available, including the supplementing of propaganda by deception and violence. This is relatively easy when only one form of official propaganda is permitted in a state.

Almost all agencies, whether public or private, are equipped with mechanisms shading over into one another, from education to public relations, and on to propaganda—sometimes almost imperceptible gradations distinguishing them.[26] "Pedagogy," says Lasswell, "is the transmission of a skill, like reading, writing, and arithmetic; propaganda strives to organize attitudes of love and

[23] S. N. Harper, *Civic Training in Soviet Russia* (1929).

[24] D. C. Holtom, *Modern Japan and Shinto Nationalism* (1943).

[25] My *Civic Education in the United States* (1934) discusses the American system in some detail.

[26] H. D. Lasswell, R. Casey, and B. C. Smith, *Propaganda and Promotional Activities* (1935); Lasswell and Blumenstock, *World Revolutionary Propaganda* (1931).

hate, divorced from the transmission of skill." But propaganda is more than this; it involves the transmission of attitudes that are recognized as controversial within a given community. Propaganda is "the management of collective attitudes by the manipulation of significant symbols."[27]

Propaganda thus develops in our day into a vast mechanism, sometimes world-wide in scope. It is fundamentally based upon modern means of publicity, upon the press, the radio, the screen, the arts of advertising, immensely stimulated in the industrial quest of consumers, to say nothing of the older forms of meetings, demonstrations, and symbolisms of various sorts appropriate to the special time and place. It should be carefully noted, however, that in a free society the techniques of propaganda are not the exclusive property of the state but the common property of all types of associations or individuals.

There has been propaganda from time immemorial, but known by no such name, and without the machinery of modern times. Rumor, gossip, and alarms of all sorts were circulated as a result of conscious contrivance by cunning managers in very early days and often with deadly effect. Our fuller understanding of psychology, of crowd psychology, and our new devices in the form of mechanisms of intercommunication have made it possible to construct far-flung systems of influencing mass action, both in peace and in war. No army is now adequately equipped without its psychological warfare division, and no operating agency, public or private, gets on without public relations and propaganda sections of one sort and another. The radio has enormously increased the range and power of such appeals, with television still to come, adding yet more to the range of machinery.

Modern propaganda is, in distinction from that of earlier times, (1) specially organized, (2) consciously directed toward definite ends, and (3) reinforced by the devices of modern technology and mass psychology. Its ramifications run through every phase of human life, for nothing is alien to the propagandist, from the cradle to the grave, from the highest and most universal truth to the deepest and blackest lie. Propaganda is not primarily an appeal to reason, or an appeal to emotions, but a total appeal to man's nature on any and every side, wherever political action may be influenced or determined.

Propaganda involves for its successful operation a fusion of an appeal to reason and an appeal to emotions through symbolic agencies of color, sound, rhythm, ritual. Propaganda may be largely or wholly true, or it may be largely or wholly false. The bare truth may be adequate by and of itself, or the appeal may be one of mingled truth, error, and deception.

In general, the appeals strive toward one of these two ends: to bring about solidarity of feeling and action through a recognition of community of interest—of consciousness of kind—with common interest, traditions, ideals, hopes,

[27] H. D. Lasswell, "The Theory of Political Propaganda," *American Political Science Review*, XXI (1927), 627-31.

and demands, or to bring about unity of purpose and action in a desired direction.

Unity of sentiment and unity of purpose and program provide a basis of action. In the case of enemy propaganda this involves, of course, the breaking-up of the enemy centers of solidarity and resistance growing from solidarity. Resistance may be broken down by the splintering of solidarity and by the despair and fear arising from conviction of error or of hopelessness.

Ill defined as are the area and techniques of propaganda, they are, nevertheless, powerful factors in our times, alike in the times of war and of peace.[28]

It is clear that consent is intimately intertwined with morale—with a feeling of well-being and participation throughout the community. All governments and, indeed, all rule-making agencies, whether public or private, strive to obtain the consent of their citizens or members. A sullen work force, a sullen army, a sullen people in general, do not contribute to victory in war or productivity and prosperity in times of peace. Every effort is made by all intelligent governments to enlist the consent and co-operation of men under any system at any time.

It is true that there are many persons who do not care to assume any large responsibility for the conduct of their government, preferring to delegate to others. They may wish to lean on others or be led by a few or one. They may not vote, and they may not care to vote if they could obtain the franchise. But even in such cases it will be found that there is an interest in consenting to the general framework of government and to some of the broad outlines of political policy. Or, reversing the method of approach, the deprivation of these rights will be resisted.

High morale is fostered by a sense of participation in a joint undertaking to which the assent of many is required, even if not through the ballot. Fear and hope are powerful incentives, but they are not strong enough to compete with an actual sense of importance in making the decision involved in a major undertaking. The day's work is, in a sense, a perpetual plebiscite in which the votes are not formally cast but in which the signs and symbols of assent and dissent are clearly understood by skilled observers.[29] Grumbling, dissent, low-level deference, ill will, sabotage, civil disobedience, resistance, nonco-operation—these are weapons readily employed by the underdog who is not consenting to the political line he is presumed to follow.

Beyond the principle of the consent of the governed, there is a wide range of devices for insuring the application of the general idea to specific situations.

[28] See on propaganda Harwood L. Childs (ed.), *Propaganda and Dictatorship* (1936); Leonard W. Doob, *Propaganda* (1935); F. C. Bartlett, *Political Propaganda* (1940); Ernst Kris and Hans Speier, *German Radio Propaganda* (1944).

[29] For illustrations of ways and means of resistance see "Poverty of Power," in my *Political Power*.

In democratic societies these methods are put in the forefront and are consciously contrived and directed toward a recognized end. In other societies the explicit winning of consent may be denied or slurred over, but, nevertheless, it plays an important role in the process of political management, not only of public but of private governments as well. Civil liberties, the suffrage, the machinery for insuring the responsibility of the ruler to the ruled, and representation and recall in various forms are the product of a long-continued attempt to bring about the effective consent of the government as a principle of political organization. Crude and defective as they may be, and perverted from time to time away from their true purpose, they nevertheless serve the purpose of presenting a principle of action generally accepted even if not fully put in practice. Even when the phrase becomes a mockery, as in boss-ruled cities of the United States or dictator-ruled areas of South America or elsewhere, the principle endures and rises again and again when it might seem to have been crushed forever.

The consent of the governed is one of the most effective tools of the political society for the execution of its purposes. Custom, violence, ceremonialism, and strategy all play their parts in the service of community purposes; but, of all these instruments, the factor of consent is the most vital and tends with the rising recognition of the dignity of man to become increasingly significant for all political societies. Consent is not unmindful of custom or symbolism, but it is more intimately related to education and to strategy in the highest sense of the term; and it is farthest removed from the lower level of violence—its precise opposite.

V. STRATEGY

An important instrument of the political government is what may be called, for lack of a better term, "strategy." Strategy aims at integration and direction in the group and includes but is broader than diplomacy, war powers and policies, or domestic tactics. It contains all of them—and more. Strategy in the state is not different from strategy in other forms of association, but the materials and the ends are different. Strategy in a sense may be said to cover all the foregoing techniques, to run through them. But it is more than that; it involves their combination and co-ordination into going patterns of policy and action. The strategy of the state and of statesmen lies in the skilful utilization of all the resources and interests of the community for the purposes of the society.

The network of integration is made up of ideological and interest appeals to special groups, to special individuals, to special regions and neighborhoods, and to the generality of citizens regardless of their group or other affiliations. The particular group in power may not be able to appeal to all these elements, but the chief political groups will be able to compass most of them and to make a working combination of strength and tenacity. When this strategy is lacking or defective, the strength of the state is seriously weakened, and its decline, if not its destruction, is imminent.[30] Notable examples of skill in this field are seen in the difficult but successful task of Switzerland, and the opposite in the failure of Austria-Hungary to maintain itself in the midst of disruptive forces. The United States of America and the British Commonwealth of Nations are other examples of strategic development of cohesion under difficult circumstances.

The rise of modern nationalism was in part a victory over feudalism by the strategic forces of the opposition, but in this case strategy was supplemented by extensive use of violence. France was an admirable illustration of the emergence of an integrated authority in the midst of regional, religious, and factional struggles that seemed irreconcilable. In the late crisis, however, the development of disintegration is equally evident. A like process was apparent in modern Italy, where competent strategy produced the union of Italy and where incompetent strategy brought it down to lower levels of strength and unity. Modern Sweden is an admirable example of successful strategy of development.

Naturally, this implement of strategy includes external as well as internal relations. The types of relationship with other powers affect profoundly the welfare and stability of the state. In a world of armed nations these relations may well mean the life or death of the state blundering its way along in the midst of potential wars. Sweden and Switzerland, in highly exposed positions, have found it possible to maintain their integrity as states, while other nations have been far less fortunate.[31] Ineptitude in this area may prove costly to the state and may even lead to its downfall and destruction. Tragically enough, the war may be won and the peace may be lost, so important are the threads of strategy in the life of the nation.

A great diplomat is a great national asset and a bungling one a huge liability. But a great strategist of and by himself is not competent to achieve results unless he has back of him a people who understand strategy and the need for its manipulations as a part of national policy. Thus the United States abandoned the League of Nations in World War I and thereby hastened the coming of another vast military struggle. In striking contrast is the diplomacy of Benjamin Franklin in the days of the birth of the nation. Disraeli and Bismarck were strategists of the old school, each in his own style of play.

But, aside from war situations, the role of strategy in times of peace is fundamental in importance. Trade, manufacture, agriculture, labor, banking

[30] Some writers, notably Smend, regard "integration" as the essential characteristic of the state.

[31] See Quincy Wright, *A Study of War* (2 vols., 1942), for illustrations of war situations and their underlying causes.

and currency, movements of population—the whole range of economic and cultural relations—are of the very highest importance to all states, rich and poor alike. National policies, embodied in laws, understandings, and practices make up a great part of the life and prosperity of the commonwealths concerned.

Above the balance of interests is the balance of organs and instruments, and above that again the balance of ends of state, the relative positions and priorities of justice, order, and freedom, and welfare security in the given political society.[32]

It cannot be concluded, however, that statesmen do nothing but balance and adjust the status quo; for they must also make decisions and inaugurate policies aimed at the dynamics of the society, if it is a progressive community. This is especially true in a period when science and technology have made possible the transformation of social and industrial relations. Especially in a democratic society common demands for services enlist the aid of the government in constructive lines of effort, in which, to be sure, lines may again be drawn between various types of conflicting interests.

In a well-organized system this strategy would take the form of organized planning at the long-range levels, as well as of immediate action patterns on other levels of immediacy. Planning involves the systematic balancing of elements in a moving program of long-time effort, directed toward a goal of community interest; and the development of special techniques, machinery, and skills for this purpose.[33]

Accompaniments of strategy on its darker side are fraud, intrigue, and deception, organized for the purpose of obtaining compliance with some political end. At all times these weapons have been means of power, both within the state and in international relations. Nor can it be truly said that these dark and devious forms of political action are absent from other social groups, whether civil, military, ecclesiastical, industrial, or otherwise. They run like a thread through all the ways of life, individual as well as collective. They are part of the strategy of good and evil as well, distortions or perversions of accepted techniques of action, banned by the conventions of social groupings but constantly recurring.

The broad plan of strategy is embodied in a program outlining the policies, balancing the interests of the state, weighing the factors affecting regions, races, classes, and interests of various sorts. There is an element of persuasion in legislation and also an element of sanction through the powers of enforcement even without penal remedies. This opens the way for many forms of compromise

[32] See Chinese and Indian literature for illustrations of their sayings counseling strategic disposition of difficulties.

[33] See Sir Henry N. Bunbury, *Governmental Planning Machinery* (1938), and my "The Possibilities of Planning," *American Journal of Sociology*, XLIX (1944), 397–407.

and adjustment dear to the heart of the statesman.[34] Without the use of violence, arrangements may be effected which provide a *modus vivendi* for conflicting groups, otherwise irreconcilable. Thus the state as a rule-making agency, along with other like agencies, may strengthen its usefulness to the community and maintain a sort of balance of power.

This balance indeed reaches far beyond the balance of governmental organs or ordinary economic interests. It runs through the whole gamut of social values as they are found in different persons and groups of persons. "The skilful statesman," says Ostrogorski, "must always be performing the miracle of the loaves and fishes in order to meet the appetite of his various constituents." The truth of this observation is by no means confined to parliamentary institutions but runs through governments of many types.

VI. LEADERSHIP

Another tool of government is that of leadership. The leader in person draws together around him and fuses many of the other elements of government into living symbolism and into ways and means of direction and control. The precise nature of leadership is one of the most difficult problems in the domain of politics or, indeed, in social action; yet it is one of the most real phenomena in political and social behavior.[35]

It is not generally recognized that leadership is not something wholly unusual and amazing. Quite the contrary, political leadership is conditioned upon the prevalence of like qualities within the community in which it is exercised. This is evident enough when we consider that a great general does not commonly emerge from a nonmilitary people, or a great parliamentarian from a people not habituated to such procedure, or a great judge where there is no refinement of the juristic techniques. The leader is original, perhaps, but not too original, otherwise he cannot be understood or followed or supported by his potential group. He leads by and through a set of key persons who approach him in equipment and understanding. The leader leads not because he is entirely different from the others but because he is much like the others and may symbolize and fuse their aspirations and desires.

In the earlier stages of leadership, force is conspicuous. In subhuman groups and among primitives of some types, force is accompanied by what is roughly called "animal cunning." Prestige may continue this superiority and supplement it, may serve as a protection for a time against a challenge and a combat,

[34] See T. V. Smith, *The Legislative Way of Life* (1940).

[35] This topic is explored in a forthcoming monograph by Louis Olom on "Leadership," delayed by the war. It deals with leadership and dominance in subhuman groups, psychological studies of leadership, including juvenile groups, and summarizing and analyzing many current investigations. Cf. Max Weber, *Wirtschaft und Gesellschaft* (2d ed., 1925), on charisma in politics.

and in some groups the actually efficient combatants may gather round the outworn prestige-holder to protect him.

But in the elders is seen the rise of craftiness, in a form of group guidance, into the making of which personal physical ability may enter very little. The leader wins for the group through brain as well as through brawn, and the fading of one may be made up by the importance to the group of the other. Thus the wise old man becomes a great asset for the tribe, as in later stages for the nation. On a later scale this rivalry is seen in the relative positions of the "frocks" and the "uniform," often competing forms of leadership, alternating with social tensions demanding one or the other—reminiscent of the remoter days when the young warrior was impatient of the elder sage and demanded more battle and less counsel.

In intergroup situations, demanding the exercise of the technique called diplomacy, the finesse of the leader becomes increasingly important to the group. Otherwise what has been won in the heat of battle may be lost in the long-drawn-out parleys of the peace treaty. More than one group has sat down to negotiate in victory, only to rise in equality or defeat.

More modern leadership exhibits strikingly the importance of two factors: the command of symbolism and facility in organization. Neither of these is entirely new in the history of political relations, but both are highly developed in modern times. Primitive symbolism was indeed highly important and broadly proliferated through the early tribal life. It was directed toward smaller groups, however, and was far less mobile in its forms than that of our times. It was in the nature of a social heritage rather than invention adapted to a newly developing situation. The symbolisms of the Soviets, of the Fascists, and of the Nazis are examples of the newer forms of symbolic interpretation of mass desires or potentialities in varying forms.

While earlier leaders wielded the ax, or invoked the immemorial mumbo jumbo of the clan, or smoked the pipe of peace in conference with their foes, the more modern type must busy himself to a great extent with the manufacture of symbols of current value in a swiftly changing world. He must weigh interests, ideologies, and personalities with a view to developing them into useful tools of social combat and organization and production. Even if force is the final stroke, the way must be prepared by attitudes favorable to its exercise, by hates and adorations, by promises and predictions, by fixation of responsibility upon unworthy holders of power, by appeals to the emotional-intellectual life of great masses of individuals.

Organization as well as interpretation is a key to the use of symbolism upon a mass scale. It is not enough to dream or devise a catching symbol, for the techniques of modern mass action, of advertising, and of assembly must be invoked, so that the symbol is impressed upon millions. The leader's followers are not now an unorganized but enthusiastic mob, but a well-officered, drilled, and disciplined army—a private army of a type forbidden to fight but ready for the modern fray of words and epithets and, most of all, for systematic mass demonstrations and efforts of every description, as may be commanded from on high.

Army organization, it is true, has been historically one of the important objects of interest for leaders, and indeed still remains so, although now eclipsed by commercial organization, labor, and school organization and rivaled by civil and party organization.

It would be an error to assume, however, that a leader must himself possess all the special qualities for large-scale organization of men, for this may be the task of an adjutant; or, indeed, the adjutant may in fact be the more powerful, with the nominal leader as his mouthpiece and instrument. But somewhere in the group of aspiring leaders there must be found the skill in mass organiza tion which has become so indispensable a part of modern social and political control, whether with Stalin, Hitler, Roosevelt, or Churchill. The co-operative enterprise presupposes a series of skills at the disposal of the government, and their distribution varies from time to time with the exigencies of the case.

Granting that the mastery of symbolism and skill in organization are emer-gent in the modern leadership situation, there are further and more specific dispositions and skills which may be found in prospective holders or bidders for power. Broadly speaking, these aptitudes vary so widely in different situa-tions that generalization is filled with many dangers, but various attempts have been made in this direction by such students as Michels, Conway, Giese, Kretschmer, Sheldon and others.[36] All these must be regarded as tentative and provisional, however, awaiting much fuller knowledge of the inner con-tent of the material dealt with by the commentators. The following series of aptitudes are commonly found in a variety of modern leaders.

1. Many political leaders have a high degree of social sensitivity, sensing what goes on around them in the field of political and social power. It was once said of President McKinley, an adroit reader of public opinion, that he had both ears to the ground all the time; and of Hitler that he said to Hinden-burg, "I may not possess your governing ability, but I can at least tell you how to make up the public mind." The leader is likely to feel the weather and know the tides that come and go in human affairs and to be able to measure the effect of special pleas directed toward representing or influencing these movements and potentialities.

2. The leader is likely to possess a high degree of facility in personal contacts with a wide variety of persons, enabling him to meet them without effort and with conspicuous success in case after case. When the cause is lost, perhaps the

[36] See my *The American Party System* (rev. ed., 1940) for bibliography; H. D. Lasswell, *Psychopathology and Politics* (1930).

personality himself may save the day in many instances. It is one of the interesting phenomena of politics that individuals are often strongly attached to leaders with whom they disagree on every major issue—attached for personal reasons, as the phrase goes. A bold, aggressive, or sympathetic, idealistic type of man may gather around him a following concerned not with alleged goals but with his own form of public activity; or perhaps seeing in him a reaching-out toward a goal to which they themselves would go if only the way were shown.

3. The leader is further likely to have great facility in group contacts, ability to know and reckon and deal with a considerable number of interest groups whose aims conflict but toward whom there must be a sympathetic attitude. This group diplomacy is of the very essence of high politics, and the practitioner in this field is well equipped for that reorganization of perplexing situations which is the very task of politics on so many dark occasions. The various races, the religions, the classes, the regions, the innumerable culture groups— these the skilful leader understands how to conciliate or to unite in victorious combinations, if all cannot be drawn in. Thus Laurier, a Frenchman in Canada; Sonino, an Egyptian-born Scotch-Jew in Italy; Hitler, an Austrian in Germany; Lloyd George, a Welshman in England; Stalin, a Georgian—all illustrate the possibilities of group reconciliation, even under somewhat unpromising initial conditions. For some purposes the outsider, or the one a little to the side, may be a better conciliator than the insider to the manner born, just because he is somewhat apart from the vested and larger interests at war.

4. It is clear from the foregoing elements that the leadership group must possess the facility of dramatic expression. This may take the form of the voice of the orator (or broadcaster in these days—and if he is photogenic, so much the better), or the pen of the author, or the dramatization of the behavior seen in large and swift adventurous movements, signalizing the individual as an unusual personality, in his experience if nothing more. Roosevelt, Churchill, Hitler, and Bismarck rank as masters in this field. And for this reason it not infrequently happens that persons without any other special qualifications than the drama of their lives are precipitated into important political positions, as in the case of Paderewski and of generals of many lands, great men so called, especially great in some form of celebrity, it matters not what. The dramatic situation comes with special power to the average man, who reads into his leader's life the unfulfilled aspirations and dreams of his own more drab existence. In the dramatic leader he follows in a way the beckoning of his own reverie life. The instinct or aptitude for dramatics fits well into the modern demand for slogans and devices lifting the individual above his daily tasks.

5. In view of the constructive character of many power situations, it is important that leaders possess some facility in invention, whether of formulas, policies, ideologies, strategy, or plans which may satisfy the requirements of

difficult situations in war or peace. It is quite possible that the nominal leader may not be the actual inventor of the new law, or the new treaty, or the new plan, or the new slogan, but it will be imputed to him, even though it has been whispered in his ear by some subtler and more cleverly reorganizing mind. In any case, he is entitled to the credit of recognizing a good suggestion and accepting and incorporating it in his political system. Napoleon was not the author of the code that bears his name, but at any rate he listened to the suggestions and approved and acted. Certainly Jefferson disclaimed originality for his Declaration. Recent research shows that some of the most interesting speeches of Mirabeau were prepared by none other than Jeremy Bentham, but not every statesman had the wit to find or use a Bentham. Naturally the inventiveness, real or imputed, of the leader must not go too far along the path of originality, or he might lose the "common touch," and become incapable of those broad and sweeping symbolisms which reach the "heart" of the masses and upon which his power may rest. He must "edge in" as a motorist cuts into traffic. He must be inventive within the framework of the power interests for whom he functions, whether as reactionary, radical, or revolutionary. If nothing is to be done in the given situation, he must invent plausible reasons for doing nothing; and if something must be done, he must suggest the something. The unpardonable sin is to propose nothing, when action is imperative.

6. The group leader ordinarily possesses an unusually high degree of courage. This is contrary to the common impression that politicians are timid and even cowardly in conduct. It is often their *raison d'être* to be conciliatory and compromising, since the knots they seek to unravel are not so easy to loose. But a closer view of the lives of leaders shows that from time to time they must throw down the gage of battle and risk their all in uncertain combat. Just as a financier does not become rich by loaning money on perfect security at a low rate of interest, so the political leader can never enjoy security and quiet, except at the price of inferior position, compensation, and authority. Within and without the party and within and without the state, there are hostile groups seeking to destroy him; and, while conciliation and patience may avail on many occasions, there are times when these fail, and the appeal to arms, politically speaking, is the only alternative. In fact, the reputation for willingness to do battle may itself save many a struggle. It is doubtless true that the conciliator may so long pursue the processes of conciliation that he may neither recognize another situation nor be prepared to have a heart and will for it; but, if so, his life and tenure are in peril, and the adventuresome spirit of someone who has nothing to lose and all to gain may drive him back from the lines of power.

The force of prestige is supplemented by the living qualities of *empressement,* tact, and humor, which tend to blend into a combination of qualities useful for the power group in the exercise of their functions. With an initial impetus of prestige the reinforcement of manner transforms an orginal investment into a growing business. What is expected appears in the flesh, and the anticipation is agreeably translated into realization. The great man, the great orator, the great figure in whatever order, with the manner of greatness, is impressive, if he carries himself with the appropriate pose. Or he may appear in an entirely different order, as in the case of Napoleon, Lenin, and Gandhi, who did not correspond to the traditional figures of power but whose unique quality made them impressive and whose manner continued the impression of the unusual, the profound, the great.

The *empressement* is by no means purely physical; it connotes a symbolic type with reflections in the lives of others; it connotes a form of what has sometimes seemed radiation or magnetism of a sort which is undefinable but felt in some fashion by those in contact with the personality. In the traditional ruling classes this quality takes the form of a gracious and pleasing paternalism, with arrogance and hauteur in reserve if need be; in democratic systems the form of a commonness, kindliness, and pervading sympathy with others. To act as a lord and as a commoner are varying patterns of behavior adapted to different phases of human social organization.

In military groups harshness and external authoritarianism survive as evidences of the belated character of the organization of control in a system which proceeds upon the assumption that fear and brute force are the controlling impulses in mankind—yet not without a touch of paternalism in the case of the genuine leaders of men whether high or low; and in democratic days with the kindliness of democracy—but always with careful preservation of the externalia of prestige and dignity of demeanor. In modern systems of cinema representation these personal qualities may now be exhibited to thousands far more intimately than in earlier times when they were limited to the relatively few.

Allied to this quality is the faculty which goes under the name of "tact." In this the quality of personal and social sensitivity is combined with that of related conduct based upon the perceptions and feelings without confusion or misunderstanding of the essential relations. It is a type of chart upon which are plotted the dangerous reefs and shoals, and likewise the clear channels of navigation. Touch is an elusive quality which puzzles observers in more than one field of action; the *tactus eruditus* of the physician may determine the difference between success and failure. The touch of the artist differentiates him from the crowd of those who fall short at just this point. The touch of the economic bargainer may mark the difference between the successful accumulator and the one doomed to toil without special benefit of the bargaining faculty. In somewhat similar manner the touch of the political leader or manager may readily mark the line between the likeable and the disliked. An intellectual slow-movie would perhaps reveal more precisely the exact nature of these differences in action and attitude patterns.

In addition to the foregoing general tools of government, there are innumerable and varied special tools. As we look over the broad sweep of political behavior from the primitive to the modern, these are so numerous and diverse as to challenge description and defy analysis. There are rules, orders, regulations, directions, commands, prohibitions, injunctions, and mandates of many sorts from the simplest to the most complex. They cover almost every phase and stage of human life at one time or another in one form or another. They are discovered and used by many different agencies and organs of government—judicial, legislative, executive—or may be the outgrowth of magic and mumbo jumbo, always declared by some person, however.

Of all the special tools of government, it may be said that law or "the Law" is of greatest importance. Many kinds of agencies have rule-making powers, generally accepted within the special group—industrial, ecclesiastical, cultural. This complicated network of rules is seldom fully appreciated by students of governance, although the rules of honor, the unwritten law, and the law of self-defense are fully recognized in human practice. Political law differs from the other laws and rules only in its relation to the ends of the political society—security, order, justice, welfare, freedom—and in the special tools utilized in its application. The "monopoly of legality" often accorded to the state is not merely a monopoly of violence, as sometimes held, but a special relationship to a special set of social ends and institutions and methods.

Obviously there are many forms of "common good," many types of agencies recognized as capable of giving laws, and many forms of sanctions which may be applied. Law in any of the series of social relationships may be derived from custom, from reason, from will, from promulgation and command, and it may be characterized by various forms of declaration and enforcement differing widely from culture to culture.

In the relatively narrow field of government there are many forms of law, public and private, municipal and international, administrative and common, civil, military, and martial. Legislators, judges, generals, administrators, and leaders make and unmake law on a wide scale. But again, without the fanfare of official proclamation and promulgation, there is the law of the land, in public law or in private law, in common law and in customary law. The law may be discovered as well as made, either by the observation of what is done or by the piecing-together of precedents piling up with the force of law.

The state may seem to have an advantage in saying "This is the law" and "This is against the law" and therefore bad. But there is also the law of God to be reckoned with and the common custom of the land and the law of the group or gang as the case may be. And the order of priorities if often in grave doubt. In some cases breaking the rival's law may be a point of honor. In war the political government absolves and rewards those who transgress the law of the enemy regarding persons and property, or in revolutionary movements likewise.

The essence of laws and rules in general is not command enforced by penalties but guidance and direction for a common purpose. There are many situations, as in traffic, in which it is not as important what particular direction is indicated as that some one direction or mode of action should be clearly and authoritatively indicated. Whether right or left is immaterial. The reasonableness of the rule and its acceptance by the group is of paramount importance. There are evil and unjust laws, but they masquerade in the name of justice and the common advantage, even if known to be evil. Nor is the essence of law found in enforcement through penalties, for if the rule is generally accepted there may be no violation of it. On the other hand, a law may be a dead letter incapable of application and in practice wholly ignored.

In the hierarchies of organization, large and small scale, there are inevitably developed innumerable forms of rules, regulations, and mandates, operating in elaborate systems of subordination, superordination, and co-ordination. The "paper work" of the military organization or of the civil authorities is replete with these diligent codings and decodings of the director and with the flow of response in return from those affected. In their least successful forms these "artifacts" become "circumlocution offices" or "bureaucracies," but under happier circumstances they are the indispensable tools of organization, clearance, and concrete action, alike in peace and in war. Special skills and facility in the development and ordering of these intricate rule systems have existed for centuries, and in modern times many similarities may be observed under widely different political systems.

Another special skill of government is that of adjudication; another is that of counsel and conciliation; another is that of management. These skills are not the exclusive property of government, for they are found in varying forms in all social groupings. Society could not exist and operate without them. But the combination of them is more highly developed in government than elsewhere.

Adjudication and conciliar skills are most highly perfected in government, while management and leadership are found highly advanced in other forms of association, for example, management in industry and the church, and leadership in every form from the family on up. Much of the governmental skill is observable in the arts of argument and persuasion, the oral dialectic of courts and councils, and of the forums of political discussion. In later times management on a large scale became a characteristic (although by no means exclusive) of governing agencies, with all the nuances of direction involved in administration.

Likewise governments have shown skill of an unusual type in the quick formulation of directives as in emergencies and crises in the assembly of essential organization, in response to social needs. In the crises of flood, fire, pestilence, war, and famine, the special skills of the governmental group are especially noticeable. In the development of special services, other qualities of the governmental appear, as in the formulation of a land policy or an educational system, of a stabilization of industry and employment, and fundamental determinations of policy from the over-all point of view of the political association.

In recent times governments have made unusual efforts and developed unusual skills in the field of the organization of consent throughout the community. Some of these qualities are observable in adjudication, others in conciliar agencies, others in sound management. But later developments are those of what has come to be called propaganda and of more rational forms of mass persuasion. The demagogue is an old type, victim of many proper satires—the reverse side of the desirable skill of facility in public relations and assiduity in cultivating and utilizing them for the common good.

Many mockeries of this skill may be observed along the political way, but these need not blind the observer to the deeper meaning of these unhappy perversions of a genuinely desirable skill, namely, that of the common denominator of the common good, exemplified in types of personalities with appropriate skills adapted to high purposes. Historically the common good might be a cover for private good and the cultivation of consent a blind for private exploitation. But as the common good historically becomes more and more a reality and as consent tends more and more to become an actuality, the inherently valuable skills of "popularity," of adjustment of diverse interests, and of making the rules and regulations adaptable to the personalities upon whom they operate become factors of increasing importance.

These qualities are sometimes lumped together as the skills of the "politician," or the "politicos" if this term is preferred. On widely varying levels and with widely varying ideas and ideals, they are the aptitudes and skills of men who are able to make contacts with many kinds of their fellow-men, to understand them, to interpret them, to negotiate, so to speak, kindliness, good will, and the commonweal. They facilitate human relationships in the realm of the political, as indeed like types do in all forms of association; for there are politicos under other names in industry, in labor, in agriculture, and in the professions both secular and sacred.

We do not have a precise and generally accepted word to characterize this ability, but anyone with any facility in observation sees the process at work day in and out. In the profoundly important task of orienting the personality in the world in which he lives, these skills are of prime significance. The emergence and early development of the personality are in great part the responsibility of the family, the school, the immediate group of friends and associates; but with maturity the worlds of government and economy loom large. Possibly

115

the personality has become so warped and twisted in early patterns of unfortunate type that frustration will cast its shadow all along the way of life. In such cases society must pay the penalty for lack of proper training. But for the vast majority of humans there remains a wide range of possibilities in adjustment and co-operation for the higher ends of the personality and the society of which they are members. It is at this point that the skills of government are called upon to do their work in producing understandings, attitudes, and good will strong enough to break up the roots of discontent and potential crime and to encourage the growth of personalities capable of co-operating in the constructive policies of statecraft required in the given society.

The skills of government when successfully used produce what we call morale—meaning good morale, good feeling, a sense of satisfaction with the ends of the community and with the ways and means of achieving these ends, in so far as this is within the purview of the political. In ordinary times all this is taken for granted, but, when the skills fail, the road becomes rougher and rougher. Under mismanagement the climate can change with amazing rapidity. Malaise, sabotage, riot, and revolution may appear as if by magic. Just below the calm surface of social order there are possibilities of savagery, cruelty, hooliganism, panics, mobs, riots—situations as startling socially as when the supply of oxygen runs out for any individual.

Special skills are found in developing each of the ends of government. The skill of the warrior is the earliest technique, developed to a high point through centuries of conflict. The maintenance of order has produced expert skills in policing and in the art of prevention of disorder in advance. Justice in the narrower sense has a series of categories all its own, as already indicated. Welfare, whether related to production as in agriculture, labor, or industry or to types of social welfare such as education, medicine, recreation, and cultural opportunities, has led to the growth of many special forms of skills. Strategy has produced groups of diplomats with skill in negotiation and in broad external policies. Internally the special qualities of negotiators, managers, and statesmen have been developed through generations of experience, producing types of men who are able to "get along" with others in a series of give-and-take proceedings. Personnel specialists have not thus far been able to break down fully the necessary qualities of such types, but they exist by general observation and common consent of observers. These qualities are also observable, of course, in the traders and diplomats of industry, in the shepherds of the church, and throughout human association.

These skills are, of course, intimately related to the tools of government and to what are called the organs of government. The skilled politicos employ the accepted agencies such as custom, violence, ceremonialism and symbolism, rational persuasion and the general strategy in which they are combined. And they make use of the special organs of adjudication, conciliar action, management, and headship in their various forms.[37]

These are the chief skills developed by governing groups and characteristic of their operations. Some of these skills are placed in various organs of government, as in war departments, strategy in departments of foreign affairs (in part), leadership in forms of executives, elective and otherwise. National consent and persuasion find a place in educational enterprises. The organization of consent in councils, of adjudication in courts, and of management in staff agencies is commonly found. Sometimes there is an office of propaganda, attempting the organization of symbolism and rational appeal at one and the same time.

But in a more general sense, these various tools run through the whole process of government, outside the special agencies to which they may be specially assigned from time to time. Custom or habit, symbolism, rational appeal, strategy, and leadership permeate the whole apparatus of politics.

It is observable that many of these same tools are utilized by other forms of association—industrial, ecclesiastical, cultural—in many ways very much like those of the political society. In the case of government these tools are, of course, closely related to the ends which government serves and can best be examined in this connection. The ends of government, the tools and the organs of government, taken together and in their interrelation, indicate the characteristics which mark the political species apart from others in the general social category.

It may be useful to set them down in opposite columns:

ENDS OF GOVERNMENT	TOOLS OF GOVERNMENT	ORGANS OF GOVERNMENT
External security	Custom	Adjudicative
Order	Violence	Conciliar
Justice	Symbolism and	Managerial
Welfare	ceremonialism	
Freedom	Rational consent	
	and participation	
	Strategy	
	Leadership	

In a later chapter (ix) we shall trace historically the growth and interrelationship of these categories along with other organs and agencies political.

[37] A. M. Carr-Saunders and P. A. Wilson, *The Professions* (1933); Werner Sombart, *Der Bourgeois* (1913); F. W. Taussig and C. S. Joslyn, *American Business Leaders* (1932); Logan Wilson, *The Academic Man* (1942); Max Weber, "Politik als Beruf," *Gesammelte politische Schriften* (1921); Alfred Bertholet, "Priesthood," *Encyclopaedia of the Social Sciences;* Roberto Michels, "Intellectuals," *Encyclopaedia of the Social Sciences.*

CHAPTER IV

THE ORGANS OF GOVERNMENT

CLOSELY related to the foregoing examination of the tools of government is the observation, analysis, classification, and interpretation of organs of the state. This has been the task of historians, jurists, and students of government for centuries, and many are the systems that have evolved as a result of this attention. As political forms and forces emerge from the obscurity of early origins, we observe focuses of activity developing in the family or primitive group in which men gather together. We may and do find forms of agency —organs—even in subhuman groups of many kinds. Animal societies reveal many interesting and useful types of leadership, authority, and division of labor instinctively followed in the mass, or group, of ants, bees, horses, and chimpanzees.[1] These groups have traits of subordination, superordination, and co-ordination; and among the ants there is seen social stratification and differentiation of status on an elaborate scale. The principal difference between animal and human groups is that in the former the behavior is built into the organism, whereas in the latter it lies in habit, custom, and culture and is transmitted through education, example, and indoctrination.

An organ is based on the division of labor in social groupings, political or otherwise. The unorganized is undifferentiated with no special duties, responsibilities, or opportunities. The organ is a persistent cluster of behavior patterns which persist long enough to be identified by the group and recognized as a part of the expectancies of daily life. The special skills of the particular types of agents are, of course, a part of the situation.

There were organs long before men gave much thought to what we now call organization. The lore of primitive groups is full of customs and terms of emerging forms of organization. The literature of the Chinese and the Indians abounds in wise sayings about the virtues appropriate to various servants of the state, and their appropriate duties and responsibilities.[2] Likewise, the governing systems of Egypt contained highly developed types of subdivision of authority both in civil and in military affairs, as well as in other branches of

---

[1] See W. M. Wheeler, *Social Life among the Insects* (1923); R. M. and A. W. Yerkes, *The Great Apes* (1929); R. M. Yerkes, *Chimpanzees* (1943); W. C. Allee, *The Social Life of Animals* (1938); Robert Redfield (ed.), *Levels of Integration in Biological and Social Systems* (*Biological Symposia*, Vol. VIII [1942]). Of special technical significance in the Redfield volume is A. E. Emerson's analysis of the significant characteristics of the societies of insects and men (pp. 163–76).

[2] On the Chinese see L. S. Hsü, *The Political Philosophy of Confucianism* (1932); on the Indians, Kauṭilya's *Arthaṣāstra*.

government, both adjudicative and conciliar. The Old Testament is an epitome of the religio-political organization of the time, rich in detail and in allusive character.

For purposes of convenience political organs may be grouped as follows: (i) organs of headship, which later become (ii) the executive; (iii) organs of adjudication; (iv) organs of conciliar type; and (v) managerial organs.

Across the face of such a classification there may be placed another arrangement of the functional aspects of government. The ends of the government—namely, security, order, justice, welfare, freedom—are realized in various agencies, such as the armed forces, the police, the courts, and in a long series of activities related to the promotion of the general welfare: education, research, health, and social security. These functions involve the co-operation of the organs of government indicated above. These activities require favorable appropriations from conciliar agencies, effective administration through managerial agencies, and adjudication at various points of interpretation and application. Research and public relations, for example, run across these lines in their span of activity. The process of voting and official selection requires rules laid down by conciliar agencies and administration by special agencies of management such as electoral and personnel devices. Conciliation and adjustment may be found running through the courts, the diplomatic services, the department of labor, in "trouble-shooters," and at almost every point in governmental contacts with society.

It is, of course, entirely feasible to classify all the numerous functions performed by governments from time to time. Under such a plan there would be set up local, state, national, and international activities of all types under appropriate headings, including perhaps several score of special forms of activities, depending upon the time and disposition of the governments described. But for this purpose of governmental analysis the categories here emphasized are those derived from generalized observation of organized political skills.

I. HEADSHIP

Headship under various names has always been found in some form or other (see discussion of monarchy as a form of state). Sometimes the head had a patrimonial-paternal origin, divine sanction, and magical attributes; at times full authority; and at other times very restricted authority. Sometimes the head was little more than a symbolic figure embodying traditions, as modern kings in general. The records of primitive groups and of all succeeding groups are full of the descriptions and accounts of the innumerable forms of chieftains who have taken the headship of innumerable political societies. Whatever else the group may or may not have, there is a chief or headman to

119

whom men turn for some form of direction and leadership.[3] "Who is the head man here?" is a question seldom without answer in any group.

What we come upon in this area is, in fact, the organization of the leader and leadership—a perennial and basic problem of politics and, indeed, of all social groupings in their respective fields. This is not only a continuing but an elusive problem, to which insufficient attention has been given by students of politics and of social relations.

In recent times leadership has been seized by the so-called "dictators" as the basis for a new and allegedly superior system of organization of authority and welfare. The newly revived "leadership principle" assumes government by the few, now known as the "élite," and the irresponsibility of the governors to the governed. Power is to be organized from the top down, in a descending scale, rather than from below up. This system also assumes the omnipotence of the state, with all power vested in the leader at the top. The leader represents no one, not even the state, but the *Gemeinschaft* or society back of the state, sometimes called the nation. In an organic sense the leader is the bearer of the might of this community, which in the Nazi theory is again based upon a special ethnic group, the Aryans, the master-race destined to power, and attaining their ends through violence in great part.

The new type of leadership, it is asserted, invigorates the political society and endows it with attributes not before possessed or, at any rate, exercised. Consent is not a factor in such a system, in which authority rests upon command, organized hierarchically from the top leader down to the humblest rung in the ladder. The old-time dictator of Roman days assumed power, full power, for an emergency only; and, when this was over, he returned to the plow or whatever he had left, as in the case of Cincinnatus. He had ample authority but for a limited period only. The new theory of dictatorship asserts the permanence of the supreme command, without time and without limit of any sort whatsoever.[4]

The Soviet dictatorship of the proletariat, however, is based upon another principle. The power of the dictator is for such period as may be necessary for the proletarian purpose and supposes the gradual development of institutions of responsibility. In the Marxian theory it is true that the state is destined to wither away in the future. But, waiving this far-distant time, the dictatorship may gradually surround itself with democratic devices such as those outlined in the Russian constitution of 1936. In the meantime, important conciliar de-

---

[3] See W. C. MacLeod, *The Origin and History of Politics* (1931); R. H. Lowie, *Primitive Society* (1920) and *The Origin of the State* (1927).

[4] On the origins of this doctrine see "Beginnings of the Anti-democratic Movement," in my *The New Democracy and the New Despotism* (1939), pp. 191 ff.; see also "The Philosophy of Pessimism and the Practice of Violence," in my *The Role of Politics in Social Change* (1936), chap. iii.

vices have been organized for purposes of discussion and determination of many problems, as in the different forms of soviet, local and otherwise. These devices do not insure, however, the responsibility of the governors to the judgment of the community on broad questions of group policy except so far as the general statement of the credo of the party may be taken as such. There is, of course, a wide range of difference between a system which is avowedly temporary in nature, designed to meet a special transition period, and a form of concentration of power and irresponsibility designedly permanent in character and professedly rooted in basic facts of human nature.

It will be observed that there is a striking similarity between this theory and that of military organization. Army structure calls for a vertical line of authority without responsibility, running straight down from the highest officer to the lowest, and without any accountability from below. Yet in most modern systems the military is eventually subordinate to the civil authority, which may remain in abeyance during a crisis but emerges as the source of finances and general direction of action. Clausewitz, the great authority on military science, conceded that many decisions in war were political in nature, to be made by other than military authorities. This is always true, to be sure, of the declarations of war and the treaties of peace. Interesting comments on borderline decisions (civil-military) are found in memoirs of various leaders such as those of Lloyd George, Ludendorff, Churchill, and others in like vein.

II. THE EXECUTIVE

A form of state organ which partakes of the nature of the policy-determining agency and the administrative agency is found in the executive, as variously organized in different modern systems. In the narrower sense the executive executes the predetermined policies laid down for him. In a broader sense, the executive, as in the United States, may participate in both these activities. The president of the United States possesses executive authority, but he also is vested with the veto power over legislation.[5]

In our time Roosevelt and Churchill stand as types of modern organization of executive authority in a democratic society. Presidential and parliamental governments present different forms of central organization. One rests the complete power of ultimate determination entirely in the legislators, and the other divides the authority among the legislative, the executive, and the judiciary. The British Parliament has complete power within the limits of the British unwritten constitution, while the American Congress and the American Executive are both limited by the nature of their constitutional authority and by

[5] See *The Federalist* for an analysis of the executive functions under the Constitution. See the *Report of the President's Committee on Administrative Management* (1937); also the *Proceedings* of the International Congresses on the Administrative Sciences, esp. those of the Sixth Congress, held in Warsaw in 1936.

judicial determination at many points. Yet the differences are more apparent than real.[6] The prime minister is the central figure in English political life, and a general election is, in some cases, much like a referendum on the minister. The fusion of powers is in his hands, subject to the overruling will of the legislative body. But, as in the case of the president of the United States, this is not a will in which he has no part in shaping. His control over budgeting, personnel, and the details of all legislation (except private bills) is more complete than that of the president. He may, it is true, be retired by a vote of no confidence, but this does not often occur. The members of Parliament may retire him, but he may also help to retire them. In the selection and election of members of Parliament, the prime minister may play a very important part, within the ranks of his own party.

There is nothing to prevent the Congress from exerting its full powers either through the budget or through over-all supervision, if it cares to exercise such power systematically and vigorously. If such powers are not regularly and diligently used, this is not an inherent characteristic of the formal system but the product of custom and use. The historical origins of diverse systems have left their mark upon present-day organization and are likely to continue to do so. The American presidency arose from a revolutionary movement against the British crown and Parliament, and later as a protest against a confederation functioning without an executive at all—none worthy of the name. It was not by accident that the president was made commander-in-chief, given treaty responsibilities, made chief appointing officer (including the appointment of judges), and given a veto over the acts of Congress. All this was fully discussed and was purposeful from the beginning. Out of this came Washington, Jackson, Lincoln, Wilson, the Roosevelts, and others who developed the experimental office to its present state.

The British system came out of a revolt against the crown by Parliament, a counterrevolution, a counter-counterrevolution, and the slow accretion of authority under the leadership of Parliament.[7] A "happy series of usurpations," someone has said, marked the rise of Parliament from an advisory agency to a dominant authority in the realm.

The accident of these origins leaves its imprint on the political processes of today and may continue to do so for a long time. Democratic processes the world over will be influenced by these systems, as the course of organizations is shaped in various nations from time to time.[8] In addition to the problem

[6] See Don K. Price, "The Parliamentary and Presidential Systems," *Public Administration Review*, III (autumn, 1943), 317–34, and Laski's rejoinder (*Public Administration Review*, IV [autumn, 1944], 347–59).

[7] Cf. Harold J. Laski, *Parliamentary Government in England* (1938).

[8] See the interesting compromise of Switzerland and that in the Weimar Constitution of Germany. On this whole subject see Herman Finer, *The Theory and Practice of Modern Government* (1932).

presented by the ends of government, the social composition of authority, and the tools of the state at a given time, the executive branch of organization must satisfy other factors—namely, relationship to other state organs and to the general judgment of the community in policy and in administration. The array of variable factors here makes the number of possible combinations very large and the range of experiment very wide. The exigencies of crisis government, of course, are always in the offing and add to the complexities of the scene.

But, different as the elements may be, it is not far from the truth to say that a skilful organizer might find concurrent lines in systems so diverse as those of Russia, England, and the United States, not to speak of the immense array of executive organizations displayed by the historians or the rise of managers in modern days in industry. Unfortunately, any strong movement in the direction of comparative analyses of systems of government and jurisprudence is lagging behind the recent and emerging systems.

The modern executive built upon the basis of technically competent administrative services and maintained with the explicit, institutionalized, good will of the community is in a strong position. The factor of continuity is enormously in favor of the popular form of organization. There is reason to believe that a strong executive will be embodied in emerging constitutions of government, along with strong legislative authority and active public opinion capable of free expression and action.

III. ORGANS OF ADJUDICATION

The practice of the techniques of adjudication and the philosophy of adjudication are as old as political behavior itself.[9] It is always counted a great gain for civilization when disputants are willing to substitute orderly adjudication for unorganized disputation and violence. The act is a tribute to reason and rational processes, no matter on what level of discourse the procedure may prove to be. In the beginning, indeed, the father, the judge, the chief, and the priest are intermingled in their functions; the same individual may act in all these capacities.

This is not the occasion for a treatise upon jurisprudence or upon legal organizations, already exhaustively considered by many eminent and competent men. That the literature of jurisprudence is overwhelming I discovered in my early studies of comparative jurisprudence under Monroe Smith at Columbia and Kohler and Gierke at the University of Berlin. The tomes of modern court reports are as impressive as they are numerous and weighty. It is not the purpose of this study to appraise or to judge jurisprudence or courts but to examine the relation of the adjudicating agencies and skills with the

---

[9] Hans Kelsen, "Law as a Specific Social Technique," *University of Chicago Law Review*, IX (December, 1941), 75–97; Roscoe Pound, *Social Control through Law* (1942).

other organs and skills of the political society in the light of the purposes of government.

The problems of adjudication are so vast that the following can be regarded only as a modest sketch designed to place this great topic in the general framework of the political, without in any sense attempting to exhaust the philosophy or the practice of adjudication as it has developed through long periods of time. This "nonlegal" discussion, as the lawyers would say, is necessary in order that the range and significance of the political may be understood.

It should further be said that adjudication is not a technique exclusively used by public government but is found in all sorts of private governments and private organizations. There are religious courts, industrial courts, courts of honor and even courts of love, prison courts, and courts of the hoboes in the jungle. The analysis of gang organization and procedure, while varying widely in different situations, throws important light upon the nature of orthodox political adjudication itself. Elements in the legal situation which the criminal groups commonly repudiate are the "unfairness" of the law and the "inequality" of its administration. Thus the law may be said to protect property which is unjustly acquired (Robin Hood theory). Its penalties are said to fall unequally upon offenders. Some escape altogether, and others receive widely different punishments for the identical offense, ten years' imprisonment for one and nothing for another equally guilty. Some escape by bribery, it is said, or by the ability to retain exceptionally effective counsel. These rationalizations are tributes to the legal theory and unconsciously recognize the basis of government and the *raison d'être* of the whole power situation. Read in the mirror, these inverted words are the most impressive eulogy of government, for their assumption is that if the law were just or justly applied, then it should be obeyed.[10]

There may be law among the outlaws—arrangements for the administration of justice even among thieves.[11] Referees, adjudicators, and arbitrators of many kinds are scattered through the organization of social behavior; umpires, referees, and "judges" emerge at every point where "trouble" is likely to break out. They are islands in the floods of disputation, unorganized and interminable. The moderating influence in social relations is enormous, so vast that it is indeed scarcely recognized—until it is gone perhaps in some crisis where there seems to be no such apparatus. What is justiciable and how, and by whom, is one of the very greatest problems of government and of social organization in the larger sense of the term. But adjudication cannot bear the whole

[10] An interesting illustration of the governmental process is seen in the "constitutional convention" held by the inmates of Sing Sing penitentiary, where a set of rules and regulations was adopted by the prisoners. Contrast K. N. Llewellyn and E. A. Hoebel, *The Cheyenne Way: Conflict and Case Law in Primitive Jurisprudence* (1941).

[11] See my *Political Power* (1934), chap. iii: "Law among Outlaws."

load of social maladjustment and, if overloaded, behaves as do other wires or instruments carrying more than they should.

The varying mechanisms of courts and the procedures evolved in various circumstances are among the most fascinating pages of political history from the emergence of tribal law, enshrouded in mumbo jumbo, on down to the organization of a tribunal such as the Supreme Court of the United States and its higher rationality. The modes of appointing judges, of organizing them, of providing for appeals, of adjusting jurisdictions, of discipline, of management—these alone would fill many volumes of political description and more of analysis. The great trials of history are among the greatest lessons in political education, and their effect is far-reaching throughout the community.

In perhaps no other area of action is the stage so well set for acute consideration of the relationship between a general and ruling principle and a set of specific facts, under the direction of specially skilled personnel. Both facts and principle, of course, must be established and made the basis of a verdict or decision. The social value of this procedure, if well executed by a just judge, is enormous in its stabilizing and rationalizing effect upon citizens. On the other hand, the unjust judge, the corrupt proceeding, or the triumph of ignorance and unreason has equally powerful repercussions of the opposite type. Happy is the community in which it may be generally declared: "Here justice is done."

What is the animating principle in adjudication and how are the special skills related to the general scheme of things political? The animating principle in adjudication is that of justice, one of the great ends of the state, and intimately related to order and freedom. Justice consists in a system of understandings and procedures through which each is accorded what is generally agreed upon as fair. It assumes the existence of value systems with value rating and value recognition upon that basis. It assumes the existence of institutions, personnel, and procedures through which these understandings may be identified and applied with even hand and with authority, in practical cases involving persons, property, or other values. This must include not only relations between citizens but also between citizens and groups or between groups or between groups of individuals and the state itself; between state organs and even between states.

Adjudication deals with such phases of this broad problem as may be accepted as justiciable. At what point do we call upon the law for help? What is justiciable? And how shall this be determined authentically? Clearly, not all questions upon which there is difference of judgment can be submitted to the judicial process, for some of them raise such broad questions of economic and social policy that their determination must pass to policy-determining bodies set up for that purpose or to the areas of private adjustment. This is not to say that in point of fact many such determinations of policy are not made in the course of a series of legal pronouncements following a special pattern or trend, especially in cases involving property rights or class considerations and racial differences or in the interpretation and application of custom.

Whether or not a line of cases is justiciable depends in part upon what the courts are willing to consider officially and in part upon the general types of jurisdiction laid down by the state. This is inevitably a zigzag line which wanders back and forth in various types of cases and conflicts. Once the lines of the justiciable are established, however, adjudication recurs to the broad principle of justice with which it is identified.

If we are to give each what is his own, then what is his own in a given situation with regard to a wide variety of intermeshed circumstances? What is a use which injures others to a point where social good requires the discontinuance of the act? Or that the state make the injury its own? What is a public purpose and how does it relate to a private right? At this point enter great social philosophies which sweep the surface of adjudication with their compelling sense of direction. The Stoic philosophy thus permeated the Roman law with its precepts regarding equality and justice. The Christian philosophy was projected through the common law. Oriental philosophies ran through the oriental law and customs.[12] The communist doctrines color the making of the Soviet juristic development, although in the beginning even the uses of "precedent" were contested.

Adjudication operates, however, not only with reference to broad concepts of justice but in the framework of a plan of law,[13] which is in course of application. "What is law?" may well be asked in this connection. There are many kinds of law and many theories of the nature of law, not all of which may be outlined or discussed here. There is common law and statutory law and administrative law and constitutional law, public law, military law, and civil law, and a long series of specially developed lines of law in many a different field of human endeavor. There is lynch law but not in the books of proper law.

And outside of these enters equity, which is not law but a close relative of law, entwined with it in the most intimate way. In adjudication equity is certainly a part of law. For equity and courts of equity may weaken the asperities of rigid law and provide remedies otherwise unavailable. The pardoning power of the executive remains a survival of royal "grace," continued as a final review of a legal verdict.

In principle the meaning of law has long been discussed and disputed. Is law "found" or "made"; is law custom; or is law reason; or is it, perhaps, the will of the authority, whoever that may be; is law what is purely conventional or what ought to be? Which of these interpretations of law applies most closely to the governmental process of adjudication in its economic and social

[12] On legal philosophy see the elaborate bibliography under "Law" in the *Encyclopaedia of the Social Sciences.*

[13] See "Modern Legal Philosophy Series."

setting? On this theme of the inner nature of law the great philosophers have evolved their special interpretations for many years—centuries, in fact—without arriving at complete agreement. Much, indeed, depends upon the angle of vision. If we look at the origins of law, there is much to be found in custom. If we look at the promulgation and enforcement of law, there is much to be said for will as the basic factor, will and the force to execute the will; if we look at the higher ends of law, reason is the all-pervading element and may be looked upon as the essence of law. But reason has many forms of expression, and the question, then, is what particular aspects of reason take on the form and color of what we call "law."[14]

Natural law has been a powerful factor in the organization of justice for centuries, especially in the period of the Stoics with their deep influence on the body of the Roman law. The medieval natural law dominated the philosophy of the time, and the natural law of the revolutionary period. the seventeenth and eighteenth centuries in particular. This was the basis of the American system of democracy. Natural law contains a series of rights inherent in men by virtue of their human nature. Equality, life, liberty, and the pursuit of happiness, the right of revolution—these are among the well-known rights arising from the fundamental law of human nature. Natural rights, it is true, are not enforceable by the courts of law, but they have a validity in the course of events and permeate the process of adjudication. They appear as compelling claims of mankind even if not always enforced by statute and decree. Tyranny, corruption, misunderstanding, and perversion may deny them in a particular instance, in a particular jurisdiction, but their value is not destroyed thereby.[15] That natural law lacks authentic statement, interpretation, and means of enforcement is in no real sense an argument against its existence and value in the political system. Both reason and experience are available for the consideration and determination of natural rights of human beings, viewing the dignity of man, his high purposes in the world, and the perfection of his personality.

The general and inexorable trend has been in the direction of what is called a government of laws and not of men. It is obvious that all law must be interpreted and applied by men, but the direction sought may be that of principle rather than an arbitrary personal decision. There is, of course, ample room for decisions which are nominally in terms of principle but actually in terms of personal prejudice or group interest. It was Holmes who said, "The life of law is not logic but experience."[16]

---

[14] "Law," says Thomas Aquinas, "is an ordinance of reason for the common good, made by him who has the care of the community and promulgated....."

[15] On natural law see B. F. Wright, *American Interpretations of Natural Law* (1931).

[16] Cf. Ludwig Bendix, *Die irrationalen Kräfte der zivilrichterlichen Urteilstätigkeit* (1927); Jerome Frank, *Law and the Modern Mind* (1930).

That the majesty of the law is often a screen for special interest rather than general good or for personal or class advantage is one of the tragedies of adjudication but is not more evident than the perversions of order, freedom, and welfare from common good to individual advantage. All the ends and tools of the state may be twisted and turned in the wrong direction, for there can be no power without the possibility of abuse of power. Even in our own day the "rule of law" is invoked by Hayek in defense of obscurantism as an economico-political policy.[17]

In what respect political law differs from other forms of rules and regulations for the common good has also been the object of much speculation. Duguit in his jurisprudence found no distinction between the rules of private and the rules of public bodies. One has no more special sanctity than another. Object and form may, of course, vary, but essentially there is no substantial difference. On this doctrine he bases his theory of the suability of the state. Obviously, rule-making authority is widely found throughout social organization and is by no means limited to the range of the political. The state makes rules, but so does the church. Industry makes rules and so does labor. Rule-making authority is a universal characteristic of organized society, and it, indeed, need not be very highly organized to have rules and regulations widespread in their ramifications. Rules are, in part, a phase of the division of labor, in part a system of status for members of the group, in part a system of expectancies related to the organization of order. These private rules and regulations are indeed accepted and applied by the courts as practices and customs in a wide variety of instances, unless they contain some element hostile to the broad purposes of the political association.

The vital spirit which the adjudicating process requires is found in the common interest as seen by reason, in the light, of course, of the special set of social and economic interests and values in which the individual case happens to be set. These rules are not, indeed, always formally promulgated; perhaps they must be found by searching. It is in this sense that the judge makes law as well as applies it. We may call this "discovery" or "projection" or "interpretation," or we may characterize the process by some other term, but in last analysis the adjudicators may be deriving a rule that never was on land or sea. Solomon's decision was not in the books of precedent; nor were those of John Marshall in interpreting the Constitution of the United States. We may, of course, in orthodox fashion attribute these principles to some established point of reference, but this does not change the essential fact of creative reasoning on the part of the court at the particular time. Adjudication, in short, is intimately related to the larger purposes of the state, in all the fields of justice, welfare, freedom, and of order and security as well. For all these are buttressed in a

[17] Friedrich Hayek, *The Road to Serfdom* (1944). See Ludwig von Mises, *Omnipotent Government* (1944).

sense of fairness which rests upon institutional procedures as well as on deep-rooted understandings and values.

The burdens of adjudication may, however, be too great for its strength in relation to the interest groups and power factors in the political society. There are other agencies in the state whose function it is to promote the broad ends of justice, welfare, security, and order. The conciliar agencies, the managerial agencies, and the *chef d'état* must carry much of the load of social and economic clash of interests. They must determine and enforce the standards of public policy upon questions which divide the community perhaps very sharply. The divisions may be so acute that all the implements of authority including force must be called upon. There are times when civil courts must close for the moment until order can be brought back, welfare and freedom secured, and social justice be put in equilibrium again.

If the burden of the courts is too great, then judicial prestige may sag and with it the strength of the state itself. Judges may be rolled in the dirt, as in Iowa, or hurled from the bench and replaced by laymen, as in Russia. The judges can adjudicate only what is accepted as justiciable. In moments of revolutionary fervor or sharp social dissension settlement must be sought in other agencies of government and other forces of the community. Adjudication as such must remain above the clouds as far as the special technique is concerned.

We may now look at the special skills of adjudication with a view to observing their relation to the other techniques of government and to appraising the special changes accompanying the advances of human thought and human invention in various fields of social behavior. If the first condition is that there must be (1) a rule or a principle agreed upon in advance and (2) an agreed organization set up in advance and assented to and (3) acceptance of apparatus, personnel, and decision, then we may proceed to ask what the special inside skills are which characterize the procedures.

In the early days there was a mixture of paternalism, mumbo jumbo, religion, magic, and immemorial attitudes of compliance with the procedures of traditional origin. To question these was evidence of an unbalanced mind or of possession by an evil spirit. In all systems, even where there was no magic, strong emphasis was laid upon the formal and the symbolic elements in the administration of justice. Justice was a rite, a ceremony, a treatment, a form through which something better might be obtained. Oaths were impressive parts of ritual and justice.

With the rise of rhetoric the jurists became more than ever formal reasoners who laid their cause before the judges or the jury as the case might be. Sophists from Greece became so skilful that they were at one time excluded from Rome as corrupters of public morals. The oral dialectic became the usual weapon and remains so down to this day in great measure.

With the specialization of labor and of subdivisions of law many changes have been made in the conduct of adjudication. Great briefs representing vast technical labors are now presented. Patent lawyers conduct their cases in a manner not so inspiring as a murder trial, to put it mildly. Oral argument is, of course, still the staple diet, but it is reinforced by other techniques.

To what extent have modern psychology, modern statistics, modern knowledge of social behavior, and modern understanding of the secrets of nature penetrated the atmosphere of the oral dialectic and the offhand adjudication by the Solomon of the moment? Enter here the array of experts testifying in special lines of cases. Physicians, psychiatrists, engineers, chemists and physicists, and statisticians with charts and diagrams invade the courtroom. Many special forms of courts rely upon quite different lines of testimony from those of the earlier days—as in juvenile courts, in insanity cases, or in rate regulations and hearings. In many cases the briefs are documents which are, in effect, elaborate treatises upon the subjects under discussion. Lie detectors, blood tests, medical examinations, engineers, accountants, statisticians, and professors lurk not far from the scene and expedite the proceedings or embarrass them as may be in special cases.[18]

Preventive justice comes in with improved knowledge of the social factors underlying crime and misdemeanor. Modified forms of punishment approach technical ground and lay a new task upon the courts as a part of the new criminology. Probation and parole begin to play important parts in the judicial machinery or on the borders of it. These new factors call for new techniques and inventions in adjudication, which are indeed developing on every hand, although preventive justice is only in its infancy.

On the border line between law and administration[19] comes a large number of rules and regulations formulated by administrative agencies under the general authority of statutes. Basic conditions may be laid down in the formal law, but many situations will be left open, and the rule-making power will enter to fill the gap. Thus there arise what may be called sublegislative powers and alongside them are subjudicial powers in the form of administrative hearings, as in civil service or taxation, among many other instances. The degree and form of administrative discretion accorded are subject to supervision by the legislative body, on the one hand, and by the judicial, on the other.[20] Perhaps more clearly than at other points in government may be observed the contrast between the characteristic techniques of the adjudicative, the conciliar, the managerial.

[18] An entertaining view of law is that of Arthur Train in *Yankee Lawyer* (1943).

[19] John Dickinson, *Administrative Justice and the Supremacy of Law in the United States* (1927).

[20] On this broad topic see Leonard D. White, *Introduction to the Study of Public Administration* (rev. ed., 1939).

Inevitably there has arisen, especially in the United States, protracted and animated controversy over the reviewability of administrative discretion by the courts, of the administrative rule-making by the legislative, and of adjudication within the administrative agencies. This discussion is characterized, however, not merely by differences and preferences as to procedure but also by broad differences as to public policy, especially in the field of industrial relations. But much the same problems arise in all systems, whether democratic, Fascist, communist, or oriental.

Much of the current discussion over the question of administrative discretion is futilitarian because it leaves out of management the element of reason and discretion. It may be assumed erroneously that managerial acts are and must be arbitrary in nature, by virtue of the character of the office.[21] While the position of administration is not the same as that of a judicial body passing upon an act, or as a legislature determining a broad policy, this does not reduce administration to the bare limits of the arbitrary and nonrational. On the contrary, the factors of common sense and of reason enter into administrative views, judgment, and action. There is an element of policy determination in administrative action and an element of administrative justice as well. No policy-determining body can possibly foresee all the situations that may arise in the course of applying practically a measure stated in broad terms. Both administrative agency and judicial alike project the intent and spirit of the law, filling in gaps and bridging over unforeseen developments. Overemphasis on detail in legislation and overinsistence on judicial review in the courts are both enemies of administration for the common good. In any government, public or private, the administration may overstep its bounds and arrogate more power to itself than was intended by the government as a whole, but such trespassing is easily remedied either by legislative action or by judicial review in a broad sense.

How the ends of government are best served in the given conditions is the real question, recognizing always the social composition of the political community and the instruments of government available and applicable in this entourage. In the democratic society the question of adjusting the proposed procedure to the general system of consent is also involved.

We may also raise the question of how the instruments of adjudication are adjusted to the general body of control in the given society. If we ask, when looking at military force, "Who shall guard the guards?" we may ask, when viewing the vast powers of the adjudicators over persons and property, "Who shall judge the judges?" Wars end, but the routine of daily tasks goes on, and

[21] See Hans J. Morgenthau, "Implied Regulatory Powers in Administrative Law," *Iowa Law Review*, XXVIII (May, 1943), 575–682, and "Implied Limitations on Regulatory Powers in Administrative Law," *University of Chicago Law Review*, II (February, 1944), 91–116.

with it the many maladjustments that must be smoothed away in working form at least.

While there are organizations in which judges hold by hereditary descent, and others in which judges are elective, the more usual procedure is that of appointment based upon special forms of professional preparation. The terms are long and the process of removal usually difficult; in elective systems, of course, the tenure of judges is at the pleasure of the electorate and some system of impeachment.

Constitutional systems have set up special mechanisms for safeguarding the independence of the judiciary against the encroachments of other agencies of government, whether legislative or executive. Public understandings of far-reaching depth and meaning fortify these structural devices by the force of public opinion. Beyond that the position of the adjudicators is based upon their professional training and the existence of general guiding principles and policies requiring elucidation and application. To some extent the adjudicators will reflect the interests of their immediate affiliations. If special interest becomes pronounced, this becomes a serious handicap and warfare the effective performance of the adjudicating function. Corruption of judges has passed by, but unconscious prejudice lingers, by the testimony of high judges themselves.

In revolutionary crises judges are likely to fare ill. I remember seeing a former judge of the highest court of Russia selling matches and cigarettes in front of the Grand Hotel in Moscow. But, whatever happens to the individual judge, the adjudicating function goes on, with relatively little change in inner content. Under military and martial law the process of adjudication is modified and abbreviated, with more swift and summary procedures. But some of the essential forms and principles are observed even in times of stress and storm, and, of course, there are military proceedings and tribunals that move with very great deliberation. The relations between military authority and local law in occupied territory, of course, raise many intricate problems of adjudication and also throw light upon many political processes otherwise not clearly exposed.

A triumph of adjudication was the establishment of one law for all men, instead of a system under which there were different laws for different classes—the high justice, the low justice, and the middle justice—or in which there was one law for the masters and another for the slave, or one law for the town and another for the gown. Equality before the law was an immense gain in setting the same standard for all men and in emphasizing the legal equality of all men, whatever social inequalities might exist. Even the Roman system, which provided equal justice for all Roman citizens, leaving large groups on the outside, was a long way in advance of other systems which did not provide so large an area of equality, even within a restricted range. The feudal system, of course, was built upon fundamental inequality in jurisdictions and judgments. It was one of the merits of the national system which replaced the feudal that one system of law—in this case the king's justice—took the place of the older inequality. Under any system of equality, in spite of all precautions, there will be inequalities arising from economic or social status, but these differentials may be overcome and, in any case, are not comparable to the outright declaration of inequality before the law.

In a situation where there is wide economic inequality, or where there are deep-seated social prejudices, equality before the law may be and is stretched to the breaking-point. Those with riches, prestige, or other effective power may break through the lines of equity and turn justice into injustice, even while announcing impeccable intentions. The very refinements of the law may be used to defeat its fundamental purposes. It should not be forgotten, however, that over long periods of time it was customary to bring presents or even bribes to the law officers pending decisions affecting the givers. It may be contended that open corruption would be preferable to secret pressure, economic or otherwise. The general trend, however, is steadily in the direction of objective and impartial justice—even in very rapid changes, as at present. It cannot be maintained successfully that the adjudicating agencies have lagged behind the other agencies of government in the race to keep up with the times and to adjust their special technique to the changing ways of living.

Nor can it be said that equality before the law was promptly accorded to women, whose rights and status lagged far behind the demands of justice; or to the rights of various ethnic groups against whom many barriers were raised in theory or in practice, as in the case of Negroes in the United States, Jews in many lands over long periods of time, and semifree persons of many varying descriptions in many areas. This dark continent of justice is still not fully cultivated and civilized, but the chief blame rests now upon lawgivers and not upon adjudicators.

We may constantly recur to adjudication outside as well as inside the political society. Adjustment by adjudication is one of the widespread phenomena of human life, finding its place in every way of life and in every form of social relationship. Arbitrators under one name or another spring up everywhere and play their part in games as well as in earnest. The complex rules of human behavior, the expectancies which everyone holds as part of his way of life— these are constantly weighed and measured by the community or by some persons in it who seem to be highly regarded. Most difficult of all rules to escape are those laid down by the community without writing and without formal means of enforcement. They constitute the unwritten law which is enforced without authorized agents, sometimes by tolerated private reprisal and violence; at other times by spontaneous mass action, exacting obedience to the rule of behavior under penalty of riding on the rail or tar and feathers or other effective means of showing community displeasure.

IV. CONCILIAR ORGANS

Councils of one sort or another have been essential parts of political society from time immemorial. Councils of war, and councils of peace, small councils and large councils, councils of the wealthy, of the wise, of racial and religious groups, of families and of empires. Some of them are imposing and others not so much so. Their debates have shaken states with their impressive nobility and again in darker moments have shamed mankind at their pettiness. The modes of selection, the units of representation, the methods of procedure, and the type of powers have all varied widely from land to land and from time to time.

What are the underlying or common purposes of these widely differing conciliar bodies? Much depends, of course, upon whether the council is advisory or possesses authority of its own. Do they merely counsel, or can they also direct and command? Broadly speaking, however, there are many similarities in conciliar groups regardless of differences in the scope of authority or organization. In the main their functions are (1) to ascertain the wisdom of the community in regard to some line of policy—for king or people as the case may be; (2) to aid in the formulation of the will of the community through definite policies of action; and (3) to strengthen community morale through the formalities of common deliberation, through consultation of agencies and interests, and through a sense of participation in the formation of common policy.

WISDOM

Councils may perform an important function in clearing up the judgment of the political society through discussion and debate over issues of meaning. Many different points of view, factual and in principle, may be brought together, and in the clash of discussion a better view of the total situation may be reached. This is true in a very small council of a small state, and it may be equally true in a larger assembly of a great state. Or it may at times be found in neither. In a conciliar body objections and advantages in policies may be found which had not been foreseen. It is not easy to distil the collective knowledge or wisdom of the group, however, under all circumstances. There may be inadequately analyzed and digested data on which to base consideration, or the atmosphere may be demagogic rather than statesman-like, unfriendly alike to facts and to reason.

A significant feature in the development of organization of group wisdom is seen in the growth of public opinion and its many and novel modes of formulation and expression through diverse groups with new techniques of propaganda and persuasion. Lawmakers are now almost overwhelmed with the weight of statistical data, of technical analyses and presentations, of remonstrances and exhortations. The press, the screen, and the radio enable many to learn of parliamentary debates where formerly only one in a great number could know; what the listener does not get, the commentator may provide for him. In our time public opinion polls are gathering judgments on proposed measures pending before the legislature, to be decided perhaps before they are presented for full consideration, and perhaps in the absence of discussion.[22] Telegrams and telephone messages may pour in like a flood.

WILL

The conciliar process affords a means of arriving at a decision, either as advisers to the sovereign or by the assembly itself acting for the community. It may be pointed out that conciliar discussions are likely to be long drawn out and to avoid rather than invite prompt decision. In many instances this is true; but in other cases the assembly forces the making of a decision which otherwise might be difficult or impossible to attain peacefully without some such method of balance and final determination by definitive vote, resolving the dispute in numerical form at least.[23] Compromise may emerge from the heat of debate and dissension.

Decision may, of course, be reached through the agency of the courts or of administrative authorities, but in neither case does this carry with it the broad quality of the genuinely representative agency consciously fixing upon a line of community policy. One is presumed to declare the law and the other to apply the law, but the council is presumed to make the law in the light of full and free discussion of the several issues involved.

The process of formal legislation is indeed a modern phenomenon with which earlier generations were little familiar. In the United States in the course of a year thousands of laws are enacted by lawmaking agencies, federal, state, and local. Some have been alarmed by this widespread proliferation of legislation, without considering however, the new complexity of social and industrial life. The learned Lecky undertook to show that democracies are essentially hostile to liberty and tend inevitably to increasing interference with community affairs.[24] The legislative body in a modern state occupies a strategic position from which it may consider broadly the ends of the commonwealth, the means available to the state, the main lines of policy to be pursued, and the conduct of administration in the large. Lawmakers have at hand or may obtain all the

[22] Ernest S. Griffith, "The Changing Pattern of Public Policy Formation," *American Political Science Review*, XXXVIII (June, 1944), 445–59; see also chap. vi below.

[23] See T. V. Smith, *The Legislative Way of Life* (1940).

[24] W. E. H. Lecky, *Democracy and Liberty* (1896); cf. Herbert Spencer on "The Sins of Legislators," in *The Man versus the State* (1884).

data necessary for decisions upon public policy. They are, indeed, overwhelmed with technical analyses and consensus. Positive decisions may emerge from the data, or intelligent compromises if essential. That this task has always been performed with complete success no informed person would contend. Yet the establishment of a deliberative body is welcomed as a step forward from the confusion and anarchy of political situations where no central decision can be reached in a manner to command general confidence and support.

Of course, if there is no community of interest strong enough to enlist general support, it cannot be expected that the legislative body will conjure such agreement from the social forces that compose the community. If there is no adequate compactness in the political society, the legislature will perhaps do no more than intensify the elements of disagreement, and this dramatizes the weakness of the state, as in Austria and later in France, or in Germany in the days immediately preceding the advent of Hitler. If two-thirds of the parliamentary body is more interested in overthrowing the political order than in anything else, the malfunctioning of the legislative agency is inevitable.

MORALE

Conciliar bodies perform a useful function in providing for participation of many elements in the shaping of decisions of general interest. Being consulted is an important part of affairs, both public and private. Not being consulted is in reverse one of the most common sources of trouble. Even the absolute ruler may well consult his subjects as does the modern boss about many matters of common concern. He may seek for information, he may try out his plans, and he may invite comment and accept some advice although not all. Only a tyro undertakes to govern alone, without advice from anyone, or of only a small circle. The army organization is the classical type of hierarchy, but councils of war give opportunity for consideration of alternative proposals.

In broadly representative councils there is opportunity not only for participation of a relatively few but for a wide range of interest in the formulation of policies and, in addition to that, a still wider range of hearings for persons and groups of all types. In this way all interests have their day in court, and many of the larger interests will be represented on the floor of the conciliar agency. Under the most favorable circumstances this provides for a wide range of participation by varied elements of the community and tends to raise the level of morale throughout the political society. This assumes, of course, that these interests are, in fact, well represented and that the tone and the temper of the discussion are not merely provocative and defiant but directed toward the common good.

But if there is only civil war on the floor of the council, it is probable that there is imminent civil war in the nation—that the bonds of unity that make a commonwealth have been snapped or are snapping fast. The conciliar agency cannot guarantee unity; it can merely help to express unity if it really exists.

Much of the discussion, to be sure, does not rise to the level of high discourse but is the exaggerated statement of groups struggling for recognition. At this point and under these circumstances the value of the discussion is in the field of morale rather than in that of wisdom. All interest will have been heard in the presentation of their special point of view, balanced against each other and against the general interest. Government "by talk" at least provides an outlet and a forum for the several differing points of view and substantial interests. They have had their day in court, their case has been stated in full, and a decision has been reached in which these groups participated, although their point of view was not adopted. This is a decided gain over nonparticipation, assuming that there is any substantial unity in the group to which appeal can be made.

One of the very gravest threats to the vitality of all types of evaluation and decision is that of too great likemindedness on the part of those who declare and decide. It is at this point that fresh, varying, vigorous ideas and views are often thrust aside, because they are unfamiliar, strange, new, troublesome. This may happen not only in government but also in business, labor, churches, and centers of learning. An opportunity for various points of view to be really heard has a sound value in all systems of direction and authority; and the legislative branch of government often serves this very purpose—but not always.

It is easy to ignore the symbolic value of a common meeting-ground for the broad interests of the city, the state, the nation, and the world—a meeting-place in which it is presumed that there are common interests, representative personalities, and common goals if only common ways and means can be found of attaining them. In dignity the rival of the political council may be the scientific or the ecclesiastical council which attains a high point of impressiveness. But other councils are also important and significant beyond question, as of labor, business, agriculture.

We may ask ourselves what would be missing if the councils no longer convened. Some might say, at first thought, "Well, very little." But on mature consideration the intrinsic values of deliberative councils or advisory councils reappear. Not even Mussolini or Hitler could have managed without his conciliar agency, with pomp in inverse ratio to its power, but still a useful instrument of state for many purposes.

ORGANIZATION

Historically conciliar agencies were early employed in an advisory capacity rather than for purposes of decision. It was many centuries before final power and responsibility devolved upon the councils themselves, either in the state or in the church. The ways and means of organizing these councils were numerous, varying widely in the selection of their personnel and in the modes of their procedure. The significant consideration in appraising these multifarious councils is not the varying forms and powers of these agencies but the recurring pattern of their function. Most of these groups were essentially advisory bodies, but with actual influence and power ranging from near zero to 100 per cent. Seniority, prestige, wealth, representation of substantial interests, "following" in the community—all these factors were of vital importance in fixing the rating of the counselors.

The arbitrary powers of a chief should not blind observers to the practical limitations of his power, to the massive resistance of dissatisfied and unfriendly groups, disaffected by the slight given to important men. If the advice of the council is never followed, its importance dwindles; and so also may the power of the chief who will not take counsel. It is one of the illusions of the unexperienced observer that the ruler rules alone without regard to those around him, because they are legally subordinated to him and therefore helpless. On the contrary, the wise leader is profoundly considerate of his group. If he rallies round him only those who agree with him—"yes men"—he will lose much of the value of his following. He may well find it useful to include some men of independent judgment, who do not fear to say what they think in critical situations. Decision may be his, but advice and counsel may be the basis of the decision. In this sense the body of counselors has a continuing and inescapable function and value. Like the function of adjudication in its field, the function of advice and counsel is recurrent in political experience. Representative government was for a long time regarded as a check upon arbitrary power of the government. This, to be sure, was not the only function of the counselors, but it was one of them.

The *chef d'état*, even if nominally supreme, must deal with the representatives of the community, and if they are selected in some orderly fashion, and independently, their position is very strong, provided they are able to utilize it. Of course, if some Mussolini is able to address the camera, saying without contradiction, "I could have filled you with bullets, but I chose to assemble you here," the effect is quite different and indeed opposite. In such cases the representatives are puppets and not indicative of any check upon the power of the ruler, except that the ruler still observes the form which has, in fact, become a sham.

In general, however, the representatives, even if not possessing large powers of decision, may present the views of the community, at least upon special subjects of great concern. As advisers they may advise upon matters of basic interest to the community as a whole or to special groups of the society, in a manner otherwise impossible of achievement. They may speak, they may protest, they may demand, they may resolve, or they may in many ways indicate their discontent, indifference, or even contempt for the head of the state, whose legal powers they do not or cannot contest.

Later, in more highly developed systems, the representatives could not only advise and protest but held in their own hands the power of policy determination and the power to change the personnel of the head of the state and his subordinates, by various no-confidence votes, in varying forms, by impeachment or otherwise. In such case the legislative might itself become arbitrary and disregard the purposes of the government and the interests of the community. Constitutional provisions, however, removed the power of the legislature to alter basic rights even by statute. What constitutes the violation of a basic liberty was left to the determination of the courts and to the general understandings of the time. In the American system the president was given a veto over the acts of the Congress as a further protection. In the British system Parliament remained unassailable legally whatever position it might take.

Whether the representative body would, in fact, represent the community in pursuance of the ends of government, or might indeed reflect the will of special groups, remained under any system a matter for practical experimentation. Corruption, incompetence, and favoritism unquestionably have been found in representative agencies set up to declare and protect the general interests of the whole community. It may also be pointed out that the same phenomenon is to be found in associations of a nonpolitical character from time to time.

Representative government appeared as soon as the size of the political community warranted or necessitated it.[25] The details of the various systems, including the unit of representation and the modes of selection and types of tenure, fill many volumes of erudition. Territory, occupation, economic status, race, religion, and other bases have served as the foundation of representation. It would be fair to say that geography and occupation have played the largest role in determination of these units. Likewise, the question of whether the representative body should be composed of one house or of two or three, and the relative powers and responsibilities of these chambers, has furnished many interesting answers, which do not agree, although the trend is toward the single chamber or the bicameral legislature at the outside. The differences are due to historical and social considerations imbedded in the life of the particular state.

The variations in mode of selection are numerous and sometimes complex—appointive, hereditary, elective, directly or by indirection, by proportional vote or otherwise, from special units or at large, for long or short terms or for life, or, per contra, subject to recall. The details of these systems are numerous and sometimes very intricate. The rationale of these variations is again explainable

---

[25] On the origins of representative government, see Finer, *op. cit.*; Laski, *op. cit.* See also Otto Hintze, "Weltgeschichtliche Bedingungen der Repräsentativverfassung," *Historische Zeitschrift*, CXLIII (1930), 1–47.

in terms of the history and social composition of the particular state but does not lend itself to broad generalizations.

The principles of representation lend themselves, however, to more generalized consideration. The general purposes of conciliar bodies have already been considered in previous paragraphs and were found to include the utilization of the wisdom, morale, and will of the society. These general considerations are, of course, balanced against the special social interests concerned in the political scheme of things. "What is represented?" it may be asked. The basic principle of representation in a political society, or in other associations, is not different from the basic principle of the commonweal, which is the outstanding, over-all consideration upon which the society rests. The common good, to be sure, is made up through persons and groups, but the overruling basis of representation is that of the state or society as a whole and its general interests taken together. It may be presumed that a full statement of all the special, geographical, occupational, or other interests affected by legislation and their interrelation would lead to a sound determination of what the general good is and what action, if any, is required. Furthermore, it cannot be that the common good is antagonistic to all the special goods or interests in the entire community; for in this case what would be the basis of the community? At some point or other, in some manner or other, the generality of special interests must be woven into a picture into which the special groups and persons fit to their advantage.

The legislator presumably knows the ends and purposes of the commonwealth in general and of the area in which he lives; he knows the relation of the general and the particular interest and is able to make a reasonable or workable pattern of the conflicting factors in operation. He represents not merely the will of the community but also its wisdom; he represents the ends of government—security, order, justice, welfare, and freedom—in their interrelations and in a particular society.

Nor is he the only custodian of the law; there is also the adjudicating functionary and the law; there is the manager and the law; there is the head of the state who also is related to the law. Representation, legislative representation in the narrower sense, is not merely an act of power in a given hierarchy but a trusteeship for the ends of government, selected in the given case involved in consideration and action. The delegation of legislative power is not only a much-disputed theme in public law, especially in the United States, but it is also a general part of the relation between a general supervisory body, such as a legislature, and the expert administrative service—an effort to apply a general rule to a line of specific administrative situations.[26] The general conclusion

[26] See the *Proceedings* of the International Congresses on the Administrative Sciences, especially those of the Sixth Congress.

of prudence is that the legislature shall lay down the general rules of behavior and the categories of action as far as they may be foreseen without burdening the statute with too great detail but that, beyond such prevision and direction, the developing situations must be handled by the administrative agencies. These agencies may lay down rules which, if the situations had been presented to the lawmakers, would have involved the making of a law; but in point of fact such situations cannot all be anticipated even by the wisest of men. More harm than good is done by overdetail, which in turn requires elaborate interpretation by someone—not the lawmaker. This is part of the broad problem of the diffusion of power which is elsewhere discussed in its general relations to government—one of the most difficult and persistent of all the many problems of all political organization.[27]

The legislative functions are often misunderstood. They are not problems of detail but of broad principle. These functions include the following: (1) formulation of broad directives of national policy in the form of law; (2) fiscal allocations of national resources for the general good; (3) general supervision of administration and development of ways and means of securing the accountability of administration; and (4) the organization of democratic controversy on a high level, where divergence of principles and policy may be clearly stated for effective national consideration.

Streamlining our legislative democracy is not primarily a matter of new laws but of new understandings and practices. I do not undertake to set up a comprehensive arrangement of new devices but content myself with a few indications of general directions. For illustration, the significance of a unified budget in the making of fiscal allowances is very great. There are now many appropriation bills in the United States, alongside a series of miscellaneous bills. These might be brought together so that the whole fiscal policy might be considered as one significant measure of far-reaching importance. In this connection the item veto might be conferred upon the president of the United States either by the long way of constitutional amendment or by the short way of house rules which might be adopted. All this would not diminish the real authority and dignity of the Congress but, by shifting the emphasis from detail to general principles, would amplify and enlarge its position in the American democracy.

In such a broad discussion the relation of national expenditures to national revenue and to total national income would inevitably be raised, and the appropriation bill would become one of the central points in national policy along with considerations of long-time planning. Emphasis would be shifted from considerations of detail to questions of broad national policy upon which the

[27] See White, *op. cit.*; "Congressional Control of the Public Service," *American Political Science Review*, XXXIX (1945), 1.

representative body, with its breadth of view, would be able to present very important considerations more effectively than in the treatment of details in piecemeal fashion.

The formulation of broad policies on a sounder basis would involve (1) better equipment of councils with technical information and the ampler use of information now on hand and (2) change in emphasis from detail in legislation to broad statement of general directives. There are, to be sure, times when a detail is inextricably interwoven with a principle, but in general this is not true. The abiding strength of councils is not in dotting *i*'s and crossing *t*'s but in lucid statement of guiding lines of direction.

It is possible to maintain effective control over broad policy through a relatively small number of directing statutes, broad in nature but pointed in direction and general purpose. The strength of a constitution is its brevity and its generality in combination. A constitution extremely long and detailed is far less effective in its impact upon national policy. The tendency of legislative bodies toward devotion to minute detail is not a sign of strength but of weakness, and continued elaboration of language indicates a drift toward inadequacy of general supervisory power, which may now be considered.

A most significant field of legislative activity is the adequate general supervision of administration. Some of the most effective work of legislatures has been accomplished by special inquiries, breaking through impenetrable jungles of confusion and secrecy, or by routine inquiries or investigations. A sound procedure would be the organization of joint committees of both houses dealing with the important problems of personnel, of budget, and of planning—these from the over-all point of view. Obviously the rivalry of two legislative bodies makes this difficult to organize or to operate, but from the point of view of the democracy as a whole, which the legislative body represents, an opportunity would be afforded for the focusing of public attention upon a broad review of administrative activities—not primarily in detail but in principle. If these inquiries are punitive in purpose or method, the results will be less satisfactory, but there is room for broad and fruitful investigations of the very greatest value to the state.

To what extent a representative body really serves as the center of controversy in the national state is itself a subject of excited discussion. Hitler evidently lost his way when he first looked down upon what he called the antics of the Austrian parliament. Many others since then have lost the way. In streamlining representation and legislation, we are met by the challenge of a revolution in modes of intercommunication. What is the bearing of the press, the radio, television, and the movie upon modern interchange of ideas and emotions? In this complex world what is the impact of intercommunication upon the representative body, and how shall it shape its behavior to meet the new demands upon it? Shall we broadcast the proceedings of councils? And, if so, what influence would this have upon the tone and tenor of conciliar debate? What is the bearing of all these new devices of communication upon the oral dialectic of legislative discourse? Or upon the committee system of preliminary consideration and recommendation? To what extent do legislative bodies under new conditions continue to be the focal points of policy determination?

We do not know the answer to all this, but we know that the answer must be sought and found. The answer will not be discovered merely in the form of a rule, a regulation, or a law but in an understanding regarding the role of lawmaking bodies. One may express the judgment that the solution will be found somewhere around the raising of the level of discussion, with broader principles and sharper definition of underlying issues. This is not the work of a legislative body alone. It can be only the result of an effective demand on the part of an enlightened community. In the long run, representatives represent what there is to be represented—not much more and not much less—not as much less as many like to say. If we do not like the picture we see in the mirror we hold up, it nevertheless is ourselves. "The fault, dear Brutus, is not in our stars, but in ourselves." In the ensuing discussion on the role of administrative management it will be possible to indicate more clearly some specific aids to intelligent and representative legislation.

In the United States the importance of organizing intelligent discussion of broad public policies is greater than in more centralized states, because no one government has full power. Effective action involves the co-operation of forty-nine governments in many cases, as well as cities and other local authorities. It is consequently important to reach a consensus widespread throughout the land and resting upon a very broad basis of understanding. Under our constitutional system both the states and the United States must agree upon many measures of social significance, as, for example, health, schools, housing, land and water use, and taxation. The foundation of such agreements may be laid in an interchange of views, a clearing of interests, a reconciliation of purposes, which a national debate may well set forth and develop. Modern methods of intercommunication present alternative procedures for discussion, but the dramatic character of a congressional debate has not yet been superseded by forums or by polls of whatever kind and value.

The important point in all this is, first, the recognition of the values of public discussion resting on the basis of adequate data and analysis and, second, the disposition to find a solution through peaceful consent rather than through division and violence. From time to time the action of legislative bodies is criticized because it is influenced by pressure groups of one sort and another— agricultural, labor, industrial, and social. This view, however, reflects a naïve conception of the political process among mankind. What type of human association is it in which there are no pressures and counterpressures for group action of one type and another? It is, indeed, these very pressures of individuals and interests that call for the balancing function of the state. If all interests and pressures settled themselves automatically, there would be no need for government at all. The stars would move in their courses without any central control.

The appearance of these social and economic interests is an inevitable phenomenon of social organization and control. In any form of government, whether that of the many, the few, or the one, these or like pressures will exist and will be reflected in one form or another. The interests may be less obvious and less public, but their activity will be observed by anyone familiar with the operations of the governing process.

Behind formal social legislation there is a large body of nonpolitical representative bodies of many types operating as a part of the public process. These groups are not repressed, intimidated, or controlled by the state, but their activity is encouraged in the interest of sound formulation of public policy—in the interest of the process of common consent to the broad policies of the nation. Some of these groups are able from time to time to dictate to the government their programs, but, on the whole, one is likely to be balanced by others, and the net contribution is that of a broader discussion of legislative policies.

The more highly organized these groups are, however, the smaller their number; and the larger their membership, the more serious the problem becomes, whether these groups are racial, religious, regional, professional, or representative of agriculture, labor, industry, or other social aggregations. In a wide range of groups their very pluralism tends to offset one against another. If, however, these corporate groups are relatively few and prefer their corporate existence and programs to those of the state as a whole, their special goods to the common good, then difficulties arise which are not readily met by any mechanism or formula. The problem under such circumstances is that of creating a genuine community, with priority of common interests over the special. There cannot be any very effective common counsel unless there is an explicit will to provide a common program in the pursuance of common interests.

If antagonistic groups, unwilling to compromise their conflicting interests, are of a territorial character, the solution may well be a geographical separation into distinct states. But if this is not the case and the groups are socially intertwined in such manner as to make segregations not feasible, then the alternative is likely to be that of violence, until such time as reason and compromise are again in position to assume the leadership of the groups. On this basis the Hitlerite state was built in Germany, and with less pretext the Fascist state in Italy.

In recent years legislative bodies have been under very heavy fire, sometimes from the enemies of democracy and again from its friends. The chief charges have been those of diffuseness, failure to keep pace with the advances of science and technology, incompetence, undue susceptibility to special interest pressure groups; and on the darker side subservience to special interests and privilege and at times outright corruption. Executive leadership in many instances has been able to muster and utilize technical information from administrative or other sources, available to legislative bodies but not organized and applied by them. Government, to realize its ends, must supply a sense of proportion, of relative meaningfulness, of broad social importance. This must rest upon a knowledge of pertinent data, a sense of social values as well as of social forces, and upon reasonable energy in decision. These are essentials in which lawmaking bodies are not always as well equipped as is desirable in view of their large responsibilities. But they are not points at which improvement is impossible under present conditions and those of the emerging future.[28]

If we bear in mind the most general purpose of government—namely, the common good and the specific ends of security, order, justice, freedom, and welfare—then in this general perspective the role of the legislative body may be seen more clearly. The gravest and most serious of all legislative difficulties is that of failure to keep the eye on the common good—the search for the common denominator of the community within which the ends of the state may best be served. Failure to find the common factor of the common good would, in the long run, prove fatal to the functioning of the lawmaking body or most nearly fatal. But precisely at this point the legislative agency is likely to be the mirror of the state itself and its manifold social forces and values. The legislature cannot reflect what is not there in unity and community of aspiration, although it may help to weave a pattern. Thus the weakness of the legislature at this point may be the index of the weakness of the community and foreshadow its decline in vitality.[29]

The legislators may, indeed, exercise an important influence in creating such a sentiment themselves, but they cannot go far byond the circle of their own social background. If there is no general agreement upon some body of policies which can be formulated, then the legislative function comes to an end, and either some other agency in the state functions or the particular state itself is at the end of its reason for existence. History is full of the graveyards of legislatures who could not agree upon anything substantial and of states which could not find their way out of their social differences, and left the way open to those who could at least through force impose a policy of order and a form of

[28] Karl Mannheim, *Man and Society in an Age of Reconstruction* (1940), Part V, chap. vi: "The History of Parliamentary and Democratic Government as the History of Social Control."

[29] See "Morbidity and Mortality of Power" in my *Political Power*.

justice and welfare. France, Germany, and Poland are striking examples of failure to find a formula of agreement at critical times.[30]

Just as we inquire as to what progress is being made in the development of the techniques of adjudiction to keep pace with the development of human intelligence, so we may ask what advances in conciliar techniques are being made by the conciliar agencies in general. And, we may add, how do these advances compare with those of other groups?

Breaking this question down a little, we ask, "What progress is being made in the organization of the wisdom of the community—one of the evident functions of the conciliar agency?" Immense masses of social data are being collected and analyzed in our time by many scientific and technical agencies developed for that purpose, as, for illustration, by libraries, by the census, and by statistical and fact-gathering agencies innumerable. These are brought together at times in so-called legislative reference services for the benefit of the lawmaker. At the same time bill-drafting facilities are provided in most jurisdictions for the purpose of insuring greater accuracy and consistency in the actual process of lawmaking.

Legislative inquiries and commissions of various types are in use for the purpose of arriving at information not otherwise available perhaps. These agencies may be of witch-hunting type, brow-beating, unfair, and domineering, or they may be full of capacity for arriving at significant data.[31] They may provide rich material through which careful review may be made of the acts of administrative or other officials in the performance of the supervisory function of the conciliar agency. Struggling in a period of swift change in the economic and social fields, with immense masses of new material constantly being developed by hundreds of investigators of many types, the conciliar agencies would do well if they kept pace with current information; and, on the whole, it cannot be said that they have distinguished themselves in this field.[32]

Again, the legislators have often encountered great difficulty in formulating broad principles of action, directives for the society in which they operate and especially for the administrative agencies of the state. They have evinced a strong disposition to deal with details rather than with general principles, to regulate the minor rather than the major affairs under their jurisdiction, to wander where power rather than reason leads them. In various interpellations under different parliamentary systems the same tendency is also observable at times. In so broad a field obviously generalization is difficult, but we may now

[30] At this point consult A. J. Toynbee, *A Study of History*, Vols. IV–V (1939) for analysis of decline of type civilizations and states. I do not agree with his analysis, but it is stimulating and consistent in its development and application.

[31] Cf., in the United States, the Dies Committee with the Truman Committee.

[32] Brilliant examples of legislative leadership are seen in the parliamentary inquiries of England and Sweden.

raise the question of whether the conciliar agencies have on the whole lived up to their possibilities in the formulation of broad legislative policies. Here again the growth of special interests based upon new technologies has given rise to powerful pressure groups with wide-reaching political powers; business, labor, agriculture, professions, and ethnic and religious groupings. Their clashes are determined, sharp, and often dangerous to the stability and progress of the community. At times they have overturned government in revolutionary movements or crippled it in divisive efforts which could not be reconciled. There are occasions when conciliation, adjustment, and compromise are of no avail. Incompatible elements put together in the same conciliar agency will not automatically be made compatible. Skilful leadership may prolong stability or delay disaster, but sometimes all is in vain, and the political society goes down.

On the other side of the picture, however, the flood of constructive social legislation during the past century has been surprising in volume, as we survey the leading states of the world. It is easy to indicate what has been done badly and to find serious omissions, but the striking fact is the great quantity of sound and useful legislation enacted in the last one hundred years. For some of this a revolutionary basis has been found neccessary, but the bulk of it has been evolved by the peaceful processes of lawmaking bodies in many lands.[83]

How far the legislative techniques have adapted themselves to the category of public participation as a function may be answered in two ways. The superior organization and the new tactics of pressure groups have made the task of participation of special groups of the community more effective than ever before. The lobby has been called the "third House." Also the percentage of population enrolled in the lists of voters has grown steadily larger, with the removal of restrictions of property, religion, race, and sex. A far greater number of persons are now represented than ever before, and they in a way participate through their chosen representatives. The "people" is far larger than in earlier times when slaves, unfree, dissidents, and outcasts of all sorts lived on the edge of political interest or activity. There are even devices for direct voting upon laws of various types, chiefly constitutional laws for fundamental measures, and many persons enter the circle of political participation by this route.

It is clear that much might be done to improve the efficiency of legislative operations, both in the field of structure and organization and in the area of legislative procedures and operations. There is much difference among experts as to whether there should be a unicameral or a bicameral legislative body, or whether the basis of representation should be territory and population, or special groups, or whether representation should be direct or proportional. Little doubt remains, however, on such questions as more elaborate technical equipment and improvements in committee organization in the direction of simpli-

[83] See the *Bulletin de la Société de Législation Comparée, passim.*

147

fication and co-ordination. There is especial room for searching of hearts and minds on the best relationship between legislative organization and detailed administration. Going deeper down is the difficult problem of continuous recruiting of representatives competent for the high task of combining into policies of common good the special knowledge of the experts with the general opinion and judgment of the public.

From time to time it has been proposed that the basis of legislative bodies should be economic, or other social units, such as labor, agriculture, industry, professions, guilds, or syndicates, which might be made the units of representation, as were the "estates" in earlier times or the corporatives in Italy under fascism. It has even been proposed that one house of the legislative should be political and the other industrial in composition and powers.[34]

But whether the representation proves to be territorial, groupistic, or proportional, or some combination of these in order, the principal problems of representation remain much the same at bottom. Changing the units will not revolutionize the task and the techniques of legislation[35] or provide any panacea for representation.

A major question is whether the mass of the community whose common good is considered feel that they are more fully represented than before; whether they feel that they are participants in the formulation of general policies. Have they faith in the general design of the legislative body, and is this a growing faith and confidence?

Looking back, we see that, when legislative bodies stood firmly against despots, they had great popular support; later, when they seemed to represent narrow electorates and interests, the conciliar bodies lost their general backing; again, with the rise of special pressure groups, the conciliar group was weakened in general esteem. In so far as legislatures enacted codes of social legislation designed to alleviate the miseries of the new time, they were again given strength; but in many cases the credit went to political leaders who were not classed as legislative leaders. This was not true, however, of parliamentary England.

It is highly significant that in the leading democratic states an executive has developed alongside the conciliar agency—in the United States from the beginning and by constitutional intent and purpose, and in England from a series of events leading to the present-day position of the prime minister now analogous to an executive leadership. In the United States the congressional agency never was the only formulator of national policy, while in England the prime minister and the cabinet gradually assumed the same position as the president of

[34] Sidney and Beatrice Webb, *A Constitution for the Socialist Commonwealth of Great Britain* (1920).

[35] See discussion under "Parties," chap. vi.

the United States—that is, an elective representative who shares in the law-making function.[36]

Nothing is clearer from the study of human political behavior than the recurrence and persistence of the deliberative council in all forms of society under all manner of conditions. If one is thrown out, another comes in. Councils may become weak, decorative, submissive, and sycophantic, but this condition cannot be reckoned with permanently; and they rise again to power in another corner and in another garb. The despot himself will call a council into being if there is not one at hand; his own council he will call it, and such it may be, for a while. He may in turn become the tool of his own council, which slowly rises to power.

The attempt of the democratic political association to bring a council into intimate relationship with the community itself, for consideration of the common good, is one of the boldest and the most difficult attempted. This experiment presupposes that the political community is capable of choosing for its representatives men of competence, character, and loyalty to the community to provide an instrument of people's control. Many exceptions and failures may readily be noted, but no other and better method has yet been devised by the mind of man to bring about representation or rapport with the day-by-day authorities. With all its imperfection, no better way has been found or is in sight.

Thus far, no political agency has been discovered which is more likely to reflect the diffusion of authority and responsibility throughout the political society and at the same time to reflect the need for integration and unification of state policies. The strength or weakness of the legislative agency is an index of the strength and weakness of the political community, at a vital point where nothing can take the place of mature wisdom, of ability to appreciate and appraise the relative claims of action and deliberation, of the general principle and the special case, of the unity of interest and the multiplicity of voices and demands.

V. MANAGEMENT

Another organ of the state deals with the application of predetermined policies—the managerial. The manager applies to a going concern policies that have been laid down by policy-determining bodies, adjusting and applying a broad principle to a series of situations many of which were unforeseen by the framers of policy. In a sense he projects the policy, keeping "on the beam," so to speak. Within the circle of the larger policy he develops smaller areas of policy on his own, subject, of course, to the supervision and review of the superior con-

---

[36] Cf. also the Swiss executive council. A general discussion of these types may be found in Finer, *op. cit.*

trols. But the manager may also suggest other and different policies for the consideration of the policy-makers.

Closely connected with managerial activity is that of the executive, separated here for the time because it deals with general headship of the state and with the work of leadership. Warning must be given, however, against too sharp a differentiation between any of these state organs, since they are all intimately interrelated. Otherwise they could not operate at all. If for purposes of analysis they are separated here, it must not be concluded that they are wholly divisible entities. In this respect the organs of the state are not essentially different from those of other societies, such as the economic or the ecclesiastical.

The fundamentals of management vary with the social techniques of the time, ranging from magic to science, from techniques appropriate to the primitive activities of undeveloped societies to those required by large-scale groups of modern days. The early duties of management were often intermingled so closely as to be indistinguishable with magic, black or white, with religion, with immemorial custom, imbedded in local tradition, all woven together. What seem to us at this distance fantastic rites and ceremonies surrounded the day's work and perhaps rendered it is exciting as a personnel or statistical laboratory of our days.

The modern interest in management is essentially a function of recent mass activity. The vast expansion of physical power in our days has been accompanied by great mass efforts. With this comes sharp specialization of labor, and with these specializations of activities comes the urgent need for new modes and mechanisms of co-ordination and management. Likewise we have given attention to organization with the rise of large mass armies. We observe the growth of intense interest in the mass developments in industry. Efficiency and rationalization have led to many and detailed studies of industrial behavior and its most appropriate organization. From another point of view there came a stream of interest arising among the biologists and the psychologists dealing with various patterns of behavior and struggling to bring them into some sort of order. In the fields of sociology, anthropology, and economics speculation over organization developed among many students of these disciplines.[37]

The earlier political thinkers used the term "organization" in the broadest sense of the term, that is, with reference to the widest aspects of the patterns of political forces in a given state. Thus a political society might be organized as a monarchy, aristocracy, or democracy, as a city-state, feudal state, a national state, imperial state, or a world state. Emphasis was also placed on the organs of organization. These came to be standardized in the course of time under the

[37] See my *Public and Private Government* (1944), chap. iii: "New Meanings of Organization."

150

categories of legislative, executive, and judicial organs, the combination of which in some form of balance was held to be the indispensable basis of sound organization.

With the development of mass action, the use of the term "organization" shifted somewhat. New points of view and new vocabularies began to appear in the narrower boundaries of administrative management. Military systems developed concepts of administrative organization related to the efficient conduct of war. Notable was the organization of the general staff in Prussia. On the civil side, in France and in Germany particularly, there developed doctrines of public administration and of administrative law, along with administrative courts. The principles and practices of administration became an essential part of the rounded education of jurists, administrators, and statesmen in these countries. More slowly in England and in the United States doctrines of administration began to appear.

To the development of large-scale economic enterprise and to large-scale military enterprise was added large-scale governmental enterprise, outside the military field, bringing numerous groups of theorists and practitioners over to something like a common ground for the consideration of organization. Enter now time-and-motion studies, cost analyses, personnel bureaus, and a whole new apparatus of measurement. Gulick and Urwick brought together in an interesting volume the doctrines of Fayol, management specialist; Henry Dennison, manufacturer; the organizational ideas of James D. Mooney, vice-president of General Motors Corporation; John Lee, controller of the Central Telegraph Office in England; and various representatives of a community of scholars including Gulick himself, Mayo, Whitehead, Henderson, and Mary Follett.[38]

Their use of the term "organization" was not always clearly defined or distinguished sharply from co-ordination, integration, management, or administration. Gulick defines organization as "interrelating the subdivisions of work by allotting them to men who are placed in a structure of authority, so that the work may be co-ordinated by orders of superiors to subordinates, reaching from the top to the bottom of the entire enterprise."[39] I shall not stop to dwell here upon Gulick's famous formula, POSDCORB, "a made-up word designed to call attention to the various functional elements of the work of a chief executive, because 'administration' and 'management' have lost all specific content."[40]

[38] Mary P. Follett, *Dynamic Administration* (1942); see also her *Creative Experience* (1924) and *The New State* (1918).

[39] Luther Gulick and L. Urwick (eds.), *Papers on the Science of Administration* (1937); L. Urwick, *The Elements of Administration* (1944).

[40] Gulick and Urwick, *op. cit.*, p. 13.

These initials stand for Planning, Organizing, Staffing, Directing, Co-ordinating, Reporting, and Budgeting. Gulick also refers to organization by major purpose, by major process, by clientele, or matériel, and by place.

The famous French industrial consultant, Fayol, means by organization "to build up the material and human organization of the business, organizing both men and materials."[41] Obviously, he thinks of organization as part of a larger process which includes planning, organizing, commanding, co-ordinating, and controlling. Almost the same use of terms was reached independently by Mooney and Reiley.[42]

The purpose of all organization in these definitions is that of unifying effort, that is, co-ordination. Co-ordination is itself a phase of authority. Thus, Leonard White speaks of the "organization of centers of decision" as a central factor in organization.[43]

John Gaus arrives at the following meaning for organization: "Organization is the arrangement of personnel for facilitating the accomplishment of some agreed purpose through the allocation of functions and responsibilities. It is the relating of efforts and capacities of individuals and groups engaged upon a common task in such a way as to secure the desired objective with the least friction and the most satisfaction to those for whom the task is done and those engaged in the enterprise."[44]

It is clear that the students of industry, of armies, and of government mean by organization the process of bringing together in working patterns the various factors of production, whether the product is a marketable commodity, a military victory, or a phase of governmental administration or management. Organization involves a combination of effort to accomplish a given purpose otherwise impossible or more difficult.[45]

Very significant are the brilliant border-line studies made by Follett in *Dynamic Administration,* by Lasswell in his several publications, especially *World Politics,* and notably by Elton Mayo in his psychomedical studies

[41] *Ibid.,* p. 119.

[42] James D. Mooney and Alan C. Reiley, *Onward Industry!* (1931).

[43] *Op. cit.,* p. 44.

[44] See John M. Gaus, Leonard D. White, and Marshall E. Dimock, *Frontiers of Public Administration* (1936), chap. v: "A Theory of Organization in Public Administration."

[45] Henry Dennison, *Organization Engineering* (1931); Gulick and Urwick, *op. cit.,* p. 113. F. J. Roethlisberger and W. J. Dickson, in *Management and the Worker* (1939), chap. xxiii, "Formal vs. Informal Organization," give an interesting and useful account of various hierarchies outside the formal arrangements in an office and their interpretation. See also Gregory Bienstock, Solomon M. Schwartz, and Aaron Yugow, *Management in Russian Industry and Agriculture* (1944).

summed up in *Human Problems of An Industrial Civilization*.[46] These lines of inquiry reach from the analysis of the personality of the administrator to his processes of administration. Even more searching analysis in these directions, difficult though they may be and slowly as advances may be made and recognized, are likely to add greatly to our understanding of organizational processes in the near future.

It is evident that magic has largely disappeared from organization, both black magic and white magic, but not wholly. Organization becomes a study of mass behavior directed toward specific ends. Leadership is involved but not superhuman leadership. Division of labor assumes a technical aspect based upon many divergent considerations. The whole process of co-ordination is broken up into its various elements in somewhat different form by various writers. The similarities in the charts and diagrams of these thinkers are, however, more notable than their variation one from the other. The information available ranges from almost microscopic inquiries, such as those of Emerson, Taylor, and Gantt, to psychomedical studies, such as those conducted by Elton Mayo. Both individual personal psychology and the total social environment have been drawn upon to provide material for more effective organization leading to the optimum operational results. It is impossible to deal here with the vast monuments of literature piled up in the last twenty years in the broad field of administration, management, industrial, military, and civil co-ordination, in academic, religious, agricultural, and labor co-ordination, and with the great apparatus of technical data, of statistics, of psychology, and of refined analysis in various forms.

It appears, then, that organization in the administrative sense involves fundamentally two processes: (1) the division of labor and duties—essentially an analytical process—and (2) the development of patterns of the elements which have been subdivided—essentially a synthetic process. There are involved many complex problems of structure and function, integration and diffusion, of staff and line, of delegation and supervision, of leadership, or participation, of co-operation, of discipline and morale, of personnel, of planning, of budgeting.[47]

What is now happening is the rise of a scientific-administrative group, broadly recruited from all classes, with a body of principles and skills, and

[46] See also the unique contributions of Herbert Emmerich in *Public Management*, esp. "Some Folklore of Executive Management," *Public Management*, XX (1938), 264–67. From a psychoanalytical point of view see Franz Alexander, especially *Our Age of Unreason* (1942). See on "mysticism" in organization the encyclical of Pope Pius XII, *Mystici corporis* (June 29, 1943), on "The Mystical Body of Christ."

[47] See the *Report of the President's Committee on Administrative Management* (1937) of which the writer was a member, along with Dr. Gulick and Dr. Brownlow, chairman.

at the service of the commonwealth which establishes them. They are ultimately responsible to the community which sets the broad lines of their support, their activities, and their personnel, and passes judgment in last analysis upon their conclusions. They are means by which the people's ends are reached.

Contrary to the general view, the defense of human liberty depends in large measure on the procedures and the spirit of public administration. The judicial agencies play their proper part in the protection of private rights, but with increasing difficulty in view of the slowness of procedure in a fast-moving society and in view of the complexity and rigidity of technical rules. The judicial agencies can do little more than outline broad principles in notable cases.

In large and increasing measure, administrative agencies supply the diffusion of power upon which the growth and play of individual initiative rely for their protection and stimulation. The degree of adaptability within the administration itself, the extent to which it is able to comprehend, sympathize with, and incorporate popular attitudes—these are factors that will be effective in determining the scope of free play of activities of the citizen in the period ahead of us.

Administration plays as large a role in government as adjudication. In administrative management there are developed types of competence upon which wisdom in decision is conditioned, a professional attitude of objectivity and fairness which is of far-reaching importance, and an over-all point of view and attitude of deepest meaning in the life of the commonwealth. Administration is akin to adjudication in many of its activities.

In many branches of administration, conciliation and arbitration play an important part, as in labor administration, where conciliators and labor boards are actively engaged in smoothing out difficulties between employer and employee. The "good offices" of many administrative agencies, beginning with the diplomats of career and running through a long series of adjusters, are utilized to bring about settlements of disputes in cases not readily justiciable in the ordinary courts of law. The skill with which this service is performed has a very important bearing upon the public relations of the persons and groups concerned. In emergencies such as war these functions become of exceptional importance, but they are operative at all times in a broad variety of forms.

Three major aspects of management operations in our day are those of (1) personnel, (2) fiscal, and (3) planning. Of these, personnel management has relied more heavily upon psychology, fiscal management upon statistics and accounting, and planning upon analyses of resources, trends, and possibilities.

Budgetary problems are usually classed under public finance. Fiscal policy in the narrower sense and national policy in the larger are in reality so intimately related as to be inseparable. Taxes, budgets, debts, tariffs, currency, and national income are part and parcel of the life of the state as well as of the common life.

Planning problems are likewise an essential factor in the development of government on all levels. In cities planning is almost universally accepted as a valuable tool of common advantage and is widely utilized both in private and in public management.

In a still broader sense management includes the total picture of administration, covering alike the fiscal, personnel, and planning and other functions in their interrelationships, whether as line or as staff activities. The general manager is confronted with the task, sometimes extremely difficult, of drawing together these different threads into a pattern of action. That dislocations, snarls, hindrances, and sticky spots develop is not exceptional in the manager's responsibility but a part of the reason for his existence. The strategy of coordination must find the way, if there is one. One may sit in the office of a highly responsible executive of a very large and intricate concern, public or private, and draw the conclusion that there is little or nothing to do until the moment for action comes. Then the manager takes charge and untangles what otherwise might prove to be a serious break in the chain of action. Or his trained understanding may detect the slowing-down of tempo and results and at the opportune time discover the remedy.

PERSONNEL

Broad personnel policies and many theories affecting them have sprung up alike in public and in private government in the last generation or so.[48]

1. The development of special groups of career persons, devoted to government or group service—the professionalization of service in fact.

2. The democratization of career service and the admission to its ranks of all classes on fairly equal terms, with many exceptions to be sure, but including women.

3. The rise of managerial personnel in considerable numbers and with greatly increased power in a wide range of jurisdictions, other than governmental in character.[49]

4. The organization of public employees to defend their collective interests—a profound change in fifty years—and the concurrent problems of overemphasis on organization as such.

It is difficult to say which of these trends is of greater significance, but it is incontestably true that, taken together, they constitute an immense change in

[48] See above on theories of organization.

[49] James Burnham, *The Managerial Revolution* (1941); Robert A. Brady, *Business as a System of Power* (1943).

155

the character of community organization, political and otherwise. Important precedents were found, however, in the organization of the army and of the church, which anticipated by long periods the present proliferation of administrative management[50] in government and in industry.

FISCAL MANAGEMENT

Fiscal management has taken on a position of increasing significance with the rise of modern industrial techniques. Modern accountancy, modern cost keeping, modern emphasis on reports and standards applicable to the large mass movements in the economy, all have left their mark upon fiscal affairs of the state. In the transition from the patrimonial state to the modern state it was relatively easy for the "management" of the day, the landlord indeed, to concern himself with the fiscal trends of his properties.[51] Democratic controls, as they rose later, were naturally directed toward supervision of the income and outgo of the government.

The growth of the present-day economic organization leads on to increasing importance of community finances. Debts became the subjects of careful organization, currencies became more and more delicate in their structure and operations, along with banking and credits of all types. Budgets began to be considered with great care and finesse as an instrument of national policy. International relations intensified the need of well-organized fiscal apparatus in the nation. Part of the appliances and understandings that came into being were legislative or policy-determining in their relations, but another part was a branch of the managerial functions of the political society.

More and more the fiscal aspects of life came into notice, as men began to link the cost of living and the wage scale together and look upon them as affected in great part, alike in peace and in war, by governmental actions. That the up-and-down turns of the business cycle could be affected by government came to be accepted as the twentieth century swept on. Governmental spendings, revenues, debts, and money policies began to be reckoned as a part of the general function of the state and held to require more and more careful consideration. What had formerly been a simple set of accounting or organizational devices became more and more complicated in structure and function, and the income and welfare of the nation were seen to be tied in with the successful operation of these new devices, so closely related to the various groups of the political society.

Thus the theory and the practice of fiscal management have grown into a development of major significance in the modern state. The ways and means

[50] Cf. the organization of the Jesuit order, and see Alfred Vagts, *A History of Militarism* (1937), for an account of the rise of military organization.

[51] Political economy in Germany was called originally "Kameralwissenschaft"; the economists "Kameralisten." See Albion W. Small, *The Cameralists* (1909).

of advances were widely disputed, but the urgency of some basically different fiscal system was no longer disputed by any form of government or any class of society.

Planning on the urban level made material progress in recent times, and special national agencies sprung up in almost every nation.[52] A planning agency may be made a central point in the coming development of public administration, serving as an adviser to those who make the ultimate decisions regarding the policy of the state, and facilitating their work.

A completed mechanism calls for an agency to deal with (1) the collection and analysis of basic data regarding resources, natural and human, and (2) the development of forward-looking policy based upon these data and their implications.[53]

The mechanism of plan-making and of planning is experimental, and clearly there may be many different forms adapted to different situations. Two main types have emerged recently: (1) the economic council, developed in France and England (earlier in Germany), designed to include representatives of various economic interests, and (2) the general-staff type of planning agency, not primarily representative in composition. The first type, the economic council, is set up as a form of representation of different interests assembling for purposes of interchange of views and of formulation of policies. The French council contained sixty-six members, distributed among the general public and consumers, production (including management, labor, and professional workers), and capital (ownership in land, industry, trade, finance, and banking). The English council consisted of some twenty-four members, four ministers ex officio, and some twenty nonofficial members selected by the prime minister.[54]

In the United States the National Resources Planning Board (of which the writer has been a member), an outgrowth of President Hoover's Committee on Recent Social Trends, was used as an advisory planning agency, dealing with the highest and best use of national resources, both natural and human.[55]

[52] Sir Henry N. Bunbury, *Governmental Planning Machinery* (1938); Ferdynand Zweig, *The Planning of Free Societies* (1942); the reports of the National Resources Planning Board, *passim;* Mannheim, *op. cit.;* and my *Public and Private Government;* "Possibilities of Planning," *American Journal of Sociology,* XLIX (March, 1944), 397–407; and "The National Resources Planning Board: A Chapter in American Planning Experiences," *American Political Science Review,* XXXVIII (December, 1944), 1075–88.

[53] See my *The Role of Politics in Social Change,* chap. v: "Strategic Controls and Planning." David E. Lilienthal, in *TVA—Democracy on the March* (1944), develops the role of the T.V.A. in practical planning in this area. See Urwick, *op. cit.,* chap. iii, on planning.

[54] See Laski, *op. cit.*

[55] See the annual reports of the National Resources Planning Board and the series of publications covering the activities of the committee since its establishment in 1933.

The committee acted as an advisory agency to the president. It was composed of three members—all chosen by the president and reporting to him. Comprehensive reports were made dealing with land resources, water resources, mineral and energy resources; with urban communities; with population; with scientific research in government; with the long-time planning of public works; with the analysis of consumers' expenditures and consumers' income; with tentative patterns of resources use; with regional, state, and local planning problems and results. This committee served as a clearing-house of planning activities in the United States—local, state, national, and unofficial as well— and dealt with the strategic and long-time problems of planning of national resources. It was given no executive or legislative powers whatever, serving solely as an advisory group for the assembly and analysis of data and for the consideration of the interrelation of fundamental and long-time national policies.

There are numerous *ad hoc* planning committees and commissions and other agencies engaged in the task of formulating long-range plans for national development in England, Sweden, and elsewhere. In this general field there are also private planning associations, such as Political and Economic Planning (P.E.P.) in England and the National Planning Association in the United States.[56] In Russia, central agencies for national control of quite a different type have been organized, with the expressed design of socializing industry.

The details of planning organization are naturally the subject of wide difference of opinion. In general, it may be said, however, that the economic council has proved a failure or a disappointment and will probably continue so in view of the fact that it sets up what is in effect a rival parliament or legislature. The economic council roots in an earlier idea of a bicameral legislature made up of an industrial house and a political house co-operating in some joint pattern of action.

My own preference is for a national planning board appointed by the executive and responsible to him, serving on an indeterminate tenure. Such an organization might act as a long-time planning agency for the co-ordination of various plans among departments and bureaus and for the elaboration of further lines of long-time national policy in the larger sense of the term.[57]

It is apparent that such an organization should not be an "economic planning" board, since this defeats the whole purpose of broader integration of national policies.[58] Not business planning alone, or agricultural planning alone,

[56] See *Planning*, organ of P.E.P., and the publications of the National Planning Association and the American Society of Planning Officials.

[57] See the National Resources Planning Board's report for 1934 and the analysis of various forms of boards there described; its report for 1943 on resources development; and my "The National Resources Planning Board: A Chapter in American Planning Experiences," *op. cit.*

[58] See Bunbury, *op. cit.*

or welfare planning alone, or educational or scientific planning alone, or even budgetary or personnel planning is adequate to meet the genuine needs of the situation in any long-time view. The value of planning in these special fields is evident, but somewhere these various separate plans must be brought together and considered in their interrelations, balanced against each other, and so organized that the different plans shall not work at cross-purposes.

FUNCTIONAL ADMINISTRATION

The functions of administration may be variously classified, depending upon the approach to the problem. There may be functional groups dealing with health, education and research, works, military activities, agriculture, labor, industry, and welfare among others. In all these fields significant advances are recorded.[59]

The military function consumes so large a proportion of community energy that attention must be directed to some of the features of commanding interest. The administration of force is one of the prime branches of management. Included here are police and custodial functions, but the military functions are of major significance.[60]

But how shall the nation protect itself against its own protectors if there arises a difference of judgment between them?[61] Evidently the effective restraint upon the power-hunger of an army will not be that of superior physical force; it must be a form of control arising from custom and wont, resting, perhaps, upon a rational basis.

If the head of the army is also the head of the state and is, at one and the same time, a general and a statesman, the solution is relatively easy—just as easy as the idea of the philosopher-king of classic renown. There are, of course, Caesars and Napoleons and Washingtons, but more commonly the virtue of the military leader and the virtue of the political leader are not the same.

One of the most difficult of all problems is, of course, that of knowing when, as technician, to keep silent and when to insist and assert. President Jefferson Davis, during the Civil War, found it difficult to determine his proper relationship with the military commanders and fell into the habit of appearing on the field of battle with a considerable staff surrounding him. But when he encountered General Lee, this military commander was outraged and asked of President Davis whose retinue this was observing the engagement.

"I do not care whose they are," he went on to say; "I do not want them here any longer." They went away, and the civil leader did not return to the field of battle under the regime of General Lee.

The recent world wars especially afford illustrations of many phases of this

[59] See White, *op. cit.*

[60] See above, chap. ii, on violence.   [61] Omond, *op. cit.*

problem of the relation of military to civil authority, culminating in the struggle between Hitler and the German army. Blum, Lloyd George, Hindenburg, Churchill, Ludendorff, Huber, Pintschovius, and countless others have contributed their accounts and interpretations of the organization of military power at a time when democratic organization and economic structure and the tissue of propaganda were all closely involved and enmeshed as never before.

But, in general, the material is ill organized, little analyzed, and wide open to fresh interpretation and, above all, to imagination and invention of new types and forms of structure, procedure, and process—new guiding principles and new modes of practical management.

The relationship between the brass hats and the frocks is a continuing one and affords many illustrations of the problem of reconciling in an action pattern the place of the expert technician and the place of the over-all director of policy. Years ago von Clausewitz, the founder of the modern art of war, recognized this problem of the interrelation of policy with military action, but his observations passed unnoticed by students of government generally.

In France, England, and Germany the relations between the army, the navy, the war office, and the parliament were of profound importance in the determination of military strategy and effective national action. Lindsay Rogers maintains that the collapse of the German fighting machine in 1918 was due in great part to the lack of co-ordination between the civil and the military parts of the war organization. Lloyd George, in particular, emphasized the necessity for repeated substitution of the civilian judgment for the military judgment at important moments of the conduct of the war. It is important to understand far better the general type and style of civil-military organization and administration, and this is one of the outstanding tasks of politics, especially in the day of democratic association and trend.

If we look at the organization of military violence, we find a very complex pattern:

1. The relationship between the army, naval, and air forces.

2. The relationship between (*a*) these military administrators and (*b*) the civilian administration.

3. The relationship between all these administrators taken together—army, navy, air, civilian—on the one hand, and, on the other hand, the economic structure and process of the nation—including relations with management and workers in the area of production.

4. The relationship between all these taken together—the military, the civilian, the economic—and the political direction of the nation.

Furthermore, there are at least three important phases of this relationship. One of them is the maintenance of preparedness in times of peace. A second is that of entrance into war and the conduct of military operations. A third is the equally important but often neglected period of demobilization—of the return of the soldier to civilian life—of the readjustment of the national economy to another phase of existence.[62]

The interrelations of all these agencies give rise to problems of far-reaching importance, especially in a period of "total war," with mass armies and mass production. The new technological developments have also upset the balances of power, particularly through the rise of air forces and the necessity of relating them to army and navy power. Amphibious warfare requires new forms of co-ordination in technology as in administration.

The relations of subordination, superordination, and co-ordination are sharply raised in military organization in the questions of hierarchy, of discipline, of obedience, of initiative, and of morale, all operating under a wide variety of changing situations. Both adjudication (military law) and conciliar (war councils) techniques appear in the armed forces under different forms and with somewhat different functions, yet directed toward the basic ends of these same techniques utilized elsewhere.

In armed forces organization is seen the historical shift from class to mass participation as officers and men and the new emphasis of problems of overhead organization. The general staff of the army—overhead organization—developed as early in fact as in industry and in advance of civil government in many instances. The struggle between line and staff is reminiscent of that which goes on in all modern establishment, public and private.[63] On the whole, the military way of life has not been well adjusted to the democratic way of life. The military caste was hostile to democratic principles and methods. The consent of the governed did not seem a basic formula for military action, although under the name of morale consent finds its inevitable place in the armed forces. But hierarchy, obedience, and discipline have always been supplemented by "morale" and in later times by propaganda. The voice of command may also use the voice of persuasion. And at all times there are values in initiative, in resourcefulness, and in forms of skepticism regarding commands.[64] The introduction of special agents of the party in Germany and Russia into military operations and authority is an interesting illustration of the difficulties on the border line of civil and military controls.

[62] Cf. Louis Brownlow, "Reconversion of the Federal Administrative Machinery from War to Peace," *Public Administration Review*, IV (autumn, 1944), 309–26.

[63] Very valuable material is found in Vagts, *op. cit.*, and the materials there used and cited. See also P. Herring, *The Impact of War* (1941), esp. chap. x. Lindsay Rogers' "The War Machine Examined," *Southern Review*, III (1938), 673–92, is significant, as is his *Crisis Government* (1934) on the whole situation. See also John H. Marion, "Organization for Internal Control and Coördination in the United States Army," *American Political Science Review*, XXXII (October, 1938), 877–97; Brehon Somervell *et al.*, "Administrative Management in the Army Service Forces," *Public Administration Review*, IV (autumn, 1944), 255–308.

[64] Emile Mayer, *La Psychologie du commandement* (1924).

In military administration, however, the problem of the place of technical experts in government is not different in principle from that of other forms of specialists, as in education and science, health, agriculture, or any other field in which there has been high specialization of technical knowledge. Important decisions must be made by chief administrators or by policy-determining bodies who make laws and appropriate funds, but who are less perfectly informed than the *expertise* with whom they may be dealing.

It may happen that official opinion differs from that of the specialist and that public opinion differs from both of them, as to military affairs, educational policies, health, or housing activities. In such cases effective decisions must be made by those who are less skilled in a specialty and presumably more skilled in generality, so to speak. The overhead decisions may well be, and often have been, wrong, but, on the other hand, the specialist may be technically wrong, since technicians may disagree, or he may misjudge the relation of his special project to the general needs and possibilities. That there are available skilled technicians in special subjects and that decisions are not made without careful consideration of technical positions is itself a substantial gain for the common-weal.

Again attention may be directed to the fact that the problem of public government at this point is not different from that of private government, or of individual decisions, when experts and broad policies conflict; on the farm, in the factory, in the church or school, or in the family the specialists' recommendations must be evaluated and adapted to the considerations of broader policy.

THE MANAGERIAL GROUP

In modern industry the managerial groups in many areas rise to a position more significant than that of the owners or the workers. Decision often rests largely in their hands, providing, of course, they are able to point to a generous measure of financial success in their particular enterprise. Wages to the workers, profits to the owners, prices and goods to the consumers—these are allocated in great measure by the managers of the concern and tolerated on the terms just stated. The managers are also prominent in labor, in agriculture, in the professions.

In the political area the managers have likewise taken over much of the decision in political relations, although the situation is by no means as notable as in industrial affairs. Have legislative bodies been on the whole less mindful and watchful of their responsibilities than boards of directors in corporations? The boards of trustees could see their profits and realize them, but the legislators were left uncertain as to their role in the determination of public policy. Had the given policy perhaps been really determined by some adroit bureau

162

head or cabinet minister who had taken the initiative or maneuvered them into the position desired?

In large-scale industrial organizations the trend has been strongly toward the rising managerial group, as distinguished from the owners or from the workers. With the increasing trend toward industrial concentration, this is a fact of very great significance for the future of management in government and industry alike and, indeed, of all social organization. In the formation of international combinations, cartels or otherwise, the tendency becomes even more pronounced and evident.

Looking at the stability of organization, however, the managerial group has not yet reached a satisfactory rapport in many instances with the workers' own organizations. Collective bargaining may be set down as generally accepted, although not in all cases; but the relation of the workers to management remains an unsolved problem in general. Even in collectivist societies, such as Russia, the relations between unions, soviets, and party leaders precipitate many severe struggles for prestige and power.[65] Decisions may be reached through the leader, but, in fact, this decision may be the climax of a long-drawn-out struggle within the organization. The managerial group develops also in other social groups as well as in industry. Labor, agriculture, and professional associations tend to set up a strong structure in which the managerial skills and personalities are very prominent.[66] In the ecclesiastical groupings this form of organization has long been evident, not only in the Catholic church but in other creeds and organizations as well. We may, of course, always raise the question—not in point of fact always raised—of what the relation of these managers is to the ends of the state or the ends of other groups and to the special techniques of the particular group and to its special social composition. In the complex power pattern of organization how are these managerial elements related to the organization of the consent of the governed, so vital a force in the life of every form of human association? In the struggle for advantage and mastery these larger factors may, indeed, pass unnoticed, but from the point of view of the student of politics and government, they are of supreme importance in judging the trends and possibilities of managerial evolution in modern society.

If we ask why cities must have managers, or the Dairymen's Association have a manager, or steel or motors have a skilled staff of managers, not so called perhaps, or the labor group, or the political party, we find the answer in the increasing number and specialization of functions and the correspondingly increasing need for ways and means of integrating these specializations. The

---

[65] See Bienstock, Schwartz, and Yugow, *op. cit.*

[66] See H. L. Childs, *Labor and Capital in National Politics* (1930); Brady, *op. cit.*; D. C. Blaisdell, *Economic Power and Political Pressures* (1941).

general staff is not a new institution but an old one in military organization at any rate. The increasing size of modern societies and the proliferation of their complex activities make new forms of binding the machinery together indispensable to successful functioning.

From very early times great estates had their overseers, who were much like managers, by whatever title known in various places. With the breakdown of the large landholdings, these types disappeared only to emerge in industrial development as "factors" of factories, as superintendents of various sorts in developing industrial concerns. Companies like the classical Hudson Bay, East India, etc., and other forms of trading companies developed special forms of structure and authority,[67] endowed in fact with far-reaching powers of a quasi-governmental nature.

It is not necessary to conclude that the managerial groups have assumed complete domination over the concerns in which they are found, although this may be the fact in various instances, but only to reckon with the undoubted truth that the managerial factor in public and private enterprise has taken on a far more significant role than before. This new role which has puzzled and alarmed the "owners" in industry and the policy-makers in government is not, however, primarily a power role but a specialization of the evolving and complex character which we now confront in our civilization. This does not in reality involve any diminution in power of the policy-determiners, provided they are able to adjust themselves to the new situation and do not struggle against the pattern which is inevitably evolving. On the contrary, improved instruments of management and administration will facilitate the work of the policy-makers and increase the range and sweep of their activities, if only they know how to make use of the new tools provided by modern organizational techniques. They clarify the business to be presented for ultimate decision.

If, however, the power-holders, the property-owners, or the policy-determiners, in whatever form of association, insist upon dealing with unessential detail, if they are unable to lay down broad lines of action, to deputize and delegate authority within these lines, to supervise in over-all manner the administration of the plans laid down—to function, in short—then there will ensue confusion and uncertainty. The managers will then perforce of circumstances assume greater and greater practical authority in instances where action is urgent and indecision fatal, or the social fabric will be torn by angry dissensions.

But all such arrangements in turn will break down or operate with low efficiency unless there is established a rapport with the mass of the workers, the voters, the consumers, a series of relationships in which all are adjusted to

---

[67] See A. C. McLaughlin, *The Foundations of American Constitutionalism* (1932); Shaw Livermore, *Early American Land Companies* (1939); Thomas C. Cochran and William Miller, *The Age of Enterprise* (1942).

the general scheme of things in which they operate. The top specialists alone will not be able to lead, except for a while in emergencies, unless they enlist the sense of justice and the sense of participation in the enterprise of which all are a part.[68] The magic word "morale" is not merely a skilful form of hocus-pocus but must be based upon a solid foundation of material and ideal interest developing in an atmosphere of confidence and trust. Statistics and psychology will not solve this equation, useful servants though they may be.[69]

It is not within the scope of this study to discuss the shop councils or the Whitley councils or the many varying devices used here and there to implement this general purpose of satisfying the sense of participation and of the fairness of wages and working conditions.[70] It is enough to state that their organization and operation are of very great importance in any system of private or of public government.

BUREAUCRACY

"Bureaucracy" is a term of ambiguous meaning.[71] At times it is used to describe an administrative system in much the same sense as the term "public administration" might be employed. At other times it is a smear word used to calumniate political opponents—the protest of the outs against the ins. At other times it is employed to indicate opposition to a particular public policy which is being administered. At other times "bureaucracy" is used to designate an undesirable type of administration.

In so far as bureaucracy is a basis of political controversy, a type of criticism of those in authority, it occupies an important part in the organization of struggles, especially in a democratic community, and serves a useful purpose as criticism of the experts and of authority. That the charges may be uninformed, unfair, or malicious even does not detract from the general value of a system in which there is free examination of the acts of authority by those who are concerned. That the facts may be twisted or exaggerated does not destroy the essential values of organized criticism by political parties or by other groups. In the course of a cycle all are at one time or another in the majority and at another time in the minority. The extremes of whitewashing and demagoguery cancel each other out in the long run, as long as there is a widespread feeling of common interest and ideals of the common good and how to attain it.

---

[68] See Chester I. Barnard, *The Functions of the Executive* (1938).

[69] See Dennison, *op. cit.*

[70] See White, *op. cit.* Cf. also Clinton S. Golden and Harold J. Ruttenberg, *The Dynamics of Industrial Democracy* (1942); and Sumner H. Slichter, *Union Policies and Industrial Management* (1941).

[71] Max Weber, *Wirtschaft und Gesellschaft* (1925), II, 650–78; see C. J. Friedrich, *Constitutional Government and Democracy* (1941), chap. ii; Ludwig von Mises, *Bureaucracy* (1944); Karl A. Wittfogel, *Studies in Bureaucracy in Oriental Societies* (forthcoming). Much useful material is found in Toynbee, *op. cit.*

Bureaucracy is sometimes attacked, however, not because of the quality of the administrators but by reason of the policy administered. For example, tax administrators may be assailed as such when the real object of criticism is the particular tax which is being applied. Or regulatory administration may be assailed when the basic assault is upon the policy itself. This led a prominent citizen of the United States to declare on one occasion that the "best government is the worst," meaning that the more efficient the regulators, the worse the system if based upon an undesirable type of policy.

Bureaucracy may also be a type of occupational disease, a standard problem arising in almost any form of organization—poor organization, poor delegation, and poor supervision, unsound personnel policies, low morale, deadwood—the types of malaise which skilled probers diagnose and for which they prescribe without great technical difficulty.[72] Alike in public and in private government, competent administrators will discover and perhaps remedy the type diseases of administration, well known to the *expertise* in this field.

We have also to deal, however, with overemphasis on routine; with lack of initiative; with indifference to the public, at times taking on the form of arrogance, and in other instances with favoritism and corruption; with types of behavior meriting the term "oppressive." There is also the delusion of self-sufficiency which often accompanies bureaucracy—a result of administrative introversion. How does it happen that division of labor may lead to routine or lack of initiative, although there is superior knowledge of special types of problems and the special opportunities for resourcefulness and inventiveness? Or how does it happen that professional servants of the generalized public—the consumer of service—become indifferent to their clients and lose sight of the common good they are set up to serve?

In earlier times maladministration was the product in part of an autocratic or despotic system in which the chief tool of the state was violence, and the consent of the governed was at the bottom of the list. In such an atmosphere personalism, favoritism, corruption, and arrogance tended to flourish. That this was an inevitable concomitant of authoritarian government, however, does not follow, since notable contributions were made to public administration by the Bourbons and by the Prussian rulers, under Frederick the Great, as well as by the Romans and later the Saracens.[73]

The official usually, although not always, starts with an advantage, namely, that the significance and the value of the office are recognized by the group in which it has been set up. Presumably there must be a reason for the office, a reason related to the better functioning of the special society, political or otherwise. The official is thus given, so to speak, a line of credit when he starts, upon

[72] *Better Government Personnel: Report of the Commission of Inquiry on Public Service Personnel* (1935).

[73] See my chapter on the "Morbidity and Mortality of Power" in *Political Power*.

which he may draw as he goes along. But this he may overdraw if he fails to distinguish between the office and himself. The official who relies upon his official prestige alone will soon be found carrying a heavy load.

The fact that reason in office may be supplemented and reinforced by "power" makes the official task at some point easier but at others far more difficult. The status of "office" cannot be drawn upon too heavily or too frequently without losing its edge. Indeed, the initial advantage in favor of the rule may be lost, and the favorable presumption may be soured into one of disfavor toward the office and the official, one or both. Incompetence, tactlessness, favoritism, corruption, arrogance, and indifference may readily start smoldering resentments. The spirit of co-operation and of leadership disappear, and M. le Bureau is left with a very difficult problem on his hands—securing united effort from unwilling men and women.

Even in the days when the master directed his slave, with powers of life and death over him, these relations of understanding and co-operation were of great importance, to overseers and managers, for the lash soon reaches its limits, if the master is intelligent enough to note the relative output of willing and unwilling workers. Now in times when the doctrine of consent is more and more widely accepted, the need for co-operation is all the greater, alike in industry and in government. Not only does a public office become a public trust, but it is understood that the public will in the long run determine the nature of the trust and how it is working in actual practice.

CONCLUSIONS

Is there any net result of all these analyses and discussions regarding the meaning and implications of management? Do the psychologists, the psychiatrists, the biologists, the sociologists, the statesmen, the students of mass management in armies, in factories, in governments, the administrators, public and private, converge in their conclusions toward any significant points of central interest? Widely divergent as the different approaches may be, they have striking similarities when viewed as part of the general development of the emerging intelligence of our day.

I. Organization now deals with new precision tools of management, with new knowledge of personalities, with psychology, statistics, more intimate studies of human interrelationships, background studies of the human environment and of the elements of organization. This huge apparatus of inquiry, analysis, and understanding is a characteristic feature of organization in the new day. It is the breakdown of primitive maxims with the addition of many newly recognized elements from which new analyses are made. The technical apparatus of modern organization is far more complicated, elaborate, and scientific than that of preceding generations. We now know how to produce,

167

how to fight, how to administer social affairs, public or private, on a massive scale; and no modern group is unmindful of the technical tools available for this purpose.

II. Organization tends to escape from its original trappings of personal authority and hierarchical rankings into a field of more truly organic relationships. Plato at an early date discussed, it is true, a crude form of psychobiological organization of the states. But this was forgotten in the later development of governmental forms. Organization became the projection of the personality of the ruler—the extension of his authority beyond his view; he divided and subdivided, delegated and deputed, his divine or semidivine authority beyond the bounds of his court, much as he might allot his distant lands and cattle to others. The central points in the picture were his unique personality as the focus of order and, of course, the difficult explanation of the transmission of power. Inequality, ignorance, and force were the tools of authority. In our own day these ancient relics still survive in the fanfare of the *Duce* and the *Führer,* and their doctrines of the inequality both of individuals and of groups of men and of violence as the mode of persuasion.

Organic theories, as distinguished from personal theories of organization, were revived and developed in the nineteenth century but were clumsy and at times even amusing in their effort to portray analogies between the human body and the body politic, whether in Bluntschli or in Spencer. In our time organization has taken on what might be called a pattern form—an organic division of labor with an organic synthesis of connecting and related items of behavior.

Emphasis is no longer laid as strongly as before upon personalized authority but upon organic position and relationship; upon the significance of the service performed by the particular persons operating in the general system with others. It is not the authority per se or the hierarchy per se but the role planned, the contribution or the service rendered—in short, the functions—that give it importance and recognition. In modern organization no man is fit to command who commands solely by virtue of his office.

This is language understood alike by the psychologist, the biologist, the sociologist, and the student of mass behavior in all forms of social relations. Organizing is thus no longer accepted, either as a personal enterprise or as primarily designed to balance or check one factor against another in some mechanical fashion, but as a nucleus of dynamic co-operation for the achievement of an organic or common purpose or design. Its difficult task is that of harmonizing, stabilizing, and energizing a series of personalities themselves not fully integrated and also a series of hierarchies running through many forms of groupings. The club will not do this—or not for long. There is needed a fusion of interests and ideals, a common sense of direction—and the direction is justice.

III. Again, the distinction between structure and function is now less sharply stated. When I first studied "civil government," it was all forms and no functions. But in a sense structure is function and function is structure. The most acute of organizational specialists love to wrangle over the disputed topic of the proper degree and type of "functionalism" in a given organization—or in general, for that matter.

Is the essence of organization the structural parts which make up the organizational pattern,[74] or is the essence of organization the function it performs in the body politic? Is the organization the convenient tool of the function? Since the rise of the common good as the goal of the political society, it has been recognized that formal structure was of secondary significance, although this was often said with the tongue in the cheek by the potentate who would interpret the common good in his own special manner. Out of the overemphasis on organization arose the special position of legal priority and symbolic precedence and eventually of special status accorded to the personal holder of the structural point of vantage and to the office itself even under democratic auspices. For in democracy as in autocracy the personal holders of special privilege may sometimes attach themselves to structural points which they hold long after the functional purpose has been served and forgotten, avoiding the test of present-day functioning.

That organization should sometimes stand in the way of the functioning of the common good is, indeed, contradictory but common. The function of organization itself is, of course, the service of the common good. Yet as not only are there awkward vestiges of survival but there are cancerous growths in organisms which turn upon and consume their own bodies, likewise in bodies politic there are inverted growths of a vigorous type which turn against the life that made them. In both cases we strive, of course, for cure and prevention. We do not yet understand virus very well, either in biology or in politics, what it is or how to prevent or to cure it.

I conclude that in recent times the significance of organization rests less upon mechanical structure and more upon function. There are more dimensions in organization than the flat surface of the chart or blueprint may indicate. Much more suggestive are the recent air maps. The fixed forms of structure are less emphasized than in earlier times, while at the same time the priority of the function as over against the structure per se and the official per se is increasingly accepted. The doctrine of "a government of laws and not of men" finds strong support in the modern inquiries and conclusions emerging in various forms of functionalism. The movement is away from arbitrary personal authority to justification on the ground of community service. The last refuge of "personalism" is seen in "leaders," so called, who admit community service as their

[74] See L. K. Frank, "Structure, Function, and Growth," *Philosophy of Science*, II (1935), 210–35.

goal, or "stewardship," or "trusteeship" but struggle in vain to escape definite responsibility for their acts.

IV. *Organization is now upside down in its emphasis and balance.* Compared with earlier positional relations, slave organization and free organization are different solar systems. Present-day organization revolves around the dignity of man, the development of human values. Production and its machinery are the tools of man. Man is not a cog in a machine, but the machinery and the organization are by and for him. Thus there is a new center of gravity in organization. This does not destroy organization and morale, but it is its modern foundation, stronger than any other.

Masses of men and women—millions of them—now know more about organization, its meaning and apparatus, than ever before in human history. Its cult is no longer secret or magic. What now appears is a reasonable expectancy by those concerned that under such and such conditions such and such an outcome will follow, in an organizational pattern, of which they are parts, and in which they share responsibility. Concretely there will be an acceptable division of labor which it is expected will be followed; workers will know what is to be done, and leaders may be expected to give directions which will presumably be followed. There will be understandings and expectancies, and there will be an authentic interpretation by some definite person or center—for the time being. There will be a general understanding of the broad directive or purpose of the undertaking, as in wartime rationing and priorities. Finally, there will be a general consent or assent to the general body of understandings and institutional and personal implementations. Intelligent assent or consent is the condition of true liberty, for it assumes a range of choice. Society is thus an aggregation not merely of bees or ants or other animal societies but of rational beings. If these reasonable expectancies, established by general concurrence, break down, the system does not function, or not effectively, or on the optimum level of operation.[75]

It is not raw and arbitrary force that really rules and gives direction. Force itself lies in established understandings and expectancies in private as well as in public government and in their flexible development in the emerging situations, stable or changing as the case may be. Of course, unreflective custom, unquestioning obedience, unwillingness to assume responsibility, fear, and violence all play a part in organizational systems, but not the principal role or the long-time role of organizations operating on the highest level of efficiency. Masses of men obey with little resistance up to a point, perhaps a tragic point; but that point must not be too closely approached or too often—whether dealing with an army, with factory workers, with government employees, or even with professors.

Complex modern organization must be rooted in understanding, in assent,

[75] See my *Prologue to Politics*, chap. ii: "The Organization of Consent."

in consent, in a full and willing spirit of co-operation. And this is not merely because our organization is complex but because it is human. Technology and mechanisms are the servant and not the master of mankind.

In more recent times the chief obstacles in the way of completely developed public administration have come from three difficulties:

1. The difficulty of keeping pace with the rapid growth of modern technology and the accompanying changes brought with it, as in health, housing, education, social regulation of innumerable types precipitated by modifications in communication, transportation, production, and the body of techniques in social science.

2. Closely related to the foregoing is the difficulty of developing a system of administration meshed (*a*) with the other organs of government, legislative and judicial, (*b*) with the common consent in a broad electorate, and (*c*) with other highly developed forms of administration and management in industry or in various pressure groups.[76]

3. A constantly recurring problem especially in times of change is that of the "neutrality" of the administrative service—the determination of the metes and bounds, if any, of the political activities of the civil servants.

It cannot escape the notice of any careful observer that much of the controversy over bureaucracy turns upon general theories of the scope of governmental activity and especially the range of governmental action in relation to industry.[77] For those who wish to restrict the policy of government in any field, every case of administrative breakdown or weakness is an argument against the extension of governmental powers, and especially so if the action is regulatory of any wide range of activity. Reasoning that collectivism can function only with sound administration, opposition may be made to the growth of such public administration. On these premises there can, of course, be no serious discussion of bureaucracy, since it is bad if it is good, and the better the worse. It should be said, however, that this is not the characteristic attitude of communities generally but only of special groups, who may fail to realize the meaning of government for the affairs of life and not merely as an opening wedge for some new form of social and economic organization. The coming state is likely to be one in which administration plays a large and increasingly important role, as important to industries or other groups as to the common good. A part of the business of business is to make adjustments with the instrumentalities of the modern state, relying upon the compatibility of the profit system with sound organization of governmental agencies.

Obviously, there are two broad types of problems involved here. One is the ways and means of dealing with the occupational diseases of management, in

[76] See *Public Administration Review*, *passim*.

[77] See *State Government*, January, 1944, on "Bureaucracy."

both private and public agencies alike—a task for the technical *expertise* and for the general public who know whether the shoe pinches or not, no matter what they be expertly informed. The other problem is of a different order, namely, what the appropriate range of governmental activity is in the broad field of social relations. What burdens do we wish to place upon the back of government?

The first of these questions was originally a part of the struggle between the many and the few, but under modern conditions of democratic organization this is no longer true. The task is that of finding the most effective tools for the performance of governmental purposes and ends.

The second problem is a by-product of the struggle between the many and the few in the industrial field, between labor and management, or between collectivism and individualism in the broader sense. But this problem is also on its way out, as a management problem, as the meaning of management per se becomes clearer in the economic-social-governmental structure of our time, and the nature of the industrial struggle is clarified. Whenever the dust of partisanship dies down, the problem becomes fairly clear in general outline, namely, the perfection or improvement of the tools of the community for the performance of community purposes. Aside from the inner problems of the *expertise* on the technical side of their work, a task equally great is the psychological problem of effective relationships of managers and public. The higher politeness and consideration for the feelings and habits of those concerned and the careful prestudy of proposed alterations intimately affecting ways of human life are of prime importance.[78] What is done is often less important than how it is done, especially in relations with organizations or individuals with large powers, such as those held by the government.

The fact that the official does not need to argue the case is an excellent reason why he should use his rhetoric for the sake of amiable relationship—emergencies excepted, of course.[79] Instead of being a person with whom it is difficult to "get along," the public official might be one with whom it is easiest to get along or, at any rate, be more than ordinarily endowed with intelligence, patience, and good will. A policeman playing Santa Claus may find this role not incompatible with discipline and order.

All the organs of government are, of course, appraised in the light of their contribution to the main ends of government as a whole—by their service to the common good, to security, to order, to justice, to welfare, to freedom, and technically by their use of the skills available to governments in the framework of the ends of the state. Management has had much to do with security, espe-

[78] See Elton Mayo, *The Human Problems of an Industrial Civilization* (1933); Beardsley Ruml, *Government, Business and Values* (1943) on "homefulness."

[79] On the effect of size of unit or organization upon the attitude of the participants in group relations, see T. N. Whitehead, *Leadership in a Free Society* (1936).

cially in the use of armed forces for conquest or defense, and with welfare services in later times.

It would be fair to say that management has utilized more generally and quickly the techniques of modern science and technology than the adjudicator or the councilor. Even a military management caste like the German did not delay in seizing upon the latest devices developed by technology, and upon education, health, and social security, as a means of providing a basis for its fighting forces. The oral dialectic is employed by administration, civil and military, but the newer symbols of idea elaboration have been utilized in the procedures and processes of administration more quickly than in the courts or the lawmaking bodies as a rule. They have made more of the values of "scientific management" alike in organization and in functional development. They have even organized administrative councils and administrative courts for the special purposes of their undertakings.

VI. THE FRAMEWORK OF THE BALANCE OF POWERS

But in a going concern like a government how shall collisions between organs of government be prevented, and how shall the higher strategy of co-operation be developed?

One way has been the "balancing" or "checking" of one agency by another. Sometimes the balance was vertical, as between central and local authorities, or horizontal, as between organs of any level of government. Sometimes the balance of powers rested upon social aggregations of many different types, as, for example, between ethnic groups, between religious groupings, between economic groups of one description and another. All sorts of combinations were possible in view of the complex factors involved in the problem.

The operations of government may be considered not only horizontally, as in the relationship of legislative to executive, but also vertically, as in the relation of the national to the local government. At each level of government the horizontal divisions of government may be again encountered, at the local and the intermediate as well as at the central. Under all systems of government and in all stages of human development there are problems of diffusion of authority and function, of center and circumference. The Roman Empire in its day was, and the British Empire in our time is, a far-reaching system of intergovernmental interrelationships of the most complicated type. This is especially true when distant lands with colonies and dependencies are involved. Elaborate theories have been evolved endeavoring to cover and classify all the different systems. Federal systems encounter like situations in which there are dual jurisdictions over the same persons and property. There are 165,000 independent governments in the United States ranging through the national, the state, the county, the city, the town or township, the school district, and many others, each with its own system of balance of powers. Distributions of territory, of powers, and of service functions are all concerned. All the factors involved in the habitat and social composition of government, in the ends of political society, in its organs and skills in the general form and spirit of the government are mingled in these intricate mechanisms and dynamisms.

Under these circumstances the "balance of powers" is really a broad problem of the centralization and diffusion of political authority in relation to many economic, social, and cultural forces at work in the given community. What is often forgotten in the whirling complex of individuals, interests, social groups, soldiers, lawyers, lawmakers, and politicos in general is the bearing of the whole process upon the ends of government and the development of the human personalities who make up society.

Just as the government provides a general framework within which the ends of political society are woven together, so the constitutional system provides a structure for the concrete organs of government. In the modern constitution there is embodied usually a declaration or bill of rights, a division of governmental powers, and a mode of amendment of the constitution itself. The powers of various agencies of government are specified and their interrelations indicated, either in a formal document or by the growth of constitutional custom. Likewise the authority of central and of local governments may be outlined. The forms in which these divisions of power and these balances between various powers and functions are set up vary widely, as the two outstanding instances of the United States and Britain illustrate. The ways of interpreting the mandate of the constitutions are also diverse, ranging from interpretation by Parliament itself, as in Britain, to interpretation by the Supreme Court, as in the United States.

In any case, the constitutional system supplies a frame of reference for conflicting powers and functions and a higher law giving a guiding principle for the several branches of the government. The essence of the constitutional arrangements is not in the precision of the definitions and divisions of authority as much as in the existence of common understandings and customs upon which the entire system must rest if it is to operate successfully. Without these generally accepted understandings, the document possesses no vitality. The first rude shock will be sufficient to jeopardize or even overthrow constitutional arrangements of a purely verbal character.[80]

In theory, of which Montesquieu was the great eighteenth-century champion, the essential balance was found to be that among legislative, executive, and judicial agencies. The famous French commentator found this balance the very definition of liberty and that, without it, nothing remained but despotism.[81] In Locke, however, the balance was that between the legislative and the

---

[80] See my *The Written Constitution and the Unwritten Attitude* (1931).

[81] *L'Esprit des lois* (1748), Book V.

executive,[82] and in reality he placed the power of decision in the legislative alone in case of conflict, with the right of revolution in the background.

The balance of powers, latterly called the Newtonian theory of government, was directed at the harmonious and consistent co-operation of the governmental organs in time alike of quiet and of tumult but chiefly intended as a defense against oppression. It was obviously more effective in preventive than in positive action. Inaction, however, or tardy action, or ineffective action may be the formula out of which despots arise, if the suffering is too great. What if the state can neither declare war nor conclude peace promptly nor act in other crises? Individual or group liberty or national security may be menaced by inaction, and the purposes of the state may be wrecked by simple failure to remove the causes of disease or danger. Generations of practical experience have shown the truth which was pointed out in *The Federalist* (1) that the absolute balance of powers with complete check and countercheck might result in the downfall of the state and (2) that the successful operation of the balance system presupposes a body of understandings in the community which will insure a certain moderation on the part of the powers concerned—a moderation which will stop them somewhere short of the precipice of disaster. Fear of authority is one great factor in political behavior, but hope from co-operative action through authority is another great element in human behavior.

The community is not concerned as much with the jealousies and rivalries of competing servants of the state as with the promotion of its own fundamental ends and purposes. The nation does not exist for the legislature or for the executive or for the courts, but these agencies are set up for the people and must operate for their general interest. At one time the executive authority forfeited the good will of communities and gave way to representative bodies; at times these agencies in turn lost popular confidence, and larger power was placed in the hands of the executive. At times the courts have risen high as the expounders of order and justice and again have lost their pre-eminence through failure to interpret the trends of the time in the light of the purposes of the political society they were organized to serve.

It may and has happened, however, that the wealth of powerful sociopolitical groups has so embarrassed the conduct of political operations as to lead to a demand for stronger political authority, with power to establish order with a heavy hand. Too great a diffusion of authority tends to create the opposite of overcentralization again; and this was the opening through which Mussolini and then Hitler came into power. Their pretext was the lack of adequate centralization in the commonwealth and the urgent necessity of unified leadership.

Modern democratic states, however, as in England and the United States,

[82] *Of Civil Government* (1690).

175

have shown the possibility of obtaining energetic and effective action without recourse to such expedients as dictatorship, without purchasing unity of action at the expense of other considerations important to the life and strength of the body politic. The constitutional organs of the state have been shown to possess sufficient authority to ride any storms of peace or war, depression or military struggle and crisis.

The balance and zoning of power always present one of the greatest of political problems—the balance between regions, interests, functions, and authorities. The overcentralization of authority may readily lead to the loss of a sense of participation on the part of the community as a whole. On the other hand, the diffusion of authority may be spread so thin that effectiveness is lost, and the whole political society may suffer from apathy, from sluggish management, from all the ills springing from lack of adequate integration.

The experienced holder of power understands how to delegate and supervise, without abdication, on the one side, or undue assumption of function, on the other. This is the *pons asinorum* of authority in all groups. The inexperienced attempts to hold every element of power in his own grasp, fears to trust any subordinate or to deputize power, destroys the spirit of responsibility through his organization, and ends in congestion, delay, and perhaps destruction. This is as true of an individual as it is of a class or a system of order and equally true of a national organization as against a local one. Overcentralism has been the cause of the overthrow of many an individual and government, by concentration against it of all the disaffected elements of excluded authority. The circumference is always against the center, even when there is no good functional reason why it should be; but, when there is really sufficient cause, the situation becomes most serious. In a period of specialization of activity and of specialization in the art of management, this tends to become increasingly true and to place all the greater obligation upon the holder of authority to adjust himself to the changing conditions.

How to find a field for the grass roots of power, for personality, team work, effective unity of action in the large-scale systems of modern power, whether political or industrial, is one of the outstanding questions of our day, as indeed of all days. The avoidance of excessive personal centralization is a question constantly confronting the holders of power and is not unrelated to the larger territorial question which has been raised in countless forms in almost every state. Concentration and diffusion of responsibility and power is a central problem within any system, local or national.

The zoning and balance of power are, then, among the major problems of government and administration, from the point of view of territorial, group, and personal adjustments. They involve the maintenance of a dynamic equilibrium in a vital world of struggling forces, not expressed wholly in laws, rules, or decisions. Formal provision may be made for the balance but may fail to secure it, or may provide against it, and yet the balance may emerge by virtue of the skilful adjustment of the holders of power at a given time, or a directing "boss" or "czar" ruling from the outside.

A special subtlety of the problem lies in the delicate and perhaps confusing interplay between juristic absoluteness and practical diffusion of authority. There may be juristic completeness of centralization and practical flexibility in adjustment, as in Britain; or there may be on paper elaborate juristic division and distribution of power and practical concentration of the most despotic sort, as in a boss- or dictator-controlled area of authority.

Trust in a considerable group of men is a condition of success in most enterprises, and nowhere is this more evident than in the field of governmental power, where so many of the rewards are in terms of prestige, and relatively so little in profits. This is one of the points where the practiced hand of experience and matured assurance makes itself most effectively felt.

Especially in a time like the present when means of communication and transportation have been revolutionized and new and larger units of operation are constantly springing up, and when social functions are more complex than ever, the problem of proper diffusion is more acute than ever before. A center of authority which was once an hour away may by now be five minutes away. An hour which once meant three miles is now perhaps two hundred miles and approaching perhaps seven hundred miles. Under these new conditions the relations between center and circumference established by long usage may be utterly inapplicable, and new customs must be devised. With equal speed medicine and technology are revising the functions of government. Under all these circumstances the adequate diffusion of authority essential to the balance of power grows far more complex and difficult. Yet the difficulty is not inherent in the situation, technically, but in the point of view shaped by long-established habit and custom.

THE "HIGHER ORGANIZATION" OF POLITICS

Much attention has been given in recent years to what might be called the "higher organization" of the state, both in the practical experimentation of modern nations and in the domain of theoretical anaylsis.[83]

In almost every country in the world there has been experimentation with and discussion of the emerging evolution of political-economic forms and forces, now everywhere challenging the peace and security of mankind—technology, cartels, unions, business and agricultural associations, armies, profes-

---

[83] See Friedrich, *op. cit.*, for an elaborate bibliography on this topic; also the *Proceedings* of the various International Congresses on Administrative Sciences; and Brady, *op. cit.*

sions, churches, schools. The problem of a socialistic or a mixed economy has led to vigorous debate not only upon economic principles but upon the whole political setting of economics. Marx has been more influential in this field than Freud.

But it is inevitable that sooner or later some of the more modern developments in the study of organization will affect the processes of the higher organization as well. The role of structure and function in constitutional or other government, the effective span of popular control in democratic societies governing the range and type of delegation and supervision, the principles governing centralization and diffusion of power in modern constitutional states, the modern ways and means of obtaining assent—consent in a modern society based upon the principles of consent or, even without that principle, upon an autocratic basis—are all under earnest consideration.

The relative roles of policy-making, adjudication, delegation, and administration in the modern state, the position of the executive and the legislative agencies in the new society into which we move, the bearing of recent inquiries and experience upon co-ordination, co-operation, span of control, synthesis of operating units, maintenance of discipline and morale, upon the processes of the present-day state, especially of the democratic type, are pressing hard upon statecraft.

From another point of view, modern psychiatric concepts, dynamic psychology and psychoanalysis, bring into the light many unexplored areas of human behavior in the realm of the personality. The relationship between the rational and the emotional, between conscious and subconscious, fixations and frustrations, securities and insecurities, dominance and passivity, "wishes," "drives," and dynamisms of many types—all these have significant bearing on political behavior which cannot be neglected. Thus far, as indicated above, only an occasional thinker, like Lasswell or Mayo, has begun to apply these recent discoveries, regarding personality, integration, disintegration, readjustment, and reorganization, to the nature and operation of social and political structure and function.

In the not distant future our knowledge of the diffusion and balance of power over areas, organs, and functions will be far more complete in analysis and in understanding, and in the light of better comprehension significant advances will be made in the grand design and strategy of government.

CHAPTER V

TYPES OF RULE

AS WE run over the picture of the various forms of government operating throughout history, their number and variety seem to defy adequate description and analysis. What is there in common, we may ask, among these endless lists of chiefs, leaders, rulers, headships, of innumerable groups with varying authorities, constantly struggling and warring even against each other for wider rule?

In all this jumble of authorities are there any clear lines revealed by close analysis and reflection? Or is the whole tragic panorama a weariness of flesh, vanity of vanities, and vexation of spirit, as uninspiring as the antics of cocks strutting and crowing in the barnyard? One might conclude from some of the ancient chronicles that begetting, warring, feasting, and dying were the principal ends of man, except for building memorials.

In looking at forms of government, it is useful to consider (1) the ends of political society in general and the emphasis in particular societies; (2) the cohesive forces involved in the social composition of the particular state, the principle or type of association; (3) the instruments or tools used in the given stage of political society; and (4) the interrelations of all these factors to one another in the end product of a special form of political authority at a particular time and place. Thus we may consider:

TYPES OF ASSOCIATION	SOCIAL COMPOSITION	TOOLS OF ACTION	ENDS OF STATE
Family-clan unit	Labor	Violence	Security
Civic	Business	Custom	Order
Feudal	Agriculture	Symbolism	Justice
National	Science	Rational consent	Welfare
Federal	Religion	Strategy	Freedom
International	Other groups	Leadership	

Out of such materials as these are governments formed and re-formed in categories and combinations that are confusing to the observer untrained in the elements of politics, but not especially complex if the proper analyses are applied to the several situations involved. It is true that form and functions of government are not readily separable, in viewing the life of the political society. The ends of government are security, order, justice, welfare, and freedom, either in general or in a particular state. To what extent the government emphasizes justice or is concerned with freedom or not, or welfare or order or security; the interrelations and priorities of the ends of the state—all these are factors of very great significance in the analysis and appraisal of political behavior. Likewise the aptitudes, ideals, and skills of the most significant groups, as the military, the clerical, the commercial, agricultural, and labor, are meaningful in any political society and may indicate its dominant color or tone, the design of the particular state in question.

However, aside from the ends of government and the social composition of the particular governmental association, it is possible and useful to consider the narrower structural aspects of the political society, bearing in mind the parallel importance of the other elements in the life of the country.

Forms of government may be classified from many different points of view on the basis of a distribution or participation in power, as government by the few or the many or the one; or on the basis of justice or injustice, as the *Rechtstaat* and the *Machtstaat;* on the basis of functions as the police state or the service state;[1] or on the basis of a dominant group as the military state, a theocratic state, or a gerontocracy.

In the earlier forms of political association the emphasis rested on age, familial relation, military skill, and magic and religion, which were all woven together in unified forms at times.[2] Later it rested upon some contrast between government by the many and the few or upon the mode of rule, as just or tyrannical, or greater emphasis was placed upon some economic factor producing plutocracy or communism.

Seniority, developing easily from family government, takes on the form of gerontocracy, or government of the elders, whose wisdom is presumed to be the safest guide in political affairs, although it might not coincide with military skill and leadership. The tradition of the "elder statesmen" still survives, although not as a form of government. Plato's "guardians of the law" were no longer young at fifty but were not selected because of age but by reason of long training and special qualifications. Gerontocracy as a form of society served a useful purpose in times past but has now no defenders anywhere as a type form.

The warrior state has a long history and survives down to the present hour. Organized violence has ruled much of the world, but generally the armed forces were characterized by some other name than that of warriors pure and simple. The present warrior state presents itself as an armed government in the interest of the community as a whole and not wholly for personal or class advantage. The warriors in earlier times were set up and equipped for combat, with a lion's share for those of special and outstanding skill in battle or cunning in suggestions of strategy. The warriors in our time require a known form of

[1] See H. D. Lasswell, *Politics* (1936); Jacob Wackernagel, *Der Wert des Staates* (1934); C. J. Friedrich, *Constitutional Government and Democracy* (1941); Francis G. Wilson, *The Elements of Modern Politics* (1936); Herman Finer, *The Theory and Practice of Modern Government* (rev. ed., 1934).

[2] Cf. W. C. MacLeod, *The Origin and History of Politics* (1931); R. H. Lowie, *The Origin of the State* (1927); Robert Redfield, *The Folk Culture of Yucatan* (1941), etc.

co-operation with the producing community, especially in what we call total war. A spear or a sword might last a long time in primitive combat, but modern artillery has an enormous appetite for ammunition which must be satisfied at once if the contest is to go forward.

The old-time formula of family, military skill, and religion might be said to have been on the way to elimination, but it has been revived in the Japanese state of our day, with all its earlier characteristics magnified and enlarged. This is likely to be the last appearance of this special and ancient form of state ruler-ship, a throwback to the earlier eras, although employing the techniques of modern times.[3]

The theocratic and the plutocratic forms of government imply the domi-nance of some special class which has acquired ascendancy over the political rulers. Property or the priesthood may, and do at times, determine the broad lines of political policy and exercise a powerful influence in administration. The government of Peru was for a long time distinctly theocratic in character. The government of the kingdom of Israel was essentially theocratic. The modern Vatican is a government conducted directly by the religious group.

"Plutocracy" is a still looser term applied to governments by men of wealth. The qualifications for office may be such as to restrict political power to the wealthy. More common are the property differentials which have accorded varying degrees of political power to different groups, depending upon their property situation, as in Greece, Rome, England, and the United States in various stages of their development. Property qualifications for voting and office-holding were prevalent in the United States for a long time, but the result was not characterized as plutocracy. Even under nominally democratic forms of government, the property groups may informally but obviously dictate the policies of the political society. Thus all the Western democracies have been assailed by their opponents on the right or left wing as essentially plutocratic in character, whatever they might be in form.

Oligarchy is another form of government in which wealth is a dominant factor, but with the added element of "bad" or incompetent government. Thus an oligarchy is a government of the few, rich and incompetent, a corruption of aristocracy.

Systematic defenders of plutocracy and theocracy are now seldom found, since what is really emphasized is the dominant influence of these particular groups rather than the responsible conduct of public affairs. Business and the church for reasons both of policy and of principle may prefer not to assume

[3] See Otto Hintze, *Wesen und Verbreitung des Feudalismus* (1929; reprinted from *Sitzungsberichte der Preussischen Akademie der Wissenschaften, Philosophisch-historische Klasse* [1929]), for the best description of the evolution of this system. See also MacLeod, *op. cit.* The Five Nations and their confederacy present one of the most interesting and illuminating pictures of primitive government.

immediate direction of affairs political, reserving the right to curb or influence the actions of others in nominal command. In practice, these lines may be blurred so that it is difficult to say which is government and which is "influence," but this is not unusual in political affairs, where indirect control is the stuff of which authority and direction are made.

Any group may control a government, occupational, racial groups, castes, classes, guilds, of endless variety, directing governmental action from occasion to occasion. What we are dealing with here is, however, not the type of pressure brought to bear on the political but the type or form of government upon which pressure is being exerted.

The classification most widely used is that based upon the breadth of participation in the exercise of control by the one, the few, or the many. In Aristotle this was modified by two other factors, wealth and "virtue," and the forms might become despotism, oligarchy, and ochlocracy. In our time we may relate the various forms to the degree in which they serve the common good and approach the ends of government.

The value of these categories diminishes with time and modern trends, since the rule of the one, it becomes clear, is less possible, if it ever was, and the rule of the many is seen to include considerations of leadership and expert ability in governmental service. The Duce and the Führer may seem to contradict this statement, but they are passing phenomena. More than that, both were obliged to maintain the democratic forms of representative government and the fiction of general suffrage. In general, the decisionism which it was thought could be obtained only through an individual chieftain, has been found attainable through democratic forms and processes, as in the case of Roosevelt and Churchill. On the other hand, the modern absolutists make at least a gesture toward popular support and trusteeship.

Broadly speaking, not only is the significant line of demarcation that of the diffusion of authority as such but also included is the end toward which its acts are directed. If the ends of the state are recognized as freedom and justice, based upon the dignity of man and his personal development, then forms of institutionalized responsibility and of general democratic participation will naturally evolve and color the whole scheme of government. The sounder classification is, consequently, that of popular government, with rulers responsible to the participating bulk of the community and directed toward the general good, and that of government of one or a few without formal responsibility, tested by their relation to the ends of government.

There are, of course, many stages between the more highly developed types on either side of the classification. It can happen that popular government forgets its responsibilities and that personal government is more mindful of them than if legally bound. There have been "good" kings and "bad" peoples in various stages of history.

I. GOVERNMENT BY ONE

With these reservations as to the value of the classification, we may now consider the three types of government of the one, the few, and the many. The government of the one is among the oldest types of rule, partly for familial reasons and partly for military reasons. The head of the family emerged into a broader paternalism or headship extending beyond the bounds of his immediate family. In early times this could be somewhat extensive, not only in the case of King Solomon but elsewhere and with less elaborate menage. The anthropologists revel in analyses of "headship" of innumerable types and colors.

Monarchy may be based upon family, upon land, upon military power, upon divine right, or upon a combination of these. Monarchy may be hereditary or elective; it may be absolute or it may be limited.[4] Of all forms of government, the monarchy has been able to utilize most successfully the factor of symbolism and ceremonialism. The mystery that "doth hedge a king" has a continuing magical power. The head was indeed in earlier times a recognized magician himself with extra-human powers.[5] The one and only possessed a position pre-eminently adapted to full ceremonial play of many most impressive forms. No matter how ill the panoply might seem to fit an incompetent monarch, the magic result was the same qua magic. An element of divinity was also added from time to time, under polytheism and monotheism, to reinforce the magical, if indeed they were not much the same in these days. The king might be the son of a god or godlet, and divine attributes might cling to him throughout his life. Family, custom, military power, magic, divinity—all these might be mingled in a somewhat indefinite but nevertheless powerful mixture of authoritarian elements out of which emerged his majesty. The medieval argument from unity which pervaded so much of the thinking of that time added logic to the power of kingship. The analogy with the one God in the heavens was also a part of the prestige situation.

When the nations began to break through the system of feudalism, the rising sovereigns relied to some extent upon an alliance with the mass of the people against the oppressions of the pettier feudal lords and thus strengthened their general position. Beyond this there were two definite gains. One was the new-found doctrine of sovereignty, which was employed to strengthen the sovereigns, and the other was the union of the altar and the throne, which now restored the divinity which had been weakened during the struggle between church and state. Thus Bishop Bossuet could declare the king to be the mortal image of God himself.

No sooner, however, was the new sovereign firmly established upon his

[4] See J. N. Figgis, *The Theory of the Divine Right of Kings* (1896), for earlier views.

[5] As to whether this was the true origin of kingship, see MacLeod, *op. cit.*

newly decorated throne than the process of restrictions on behalf of the community began. Civil liberties, representative governments, and constitutional processes were invoked by the mass of the people, and the king became, little by little, as in England, a constitutional sovereign without the arbitrary authority of earlier times.

Even in Bodin's sixteenth-century theory of sovereignty the sovereign was bound by the custom of the land and the laws of nature and of God. Absolutism was gradually but surely whittled down in England until only a shadow of early authority remained. Ceremonial and symbolic significance survived the loss of juristic and military power, however, and remained as a basis for monarchy after the substance of authority had long been shorn away. In Germany the emperor was no longer absolute but was made a part of a constitutional system. "Nichts ohne und nichts gegen den König" was the slogan of the time—"nothing without and nothing against the king."

The advantage of unity and continuity likewise remained, but continuity was seriously disturbed by the principle of heredity, which often failed to serve the purposes of the state. With breaks in the line, with regencies, with incompetent holders of authority, these advantages were sadly shattered. The modern kingship was never better characterized than in the phrase that "the king reigns but does not govern."

In Japan alone did the ancient form of monarchy retain its earlier position of divinity, mystery, absolutism. Even there, however, forms of constitutional government began to spring up and, until recently, to develop no little power. How far the present emperor retains the substance of power, or the shadow of it, is not wholly clear. At what point and to what extent may the advice tendered him by military, familial, and industrial magnates be rejected or modified with ease or impunity? In general, the Japanese government is more nearly an aristocracy governing through the screen of an implied divinity or divine influence.

The latest form of one-man rule with its demand for absolutism and irresponsibility is seen in the newly risen dictators. They abandon, however, the tradition of heredity and of mystery which was always the property of the traditional monarch. The leadership principle, as it is called, provides for centralization of authority in one person and reverses the scale of authorities, in that power comes from the top down and not from the bottom up. The leadership principle also is tied closely to two other doctrines and practices of very great importance: the omnipotence of the state and the glorification of government by the few. This latter doctrine of the élite will be considered under the head of aristocracy later in this text.

These wide-sweeping powers of the state are to be concentrated in a single-headed executive in whom the totalitarian powers are vested. The legislative remains formally, but for purposes of discussion, not of ratification. Likewise a party and a voting system remain, but under restrictions that deprive them of responsibility. The head of the state is the old-time despot ruling without legal limitations upon his authority, either in civil or in military affairs. This despotism is not founded upon the ownership of land, upon hereditary descent, or upon divine sanction but upon the assumed trusteeship of the nation, vested in himself by his own decree.

The theory is not that of classical dictatorship, since the ruler is in no sense a temporary figure, as were the dictators, but the permanent head of the state, after the fashion of the historic autocracies or despotisms. Neither in Germany nor in Italy was the autocrat termed a dictator but "Duce" in one case and "Führer" in the other.

The general theory of "leadership" rests in first instance upon the alleged necessity for unified centralization of authority in one point. It relies further, however, upon a theory of political inequality, in many ways like the old system of feudalism. The consent of the governed is eliminated as an undesirable and unworkable element in the political organization, and the irresponsibility of the rulers is substituted as a principle of association.

The essential principle of the new autocracy is, then, the irresponsibility of the governor to the governed. He is their interpreter but not their representative. He promotes their interests but not in accordance with their mandate or their power of review.

The democratic doctrine of the value of mass judgment is repudiated flatly, and the countercontention is made that the mass are incapable of understanding their own interests, of choosing agents to act for them, or of reviewing the acts of their leaders. Further, it is held that the masses are not interested in control over their leaders but are content to follow. The one-time voters are no longer troubled with the making of decisions regarding personnel or policies but pass over the task of political decision to their superiors or to the one superior—at once legally omnipotent, morally unassailable, and politically irresponsible. (Paradoxically, however, they still vote.)

Thus liberty, equality, representation, and responsibility are at one stroke wiped out. Justice[6] and order will be interpreted by the leaders as the ultimate molders of the national interest and destiny. But they are, theoretically, in no sense responsible to those in whose interest they act. The relation of ruler to ruled is that of freedom from judgment by those of inferior rank. What the nations need, it is maintained, is interpretation by the few and not representation by the mass—the leader principle rather than the "consent of the governed."

It may always be asked, "How do the leaders come to be leaders?" Whatever the answer may be finally, the answer now is, "They are."

[6] Giorgio del Vecchio elaborates the new theory of justice in modified Hegelian fashion, *Saggi intorno allo stato* (1935), pp. 149–70.

The general theory upon which such organization rests is that of lack of confidence in the competence of the community to choose representatives adequate to express its interests. The alleged proofs are deduced from the acts of contemporary legislative bodies found to be ignorant, corrupt, and dilatory in their behavior. In Italy argument is made in behalf of the occupational organization of representation through the various corporatives, but it is not conceded that these agencies should possess any genuine legislative power independent of the will of the head of the state.

Voting is also retained, but freedom of discussion is not permitted nor is freedom of association. The whole polling process goes on under the shadow of intimidation, direct or indirect, with the terror not far in the background. Voting is not merely possible at times but obligatory or at least salutary—a form of insurance which apparently costs nothing. One is reminded of voting under the Second Empire in France, which was termed the "plebiscite pour le rétablissement de l'opinion."

Government by the few, then, headed by a dictator is a mode of organization and process of action, with ultimate concentration of government as the final goal and possible toleration of a form of democratic consent as an intermediate stage.

In general, the new autocracy places strong emphasis upon the role of force in political affairs. Within the state, force is to take the place of consent as a factor in decision; and externally force is to take the place of the international jural world order advocated by the democratic theorists. Autocracy and autarchy are made to go arm in arm—despotism within and isolation without. The Terror within and War without. In either case, the "softness and persuasiveness" of the democratic process is to be avoided and the sterner rule of violence substituted.

In any event action is better than thought, it is held, and decision is superior to deliberation. Impatience and autocracy are happy companions. They make possible swift, stern, and ruthless decisions which promote the welfare of those whom it may concern, it is said. "We think with our blood," runs one formulation of the new doctrine of activist autocracy.

Obviously, this does not mean that there is no room for reflection in the new despotic regimes but that reflection on the acts of the governors by the governed is unnecessary and superfluous—and even dangerous. There were many well-trained and competent minds in Germany and Italy, but their thinking could not stray beyond the bounds set for them by those who arrived at the final decisions as checked by the secret police. If we ask, "By what process are these final decisions reached by the few?" the answer is vague; even more, the question is irreverent and unhygienic perhaps. "Creative skeptics" are not needed in the moments when the great decisions are being made by those who are entitled to make them in their own right as determined by their own personally made law. The king could do no wrong, and the modern autocrats can do no wrong—by definition—because they are the law.

II. ARISTOCRACY

The government of the few has a long history and a persistent philosophy, perhaps the most persistent in the world and the most subtle and pervasive—so easy is it to find reasons for the continuation or perpetuation of advantage and interest of some favored group. Further confusion is caused by the fact that in most governments actual officialdom is in the hands of relatively few persons who act for the community. In the divisions of labor the task of governing naturally devolves on a small number who may be identified as the superior few, but, in fact, they may be merely selected persons functioning for others. These officials may be in no sense superior to the average citizen and, in fact, may be performing work for the government which is the same as private employment, as in the case of public works. Or again the officials may be responsible to the community for the agency, constituting what Jefferson once called an "elective aristocracy," different in principle from aristocracy as a special form of government.[7]

It would not be far from the truth to conclude that most governments have been aristocracies, including the undemocratic democracies, on the one hand, and the monarchies, which were really the government of a few surrounding the king. From the point of view of immediate decision, especially of the military type, there were many systems in which power was sharply focused in one man, but even here long-range plans were determined by a group around the head of the state. When rulers were too old or too weak, obviously authority was vested almost wholly in the regent or regents surrounding the chief and acting more or less in his name. The leaders must even decide whether their ruler was capable of continuing in his position in case of borderline disability. Likewise small groups, ruling in the name of the majority or the mass, often carried on blandly without much regard for the mass in whose interest they professed to be functioning and without any real responsibility to those they appeared to represent. In point of fact they might be merely a group of militarists or of landed or other property interests or some small ethnic group holding the seats of power in the name of many—but only in name.

Aristocracies vary widely with the ends of the state in which they are concerned, the instruments they use for the realization of their purposes, and the social composition of the civic community in which they operate. The few may be based upon birth, upon age, upon military prowess, upon property,

[7] For discussion of aristocracy see my *The New Democracy and the New Despotism* (1939), Parts II–III, on the background of the "noble few," pp. 191–207.

upon race, upon cultural attainments, and upon religion, or the few may rule for the logical reason that they do rule, as some élitists maintain.

Their defenses range from the famous passages in Plato's *Republic* to the declarations of Pareto, Michels, Mussolini, and Hitler. Between them stretches a long series of portrayals of the advantage of aristocracies—defenses not necessarily coherent or cohesive, since the types of aristocracy to which reference is made are so widely different in form and purpose. Further difficulty is caused by the fact that aristocracies, calling and feeling themselves "democracies," omitted whole ranges of persons from their consideration, as in Athens, Rome, England, and the United States at various periods of their respective histories.

Dominant racial or economic groups have held themselves in power with right good will, stressing their own competence or preference in the given situation. Barbarians in Greece, workers in England, and Negroes in America were not merely thrust out of the circle; it was simply assumed that they did not "belong" politically or otherwise.

We may proceed to inquire what the premises are upon which an aristocratic system is constructed and operated and what the underlying considerations in the ideology of the aristocrats are.

1. The first premise of aristocracy as a type of political association is that there are well-defined differences in the political capacity of individuals and that these differences may be identified and validated. What are these political differentials?

2. Closely related to this assumption is the kindred one that the superior types may be selected and continuity obtained by some adequate procedure without definite political responsibility to the commonwealth and that this leadership will be recognized by the community widely enough to insure the maintenance of security and equilibrium. What are these methods?

3. It is assumed that the *aristoi* will accept responsibility for some form of community policy. What is the nature and scope of this "irresponsible responsibility"?

How shall these various assumptions be validated in an organized and operating system of aristocracy? This is the continuing task of the few who are to maintain themselves in a changing world.

1. The differentials in human ability—and especially in political ability— must be well defined and commonly understood, and they must be validated by general understanding of their soundness and by general acceptance as a basis of authority. What shall be, then, the special qualities of the few by which we shall identify them and, having identified, worship them or accept them without worshiping? Birth, seniority, wealth, arms, special skills, personality, attitudes, and habits may alone or in combination supply such a basis of widespread acknowledgment. Heredity is by this time discredited and abandoned by some of the apostles of élitism themselves. Wealth is a fluid claim to service—

if honored by those to whom addressed—but more uncertain in modern times than in earlier years. Arms are an element of strength. But the fact that rulers have arms is not enough. Long ago Rousseau said: "The strongest is never strong enough to be always master, unless he transforms his strength into right, and obedience to duty." We yield to the force of the robber but at the first opportunity turn to trap him and disarm him. If a few great ones had title to every last penny in the world, would they feel secure? Or if a few great ones commanded an army containing every able-bodied man and woman in a given state, would they be or feel secure—or shiver a little as they reviewed their own? A great commander might feel secure—a Caesar, an Alexander, a Napoleon—but not one who merely dreamed the dreams of these men. A great producer of human wealth might feel some confidence in his security, but not a fortune-maker such as Insull or Krueger—a dreamer of Croesus dreams in a world of speculation, running close to the borders of fraud and gambling.

The credentials of the *aristoi* are not easily read thus far, whatever later theorists may develop in the form of indices of difference. The heir apparent in China was told that a special mark on the palm of his hand indicated that he was predestined to rule. In India there was the story that if a child was seen protected by the hood of the cobra against the sun, he was destined to become a great ruler; and it is said that rulers have been so discovered.

Aristotle lamented that there was no sure distinguishing mark to serve as the infallible index of the slave nature, although he thought that in general this might be found in the cringing manner of the inferior. Slaveholders of the South found the missing link, they said, in the color of the Negro. In more modern times the Germans have found the mark of superiority in the alleged characteristics of the Aryan.[8]

Plato faced this difficult situation squarely and set up his indices of superiority, further indicating the ways and means by which selection of the adequate might be made. But in this he has had few successors who have been willing to face—or pass—the tests he set up.[9]

A precise study of the human differentials is on its way but is still far from the goal of adequacy. The psychologists, the biologists, the psychiatrists, and the psychoanalysts have developed tests and "batteries" of tests of many types. But the battle still rages even on the relatively simple ground of the I.Q., while little advance has been made in dealing with complex social characteristics and aptitudes, and still more scanty is the material dealing with the narrower range of political capacities. And in the political field, while progress has been made with personnel studies revealing individual differences and skills in public

[8] H. S. Chamberlain, *Die Grundlagen des neunzehnten Jahrhundert* (1899); H. F. K. Günther, *The Racial Elements of European History* (London, 1927).

[9] See Michael B. Foster, *The Political Philosophies of Plato and Hegel* (1935), chap. i, on difficulties encountered by Plato at this point.

administration, the determination of the traits and abilities of governors in the larger sense of the term is not yet developed to the point of exact or approximate identification. If it should be conceded that the making of the administrator is understood, there still remains a long road to the identification and training of the leader.

The analyses of writers commonly associated with the idea of aristocracy show that they are meager in the range and precision of their descriptions of the *aristoi* whose rule they advocate. Close inspection of their interpretations of the chosen few are indeed so disappointing as to make it well-nigh incredible that these doctrines should ever have been accorded any serious consideration. This is notably true of Pareto, foe of democracy, whose analysis of the characteristics and skills of the élite can scarcely be considered as more than elementary, if not indeed trivial. It would not be far from the truth to say that in Pareto's theory the élite are the élite. Those are competent to rule who do rule, and the test of their capacity is the fact of their governance. But, obviously, the fact that the rulers rule gives no answer to the question. It is interesting to note that the two founders of élitism differed widely on whether the Fascists were really the élite or not. Mosca said no, and Pareto said yes. The doctrine of *Führerschaft* is not subjected to acute analysis. If we ask how these leaders are to be known, the theoretical answer is not clear.

Since it may be assumed that some of the superior will always be found on the outside of the governing circle, may it not be possible to define the governing class as a group rather than in individual terms? The readiest answers from this point of view are found in birth, property, occupation, some common cultural mark. Seniority and intelligence might perhaps be included in this list but are not seriously considered in the modern presentation of the claims of aristocracy, at least not as distinctive marks. The bonds of birth and blood were emphasized in the German Nazi theory but were rejected in the Italian version as irrelevant. Hitler found a special criterion of aristocracy in a "pure race," Aryan in its German setting, while Mussolini discovered no such mark. "Race," said Mussolini, "is a feeling, not a reality; ninety-five per cent at least is a feeling. Nothing will ever make me believe that biologically pure races can be shown to exist today." Later he followed Hitler.

The theory of racial or national superiority does not solve the problem of individual position within the nation or help to draw the sacred circle around the naturally endowed rulers. The question still remains, even in Germany: "Who is the *Führer* intended by nature for leadership, and how shall we find a classifying principle?" What is it that marked out Hitler, Göring, and Goebbels as over against Brüning, Braun, and Severing, making one set the leaders and the other the followers?

The doctrine of "personal" biological descent is repudiated in the modern systems of aristocracy. Clearly this would have eliminated Hitler, Mussolini, and a great body of the circle of *aristoi*. If hereditary differentials were firmly established on a scientific basis, and if it were shown that political qualities were transmissible, the geneticists might be called upon to trace the biological transmission of such predispositions, if any. But none of these steps has thus far been taken, and there are no data upon which a system of aristocracy may now be constructed. Nor is there yet any assurance or reasonable expectation that such discoveries will ever be made in the domain of biology.[10]

The same may be said of the psychoanalysts' development of master-slave natures or inferiority-superiority complexes or "aggressiveness," as distinctive marks of capacity and incapacity for rulership.[11] These attitudes or dispositions are set in the framework of a many-sided system of personal and social values and are not specifically political in their significance. Recognition and satisfaction may prove adequate to the needs of the individual in any one of a long series of prestige systems, and the political may not be of prime significance in a particular individual's scale of values. He may prefer to lead an orchestra or a bowling team and be well paid in the applause of his fellow-men for any one of a thousand skills found in the wide range of work, play, art, or relationships innumerable. But thus far none of these developments plays any role whatever in the emerging theories of aristocracy.

Property as a distinguishing characteristic of the ruling group is rejected by the modern *aristoi* along with biological descent. When the land and the title to rule went along together, the description of the "lord" was relatively easy, but in the present system of aristocracy neither of these factors is admitted as decisive. No system sets up the possession of wealth, measured in our pecuniary order, as a title to political recognition in the official sense. Hitler had indeed announced that he had not even a bank account. Nor do the traits and skills by means of which wealth is obtained play a large part in the description of the natural élitist. It may be borne in mind that the larger holders of property and industrial power often regard these possessions and position as evidence of their right to influence and even to control the ordinary government, but this rarely enters into the modern theory of aristocracy. It may be noted that the Soviet system attached a negative significance to property, in that the possession of property used for the purpose of enabling the owner to live on the earning of others was set up as a disqualification for political activity of every type, including even suffrage.

Nor has any occupational basis been accepted as a means of entrance into the charmed circle of the aristocracy. Plato proposed the creation of a special

---

[10] See Aldous Huxley's ingenious outline for organization in the event that such discoveries are made, as described in his *Brave New World* (1932). See also H. S. Jennings, *Prometheus* (1925); *The Biological Basis of Human Nature* (1930).

[11] Harold D. Lasswell, *Psychopathology and Politics* (1930), and *World Politics and Personal Insecurity* (1935).

class of guardians and specifically set up their characteristics, but this early advice has not been followed by the modern apostles of aristocracy. The use of technical experts in the direction of administration is important but does not reach the problem of political leadership.

In a situation where the direct appeal to force enters largely into the argument, it might be presumed that the military profession would automatically be counted in as a part of the governing élite. But there has been no disposition thus far to accord recognition to the occupation of arms or any natural right to political leadership of the military class. In none of these cases, however, was there any development of the underlying philosophical assumptions of the Fascists or the Nazis. Mussolini and Hitler reached the rank of corporal, and Hitler purged the generals. In the philosophy of neither of these men was there any effort to incorporate the military class into the inner circles of the upper superiors. Quite the contrary, their purpose was to utilize the armed forces, while keeping them away from the center of actual political authority—a balancing feat of supreme difficulty, especially where there was the enormous prestige of the army in the background. The military class is likely to find its defense in arms rather than in philosophy.

The development of technocracy as a proposed system of industrio-political government gave an opportunity for the elaboration of a theory of the superior, but little progress was made in this direction by the proponents of the new system. Chiefly engineers interested in the problem of production of commodities and of services, they did not address themselves primarily or adequately to the governmental implications of the new regime which they advocated.[12] Sweeping charges were directed against the political and industrial leaders of contemporary significance, but surprisingly little was said of the types to replace them. In general, attention was fixed on engineering production rather than on social or political efficiency. Estimates of possible production, discussions of new types of value measurement in newly devised units, and pictures of the social advance to be made were freely projected; but the job specifications of the technocrats were in the main lacking. Doubtless they must be managerial in their capacity, adventurous in their disposition, and representative of the most highly developed technique of production, but beyond that the specifications of the technocrat were not subjected to much analysis or exposition. It would have been possible, indeed, to specify the professional training of an engineer, but, in fact, this was not done explicitly. When such attempts were made, they fell far short of an appreciation of the requirements of the problem of governmental organization. Technocracy was weak here. It gambled on capacity to interpret "ergs," not to co-ordinate interests. In a

[12] Harold Loeb, *Life in a Technocracy* (1933), based on the ideas of Howard Scott; James Burnham, *The Managerial Revolution* (1941); Robert A. Brady, *Business as a System of Power* (1943).

technocracy "corporate monopolies" would be the government, with a "coordinating industrial board." The chairman of this board would be the "highest official in the territory and would have certain fiat powers for emergency use—a most undemocratic system." In some vague and ill-defined manner the consumers or the stockholders would exercise some undefined power of control over the officials, but the scope and method of the control remain wholly hazy.[13]

It may be concluded that the identification of the *aristoi* is far from satisfactorily developed thus far. The Platonic analysis, by far the most complete yet presented in defense of the rule of the few, is disregarded almost as if it did not exist. It is a far cry from Plato's guardians to Hitler's assertion that the basis of authority must be popularity and force, or to Mussolini's fierce scowl, outthrust jaw, pouting lips, and heavy tragedian manner. One might almost conclude that the chief skill of the élite was histrionic, and hence the ablest actor the most desirable leader.

The most conspicuous of the modern élites have been somewhat embarrassed by the fact that their leaders were set forth as *sui generis*, geniuses of an exceptional type. In such instances the leader cannot be replaced, and even to suggest this is to question the superhuman basis of the whole plan of political salvation. There can be no other Mussolini, no other Hitler, it is argued.

Aristoi really do not need dictators who are more likely to devour them than to nourish them. The elevation of a dictator is a momentary abdication which may become permanent—unless a curtain is drawn on the dictator's show.

2. Assuming that the political characteristics of the aristocracy have been fairly well identified—a goal thus far not attained—how shall the *aristoi* be selected? How shall the smooth flow of continuity be maintained?

For a short time, in periods of great tension, in mutual fear of external attack, it is possible for an "aristocracy" to maintain a fairly solid front; but there can be no guaranty that this will endure. The characteristic weaknesses of the *aristoi* have been, as pointed out by Montesquieu, jealousy and rivalry.[14] One faction may appeal to the mass as against the other; one faction may set up a strong man as against another; one faction may fear and attempt the annihilation of another. Hitler's bloody purges of 1934 and 1944 are only modern illustrations of what has happened innumerable times in the history of the anxious

---

[13] "Political government" is out of date, it is held—an institution which has no engineering significance. If political government is retained, "its function would be showmanship. The routine of its executives would be made up of receiving distinguished guests, laying corner stones, making speeches about the rights of man, American initiative, justice. Its offices would be elective, thereby titillating the egos of those who like to think they are running things. Prominent clowns will, doubtless, be frequently elected" (Loeb, *op. cit.*, pp. 102–3).

[14] See discussion of Montesquieu in *The Spirit of Laws;* Machiavelli, *The Prince;* Aristotle, on aristocracies, in *Politics*.

élites who could not trust one another—or perhaps trusted too fondly, as in Machiavelli's case of the leader who invited his rivals to a peace party which ended in the death of all the undesirables.

The loss of hereditary distinctions as a mark of aristocracy and the decline of wealth as an index make the status of an aristocracy extremely dubious. Military prestige is always uncertain, in that no one knows when or where it will spring up, often at some inconvenient point, upsetting the balance of the comfortable occupants of the bowers of authority.

Once it is accepted that the few are to rule without legal responsibility to the rest of the state and further that neither birth, wealth, electoral choice, nor standardized merit shall govern the line of successions, what shall be the means by which the allegiance of the bulk of the community is held in line for the support of the superior? How shall stability be insured for aristocracy? Even Plato was driven to say that he would start his ideal state with "one royal lie," namely, that the various classes had been born as they were. But in modern times this is not an adequate answer.

In modern terminology this is a large-scale problem of morale—of the maintenance of such a driving form of *ésprit* that the community will produce, will fight and work, will be happy, and, above all, will accept the sway of the aristocracy as one of the major facts of life. The alternative presented is a dark picture of malaise, discontent, and actual or threatened revolution. And if the institutional channels of responsibility are clogged, the only way of action will be the channel of force.

With this in mind, all aristocracies have studied the problem of pleasing those over whom they rule, of charming those whom they command so that they will obey; of combining the club and the charm in the most acceptable manner, of developing a vast apparatus of symbolism and ceremonialism. In a sense their tenure of office depends upon the outcome of a perpetual plebiscite. The masses of the inferior do not vote, but they cast an informal ballot expressing their attitude toward the superior power. These ballots are not counted directly but are reckoned in terms of crowds, hurrahs, applause, readiness to serve, and the absence of resistances and revolts. One hiss may count as much as the loss of a seat in the legislative body; one boo may sound like a revolt.

The appeal may always be made to the higher levels of statesmanship shown by achievement. The few may appear as the continuing benefactors of the community of which they are the heads. More territory, more loaves and fishes, and more expanding sentiments of group prestige may be the fruits of their rule; and this may be appropriately presented as a justification. Or inferior achievements may be magnified until they seem important.

All this is, however, an appeal from the minority to the majority, as if they were the competent judges of what is good. Hence it contains within itself the seeds of some form of popular responsibility—to be avoided in the most complete form of superiority which assumes not merely superior power but superior competence in judgment of community affairs, and which avoids institutionalized responsibility.

The electoral device, however, the modern élites are reluctant to abandon wholly. It may reasonably be asked: "Why do the modern aristocrats play with the electoral system in their organization after repudiating it as a useless device of outworn democracy?" Mussolini once said, by way of illustration, that the Italians might vote until sick at the stomach but that the inner circle would determine policy. In general, he protested against what began to be termed "electionistic" tendencies, meaning thereby too great emphasis on electoral devices. The answer may be, from one point of view, that the use of elections is merely a device of a transition period and that the machinery of counting will be abolished in the fulness of time and with the perfection of the system. Or, from another point of view, it may be said that the electoral device is useful in creating a feeling of popular participation in the government—as a means for improvement of general morale, although in fact the important decisions are made in another fashion. Elections from this point of view are morale mechanisms rather than modes of selection of personnel or determination of broad policies.

3. The superiors assume the trusteeship of the community, with a general responsibility for the well-being of the nation or other political unit in which they function. They may determine their own position in the general scheme of things political, and they must observe the relative position of all others in a broad scheme of values over which they stand in general charge.

Shall the supermen assume that the welfare of mankind is best served by their own superdevelopment, with the benefits trickling down to others as time goes on? Or shall they undertake some more immediate and direct diffusion of the gains of greatness for the weak? Or shall they perhaps assume that their own glorious development is itself a flower which may well satisfy the imagination and the desires of all the others? Perhaps others do not matter at all but merely serve as the clay from which the figures of the truly superior are shaped.

What theoretical account of themselves shall the politically unaccountable give in their philosophical moments? And what shall be their program?

Shall they decide to educate the masses of the people in such a way as to fit them ultimately to become *aristoi* or in such a manner as to render them ineligible and content with a humbler lot? Shall they educate for class status on the whole or for mass status? At this point they may predetermine the destiny of the oncoming generation in great measure.

What type of race will they choose to breed, if they better understand the art of eugenics? Will they give preference to breeding of superior types, or might they conclude to grow morons as once suggested by a psychologist— morons to do the hard work of the world, while others live upon the fruit of their labors? Shall they breed a class or a special race or breed for mass development upward toward final universal éliteness?[15]

Shall they early begin to train men for special occupations, adapting them to some standard status, or shall they leave open the door of hope to all? Shall they approximate something of a caste system or shall they assume that modern society requires more opportunity for adaptation and advancement on the part of the many?

Shall they regard the economic field as essentially a free struggle for survival of the fittest or supervise it to the extent at least of making sure that it does not undermine the prestige or position of the *aristoi*, political and otherwise?

How far will they go in the assumption of responsibility for direction of control over the instruments of production, the processes of distribution and consumption, and of standards of living? What shall they say to capitalism and to communism in developing national policies appropriate to the domination of the few? Theoretically they might go either way—a long way—or they might go another way which was neither one nor the other in form or process.

Practically, the recent élites of Italy and Germany have balanced capitalism against socialism, although favored and supported by the former, but in so doing it must be observed that they have made an appeal to another form of loyalty in the shape of modern nationalism. The nation itself is, however, a mass phenomenon, and continuing appeal to the mass is full of peril for an association based upon the principle of class, even if repudiating any specific responsibility to the masses. This accounts undoubtedly for the retention of the forms of plebiscite and pseudo-voting in these places.

Nor is there anything to prevent an élite from taking on a religious color and affiliation, improbable as this might seem in view of the warfare with the church in Italy and in Germany. It might, indeed, be maintained that the only sure basis for an élite lay in the cultivation of religious values and interests as a continuing bond of allegiance. The caste system, which held sway over the world for a long period of human history and still dominates the daily lives of millions of our fellow-men, was given the aura of religion and found this the strongest support in its most difficult hours. It is entirely possible that a state church may emerge to bless the new leaders, as in earlier days the Anglican and the Gallican churches emerged.

It is evident that aristocracies are seriously embarrassed by the following uncertainties:

1. *Uncertainty as to the precise characteristics of the aristocrats, or of any working group of them.*—The picture of the aristocracy as our natural rulers lacks the identification upon which a system must rest, or the scientific validity.

---

[15] See Huxley, *op. cit.*, for ingenious suggestions as to possible policy. H. G. Wells (*The Shape of Things To Come* [1933]) has described the "Air Dictatorship" and the "Modern State Fellowship."

Most élites seem indifferent to the elevation of men with special aptitudes and skills making for mature and stable statesmanship. Who are the aristocrats? What warrant is there for assuming that the unfit will not emerge and occupy the seats of authority; that the *aristoi* may prove to be common gangsters dressed in a little brief and bloody authority?

2. *Uncertainty as to the selection and continuity of the superior ones.*—If we know that we belong to the aristocracy, how can we be sure that others recognize our natural pre-eminence? If birth or status is abandoned, and if elections are repudiated as ineffective, the labeling of the aristocrat is made difficult. Who, then, shall choose the few—and the successors of the few?

3. *Uncertainty as to the nature and administration of the trusteeship of the aristocracy.*—Shall the aristocracy hold their trust to be that of the development of the whole community over which they preside? Or perhaps their own energies and their development are the end of the mass of the community—their highest and best satisfaction.

The devotees of aristocracy must make a series of fundamental decisions in the establishment of their authority. Their relations to religion, to science, and to industry are involved; still more difficult, their relations to the mass movement are involved in nationalism, with its heavy trend back to massism and democracy. What is the program of aristocracy? What safeguards shall they build against the shock of military defeat, against the cycles of economic depression, against the outbursts of suppressed freedom of speech and thought, against the silent persistence of religious values? If aristocracy is merely another name for personal adventure, if its methods are chiefly violence and propaganda, if it reflects largely national impatience in a moment of despair, then it may be so judged. But if the government of a few is really the generalized goal, then the criteria of excellence must be identified, ways and means of selection and continuity must be evolved, the relation of the few to the many must be defined and interpreted, and types of programs must be developed.

Thus far indeed in modern times the advocates of aristocracy have been most conspicuous for the use of violence rather than reason, for bombastic appeal to the very masses they affect to despise, for pseudo-voting rather than genuine electoral processes, for attacks upon rational political choices rather than for their recognition and incorporation in a system pre-eminently requiring these traits and skills.[16]

---

[16] "If you want to get men to act reasonably," says Huxley, "you must set about persuading them in a maniacal manner..... What we want ....is a sane and reasonable exploitation of the forces of insanity" (*Crome Yellow* [1922], pp. 228–29). For this purpose he suggests three main species of men: the directing intelligences, the men of faith, and the herd. Cf. H. G. Wells's prescription for recruiting the new élite (*What Are We To Do with Our Lives?* [1931] and *The Shape of Things To Come*). Pareto's doctrine of the élite is weak and unconvincing; only the word will survive, semantically, so to speak.

If the superior are really superior in the light of modern intelligence and science, why do they employ so extensively the weapons of force and ballyhoo? Why have they so little confidence in their own inherent qualities? If it is qualities of will and of activism they seek to emphasize, then the questions may be asked: Has it been found impossible to unite intelligence and will in a formula of personality or a pattern of behavior? If the loudest shouting and the bloodiest shedding of blood give the title to the new leadership, will not the trend be in the direction of still louder shouting and still more savage policies?

The historic categories of aristocracy point either in the direction of intelligence and personality demonstrated by long training, as indicated by Plato, or in the direction of a group inspired by religious ideals; but neither the philosopher-king of the classical period nor the prophet-priest type is seen in the aristocracy of the modern day. Neither military force nor economic wealth offers a solid and enduring basis of an aristocracy that professes to rest upon any rational view of life.

It may be said that nationalism or proletarianism affords support for a group of leaders, but the underlying trends of modern nationalism and of modern proletarianism are at bottom mass-driven and over a long period of time are untrustworthy for those who affect the cult of aristocracy. Dictatorships of the few, resting upon mass movements, are built upon foundations of sand, for ultimately the nation or the class may decide to take charge of their own estate. If the test of the validity of authority is force, then the mass may ultimately have the superior argument; and if it is ballyhoo, how long and how effectively may it be maintained?

We conclude that we are a long way from knowing the differentials in human capacity and in political capacity; from knowing adequate methods of selection and continuity of desirable persons for political leadership; from being in a position to outline the scope and method of their "irresponsible responsibility" to the commonweal; from faith in the equipment or the intentions of the *aristoi*.

The curse of aristocracy is not that great men fill great places but that small men fill great places and piece out their inferiority with arrogance. Truly great natures are likely to find a response in the mass of mankind. They need not fear the many as much as the jealous few. In the very nature of aristocracy it is difficult, if not impossible, to appraise the position of the *aristoi* properly, to be as expert and responsive to the problems of equitable distribution as of production. In dealing with the ends of government, aristocracy tends to identify the public good with its own material and spiritual values. But can aristocrats know what justice is when they are judges in their own cause?

III. DEMOCRACY

The democratic form of government, like the monarchic and the aristocratic, covers a wide range of variations, which at times seem to include so many blurred patterns as to make generalization difficult. But democracy encounters far fewer difficulties when the ends of government are considered. The social composition of democracy, its special implements and tools, its relation to the ends of the state—all these are factors which, taken together, illuminate the growth, trends and rationale of the democratic system of organization. A regard for the equal dignity and worth of all human personalities, reliance upon the consent of the governed as the basis of justice, and the development of institutions and procedures for the purpose of the true ends and means of government are the characteristic lines through which the development of the democratic process and forms may best be traced.

Democracy is a form of political association in which the ends of government are habitually determined by the bulk of the community in accordance with appropriate understandings and procedures providing for popular participation and consent. Democracy is contrasted with other forms of political association in which the ends of government are habitually determined by a relatively small group in accordance with appropriate understandings and procedures providing for autocratic, aristocratic, or other forms of minority control and direction.

The principal bases of democracy are as follows:

1. The essential dignity of man, the importance of protecting and cultivating his personality on a fraternal rather than a differential principle, and the elimination of special privileges based upon unwarranted or exaggerated emphasis on the human differentials.

2. Confidence in the perfectibility of mankind.

3. The assumption that the gains of commonwealths are essentially mass gains and should be diffused as promptly as possible throughout the community, without too great delay or too wide a spread in differentials.

4. The desirability of popular decision in last analysis on basic questions of social direction and policy and of recognized procedures for the expression of such decisions and their validation in policy.

5. Confidence in the possibility of conscious social change accomplished through the process of consent rather than by the methods of violence.[17]

[17] For some general discussions on the assumptions of democracy see James Bryce, *The American Commonwealth* (1888) and *Modern Democracies* (1921); Hans Kelsen, *Vom Wesen und Wert der Demokratie* (1929); Harold J. Laski, *Democracy in Crisis* (1933); John Dewey, *Democracy and Education* (1916), *Individualism Old and New* (1930), *Liberalism and Social Action* (1935), and *The Public and Its Problems* (1927); Richard Henry Tawney, *Equality* (1931); Célestin Bouglé, *Les Idées égalitaires* (1899), *La Démocratie devant la science* (3d ed., 1923); Thomas Mann, *The Coming Victory of Democracy* (1938); Ordway Tead, *New Adventures in Democracy* (1939); Eduard Beneš,

These principles constitute the theoretical basis of democracy. The program of democracy is directed toward their validation through specific mechanisms and in particular programs. But the underlying principles are standards by which special procedures and the policies of the moment are to be evaluated. Taken together, they make up the working philosophy of democracy, as it is evolving historically.

We may raise the question, "How shall these conclusions be tested in the light of our present knowledge, and how do they differentiate democracy from other alternative types of political association?" This validity is, of course, subject to examination by any of the means we utilize in the testing of knowledge. For the proof of some of them we should look primarily to rational and ethical analysis and to the body of observations, analyses, and conclusions accumulated by modern social science; or both methods may be applied.

Thus, the dignity of the human personality may be regarded either from the ethical-rational point of view, or from the point of view of the student of groups in their relation to their members, or from that of a student of morale, such as Mayo or Urwick, who considers the meaning of the "satisfied personality" in the organization of association. The "continuing perfectibility" of mankind may be explored through the data developed by science, technology, and personality studies seen in the ranges of social science. Likewise the generalization of mass gains may be approached from the point of view of studies of the nature of association, by the students of groupism, or from the point of view of a rational analysis of the nature of a community and the commonweal. The same process is applicable to the possibility of conscious control of social affairs and to the role of violence in this field. The value of mass judgment and the meaning of the consensual arrangements designed for that purpose may be scrutinized by a variety of approaches, including rational analysis, observation, and experiment. All these types of treatment have been applied from the days of Aristotle down to modern times.

We must, of course, allow for the historical fact that many regimes—autocratic, aristocratic, and other—have proclaimed from time to time their adherence to one or more of these democratic assumptions but in practice have paid little heed to them. Benevolent despots have arisen who took seriously the task of protecting their subjects, and nourished them as they would their flocks and lands—and perhaps with right good will. But they wished to remain irresponsible to their people, and ordinarily their regime at best was neither fraternal nor peaceful. The governments of the few or of the one have often assumed a general paternal attitude whether from the patrimonial point of view or the

Democracy Today and Tomorrow (1939); Reinhold Niebuhr, The Children of Light and the Children of Darkness (1944); Mortimer J. Adler and Walter Farrell, The Theory of Democracy (forthcoming; the first parts have appeared serially in the Thomist, Vol. III [1941], No. 3, through Vol. VII [1944], No. 1).

military, the industrial, or the religious, or the view of nationalistic proprietorship. But commonly they were unconcerned with liberty or equality or the protection of human personality, or with normally peaceful change, or with ways and means of responsibility of the ruler to the ruled. Sometimes, indeed, they were practically unconscious of these ideas or were indifferent or cynical; or, again, were positively antagonistic to them; or, in a more cheerful mood, looked upon them as ideals impossible of attainment in any practical span of time. All this attitude was set, of course, in a framework of vested interest which made the rejection of democratic ideas not only logically inevitable but also profitable and pleasant in the immediate present.

It is also true that so-called "democracies" at various times have fallen far short in practice of the goals indicated in the assumptions of their basic form of political association. Even in our own day there are nominal democrats who do not intend to allow their democracy to interfere with their preferred position in society, and the protection of the special values they cherish whether in the form of property or prestige.

On the whole, the democratic theory affirms that the democratic group of assumptions, as to both ends and means, constitutes a unified program which may be taken as a way of political life. Other systems are differentiated from it either by different ends or by different means, or both. The disunity of ends and means constitutes one of the most serious obstacles to the development of democratic institutions.

The prime factor in the maintenance of democracy is the unification and application of the assumptions of democracy in a working program—the general recognition of the meaning of these assumptions and of the importance of realizing them in practical affairs, internal and international as well. Democracy will be at its weakest when these ideals are imperfectly or weakly carried through, and strongest when they are energetically advanced in comprehensive, systematic, and persistent fashion.

It is important to observe that many of the older criticisms of democracy are no longer seriously considered.

a) In view of the far-flung territory and population of the United States and of Great Britain, it is absurd to maintain the older thesis of the incompatibility of democracy and the large-scale state. Yet as late as the end of the eighteenth century, and even in the United States at that time, doubts were expressed as to the possibility of any other than a small-sized democracy. There is democracy in relatively small areas such as Switzerland and Sweden, but there is also democracy in Australia and Canada. In neither instance does the area or the numbers seem to be the conclusive consideration.

b) It is no longer confidently asserted that a democracy cannot survive in military struggle against monarchic or aristocratic contenders. In modern times the life-span of mass rule seems as good a risk as that of any competing form of government, and better than some. In the first World War it was Russia, Germany, and Austria who collapsed under the strain of the long-drawn-out struggle. France and England were able to weather the storm, to organize and utilize vast military and naval forces, and to maintain their morale under very difficult circumstances. Whether or not the essential differential was the form of government or not, it cannot be denied that the democracies were not shown incapable of maintaining themselves over a long period of intense military activity.

c) It is no longer confidently asserted that democracy can produce nothing beyond the rule of incompetence and ignorance, as was positively declared in earlier times by the advocates of the few. In the face of competent governments such as those of Sweden, Switzerland, England, France, and the United States such a position is no longer tenable and, indeed, is no longer advanced seriously. There are weaknesses of democracies in special cases—but the old-time generalized assertion that no democracy can ever produce types of competence under any circumstances is now difficult to sustain.

In short, the classical arguments against democracy based upon necessary limitation to small size, upon inability to survive military struggle, and upon general ignorance and incompetence have been abandoned as a result of the experience of recent generations with democratic types of association, even when not fully democratic in horizon of participation. Democracy has been acquitted of these charges and a new indictment framed.

Much confusion has been caused by failure to distinguish between the essential elements of democracy and special features of democratic organization, program, or social background. The general principle of community control over essential community problems for community ends is in this way lost in the controversy over special and temporary features of a general system.

In general political theory, democracy is not identifiable with (*a*) any special size or area of association such as city, state, nation-state, or world state; (*b*) any form of economic organization, such as agrarian, industrial, capitalistic, socialistic, state capitalistic, or otherwise; (*c*) any special form of centralization or decentralization of powers or functions, as federal or centralistic, or any special form of the separation or balance of power among agents of authority; and (*d*) any particular form of representative or executive organization, such as unicameral, bicameral, multicameral, regional or occupational representation, or special type of administrative or managerial arrangement, or of parliamentary or presidential government.

In various modern situations—American, Swiss, English, Swedish—democracy is associated with special types of machinery, program, and cultural background. But the general principle of democratic association and purpose lies deeper down than these special forms and problems, however important they may be in a given phase of social development in a particular territory or people.

The principle and the practice of democracy may be found in many kinds of social, economic, religious, racial, and cultural situations; they may be found in many varying types of governmental organization; they may be found with many widely ranging programs designed to carry out the principle of democracy under very different circumstances. But these different social settings, varying mechanisms, and diverse programs are not to be confused with the underlying system of common determination of the commonwealth organization and action for common ends.

Further confusion arises from the wider or narrower range of democratic participation in various times and places. From time to time the horizon of democracy varies. A small section or a very large section of the community affairs may constitute the area of democratic effectiveness. The inclusion of the whole adult population is a relatively recent phenomenon, for most historic democracies so called did not include more than a minority, and sometimes a very small minority, of the political community.

The fact that within these narrower ranges of population with imperfect democracy lies much of the practice of popular government tends to confuse the general principle of democracy with special times, places, and programs. What we observe historically is the development of democratic principles and forms within aristocratic society, which affirms the theory of democracy while retaining the aristocratic form of association and tradition.

In recent years it has been the habit of some thinkers to relate the democratic system of government to a special form of industrial organization and, in particular, to capitalism. It has been held that there is a close analogy between the free competition of the economic world and the electoral process of the political, and the conclusion has been drawn that one rises or falls with the other.

A view of the historical development of democratic ideology and institutional forms shows that they have sprung up under a variety of conditions, sometimes rural and agrarian and at other times urban and industrial. Aristotle enumerates different varieties of democratic rule in his *Politics*—a democracy of husbandmen, of shepherds and herdsmen, of mechanics, exchange men, and hired servants.

The history of the world since the great Greek illustrates still more fully the possibilities of varied types of democratic states, as in Switzerland, in Australia, in Canada, in the United States, rural and urban and industrial—under a wide variety of economic backgrounds so numerous as to make it perfectly clear that essentially democracy is not dependent upon any particular form of industrial or economic organization. All the burdens of unorganized urbanism and of unorganized laissez faire economics were imposed on the development of mass rule, and the inevitably ensuing problems were charged wholly to these democratic institutions without regard to the special circumstances under which one form of democracy grew up. Additional basis for this position was given by the fact that the "natural law" theory of government was confused with the "natural laws" of economics, as they were called. There was an effort to identify liberty in the political sense with economic liberty. It soon became evident, however, that the "natural law" system in politics led straight to the establishment of government, whereas in economics it led to the boycott of government; and, further, that the "natural liberty" of politics soon resolved itself into a system of political liberty, order, and justice, whereas the "natural liberty" of the economic world tended to resist governmental and social regulation and often led to inequality and injustice and indeed to monopoly.

Within modern society there developed new concentrations of commercial wealth which began to menace at many points the workings of a political system not prepared for such powerful elements. These new industrial units in a sense took the place of the old landed group—the landlords—who in the preceding period had dominated the economic and the political life of the community. Mobilizing quickly and often acting with great ruthlessness, these new forces were able in many instances to dictate terms to government and to obtain either special subsidy, privilege, or immunity from regulation by the state. Their powers over trade and commerce enabled them to fix wages and salaries, to determine prices, and to monopolize or control the amount and type of output over wide ranges of industrial activity. Under the protecting shelter of laissez faire[18] they often made politics in a sense a branch of economics.

All this led many to the conclusion that democracy was only another name for oligarchy—or, in the later terminology, plutocracy—using the forms of democracy while enjoying the substance of aristocracy. Marxians, indeed, were so confused that they identified the entire state with a mechanism for the use of violence in support of the bourgeoisie and therefore demanded its destruction. Critics attributed to democracy all the perplexities of society both economic and governmental as well, although many of these problems were presented primarily not by any form of economic or governmental organization but by the emergence of human science and the development of new technology.

The greatest threat to democratic development was not the lingering distrust of the many by the few. This had always existed but was always overcome by greater distrust of the policies of the few. In reality, the greatest menace to democracy arose from the widespread feeling among masses of men that democracy was a set of forms, rules, and declarations which in practical operation favored the few rather than the many. If the great landlords were to be followed by the great financiers, if the gains of civilization were not to be effective in the daily lives of men and women, then the question might be raised and was raised, "How are we better off than before?" With this might

[18] See my *The Role of Politics in Social Change* (1936), chaps. i and ii.

come a decline of the supreme faith in democracy which had made the most revolutionary force in recent history. Thus the Marxian, on the one hand, and the Fascist, on the other, and the cynics at all times combined to attack the whole democratic system itself and to cast aside liberty, equality, and peace as ways and means of social advance.[19]

Others drew the conclusion that formal mass rule could never signify anything but plutocracy. That America, the amplest home of democracy, was also the home of industrial concentration appeared as an additional proof of the intimate and necessary interrelationship between the form of government and the form of concentration of capital. That capitalism had developed in like form in Germany under another system and in Japan under still another was blandly ignored in these hasty calculations. This type of reasoning often made it possible for opposites to unite in attack upon popular rule, one side denouncing democracy on the ground that it was not democratic enough, and the other because it was or threatened to become too democratic. Thus the Communist and the Nazi might combine against democratic government, as they did in Germany in the period just before the advent of Hitler. In general political theory, however, there is no necessary relationship between democracy as a form of political association and economic association or organization. Whatever the form of government, it is obliged to bear the burden of adjusting the balance between modern technology, industry, and government.

Equally naïve are those who assert that democracy cannot survive in an industrial society in which large-scale production is found. This is not unlike the earlier doctrine that democracy cannot work on a widespread territory but must be confined to tiny areas. The size and complexity of industrial production do not condition the operations of the consent of the governed. The broad decisions as to the function of the democracy may be made whether the industrial organization or territorial area is small, middle sized, or large. The task of the people consists in outlining the broad policies to be followed and in exercising general and not detailed supervision over the personnel and the policies they have set up. It is no more difficult to accomplish this result in a large territory than in a smaller one, or in a large-scale industrial organization than in a smaller-sized one.

An underlying problem in respect to industrial units is the optimum size of operating units from the point of view of the commonwealth, and this may vary widely in different ranges of industrial production. The real difficulty arises in the minds of those who are so bewildered by size, or confused by complexity, or overwhelmed by nostalgia for the primitive that they are unable to apply organizational principles to the essential problem—which is the or-

[19] Even James Bryce plaintively queried why democracy was not satisfied with machinery but demanded the use of democratic mechanisms for social and economic purposes (*Modern Democracies* [1921], chap. lxxx).

ganization of policy-determining bodies for the statement of general laws and principles and the organization of administration for the purpose of management, and the role of the policy-determining agency in general supervision of the administrative agencies.

IV. THE NEW DEMOCRACY

The modern long-time trend is in the direction of democracy. Pointing this way are the advance of science and education, the growth of respect for human personality, the decline of brute force, the growth of world jural order, the nature of massed industrial life, and the reorientation of our modern value systems.

Once the principle of democracy is firmly established in institutions and understandings, it is possible to achieve the recognition of the genuine elements of social and political intelligence found in a given community at a given time. It is not necessary to set up a detailed comparison between the systems of autocracy and democracy at all the various points where contrast might be sharpest. I choose for the moment the category of the maintenance of the balance between justice and order. Order makes possible an integration of external behavior in patterns that may be counted upon by the citizenry. Justice makes possible or facilitates an inner integration of the personality and the development of community morale.

In any case, the balance between order and justice is one of the basic elements in stability and progress. Authoritarians are likely to place order first, and it is, indeed, of urgent importance in any scheme of affairs. Autocracy is also likely to place order first and allow justice to come along afterward—but perhaps forgotten in the meantime. The few are likely to fear the many and to interpret causes in their own interest. The mass is confident in its own strength and not likely to precipitate action from nervous fear that they may be too late.

Another great object of government is the organization of stability and the organization of change. It is plain that the mass may promote stability while recognizing genuine variations. The fatal weakness of the autocracy is the prolonging of power after its justification has gone—of preserving the authority that once rested upon superior capacity long after the element of superiority had faded out. The brain that won the battle or the war, the hand that waved the wand of economic production, the intelligence that understood the secrets of statesmanship and its practice—these pass away and their successors cannot carry on, except as they cover their inner weakness with the glitter of decorations. Weakness contrives the appearance of strength, encouraging belief in skill that is actually gone. The continuing mass, however, has no reason to deceive itself as to outworn capacities but may recognize the flux of the difference in human capacity, political or otherwise, and adjust its affairs accordingly.

Those who assert that democracy cannot organize effective management forget that scientific management is the very child of modern democratic societies and that executive leadership is the great contribution of modern democracy to statesmanship, notably in the United States.

Those who assert that democracy cannot organize and utilize force are unmindful either of ancient predictions of democratic incapacity to survive or of recent military events demonstrating democratic strength. The gravest danger threatening the peace of the world today is the illusion that democracies will not and cannot fight because they do not like to fight. This is the philosophy leading to the cemetery—the rendezvous with death—in Belgium or elsewhere.

Those who assert that force is the only solvent of industrial and social ills ignore the history of social legislation and its wide achievements and possibilities. Morale is a basis of group life, and common counsel the mode of its achievement and expression. Constitutions, congresses, courts, and civil liberties are ways of reaching the goal of common consent—the soundest foundation for the superstructure of the modern state.

Those who assert that democracy cannot organize to meet the insistent demands for social change, for the recognition and adaptation of the new, and who therefore rely upon the sword within and without, ignore the essential nature of our modern difficulties. Our social, economic, technological, and philosophical problems are not capable of complete solution by brute force but require the exercise of the highest intelligence, the highest wisdom, the greatest patience and skill. Autocracy in regard to economic and social affairs is not an open road to a secure retreat from trouble.

The conclusion is that, under modern conditions in civilized states, it is easier for the many to maintain efficient administration with responsibility to the community than for the few to develop an autocracy that is at once socially efficient and a wise judge in its own cause. Either might maintain an effective administration, although autocracy has usually developed class administration, but in the field of political leadership the responsible choice of the mass is likely to be superior to the irresponsible choice of a few.

If great political messiahs emerge from time to time out of troubled periods, they may, perhaps, choose themselves and function in some crisis in the national life. But the followers of the great are seldom equally great, and their successors are better selected by the people they serve through some line of established responsibility. America has shown in Washington, Jefferson, Lincoln, Wilson, and Roosevelt the vast possibilities in the field of democratic leadership, ready for the darkest hours of national difficulty and for periods of peace and prosperity. The history of democracies is full of great men who rose and retired in the framework of popular organization and approval.

In the near future several factors, among them the following, will make the task of democracy easier than before.

1. *The emergence of superior forms of public administration.*—In earlier times administration was the creature and the servant of the autocrats—the Hohenzollerns, the Bourbons, the Stuarts—and was recruited from the few. But in our day it comes from the mass, is the tool of the mass, and stands at their service. Administration is not only the channel of continuing efficiency but also the open way for the influx of new scientific intelligence in the domain of social affairs. The bulk of government is administration. The new kind of administration will command not only the services of the old-time jurists but also the new-time scientists, educators, engineers, doctors, technical workers, and managers springing up on every side in modern communities and constantly recruited from the ranks of the people through a system of general education for all. Those who assert that democracy cannot utilize intelligence in its service are unmindful of the possibilities and actualities of modern civil service, as seen in England, Sweden, France, and elsewhere.

This is not to say that lawmaking agencies will not function. On the contrary, they will work more effectively than ever before. Lawmakers are greatest when they deal with general principles and policies and weakest when they enter into minor details and management.

Furthermore, the development of executive leadership—one of the great contributions of modern democracy to government—will make the task of mass politics easier than before. This form of organization has been most fully developed in the United States, but closely related systems are seen in the prime ministry of England and other countries. Through this type of organization it is possible to blend the elements of effective popular responsibility with those of unification of action, both in peace and in war. An executive of this type, resting on a genuine system of institutionalized responsibility, is a factor of vast strength in the future development of government. In wartime such an executive is able to deal effectively with the aggressiveness of military authorities, on the one hand, and the sensitivity of representative agencies, on the other, while maintaining the general framework of understandings and agencies in which mass rule is embodied. In peacetime he may provide the energetic leadership and power of co-ordination required for the development of constructive policies, for dealing effectively with vested interests resisting change for the common good, for application of policies determined by commonwealths. President Wilson is an example of war leadership and President Roosevelt of social leadership in an industrial emergency and of war leadership.

2. *The growth of education.*—Another factor of far-reaching significance in mass rule is the spread of universal education. Most of the time in the history of the world, most men have lived and died in ignorance, excluded by class or caste barriers from the circle of trained intelligence of their time. Reading, writing, and "schooling" were the marks of the gentleman and the ruling

class. As late as 1807 it was said on the floor of the House of Commons in England:

"However specious in theory the project might be of giving education to the labouring classes and the poor, it would, in effect, be prejudicial to their morals and happiness; it would teach them to despise their lot in life instead of making them good servants in agriculture, and other laborious employments to which their rank in society had destined them; instead of teaching them subordination, it would render them fractious and refractory .... it would enable them to read seditious pamphlets, vicious books, and publications against Christianity; it would render them insolent to their superiors; and in a few years, the result would be that the legislature would find it necessary to direct the strong arm of power toward them....."

Education will provide outlets for the discovery, the expression, and the realization of human capacities in a manner hitherto unknown, and it will equip the generality of the community with standards of, and equipment for, critical judgment on the basic policies and key personalities of the community. In the first stages of growth it is not unlikely that shallow and superficial education may serve as a basis for shallow judgment, but in the long run the general spread of intelligence through both formal and adult education will result in higher levels of appreciation, criticism, and judgment. The quality of education itself shifts from the traditional to the transitional and prospective point of view and to new forms of insight, appreciation, and capacity for adjustment.

3. *The emergence of the era of abundance.*—The vastly increased productivity of mankind fundamentally changes many aspects of human behavior. It particularly diminishes the role of fear and force in human relations and narrows the field of human domination through exclusive possession of some very limited commodity or utility. Land hunger, poverty, unemployment, and insecurity were the easy road to slavery and submission for centuries of human existence; the differentials in capacity were under these conditions readily magnified into wide disparities of political position and translated into terms of brutality and neglect. The philosophy of submission, instead of consent; the justification of brutality as a necessary mode of social discipline and integration; the rationalization of poverty and destitution as the inevitable burden of existence—all these now come out into a new domain where land and commodities are more abundant and where insecurity in the older sense lacks a reason for existence. This profoundly modifies the whole basis of human life, and makes the way far easier for the development and application of the doctrines of democracy. It is easier to be good neighbors when there is enough to go around.

4. *The emergence of industrialized democracy.*—The burdens of the democratic state will be easier to bear when the commonwealth performs avowedly and actively the function of validating the tenets of democracy—particularly that the gains of nations are essentiallly mass gains and should be distributed through the mass of the community as rapidly as possible. Modern democracy escaped from absolutism, which was established on the ruins of feudalism, only to fall foul of the snares of plutocracy from which it is difficult but not impossible to escape. The transition of modern democracy from a landed base to an industrial base has been a long and severe one; but as this crisis passes and industrialized democracy emerges, the strength of the mass position becomes clearer and stronger.

That a transformation is on its way is clear to anyone who observes the signs of the times; the increasing tempo of scientific invention and technology; the displacement of personnel and capital resulting therefrom; the disunity in social, economic, and political life and the ensuing trend toward mass integration and unity; the disjointed experiments in social legislation; and, finally, the emergence of central planning.

The type or types of association emerging cannot be predicted confidently by any responsible person; but the indications are that the units will be the nations, set in some jural order, and that the basic type of organization will be the rule of the many in one form or another. The precise form of this reorganization is far less important than the general principle, the common understanding regarding the goal.

The exchange of the values of liberty, equality, consent of the governed, rational discussion and persuasion for despotism, inequality, irresponsibility, the terror within and war without, anti-intellectualism, and shrill emotionalism is not a bargain in our time. The price is high, and there is no guaranty that the goods will be delivered.

The task of the modern state in readjusting its ways and means to the urgent demands of the new technology, to the new inventions in natural and social science, is a vast one; but there is every reason to believe that the problem may be solved within a reasonable period of time and within the general framework of free institutions. The shift from an economy largely agricultural to one largely industrial is fraught with many difficulties but in no sense impossible to accomplish within the limits of order, justice, liberty, equality, and consent.

The Jeremiahs are, in general, those who undervalue the capacity of the state for promoting the commonweal by the balance and integration of social forces within its area and people. Or, on the other hand, there are those who think of the state in terms of its primitive tools of force and violence. Thus the communists reject the state altogether, and the new autocrats deify the state. There is a zone of moderation between them in which the destiny of mankind will be worked out. Both rational analysis and broad long-run historical trends show that this zone is not that of absolutism and irresponsibility, of force and terror, but one of consent, discussion, persuasion, of expert knowledge under the general guidance of the common judgment.

5. *The growth of the more abundant life.*—Finally, the dawn of the creative role of mankind is just beginning to be dimly seen, as we observe that the bonds of tradition are being broken in many places and that the role of change in human affairs is being recognized in modern times. The opportunity before us is not merely that of adapting ourselves to necessary change but a prospect of constructively shaping the course of affairs and events. The new knowledge of the modern world not only enables us to avoid dangers. It is not enough to learn now to step aside from an automobile. We may control the conditions under which the traffic risks arise. The avoidance of death is the negative side; the positive is the growth of the more abundant life.

The weaknesses of democratic government, and they are many, are not in principle but in practice; not in its relation to the higher ends of government, to the common good for which governments exist, but in the details of programs attaining these ends. The equality of all men, the dignity of all men, the value of the consent of the governed as a principle of action—these are basic in democracy. They provide not only a foundation in practice but faith in the possibilities of the commonweal.

Of the many diseases of democracy—corruption, boss rule, demagogery, low-level interest in common affairs, immature susceptibility to foolish or cunning approaches to disaster—all are irritating and some are fatal. Many democracies have gone down or become only travesties of popular government.

Democracy is the best form of government yet devised by the brain of man. Some better type may yet be found, but it has not thus far been discovered. If there is no vivid appreciation of the common good and practical interest throughout the community in achieving it, the prospects for any good form of political rule is gone; while if these qualities and attitudes prevail, the community will then be likely to take care of the common good itself through some process of the consent of the government.

CONCLUSIONS

In the preceding paragraphs some of the implications of democracy have been traced in broad outline and in general principle. Particular policies and programs will vary widely with the special situations arising from time to time, but the general direction and trend will be of the broad type indicated.

The short-time program of democracy, based upon its assumptions, may be summed up with reasonable clearness in general terms. There is involved:

1. A positive social program including the guaranty of full employment, of economic stabilization and security, of increasing productivity with equitable

distribution of national gains; and a guaranty of minimum standards of living appropriate to our stage of civilization.

2. Adequate machinery to make democracy work, including suffrage and civil rights, the sharpening of legislative organization and objectives, the further development of public administration, attention to plan-making, and planning of national resources.

3. The development of a system of jural order in the world, maintained by force if necessary, through which war may be outlawed as an instrument of national policy by some effective form of understanding or association and, in the interim, more intelligent adjustment of the relations between the organization of violence and the organization of consent in commonwealths.

4. Faith in democracy's political ideals with (a) greater stress upon human values in the larger sense and (b) greater emphasis on the broad possibilities in the coming era of abundance.

Democracy's program must conform to the newer ideals and possibilities of our new day. It must guarantee a fair share of the vast gains of civilization, material and higher, to members of the democratic society if it is to survive under modern conditions. It must validate the assumptions of democracy in the everyday life of the community.[20]

CHAPTER VI

FORMAL AND INFORMAL GOVERNMENT

ORGANIZED government is always accompanied by much less highly organized forms of political participation, ranging from the somewhat formal to the highly informal, from the quasi-governmental, such as the political party, to the diffuse influences of public opinion. This is not a new situation but one of the very oldest in government. In primitive groups it often happened that formal control and custom were difficult to separate. The rulers, indeed, might merely declare the custom to be the rule. And even with more highly developed systems of social organization, custom might be regarded as law, as in the Confucian system, where the law was looked upon as the personal declaration of the existing customs;[1] and in all systems custom may become law.

The same social need that gave birth to central authority also produced a set of attitudes and observances, institutionalized or otherwise, which operate to diffuse and condition authority in many different but effective ways. The social situation that sets up authority sets up the conditions on which authority is

---

[20] This study is a discussion of democracy in generalized terms only. Special comment on the trends and program of democracy in the United States is reserved for another study.

[1] See Lin Mou-shêng, *Men and Ideas* (1942).

212

exercised. This is true no matter what the form of government may be or how autocratic and irresistible the bearer of authority may appear to be. In our own time political parties are in part organized agencies of government, at times very highly developed and in fact recognized as parts of the government as in the United States of America, while public opinion is solid in its effects but tenuous in its organization. In Russia, Germany, and Italy the party became in effect the government.

These various types of informal government shade into each other and overlap at many points. For purposes of this discussion I am examining basic understandings, resistance and revolution, bills of rights, public opinion, voting and parties, public and private government—in all of which there is participation in the governing process by persons not formally recognized as responsible parts of the regular government.

I. BASIC UNDERSTANDINGS

At the base of any system there is a broad body of attitudes and understandings regarding the nature and limits of authority within the given state. These understandings may be implicit in the practices and conventions of the group behavior pattern, or they may be explicit in written documents such as constitutions, fundamental agreements, and charters in which are written down the general understandings regarding the nature of subordination, superordination, and co-ordination in the political community. Special machinery may be set up for the purpose of making the understandings effective, but the understandings are more important than the mechanism.[2] The nature of these understandings will vary widely with the history and culture of the political community, the degree of political consciousness and interest, the capacity for internal and external relationships of a political nature, and the special skills of management and co-operation.

Ranging over the modern world, to say nothing of the earlier years of human history, these understandings and their implementation have an enormously wide spread of possible and actual variation. At the root of all authority, however primitive, lie basic customs which authority cannot successfully contest. The political "conventions" are a part of the social conventions upon which the whole society rests.[3]

In early forms of government these political understandings are not written or very explicit. They are in the nature of traditions handed down from one generation to another as a part of the wisdom of the elders. The details of these understandings may not be generally known or clearly understood; they may

[2] See my *The Written Constitution and the Unwritten Attitude* (1931).

[3] See W. C. MacLeod, *The Origin and History of Politics* (1931); R. H. Lowie, *The Origin of the State* (1927); Gunnar Landtman, *The Origin of the Inequality of the Social Classes* (1938).

be veiled in secrecy and ritual, religious or secular. What is important is the general understanding that there are such fundamentals of political behavior and that there is someone to interpret them and apply them as occasion requires. Dimly, perhaps, these understandings are related to the general purposes of government, checked by simple terms characterizing the conduct of governors, as just or unjust, weak or strong, good or bad. Formalized codes of laws develop later in innumerable forms—the Code of Hammurabi, Solon's laws, Chinese and Indian collections of maxims and understandings. These in turn lead to the formulation of great monuments such as the Roman law in Justinian's *Digest*. In modern times there comes a long series of codes and fundamental laws of many widely differing types. These early formulations often deal largely with codes of behavior as between individuals with relatively little emphasis on the state, but, as time went on, this was changed. In the course of time, constitutions appeared with formal statements of the rights and duties fundamental in the community, with what is called "constitutional custom" alongside the written texts.

The problem of "understandings" is not at bottom merely that of a legalistic formula but a psychological problem. What are the command, obedience, cooperation, and consent attitudes of the persons in the particular society under consideration? Little such material is at present available and may not be found for a long time to come, until psychology and anthropology have done their more perfect work; and, of course, one might say, until the students of government have provided us with better patterns of political behavior.

Civic cohesion and propulsion are not based upon rational analyses and conclusions alone but upon impulses and instincts. But the sum total of behavior is included in the political view, whether rational or nonrational. Both enter into the formation of what we have called custom, or into the custom of the constitution. The discovery of Pareto that there is logical and nonlogical behavior is not newer than the dawn of history. The mother of any family could have supplied him with the same information based upon her observation, experience, and experiment.

Any observer is aware that some men are more rationally inclined than others and that political processes must be arranged accordingly; but the political observer also understands that the high I.Q. in intelligence may have little correlation with political I.Q. Pareto himself is a witness of the truth of this, for his intelligence did not protect him from naïveté and absurdity in the realm of the political.

But it must be noted that if we are aiming at an appraisal of the political process, the general understanding is more important than the form in which it is embodied, whether written or unwritten. The unwritten constitution is full of meaning for the student of political behavior. These basic understandings are rooted deep not only in the political life of the people but also in its economic and social life; they are the attitudes, expectancies, and reactions which characterize the mass of the community, or of the politically conscious and alert in the community, and will determine its course of action from year to year.

To misunderstand the understandings is the greatest fault a political leader may have and will destroy him if he persists. This is not to say that general understandings may not be changed or modified but that adaptation must be in the general tone of the community, unless, indeed, the movement is a revolutionary one. Even so, revolutions are usually directed against a limited series of abuses and evils, assuming that these abuses and evils violate a pattern upon which there has been agreement.

The democratic revolutions of recent times, the communistic revolutions, and the Fascist revolutions were all obliged to break with important lines of general understanding; but in all these instances there was an appeal to rights and claims which were violated by the political system against which the attack was directed.[4]

The whole problem is enormously complicated when, in addition to bringing about more narrowly political understandings, there is added the load of ethnic differences, religious differences, and economic class differences. It was said of the Austro-Hungarian situation: "Elsewhere the descendent has an easy task in entering the heritage of the fathers because it contains a single will and a uniform sense. In us, however, shout a hundred voices of the past, the struggle of the fathers is not settled, each must decide it anew, each must choose among his fathers, each must for himself pass through the entire past again."[5] When we consider the tangled skein of allegiances and loyalties in any political community, the marvel is that general agreement may be found on any large body of central directives generally accepted by the bulk of the community.

What do we understand by an understanding? It is possible to analyze these understandings more specifically by breaking them down in the light of the ends of government, of the social composition of civic cohesion, and of the instruments of the state for support of its policies. How do these understandings fit in with the general principles and types indicated in these classifications of fundamental aspects of political behavior? How are they related to security, order, justice, freedom, and welfare; how are they related to the component social elements of the society in which they operate, and how are they related to the basic implements of the political society in effectuating the will of the community? All this will not reduce the understanding to the precision of a formula, but it will help clarify the problem.

[4] See my *The Making of Citizens* (1931), pp. 128–45, on traditions in civic training.

[5] Cited by Oscar Jászi, *The Dissolution of the Habsburg Monarchy* (1929), p. 130.

215

Modern statistical techniques, modern techniques of psychology, recent insights into social and cultural relationships, a vast mass of accumulated social data—all these are increasingly available to provide clearer understandings of trends and indicate alternative lines of action more surely than ever before. Without such guides the visibility is very low and the prospects for social planning are very poor.[6]

II. RESISTANCE

The validity of general understandings is enforceable by resistance and revolution. With rulers controlling every known implement of power in the state, nevertheless from nowhere arise the forces that bring authority to book. "How can this be?" the authoritarians cry. And the historians spin the tale for posterity, showing how the mask of power had become the cover for futility. Nowhere are there more dramatic tales in history than in the accounts of falling rulers, fleeing from every emblem of their own authority as from the pestilence itself. But, long before revolution is reached, we come upon the evidences of resistance.[7] Some of its indicia are: low level deference, with grumbling, sabotage, sulkiness; organized disobedience without violence; organized nonco-operation without open disobedience—and then we come upon organized resistance. (Revolution is discussed in chap. vii.)

In more recent times the techniques of resistance have been developed more fully than ever before. In the industrial field the strike, in many forms from the intermittent to the general strike, has been invoked as a means of protest against the conduct of the employers or of the governors at times. Sabotage has been utilized effectively to cripple or obstruct the complicated machinery of production. Notably in the recent war, saboteurs have played a vital role.[8]

The broader freedom of speech, press, and association has made possible many new methods of indicating dissatisfaction with the powers that be and their ways. This might always be done through the agency of gossip, but the modern methods of communication have very greatly increased the possibilities of such resistance to the acts of authority. In the last five years the chronicles have been filled with the history of the underground in many lands—in Norway, in Holland, in Belgium, in France, in Poland, in Yugoslavia, in overpowered countries of many types and against the serious efforts of a well-

[6] Of special value are the analyses made by James Bryce, Graham Wallas, and Max Weber and studies of the anthropologists in the area of the primitive. My series on *The Making of Citizens* (1931) develops data on this subject in several states.

[7] See the chapter on "The Poverty of Power," in my *Political Power* (1934).

[8] I have discussed this topic in my *Political Power* in chapters dealing with "The Shame of Power," "The Survival of the Fittest," and "The Morbidity and Mortality of Power." See also Pitirim A. Sorokin, *The Sociology of Revolution* (1925); Lyford P. Edwards, *The Natural History of Revolution* (1927); George S. Pettee, *The Process of Revolution* (1938); Leon Trotsky, *History of the Russian Revolution* (1932).

organized and resourceful conqueror. Again and again the helpless have baffled and thwarted the mighty in incredible ways. Newspapers were published and circulated, radios operated, and guerrilla bands were active behind the lines. The fifth column has become another of the resources upon which military leaders may count at times.

The nonco-operation of Gandhi and his followers has been successful in paralyzing wide ranges of industrial and political activity in India.[9] Gandhi, the Hindu, trained in the theories of Tolstoy, in the doctrines of Jesus and Buddha, in the English school of law, and in the hard school of practical experience in South Africa and India, evolved elaborate and refined methods of nonco-operation. Among the more striking of the special forms of protest were: wholesale submission to arrest, as in South Africa, and the consequent flooding of the prisons; wholesale evasion of the salt tax; refusal to accept office under British rule; days of fasting designed as mass protests against the prevailing power group; boycott of British textile industry by use of the spinning wheel; and the use of the hunger strike (employed on other occasions, however). These devices may be summed up in what is termed "soul force," by which is meant the use of moral pressure against physical force or violence—the conquest of the lower through the higher nature. These constitute an elaborate and in many ways effective system of what may be called "civil disobedience" within the borders of legality. The ingenuity with which these measures have been devised and the magnitude of the support accorded them have been puzzling in the extreme to the powers that be. Here again, however, the employment of crass violence only strengthens the impression of solidarity which these very policies are designed to foster and reinforce and in a sense drives the barb more deeply in.[10]

Of passive resistance, Gandhi says: "Its equivalent in the vernacular, rendered into English, means Truth-Force. I think Tolstoy called it also Soul-Force or Love-Force, and so it is. Carried out to its utmost limit, this force is independent of pecuniary or other material assistance; certainly, even in its elementary form, of physical force or violence. Indeed, violence is the negation of this great spiritual force, which can only be cultivated or wielded by those who will entirely eschew violence."[11]

The range of possibilities in this direction is very great and has never been thoroughly explored even by the most adventurous student of tactics or of political organization. The opportunities are as wide as the sphere of social relations, including sex, the social amenities, religious relations, business contacts, sport

[9] See my chapter in *Political Power* on "Abnegation and the Road to Power"; Richard B. Gregg, *The Power of Non-violence* (1934).

[10] Mahatma Gandhi, *Sermon on the Sea* (1924), chap. xvi: "Brute Force"; chap. xvii: "Passive Resistance."

[11] *Mahatma Gandhi, His Life, Writings and Speeches* (1923), pp. 95–96.

217

relations, and recreation generally; in short, the caste situation reversed by the pariahs as against their masters.

The continuing will to resist, however, may not be present. Leaders may be won over, the fainter-hearted may give up, the fearful may yield to force; and the counterpropagandas and counterpressures of the power groups themselves may wear away the attitude and the behavior pattern which began so bravely.

Just as the official who attempts to exercise power outside the field in which he "belongs" may encounter difficulty, so the resistant who has back of him no large social interest which he reflects or represents, or who is not skilful in his devices, will find himself in a difficult position. Instead of appearing as a social benefactor or a martyr, he may find himself classified as a common nuisance, deserted and derided by his friends, while he is punished by his foes.[12] Neither the arrogance of the unrepresentative official nor the impudence of the unrepresentative resistant is any guaranty in itself of a successful outcome, for the group is not primarily interested in either and, indeed, looks upon them both as excrescences upon the body politic.

It may be noted, however, that "civil disobedience" is a phenomenon of private as well as of public government. In the family, in the school, in the church, and in industry methods of neutralizing authority may be found in profusion. One may see children at a very immature age finding ingenious ways and means of evading the rigors of parental discipline. Overworked or discontented slaves have lines of protest. Prisoners even may strike, and workers of high and lowly status may defy and obstruct the policies of authority. It is not necessary to disobey; a literal execution of a wrong order may be even more successful as a protest.

Thus it is clear that there is a wide range of consent of the governed, even when there appears on the surface no such possibility, so fundamental and universal is the feeling that authority must unite justice with force in human relations.

III. MIGHT AND RIGHT—THE RIGHTS OF MAN

That there is right outside of legal right has long been the standing trouble of the formalists and the strict authoritarians who find their support in the letter of the law and the technical authenticity of authority. But the basis of authority lies outside formal government in judgments and conclusions reached through other than legal channels. These conclusions spring not alone from moral values of the higher type but from political values not included in the current scheme of authority at a given time. This may be termed the "range of political ethics," but in truth these values are reached by observations and reflections largely within the field of politics and government. They are

[12] Henrik Ibsen, *An Enemy of the People* (1882).

idealisms which can never be understood by limiting the view to formal institutions of the established type.

The most notable and effective expression of these extra-governmental political values is seen in the rights of man, at first only assertions or unorganized claims, but later taking on more systematized shape in bills of rights. These were in part bills of wrongs for which there seemed to be no remedy in the existing system, but which nevertheless possessed validity of their own, in their own right, so to speak, whether recognized by existing law or not. The shaping and custody of these rights have been assumed from time to time by representatives of established religion, by moralists as such, by philosophers, by jurists, sometimes by revolutionaries from without the walls and sometimes by liberals from within the walls. But right without might was their central theme—and how to unite right and might in a formula of co-operative authority.

In the course of time broad and general understandings as to the nature and limits of authority are supplemented by more institutional developments. Here are included the rights of man in the theoretical sense, the civil rights of men expressed in law. Later came the ballot, the party, and the growth of public opinion. In all these developments there was inevitably much overlapping and confusion of pattern but always a sense of direction which was unmistakable.

What should be or ought to be is often despised by authoritarians, but no student of politics will fail to accord to the idealistic demands of men their proper place in the evolution and operation of governmental affairs. The urge of the human personality for expression and recognition is clearly outlined by observation, experience, and reflection as a basic factor in political relations. Government is a device designed for the attainment of security, order, justice, welfare, and freedom, and ceases to have any warrant for existence to the extent that these ends are turned away from rights. Political faith and hope have their place in governmental affairs, and the authoritarian who overlooks them builds upon the sand. Even on the level of manipulation alone as a characterization of the political, faith and hope are also instruments of manipulation and action, dynamics in war and peace alike.

From time immemorial the rights of man derived from the law of nature, from Christianity, from human experience, observation, and reflection, and have been a refuge against human authority. These rights have provided an altar to which men might flee, a rallying cry for resistance to tyranny or oppression or against officialism in its worst forms. When law and force and even custom provide no last defense for the human person, he may still appeal outside the law to his claims upon humanity. In the darkest hours of the desolation of destruction, rights are not obscured; they may shine the more brightly in the gloom.

As time went on, these rights were brought together in more systematic form. They found their way into the Roman law; they flowered in the natural law when almost forgotten by governments; they became the basis of revolutionary movements against absolute despotism and the cornerstone of constitutional democracies everywhere.

Over many centuries it has been contended that these rights are not true "rights" and have no validity in the governmental field. It has been said that there never was a historical "state of nature" in which such human rights existed prior to the establishment of civil government, that such alleged rights have no efficiency without legal enforceability, and that they possess no special value for political understanding.

But both reflection and experience show that these rights of man have increasing value. Their foundation rests in the rational nature of the human personality. The validity of these claims of human nature is not dependent upon the particular interpretation or application given by a particular agent of authority at a given time, important as this may be practically, but upon the rational and historical value of the human claim in the framework of advancing civilization. They are an affirmation of the value of the ends of government, an assertion of confidence in the principles upon which all political associations rest in last analysis. That rights have not yet been fully realized does not take them from the field of the political, for politics deals with ideals as well as with realities. Ideals, indeed, are themselves realities.

These broad rights of man are, of course, a part of a far-reaching system of customs and emerging procedures for enforcement. In a sense they are generalizations from long-established customs or idealizations of ancient practices projected toward fuller and finer realization. They rest upon experience and observation as well as upon reason and faith. Long-established custom, prolonged adjudication, and violent revolution are all involved in the evolution of human rights in various political systems. In parallel courses in my day we studied comparative jurisprudence, on the one hand, and the philosophy of law, on the other, and the interplay between them; both, of course, to the accompaniment of the history of legal, political, and social institutions.

It cannot escape notice that rights are not only claims against the community or the state but also claims against other individuals or groups with demands for protection by the state if necessary. The person demands protection for his property or his person, his set of values in life as a right to be enforced by the power of the state if required. In this way rights are not merely counterbalances to the centralization and integration of political power but also tend to strengthen and protect the just agency of authority. Hence the rights of man are not antistatist but look to an interpenetration of community and individual position and prestige.

This is all the more true, since the individual cannot assert a claim against others without admitting at the same time a similar obligation under like circumstances. There cannot be a society of persons who have rights but no corresponding obligations. Thus a system of rights, while providing forms of protection against unjust authority, at the same time provides for interrelation of rights and responsibilities. But this is the very texture from which political association is itself made up. In protecting the rights of the personality, the political society protects itself and performs the very function for which it is set up and on the basis of which its existence is justified.

While this process is most clearly institutionalized and observable in the political society, it may also be seen in other social organizations—religious, economic, cultural—in which rights and duties are developed and maintained. In the canon law, in guild law, in corporation law and practice, in educational and cultural organizations, the same process is at work, operating on much the same general basis.

In the course of time these protective procedures began to be organized in formal fashion with agencies more and more elaborate, slowly constructed for the purpose of protecting the citizen against another citizen, or against the state. This list came to include the right to a legal personality and status, trial by jury, and special writs and remedies against arbitrary procedure. These observances came to be called a body of civil liberties, and their enforcement was vested in special agencies—the courts of law. With more direct bearing upon the nature of authority came the special rights covered under freedom of speech, freedom of the press, freedom of religion, and freedom of association. These rights were designed to insure conditions under which the citizen might maintain the consent of the governed, without which authority might not express the common good.

Forms of adjudicating and adjusting the claims of individuals against each other and against the government have been established from time immemorial, and from very early times there were ways and means by which the head of the state might be called in question at the behest of his subjects, particularly in the domain of property and personal rights. In general, neither life nor property nor person could be seized and commandeered without regard to the prevailing customs of the group, whatever it might be. Magic, taboos, and religion surrounded and protected the humblest in his domain.[13]

For those approaching the top of the hierarchy the degree of consideration was much less sharply defined. The remedies, to be sure, were not always strictly juristic but might be achieved by violence and revolution, as when the Greek king invited his subject to dine on the subject's son. The barriers of sex, slavery, and private property possessions were always present, however feebly defended at times. The absoluteness of absoluteness is always likely to be exaggerated, for the custom of criticism and challenge grows rapidly.

The mere writing of these declarations in a document, however, has little value unless there is to be found the custom and the will to make the guaranties

---

[13] See MacLeod, *op. cit.*

effective in practical affairs. Freedom of speech, freedom of the press, freedom of religion, and freedom of association mean nothing if they are not really or readily available to the citizen.

The most notable collection of human rights is that of the American Declaration of Independence. "We hold these truths to be self-evident: that all men are created equal; that they are endowed by their Creator with certain unalienable Rights; that among these are Life, Liberty and the pursuit of Happiness .... to secure these rights, Governments are instituted among Men, deriving their just powers from the consent of the governed,"[14] with the right of revolution as the ultimate appeal. With this we may compare the French Declaration of the Rights of Man and Citizen (1791) and a wide range of modern constitutions.[15]

In the Atlantic Charter these rights took the additional form of freedom from fear, freedom from want, along with freedom of worship and of press.[16] President Roosevelt declared further (1944):

"We have come to a clear realization of the fact that true individual freedom cannot exist without economic security and independence. 'Necessitous men are not free men.' People who are hungry and out of a job are the stuff of which dictatorships are made.

"In our day these economic truths have become accepted as self-evident. We have accepted, so to speak, a second bill of rights, under which a new basis of security and prosperity can be established for all—regardless of station, race, or creed.

"Among these are:

"The right to a useful and remunerative job in the industries, or shops, or farms, or mines of the nation;

"The right to earn enough to provide adequate food and clothing and recreation;

"The right of every farmer to raise and sell his products at a return which will give him and his family a decent living;

"The right of every businessman, large and small, to trade in an atmosphere of freedom from unfair competition and domination by monopolies at home or abroad;

"The right of every family to a decent home;

[14] See George Jellinek, *The Declaration of the Rights of Man and of Citizens* (rev. ed., 1901); Beardsley Ruml, *Unfinished Business* (1943); my *On the Agenda of Democracy* (1941), chap. v, p. 99; Georges Gurvitch, *La Déclaration des droits sociaux* (1944).

[15] See also bills of rights in state constitutions in my *A History of American Political Theories* (1931).

[16] See National Resources Planning Board, *National Resources Development—Report for 1943*, Part I: *Post-war Plan and Program* (1943), p. 3.

"The right to adequate medical care and the opportunity to achieve and enjoy good health;

"The right to adequate protection from the economic fears of old age, sickness, accident, and unemployment;

"The right to a good education.

"All of these rights spell security. And after this war is won we must be prepared to move forward, in the implementation of these rights, to new goals of human happiness and well-being.

"America's own rightful place in the world depends in large part upon how fully these and similar rights have been carried into practice for our citizens. For unless there is security here at home, there cannot be lasting peace in the world."

There is also in process of formulation an international bill of rights in the light of international law as developing in our day. This would set up a series of rights to which all men are entitled and which would be enforced by an international jural authority, through diplomacy, national legislation and adjudication, and international and world jurisdiction.[17] (See chap. viii.)

The rights of man provide the domain of faith and hope in government, the court of appeal which is never closed, the law beyond the law and the jurists, the lawmakers, the managers, and the adjudicators. Friend of all outlawed persons and groups, the rights of man are claimed and acclaimed by many from time to time and again rudely silenced and repressed. The institutionalized friends of the rights of man may be as dangerous at times as their friends; the ecclesiasts may insist upon their own authentic interpretations of rights, invoking the supernatural; the jurists may entrap rights in their mechanisms for purposes of vested wrong and defy conflicting interpretations by the outlaws; the formalism of political right may strangle substance by form and exalt the strictly formal against the human side of living. Philosophy and morality, caught in a context of vested interests, may come to their rescue. But the rights of man go deeper down and higher up than institutional devices for interpreting or applying them, whether religious, juristic, economic, moralistic, philosophical, or other. They illustrate the recurring poverty of power which is the hope of freedom in all times.

IV. PUBLIC OPINION

Public opinion comes in to supplement what have been characterized as "understandings." What are these early conventions, customs, and understandings but public opinion, however crudely and slowly formulated? Trivial custom might change slowly and imperceptibly, and its interpretation might rest in the hands of special experts who were perhaps not conscious that they

[17] Cf. Quincy Wright, *Human Rights and the World Order* (1943). See below, chap. viii.

223

were making new rules of the game. Nor was the group aware of the making of a new rule or variation of the old rule.

For centuries means of communication and transportation were slow, general education was uncommon, and much of public business was veiled in secrecy, either from necessity, as in war, or from proprietary pride of the talent who possessed the lore of government and were not disposed to share it with many others. But still there was room for general group opinion.

With the dawn of higher intelligence and with the rise of group consciousness, the ways and means of control over the integration of authority and political personnel became more and more obvious. Those who were to obey discovered methods of baffling those who were to command, and those who were to command began to study methods of holding their subjects in check. The technical devices for securing diffusion of power and for reviewing and restraining rulers are more readily seen, but the slow massing of elements of direction, outside organized forms, are more difficult to observe accurately.

Aristotle early discovered the values in mass judgment which he set down as one of the strong points of the democratic system which relied upon the validity of such judgments. The Roman system gave lip service and sometimes more to the basic reliance upon the popular origins of law, but rights were made explicit in formal fashion rather than through the more intangible mass opinion. Indeed, it may be said that the rising emphasis upon formal restraints on authority often tended to distract attention from the informal restraints which had long existed and still continued to operate behind the scenes.

In the long-drawn-out struggle between the absolute monarchs and the mass of their peoples, heavy weight was given to natural law, natural rights, and the right of revolution as counters to the divine right of kings and the legalists' version of juristic sovereignty and immemorial custom. The absolutists cried down the people, the public, as from one point of view an unreality, an artificial person, and from another point of view adverted to the inevitable ignorance and incompetence of the mass—the group which Hegel declared "knows not what it wants." The group was thus depicted as unreal and incompetent. Custom, history, and tradition were now appropriated by the established regime for its own authoritarian purposes and defense.

Custom was invoked by Burke, Savigny, and others to sustain hereditary rule, nobility, feudalism, and, in general, the interests of those in the seats of power. Customary law was invoked, for illustration, as against the artificial law of constitutions—made to order, it was said. The great struggle over codification of law was carried on by conservative defenders of customary law as against the radical demands for conscious remaking of the law in modern terms. It must be noted, however, that the English common law was more adaptable to the changing circumstances of the time, introducing significant changes along the way.[18] But Rousseau's championship of the "general will" appeared as a basis of democracy.

In no area has there been more concentrated and bitter attack upon democratic rule than in the sector involving the formation of mass judgment upon questions of public policy. Beginning with Plato and Aristotle, with Buddhist and Brahman, this controversy has been continued for over two thousand years. It has been maintained that there is not and cannot be any informed body of judgment in the mass from which we really get enlightened and continuing judgment. Incompetence and irrationality, it is maintained, are the characteristic and ineffable marks of the mass and the unmistakable cue for the entrance of the few who inevitably must intervene to provide the essential leadership. Mass rule is mob rule, it is asserted; what can the mass know or what policy can it originate or identify as well as could the *expertise?*[19] Tariffs, currency, treaties, budgets, regulation of industry, health and education; what can the mass know of these topics that would help in the solution of the group problem?

It has been held that the social group has no real existence, except as an artificial person, *persona ficta,* and consequently cannot be a subject of authority or responsibility. In our own day Hayek has declaimed against the dangers of "conscious social control"—to him the very definition of unreason and anarchy.[20]

In so far as these arguments are not merely the slogans of the power-hungry, they rest upon inadequate knowledge of the trends and possibilities of emerging modern organization and management as well as upon ignorance of the psychology of the many. The vast and rapidly accumulating mass of data bearing upon economic and social problems can be analyzed and digested in our time as never before and made available to the partisans of various causes. The division of governmental labor following modern lines of simplification, as in England or the United States, enables the citizen to make broad choices in personnel and policy, through which broad direction may be obtained. Modern means of communication and transportation make possible the dissemination of information and ideas in incredibly short time. In the slow-moving systems of a thousand years ago, perhaps no one knew what happened one hundred miles away; today the flash will reveal almost instantly what goes on around the world if need be. There is, therefore, no sound reason why the mass cannot be informed on the progress of events and pass broad judgments upon them through the electoral process from time to time.

The systematic study of popular psychology began only at a later time, de-

---

[18] See Sir Frederick Pollock, *The Genius of the Common Law* (1912).

[19] Walter Lippmann, *Public Opinion* (1922).

[20] Friedrich Hayek, *The Road to Serfdom* (1944).

225

veloping chiefly in the field of sociological inquiry. The methods of approach, the data accumulated, the analyses made, and the conclusions derived are all of great importance in appraising the force of public opinion in relation to the diffusion of authority.[21] These inquiries have ranged over a wide field, from anthropology to social psychology, to psychiatry and psychoanalysis, attacking the problem from many widely scattered points of view, in terms of races, groups, classes, nations, individual persons, and frustrations, personal and group. Gumplowicz, Ratzenhofer, Tarde, Le Bon, Durkheim, Sombart, Simmel, Ross, Lasswell, and many others have dug into the underlying secrets of crowd or mass psychology, endeavoring to fathom its mysteries and determine its laws.[22] The recent developments of Nazi and Fascist political theories and practice have stimulated another series of inquiries into the nature of the mass over which leadership is to be exerted. Nazi theorists tended to fall back upon *Gemeinschaft*—a *Blut und Boden* type—which requires the guidance of a *Führer* in order to fulfil its destiny.

Many of these inquiries have appreciably added to the understanding of the problem, but the multifarious aspects of public opinion, baffling to trained sociologists, and the varied approaches to the broad subject have made progress slow in this sector. Le Bon struggled with the psychology of particular nations, not very successfully on the whole. Others have dealt with mobs, crowds, and mass phenomena of many types in the pursuit of the higher understandings. Psychoanalysts interpret the mass in terms of their special approach to understanding through "identification" of the many in the form of symbolism in which expectancies and demands play their important role. Lippmann has questioned the existence, or validity if existing, of public opinion, preferring special group opinions, which, of course, may be broken down again.

On the whole, there is yet broad room for improvement in our technical knowledge of public opinion. But, for the immediate purposes of this inquiry, there is no doubt of the significance of this social force, unorganized yet active, in controlling the direction of the political association. Difficult and elusive though it may be in scientific study, the practical force of something called "public opinion" is of indubitable importance—whether regarded as a unit or as a congeries of groups of opinion and interest.

The manipulation of mass opinion has been a favorite device of power-seekers for centuries, playing upon every impulse and interest of the body politic, whether rational or irrational, high or low. The power-hungry have declared, and sometimes believed, that they could reflect the interests and will of the community more accurately and effectively than through election or

[21] See C. E. Merriam and H. E. Barnes (eds.), *A History of Political Theories: Recent Times* (1924), chap. x, on "Social Psychology and Political Theory"; F. W. Coker, *Organismic Theories of the State* (1910).

[22] Lippmann, *op. cit.*; John Dewey, *The Public and Its Problems* (1927).

like process. Hitler maintained that he personally was a more useful representative of the German people than any representative body chosen by the mass and, with the techniques of violence and propaganda, undertook to establish his regime.

In the consideration of informal governments, public opinion is clearly established as a political force of prime significance, to be reckoned with under all modern systems of political association. Neither the formal organs of government, including the legislative, nor elective executives, nor judges on the bench, nor the private pressure groups, however strongly rooted, nor the political parties, semigovernmental and semiprivate, are able to brush aside or to stand against the force of a public opinion fully aroused and dynamized. Public opinion tends to be an agency for the expression of the common judgment regarding the common good, cutting across the lines of formalized institutions at times, recruiting its strength from nowhere apparently, yet projecting its force often irresistibly. What happens in these instances is the formation of a common denominator derived from many elements, a common rallying point for the expression of rights and wrongs, of policies and programs, common to the participants.

Public opinion thus supplies a check on the excesses and extravagances of guildism, using this as a term to cover many forms of interest groupings, on the one hand, and of formalized government, on the other. Demagogues and charlatans may utilize this agency at times, but by and large it is an instrument for statesmanship and intelligence. In a democratic society this corrective is invaluable in maintaining participation in power on the part of those who are in the society but not of the government.

V. VOTING AND PARTIES

Voting and parties are more fully formalized and institutionalized and might well be treated as parts of government. The voter is not in continuous action, but the political party does not adjourn; and in some jurisdictions, as in Nazi Germany and in Russia, the party is the government in reality.

The origins of the technique of voting go back a long way in human history. Voting with black and white balls, voting with shells, viva voce voting, show of hands, rising voting, open voting, secret voting, machine voting, electrical voting—all these and other related methods have been utilized.[23] In some early phases of development the ballot was closely linked with choice by lot. Chance was early looked upon as a form of choice, in which the selection was really made by some outside superforce or superfate. Selection by lot was not uncommon and, indeed, is still found in some situations. In this sense the use of lot was not far removed from the determination of courses of action by

[23] See Harold F. Gosnell on "Ballot" in the *Encyclopaedia of the Social Sciences* and the bibliography there cited.

reading the signs and auspices, by oracles, prophets, and the like, in many varying types in different cultural patterns. The experts were able, it was thought, to interpret the will of the superpowers through signs obscure to most men but discernible by the wise ones. Later there came to be forms of selection in which lot and vote were combined into a double system of lot and choice. It still happens, to be sure, that, in case of a tie vote, lot may determine the choice.

The vote is a standardized instrument for participation in authority. Voting is a symbol of participation in decisions of all groups, political and otherwise. When a community arrives at a point where violence may be replaced by forms of balloting, a substantial gain in orderly procedure has been made. From time immemorial the vote has been a symbol of willingness to take part in proceedings and to agree to the conclusions of those participating—whether by majority, by extraordinary majority, or by unanimity. But votes taken without any binding decision, merely as advisory, have their value.

In early times mass voting might be little more than an expression of assent or dissent, evidenced by volume of noise in approval or disapproval. Viva voce voting continues in special instances to this day in deliberative bodies, in town meetings, or like mass meetings, and as a regular practice in some areas.[24]

We may now consider (1) what the general significance of the ballot is; (2) who are included in the circle of voters and on what principle; and (3) to what phases of state activity the vote is adapted, i.e., what is votable?

1. We do not understand very well the early meaning of the vote. Was the vote counted or weighed? Was the superior vote an index of physical superiority, of the preponderance of judgment and wisdom? Was it an indication of what the ruler could count upon in the way of material and military support, of men and morale, of enthusiasm or lack of it, to be spelled out later? Or to what extent was the vote a mode of determining the will of the superpowers or the voice of the people as the voice of God? It is significant that, with the rise of democratic systems, the vote becomes generalized and also equal, as distinguished from a limited franchise or a ballot weighted in favor of the few. This is a fact of far-reaching importance in the organization of consent of the governed and in the direction of the recognition of the dignity of man.

In systems where the broad outlines of the general welfare are determined by the bulk of the community, the vote is the symbol of participation in the organization of consent. It marks the recognition of the dignity of man, of his importance as a part of the process of government, of his membership in the community. The vote is a part of the process of consent, a claim of the citizen against the community—a claim which may or may not be recognized. The minor terms and conditions of voting will, of course, be subject to various forms of local regulation, wise or otherwise, in their design and application. Votes

[24] On "Voting" see the *Encyclopaedia of the Social Sciences*.

may be weighed or loaded in accordance with some system or other, for there are many such devices in history and in operation, as in a three-class system, proportional voting, or in some method of indirect election.

2. Speaking broadly, the dictum above stated requires the inclusion in the electorate of all the mature citizens of the given community, without regard to race, sex, property, religion, or other exclusive requirements. Viewing historical experience, however, this has not been the range of voting, but various restrictions have been laid down from place to place and from time to time. The early democracies, including the United States and Britain, long restricted the electorate, on one ground or another, to a small minority of the citizens. Race, sex, and property played an important role in all the heated discussions upon the vexed question of the circle of voters, even in a democracy; and they continue down to the present at one point and another. Restrictions based upon maturity, residence, sanity, and minimum intelligence are, of course, of a different category, in detail open to long-drawn-out discussion.

In general, it is fair to say that the lines of cleavage have often been drawn with regard to the special or vested interests of holders of power reluctant to give it up and with prediction of dire consequences if the electorate was broadened. In the abolition of property and sex requirements this trend was particularly evident, but it is also clear in discussions over race relations that the dignity of man is not as often the dominant consideration as is the prestige of the upper group.

3. To what aspects of state activity is the ballot most clearly applicable? "What is justiciable?" the lawyers ask. "What is votable?" the statesmen may inquire. The broad answer is easier than the detailed application of it. Broadly speaking, the vote is applied to such participation as is necessary for the preservation of the ends of the state: security, order, justice, freedom, and welfare for human personalities.

This calls for the installation and review of such personnel, measures, and means as are essential to these purposes. Obviously this does not involve the election of all officials or a vote upon all measures, for this would defeat itself before it started. But, on the other hand, it is not met by yes-or-no vote favorable to a regime for a long period of time with no opportunity for review, reprimand, or reversal. Between these extremes lies a mean within which the key points are placed in the direct range of the voter. The representatives, often the chief executive, basic measures for direct consideration—these are the usual province of the votable. The vote is set up to compass the range of effective control and general direction of operating authority.

The whole problem of the relation of the expert and the layman in governmental affairs, their respective competences and roles, is involved in the determination of the forms and processes of political consent and in particular of voting. How can we make sure that the will of the community and the wisdom of the community are effectively united, so that the force of will, the cutting edge of intelligence, and broad human considerations are utilized in a final end product of human personality in association for the common good?

The citizen may vote one way today and be of quite another judgment on another day, or he may vote strongly or feebly, unanimously, so to speak, or with only slight preponderance of opinion in his own councils.[25] There is in a sense a continuing, unrecorded plebiscite on the personalities and policies and administration of government. Between votings the citizen may offset his vote by pressures of many types, generally through public opinion and through special agencies and groups.

It is not the mechanical voting alone that is important but the symbolism of popular consent and control, the free and open discussion of pending problems, in their relations and in their priorities, the nature of the ruling personnel and the alternatives available, and the general course of administration and its effectiveness or ineffectiveness in the light of the grand design of the political society.

The weaknesses of ballotage are not difficult to observe and classify. They include nonvoting, fraudulent and corrupt voting, frivolous and unintelligent voting, and voting reflecting ignorance, bad judgment, or personal interest. The power of money, of gangsters, of bosses and machines, the emotionalism of religious, racial, and class groups, is evident in many voting arenas. If this were all, voting would doubtless come to an early end. But, on the other hand, there is observable, in my own experience, as a candidate and otherwise, alert, intelligent, and discriminating judgment on personnel and issues, under many difficult situations, such as the Civil War and World War II elections in the United States. Demagogues, gangsters, and ill-balanced representatives of special interest groups are parasites on the electoral system, possible only on condition that the bulk of the community is of the contrary type and temper. If all the community were corrupt, selfish, or puzzleheaded, elections would not signify much in any body politic. So it happens that in well-governed communities the moments of electoral despair are turned into triumphs, and the ends of government are reinstated in the public office.

On the negative side, what would happen if there were no voting at all, and what alternative method would be available for checking and warning authority against wandering from the path of the common good and against preserving the balance of might and right in the composition of authority, for rallying support around trusted and tried leaders of the community?

Of course, if violence determines or largely influences the course of voting, the value of balloting is destroyed. Violence and voting are incompatible tech-

[25] I have sometimes found in experiment that if all the factors involved in an election are agreed upon and weighted, the citizen then, upon adding the factors, is voting against himself.

niques. All that remains of value in the ballot under the rule of force is the implicit tribute to the symbolism and social significance of the vote—the tribute of hypocrisy to virtue.

In general, the intelligence and judgment of voting reflect the community level of intelligence and judgment in common affairs politically. If the supremacy of the common good is fully recognized by the bulk of the community and if the ends of government are understood, if there is faith in the validity of the electoral process and willingness to accept its results, the usefulness of the ballot will be evident, not without disillusionments and disappointments, however. If the mass of the community is not willing to assume the responsibilities of self-government, mere voting is no panacea. The real test is not one of general intelligence or wealth or leisure but of undoubted devotion to a common interest, undoubted faith in popular capacity, and undoubted will to pursue common aims.

What is true of electorates is no less true of representative bodies or councils of various sorts. If racial, religious, and class interests seem more important than the commonweal, the structure of voting breaks down quickly, whether in a small body or in a large electorate, and for much the same reasons. Even in small communities the effectiveness of the voting technique may crumble without some preponderant community of interest greater than personal or special interest. Treacherous as are the currents and reefs of voting, it is the only channel thus far devised that makes possible passage into the port of self-government, assuming this as the direction and end desired.

The application of the voting system is not, however, one of simple unitary ballotage, for individuals vote as members of a variety of social groupings—regional, occupational, racial, religious, cultural. Factions and groups have always existed and, indeed, were sometimes termed parties, but the modern political party dates from the modern period and the rise of democratic government.[26] The party supplies a rallying point for those groups and individuals who are concerned with the over-all policy and the personnel of the political society, and organize for the purpose of promoting their policies and making them effective in the life of the state.[27]

These groups are made up of widely different types of adherents. Some are influenced chiefly by broad principles and ideals of political policy; others, by more special interests in special types of policy; and others are concerned, on the shadier side, with the patronage or spoils of office. Once the group is established, it may be swept along by a tide of custom, with masses of adherents who inherited their party beliefs. In general, the party undertakes to provide

[26] See C. E. Merriam and H. F. Gosnell, *The American Party System* (3d ed., 1940).

[27] See also C. E. Merriam and H. F. Gosnell, *Non-voting* (1924); C. E. Merriam and Louise Overacker, *Primary Elections* (rev. ed., 1928); my *Four American Party Leaders* (1926).

a solution for broad national (or local, as the case may be) policies with which great masses of voters are concerned. Organized efforts for the election of personnel to office and for the formulation and administration of policies are made by these groups in their party capacity.

In addition to aiding in the election of public servants and in the formulation of political policies, the party also operates (1) as a critic or conductor of policy, (2) as an agency of political education, and (3) as an intermediator between government and citizen from time to time. As a conductor of government in the name of the party, the party leaders must present and defend, or in the opposition criticize, a broad range of governmental purposes which are stated, formulated, and also administered, subject to the judgment of the electorate as a whole. Public interest and enthusiasm are enlisted on a large scale in these enterprises and over broad ranges of time. By and large, the party serves as an immense stimulator of general interest and responsibility throughout the commonwealth. A great void would be left without the activities of the party at this point. It is true that the level of education under partisan auspices may at times fall very low; again, it may be very high.

At times parties fall to the level of organized appetites for public exploitation, as in the formation and operation of corrupt machines. However, these groups are not genuine parts of the party system but parasitic upon the general body of public interest. They do not help the party. They hinder its operations in the true and proper sense of the party as a functioning agency in a community.

The relation between parties and "pressure groups" varies widely in differing types of situations. In multiparty systems the tendency is for parties to correspond to pressure groups themselves, as an agrarian party or a labor party, or a racial party, or a religious party. In the two-party systems, however, the party is presumably broad enough to encompass the various pressure groups or a considerable number of them. Thus in America neither of the larger parties abandons labor, or industry, or agriculture to the other party but endeavors to divide the various groups, even if not successfully. A highly organized and successful pressure group does not aspire to become a party but to dictate terms to established party groups—both of them if possible. Broadly speaking, in a two-party system compromises and concessions are made before elections in platforms and campaigning activities; but in multiparty systems compromises are made after the election, when the relative strength of the contending groups is known, and the combinations required for control are effected.

The successful operation of a party system requires a high degree of sophistication, adapted to a plan of popular control through an organized system of consent, habitually accepted as the common procedure. A party system will not operate at all unless there is (1) a general agreement upon certain broad principles of common policy and (2) a willingness to accept electoral results as decisions for the time being. If all or several parties are anxious for revolution, as I observed in Germany in 1932, where Communists and Nazis were openly concerned with the overthrow of the government, awaiting only a convenient moment for the revolution, the success of any party system is out of the question. The stabilizing elements must be very strong numerically and as determined as they are numerous. The party presumes basic agreement upon broad lines of policy and willingness to accept peaceful methods of solution for problems upon which there is no agreement. Otherwise the outcome is civil war, with bullets instead of ballots as the final arguments.

How to reconcile flaming party spirit in the conduct of campaigns and a spirit of compromise afterward is not an easy accomplishment for the inexperienced; and, indeed, to some this may seem the high point in insincerity or hypocrisy. But as in organized sport we do not aim to kill or maim our opponents but only to surpass them in a given play, so in party warfare the aim is not the death of opponents but their relegation to political inefficiency for the time. To those who, knowing the rules of the "game," regard the play as hypocritical or unworthy, then it is, of course, such for those who so feel. But to others who understand the rules and accept them, the "game" may even be exhilarating. The defeated partisan does not resort to assassination and revolution but accepts the verdict as the voice of the community for the moment. The minority party proceeds to devise ways and means of altering that verdict on the first possible occasion. All this really rests upon confidence in the justice of the community, finally expressed in a deferred verdict. If this seems extraordinarily complicated and difficult beyond measure, the answer is that this experience is precisely analogous to that which is found in many another way and walk of life—in the family, in the club or society, in the corporation or the union, wherever minorities are found who accept judgments against them but await another day. The minority can never hope to become an operating and successful majority peacefully unless it can anticipate that the present majority or its leaders will in turn accept the new verdict of the new majority.

The role of the party is evident when we consider what would be missed in its absence. The electorate confronted with the choice of personnel and the selection of policies, the representative body confronted by the whole problem of organization and program would, if starting *de novo*, fall into sundry groups and cliques attached to individuals or ideas. Combinations of these groups would begin again under one name or another. It is, of course, possible that new groupings would arise under some other name than that of party, but political behavior would be unchanged essentially. The party provides a continuity in responsibility for selection of personnel and for advocacy of policies or their opposition. Conceivably the whole process of choices and accommodations might begin again on every new election or occasion, but habits of continuity and of association in responsibility or in criticism of action have their value in the organization of consent and the formulation of issues affecting the common good. From time to time this function of the party association bogs down into irresolute, futilitarian, or even corrupt behavior, amounting to a perversion of the party function in free association. The so-called "party" may be nothing but a name for power-seekers masquerading in the name of some factional group—power-seekers who wait only the convenient moment for revolutionary action. Merely to adopt or to impose a party mechanism on an unwilling community would have no useful effect whatever. The party cannot grow unless in a favorable climate.

Group representation may be obtained through the device of proportional representation (in many varying forms) by means of which the voter is able to express a special preference for a particular political group, or individual, registering this preference in various differential forms.[28] The merits and demerits of this system of voting and representation have been widely discussed and with no general consensus of judgment thus far. Where there are very special groups willing to place their special interests in the foreground as against all other considerations, they will find representation, regardless of the system adopted.

In more recent times there has appeared the one-party system. Here one party has a "monopoly of legality," and no other competitor is allowed to function as a party. This has been the system in Russia with the Communists and was the system in Germany with the Nazis and in Italy with the Fascists. The one party assumes the responsibility for the operation of the government, including personnel and policies. Discussion of general public policy can go on only within the boundaries of the party. Its decisions are final and binding upon party members as well as the members of the society. Evidently the operation of this system requires a condition in which freedom of speech, press, and association is barred by the force of the state. The party under such circumstances is a political association, but the system is not applicable to a free society.

All these systems—the two-party, the multiparty, the one-party—are experiments in the direction of developing some medium between the formal government and the mass of the community, some mediating agency, somewhat less authoritarian than governmental structures and personalities, and yet somewhat more formal than the pressure groups found throughout the community. In the one-party system the emphasis is clearly on the side of the authoritarian, and in the case of the others it is distinctly nonauthoritarian, although the partisans may in various instances be members of the governing body, especially on the legislative side, but also on the executive when there are elective executives, as in the United States.

With all their multifarious and often contradictory maneuvers and wander-

[28] On proportional representation see Ferdinand A. Hermens, *Democracy or Anarchy?* (1941).

ings, parties are moving in the broad general direction of the organization of general consent to government through informal ways. Through these channels the flood of public opinion may flow with great force—with compelling force in many instances—although in another season the particular party channel may be found dry or almost empty.

Where there is not a monopoly, legal or otherwise, the party system tends to keep alive the spirit of competition in the political field. Political figures are encouraged to emerge and to become active, arousing political interest as they go and stirring up public discussion and forms of political education, even on a relatively low level.

This formal-informal status of the party, this responsible-irresponsible position in the political society, this uncompromising-compromising attitude, may seem to some to be inconsistent with the genius of organized government. If we think, however, of the necessity of combining right and might in authority, if we think of the desirability of organizing the consent of the governed and yet maintaining a government which cannot stop to ask consent for every act, the role of the party becomes clearer. Without the party, centralized authority may be able to bear down opposition too easily. The pressure for more and more is likely to be met by less and less effective opposition. With the party, however, the criticism and opposition of the "outs" may grow more and more as important groups and personalities are kept longer and longer out of political responsibility. The overthrow of the ruling party becomes more and more likely under such conditions, unless indeed material concessions are made by those in authority. In any case the spirit of criticism of government, as well as that of responsible defense, is kept alive, even at the price of unfair criticism and unfair defense. The important goal is not, however, keeping the party as such alive as it is keeping the consent of the governed alive—reconciling the formal with the informal government.

The party is not a fundamental end of man or of government but a useful tool, if properly employed, for practical purposes in subordination to the larger ends of the common good. A party may become a vested interest in the way of progress, an organized appetite only, a cover for gross thievery, masking for military designs, for thinly covered personal and group plunder.

Parties can be useful to the community, only as there is general subordination of private to public good, as they aid in the development of personalities and the shaping of issues of general concern and value, and as they rise above regional, racial, class, and cultural differentials and make the general good the paramount concern, in fact as well as in declaration and protestation. Unless there had been many such evidences of willingness to place the public first, parties would not have survived the experimental period.

It is also important to observe that parties cannot be forced upon a community by legislation or constitution. Unless the given political society is on the whole disposed to put in practice the common-sense ways of the parties, as seen in their best estate, the system will not work with any degree of success. If loyalty to party is not higher than loyalty to class or group, and yet yielding to loyalty to the common good of the community, there is no guaranty of a party system operating on any considerable scale of effectiveness. I am not including here the one-party system, which is not a party system at all, but another form of aristocracy, even though temporary in nature.

There is little basis for forecasting the future forms of party organization and action. In democratic states the party has often rendered invaluable service as a broker between formal government and informal public opinion. It is possible that some better instrument may be found than this admittedly difficult tool of association, but thus far none has been discovered.[29] Nor is any in sight.

VI. PUBLIC AND PRIVATE GOVERNMENT

At this point we come to the borderlands of public and private government— often difficult for the ultraformalists to understand or to appreciate in relation to the political.[30]

A congeries of associations operates to produce the net result in the community. Many of these associations have their own parallel plans for social action of their own special genre—in family, church, industry, agriculture, professions. Methods of initiation, assumptions of responsibilities, opportunities, duties, forms of discipline and reward, ways and means of meeting the crises of life—all these are the commonplace of all associations. Sometimes they are very explicit, and again they may be very vague, existing in understandings which, however, may be extremely powerful in operation. Government is intimately related to all these cross-sections of social living, and its devices must be closely enmeshed into the others.

In the main, social groups govern themselves and have always done so, from the family on down to the present time. Every one of these groups brings pressure upon the conduct of government from time to time in many direct and indirect ways in pursuance of its interests and values. Individuals do likewise. This is not an occasion for alarm but an observation on the nature of human society and the unending competition for recognition and expression. Danger arises only when identification with and the devotion to individual or group interests becomes incompatible with the common good expressed in the larger community. If there is no outstanding good, but only a series of special goods and interests, the basis for community organization and action does not exist, and the larger group has no reason for further operations. Austria is a striking modern example. Observation shows that this has happened again and again

[29] For suggestions regarding the reorganization of the party system in the United States see Merriam and Gosnell, *The American Party System*.

[30] See my *Public and Private Government* (1944), chap. i.

in human affairs and that the state has been dissolved or disrupted in a long series of internal struggles. Incompatibility of race, religion, economic interest, and general and special loyalties is the formula for disintegration. Since one of the tools of government is force, commonly an attempt to seize this force will be made, and thus the struggle is transferred to the battlefield.

That public government is somehow aloof from all these permutations and combinations of private governance is one of the great illusions of shortsighted observers, some of whom deify the state while others diabolize it. The truth is that the state is neither above humanity nor below it. The government is of the earth, earthy, but it also embodies the aspirations and ideals of men.

The government is the instrument of all these groups taken together for the realization of security, order, justice, welfare, and freedom within the framework of the common good. The formalities and juristics of government are only the agencies through which the community operates to effectuate its interests and values in personalities and policies, in directions, tones, colors, and types of social effort. Far from attempting to reduce all these associations to a common type and intimate control, as in the *Gleichschaltung*—"assimilation"— of the Nazis, the state might more usefully encourage richness of variety. Especially in a period of rapid development and of division of labor, the proliferation of diversity is more important than the effort to bring about a monolithic form of social organization. Personalities and groups of personalities may be self-governing in what essentially concerns them functionally within the broad range of the commonweal. The difficulty lies not in the self-government of associations but in their desire to impose government upon others, or adopt courses of action hostile to the rights and position of others. In a sense the bulk of government is nongovernmental; functions rather than structures and forms are the staple of social directions. Military and juristic pressures are alike deceptive in their appearance of omnicompetence and omnipotence. The real directives come from social techniques such as education and medicine, from new inventions for the expression and expansion of personality as seen in production of materials, goods, and facilities of many types, from the higher ideals of men in the political field and beyond in other realms of values.

To formalize these multifarious associations into responsible political governing agencies would accomplish nothing. A guild of agriculture, industry, and labor would be supplemented by law, medicine, engineering, and education, and these again by several religions, and again by races and colors, and again by regions, and again by urban and rural areas, and again by cultural and fraternal associations of many forms. Our present types of government would begin to look very simple again. With the proliferation and professionalization of occupations and activities, the task would become increasingly complex and unworkable. Once direct political responsibility was vested in these groups, the struggle would begin all over again for domination and control of the groups or guilds—under other names.

Interchange of experience and ideas among persons and groups is increasingly developed through modern agencies of communication, with the press, including journals and books, the radio, and the screen supplementing the forum and other agencies of earlier times. Occupations and interests, it is true, color these communications, as in the case of trade and nationalistic publications, but in the main the characteristic feature of communication in our day is its tremendous outpouring across all group lines and across all space as far as that is concerned. [31]

Signs and signals flash by day and night throughout the community with many implications for human behavior. Communication alone will not of itself produce a community, but it may facilitate the process, although at times it may also prove disruptive to common purposes by the development of special dissensions. It might be said that communication has no more value than the old-time buzz of gossip or that completely controlled communication would place social control in the hands of the owner or director.

Whatever the merits or level of communication may be, and its possibilities for advance are very great, there can be no question that communication cuts through the lines of special and group interest and association and opens the way for interchange of ideas, values, policies, and appraisals relating to the common good of a given jurisdiction. If government, as one of the agencies of the common good for certain common purposes, is able to adapt itself to this new phase of communication, its value to the society will be immeasurably increased. Protests, complaints, inventions, suggestions, and reflections of a thousand types will be streaming through the air, diffused on the screen and in the press, awaiting the touch of those who know how to catch and use them for common purposes. Much of this process will elude the agencies of adjudication, counsel, and management unless they are alert to their new opportunities and responsibilities.

Demagogues, despots, and mountebanks may seize the machinery of the radio, the press, and the screen, as well as wise men of the state, and scatter misrepresentation, confusion, and hate to the detriment of the political society. Gangsters of the Hitler-Goebbels type have already shown the power of ruthless use of agencies such as the radio and the press and have boldly attempted to justify their behavior on the ground that their representation of the general interest was more genuine and effective than that of governmental agencies under other systems of government. This was false, but it nevertheless illustrates the possibilities of the use of communication techniques. The first *coup*

[31] See Charles W. Morris, "Communication: Its Forms and Problems," in *Approaches to National Unity: Fifth Symposium of the Conference on Science, Philosophy and Religion in Their Relation to the Democratic Way of Life* (1945).

d'état in Austria, it will be recalled, was accompanied by the seizure of the radio and an impersonation of orders from the deposed chief of state. Special interests of race, religion, region, and occupation may also seize the means of communication and utilize them for special purposes, notably in the case of the press, or may exercise so many vetoes on free discussion as to obstruct the rational formation of judgments.

Beyond all this, there is a basic challenge to reason and good will in government to make full use of the new scientific agencies for intercommunication between persons and groups in the newly emerging society into which we come swiftly. Neither in public nor in private government can we expect that the common good and the ends of association will follow only the old channels of relationship in view of the mighty changes going on around us. Now that new vistas of communication are opening out, it is possible to achieve the more complete understandings upon which the general good depends. But the mechanics of communication alone will not solve the problem. There remains the question of the content of communication and the ends toward which it is directed. Auditory and visual acuity are not ends in themselves but implements of the higher values for which association comes into being and is continued. There could be no graver error than to conclude that perfected mechanical communication per se would solve our social problems.

VII. CONCLUSION

Participation in authority is unavoidably one of the most difficult of all the problems of political or other forms of association—far more difficult than the formal balances of power. The development of central focuses of authority, the establishment of rough forms of command and obedience either by custom or from fear of subordination and superordination, is a fundamental task—on the "must" list of any community. But the sharing and diffusion of authority, co-ordination, and co-operation are far more difficult and involved, requiring the concurrence and co-operation of many different and often opposing elements and their fusion in a going concern. So delicate is the set of balances involved that catastrophe or even dissolution is never too far away. In our own time a strong France seemed to break to pieces for the moment in a crisis.

In view of the difficulties in the composition of authority, it is small wonder that failure has often marked the trial. Authority and antiauthority, center and circumference, and techniques, devices, forms, structures, and procedures exist for the growth of the human personality in the framework of the common good. This is a hard saying for some formalists who find the form more important than the purpose for which the form exists—the means more to be considered than the ends.

Adjudicators may forget that there are adjudications behind and beyond the

239

formal law; administrators may forget that management is not a monopoly of formal managers but a commonplace of social organization; legislators may not see beyond their formal statutes into the unseen lawmakers busy every day with lawmaking and application in their own areas of jurisdiction, weaving custom and reason into behavior. Warriors may see in steel and high explosives the ultimate reason, forgetting that obedience to orders is not made of steel but of custom and morale. To the trained observer of political behavior and its ultimate ends, government may be seen for what it really is—as one phase of subordination, superordination, and co-ordination among men, as a cross-section of social behavior, as one instrument among many for the expression and elaboration of human personalities in the framework of the general good.

The preceding pages have presented an analysis of the ways in which formal and informal government unite for the promotion of the ends of society, for the establishment and maintenance of authority which contains the elements of right and might. We have noted the vast body of custom from which come law and policy as parts of a way of life deep down below the surface of the formal structure of government; the areas of resistance which dull the edge of the sharpest instruments of oppression and arrogance and at times flame out in revolutionary movements; and the refuges on the altar of the rights of man of political faith and hope beyond the reach of brutality and power. We have noted the subtle but massive influences of public opinion, despised and flouted by authority from time to time, but powerful when aroused, driving all before it, when its majesty is fully asserted. Finally, we looked at more definite ways and means of reconciling formal and informal government, at the ballot and its significance, at political parties as instruments of politics, and at the vast areas of private-public government in which so large a measure of human life is contained.

This is a body of considerations which many political scientists have discussed from the days of Bodin on through Montesquieu and down to the modern researches in sociology and politics but one which is often neglected both in theory and in practice by those whose attention is fixed upon forms of government rather than upon the functions and purposes for which the forms exist. Government and law are from one point of view specializations of human behavior—but specializations which have their roots in society from which they spring and their relationships to general patterns of human nature and aspiration.

This is what Bagehot had in mind perhaps when he referred to "illogical moderation" as one of the causes of British success in politics, or what Dicey meant when he referred to the "custom of the constitution," or what Holmes saw when he said that the life of law is not in logic but in life and experience. Significant as these important observations were, it is not necessary to set up opposition between logic and life or logic and custom. The reasoning of custom may not be highly formalized, but reason may still underlie and condition the generalizations made in its origin and evolution. Mere custom may become unreasonable if it becomes repetition without reference to change, just as reason may become unreasonable without reference to the data upon which it operates.

Informal government, which is often the despair of the formalists, is full of meaning for the realization of the ends of government. The custom of ignoring custom has been the downfall of many a measure and many a man and many a power system.

CHAPTER VII

STABILITY AND CHANGE IN GOVERNMENT

CUTTING across the lines of government just considered there is a major task of the political association—the constant adjustment of its organization, procedures, and functions to the changing techniques and patterns of the society in which it is set—the perennial task of maintaining a workable equilibrium between the requirements of stability and change. This is notably true in dramatic periods of crisis but also in the less exciting stream of more slowly moving variations in social forces. One of the very reasons for the existence of government is the subdivision of human labor and the political function of continuing guardianship over the relation of the common good to changing factors in the society. The political authorities cannot say of startling events, "How passing strange." "Never unprepared" is, in a sense, their motto, although by no means their unbroken practice.[1] It is too much to say that crises are the commonplace of politics. But fire, flood, famine, pestilence, war, unemployment, if not customary, are nevertheless occurrences for which the state must be prepared. In a sense there should be no crisis which the well-organized government has not anticipated, if within the range of reasonable anticipation. Earthquakes, tidal waves, volcanic eruptions, and other incalculable events may well find the governors unready. But, in general, preparations may be made for most emergencies. War upsets many of the routines of the state as well as of private agencies, but for war there are always forms of readiness, however inadequate.

The general considerations underlying political change may first be analyzed as a basis for more specific inquiry.

[1] Lindsay Rogers in *Crisis Government* (1934) is one of the few writers who have considered the extraordinary functions of the government.

I. THEORIES OF CHANGE

The classical theorists assumed that they could discover a form of political association which, once set up, would never need to change. Systems were constructed by Plato and Aristotle in which they undertook to devise means by which change might be successfully resisted in practice. States were to be set back from the sea to avoid the drifting populations found there; songs and dances that might stimulate restlessness—the jazz and boogie-woogie of their day—were strictly prohibited. Only mature persons were to go abroad, and, when they returned, they must sing the praises of their own country. The beginnings of change must be studied with the utmost care and every precaution taken to extinguish any flames, however insignificant.

Beginning with Bodin in the sixteenth century, however, the students of government recognized the inevitability of change and the desirability of preparing for it through regular channels of modification. The natural law philosophers built upon the permanency of general principles of politics but admitted the value of wide variety of structure and processes upon these foundations. In Montesquieu "the necessary relations of things" became the essential element in the *Spirit of Laws*.

But in the eighteenth century revolutionary struggle the possibility of political change by conscious control of men was as sharply challenged by Burke and others as it was defended by Jefferson.

A revolutionary factor in the field of social change was the appearance of the Darwinian doctrines. Here was a theory of growth in terms of evolutionary development—a picture of human life and indeed of all life, human and other, as a constantly unfolding process of mutation, adaptation, and adjustment. Here was a doctrine with wide-sweeping implications for biological study, for theology, and for social science.[2] Two opposite interpretations of this idea spring up in politics. One asserted the complete vindication of the doctrine of laissez faire as the struggle for survival; the other, the validation of the political process as that of unending change. These opposing ideas are nowhere more effectively stated than in Spencer[3] and Huxley.[4]

The doctrine of the survival of the fittest was employed to justify noninterference with industrial arrangements, and the whole classical economic theory was restated in terms of Darwinism. What can be more futile, said Spencer, than to hope to advance by violating the most fundamental law of nature—that of the relation between conduct and consequence? Political puttering can do nothing more than block the way of nature. The strongest survive; the fostering of the weak only delays the inevitable triumph of the fittest. Even in

[2] David G. Ritchie, *Darwinism and Politics* (1889). See also Richard Hofstadter, *Social Darwinism in American Thought, 1860–1915* (1944).

[3] Herbert Spencer, *The Man versus the State* (1884) and *Justice* (1891).

[4] T. H. Huxley, "Administrative Nihilism," in *Method and Results* (1893).

Spencer, however, the significance of some change was admitted, but it must be change of the "natural" order and not of the man-made kind.

On the other hand, the conception of life as a vast process of evolutionary change stimulated the imagination of the world, parallel as it was with the titanic drama of the Hegelian dialectic, which depicted the course of history as the progressive development of human liberty, and with the Marxian dialectical materialism. The stability of institutions was no longer safely based upon time, custom, and status; they were henceforth subjected to the constant test of their validity. Their sacrosanct quality was gone, and it was open to every rival group to envisage its own chosen type of social organization as an evolution—the evolution of democracy, of socialism, of aristocracy—the logic of whatever you like in the light of the "irresistible trends of evolution."

Even more significant, however, was the conclusion now reached that man might direct the course of change within limits. It was seen that, while on the lower levels evolution is an unconscious process, on the higher levels of human life it becomes a conscious process of adjustment, subject to the intelligent direction of men—an emergent evolution. The brutality and blindness of nature may be directed by the human intelligence, as pestilence, famine, plague, and fire are controlled by mankind; and the wild forces, formerly thought of as devils or evil spirits, may be tamed to the service of man.

Instead of a theory of fatalism on the part of the state or of society, we arrive at a theory of conscious control over the course of human evolution. Instead of the deterministic survival of the fittest, we may have the voluntaristic control over various lines of human evolution, through human contrivance and design—within limits to be sure. The permeation of this idea through human thinking was of monumental meaning, for it established (1) the normality of change in institutions and (2) the possibility of conscious, directed change in social attitudes and in institutions.

Coinciding with a period of incredible speed in technological change, and with the rise of democracy, this new doctrine opened the way to a new heaven and a new earth. It was not merely revolutionary in the usual sense of the term, as when we speak of the French Revolution, but revolutionary and radical in the sense that it went down to the bases of human attitudes toward social change. It was a revolution that went down far below the surface of ordinary conflicts—revolutionary as were the doctrines of Socrates, of Jesus, of Galileo, of Columbus, in their respective times and areas of action.

II. CONSERVATION AND MUTATION

The contending forces have often forgotten in the heat of their controversy that evolution consists of conservation and mutation as well.[5] Science itself

[5] See the discussion in *The Obligation of Universities to the Social Order: Addresses and Discussion at a Conference of Universities under the Auspices of New York University* .... (1933).

staggered at mutation, uncertain in the war of geneticists and environmental-ists, still unable to identify the situations under which mutations take place, except in a general way. Upon this might turn in last analysis the control of mutation, the limits of modifiability, and the ease of and resistance to change.

That there are broad ranges of modifiability has been shown in animal and vegetable alike. The biologist can turn the cock into a hen, and a Burbank can grow unbelievable forms of vegetable life.[6] Leaving out of the question the finality of type forms, it is clear that there are areas of modifiability in human nature which may be discovered and which vary in resistance to modification by nature or design of man. There are diverse processes of metabolism and processes of mutation, of renewal and of variation. There are values which we wish to conserve, some of them, or to modify. It is important to consider, then, what elements are relatively permanent and what elements may be changed, although with much difficulty. By way of illustration, it is possible to say of humans that bisexual reproduction cannot be changed; that the law of divorce may be altered with relative ease; that the complete abolition of the family would be accomplished only with very great difficulty in modern society. It is comparatively easy to induce a modification in church procedure, difficult to break up an existing ecclesiastical institution without great disturbance of the community and large wastage of social energy, and impossible to suppress religion altogether.

Neither in nature nor in human society is the essence of mutation well understood, and "sport" individuals or "sport" types may at any time emerge with startling consequences. But both in nature and in social relations progress has been made in the understanding of variation and in its manipulation with-in certain limits. The biologist, the botanist, and the breeder may evince a high type of skill in the reorganization of types by conscious design and planned effort; and society itself has undertaken methods of management of one form or another, such as prohibition of marriage within certain ranges of con-sanguinity, the exposure of the weaker infants, prohibition of the reproduction of various types of defectives, devices of birth control, and encouragement of birth rate.

The metes and bounds of modifiability are written large in the records of many revolutionary movements and in many abortive attempts at social change, whether by state, church, or cultural group. We do not have, however, the exact indices of modifiability, and herein lies the possibility of deep-seated antagonisms in proposals for social alteration.

III. CONSERVATISM AND RADICALISM

Unfortunately, conservatism, presumably the official custodian of conserva-tion, does not deal uniformly with those basic elements in social values and

[6] John C. Merriam, "Conservation and Evolution in a Changing Social Program," *Proceedings of the American Philosophical Society*, LXXIII (1934), 351–70.

institutions which might most advantageously be conserved. Conservatism often turns to the defense of vested interests not functioning well and hence requiring artificial reinforcement, such as slavery, serfdom, or modern industrial privilege. The very areas in which change is indicated—the areas of decay—resist the modification of the social pattern, surviving their functions, projecting their prestige beyond their social utility. This situation may be seen often in business, in government, and in church as well as in the state.

This is age lingering too long; it is power refusing to delegate; it is privilege acting as judge of its own share of the social dividend; it is the extension of the dead hand into living relations. Thus, true conservation may find it necessary to fight its way against conservatism, strangely enough. The nation may defend its forests, its mines, its minerals, and its human resources against the special interests that waste them.

Conservatism might appropriately direct itself to the wisest ranges of practical modifiability, to appropriate rates and the wisest modes of change. But the practice is often quite different, amounting to a flat defiance of change impinging upon particular interests, even though the general interest may be advanced.[7] So professional conservatism comes to be arrayed against conservatism in the broad sense of the term. This is conspicuous in the industrial world, where business is often conservative in the sense of protecting vested interests but intensely radical in change of machinery and organization.

Radicalism, on the other hand, may be found in opposition to social change indicated by the trend of the time and may protect its own immediate interests as against the broader interest of the group and of posterity. It may reject the advance of mechanization; it may oppose the newer forms of industrial organization. Labor opposed the corporation originally as vigorously as capital opposed the trades-union. Unfortunately, the social implications of invention have never been carefully scrutinized, nor has society adjusted itself to the displacement caused by new technologies, which help the race but ruin the individual worker affected.

Radicalism may confuse a value with a prejudice, as when the Marxians undertake the destruction of the state, fearing it as an instrument of capitalism; or the anarchists attempt the destruction of education and science, fearing it as the instrument of capitalism; or the overthrow of religion as the enemy of the proletariat; or labor-saving machinery, or modern production. A long catalogue of bourgeois practices was on the list of the Soviets but later relinquished as hatred died down and a sense of proportion returned. It was proposed to abandon precedent in law as a bourgeois institution; to forbid dancing as a bourgeois institution. But, on the whole, the later Soviet attitude and policy have been highly favorable to innovations of the most sweeping and fundamental nature, in wide-ranging areas of activity.

[7] Lord Hugh Cecil, *Conservatism* (1912).

Radicalism may resist useful social mutations, either because they are misunderstood or because they do not fit in with the program and strategy of the group in power at the particular time. Radicalism may find itself at war with radical change, just as conservatism may find itself at variance with conservation.

The difference, then, in modern politics is not that between one group's looking skeptically at all proposals for change, demanding great circumspection and prudence in change, and another group's optimistically regarding possible change, and somewhat less critical as to the ways and means of change. These attitudes are not monopolized by either party in the social conflicts of our own or other days. Not only are there many radicals in all conservative movements, but there are also many conservatives in every radical movement. It is to be expected that those displaced or disinherited by change should resist until a way is found by which the gains of civilization shall not become a loss to them.

This is not a criticism of these attitudes but an analysis of their relation to the great political and social problem of the relation between conservation and mutation.[8] It is in the nature of party movements that compromises should exist in order that special groups may be satisfied and that parties may persist. But it is important for those not at the core of these groupings, and even for those at their center, to have in mind the problem of conservation in its largest meaning, in order to preserve the critical judgment and choice which underlie all systems of general control.

IV. ROLE OF INVENTION

It cannot be too strongly emphasized that the building of modern civilization was in great part the work of the discoverers, scientists, and inventors. It was their initiative that made the wonders of the modern world. The seeds of our civilization were not sown primarily by the warriors or the entrepreneurs but by the technicians and organizers whose intelligence penetrated the hitherto unknown and brought forth hidden treasures for mankind. The recent discoveries of the human mind are not accidental but projected from a high mental plateau attained by the human race after centuries of previous effort. They represent the possibilities in an era supplying reasoning power, scientific education, and public order and displaying keen interest in the outcome of scientific inquiry on a large scale—of a civilization which is essentially nontraditional, irreverent, imaginative, and bold on its material side, however it may cling to the opposite set of traits on the other.

These technological changes have been far more revolutionary in their immediate effects and in their wider implications than the bloodiest revolu-

[8] John C. Merriam, *The Inquiring Mind in a Changing World* (1934); T. V. Smith, *Creative Sceptics* (1934).

tions of any time. They have multiplied the productivity of the soil, the output of factories, given the hand one hundred times its former power, opened out materials and processes of incalculable value to millions of persons, and cleared the way to a wonderland of achievement in health and well-being. In their immediate channels they have swept aside superstition, prejudice, misunderstanding, ignorance, sometimes with little and again with much resistance, but with the inevitable conclusion emerging. The distribution and application of these gains of civilization is another story full of sorrow for millions of the disinherited, but the accumulation of vast riches for the race is incontestable. The lag between what might be and what is, technically, is one of the tragedies of the time, but the piling-up of the treasure heap is beyond doubt a fact with which politics must deal. I pause only to emphasize the sometimes forgotten truth that change may now involve not merely redistribution of what is but the vast expansion of what is into far more. It is within the scope of modern government to reckon with this basic fact and to express it in realistic forms.

V. WAYS AND MEANS OF CHANGE

We may ask, "What are the types of change most likely to be considered by governments in the period into which we come?" These changes will, of course, be the result of variations in technology, in social invention and control, in social directives.[9] New machines for controlling our physical resources, new modes of re-educating men, and new patterns of social invention seem to lie on the horizon, assuming that our civilization does not bog down of its own weight in the swamps of violence and strife. It would be impossible and, indeed, an impertinence to undertake to say what the future contains in the apparently inexhaustible fairyland of control over natural forces. The finger of science does not tremble as it points in the direction of conscious control of evolution and the triumph of intelligence in human relations. The types of change growing out of this process are fundamental to all political speculation and programming.

In the rational control of the processes of political change lie some of the richest possibilities for the human race and, at the same time, some of its blackest dangers. Those who wish to accept the cult of violence may find on the pages of history enough of fire and sword to occupy all their reading hours and confirm them in their conviction of the inevitability and priority of violence in social change. But a student of government will indicate alternative

[9] A résumé of such predictions is found in E. P. Dutton & Co.'s "Today and Tomorrow" series, covering the future of science (Haldane and Russell); of man (Schiller); of morals (Joad); of women (Ludovici); of Darwinism (Brain); of biology (Jennings); of intelligence (Lee); etc., in some fifty small volumes. See also H. G. Wells, *The Shape of Things To Come* (1933); Lancelot T. Hogben, *Science for the Citizen* (1938); Edward L. Thorndike, *Human Nature and the Social Order* (1940).

possibilities while not denying war and riot their relaxation in volcanic hours of smoke and death.

The channels for effecting social and political change are numerous and varied as the social texture in which the government functions. They may range from slow and almost imperceptible variation to the wild and violent storms of revolution; they may be brought about by constitutional methods and through the processes of social legislation, which is partly lawmaking, partly management, and partly adjudication.

A. REVOLUTION[10]

What constitutes a revolution may be subject of much discussion, for many fundamental changes are made by wholly peaceful methods. In general, the use of violence or the threat of violence is a connotation of revolution. In any case a revolution involves basic changes in structure or policy in a given governmental pattern, whether sudden or long drawn out. Revolutions, it may be noted, are not peculiar to government but the common property of all forms of human association, secular or ecclesiastical.

Revolution may seem to be an outsider in the show of government, but with lightning rapidity it may enter and take possession of the seats of power. At what point authority crumbles, at what point applause fades away and turns to hissings and reproaches, at what point obedience turns to defiance, at what point the soldier will not fire when commanded—these are factors making it true that "uneasy rests the head that wears the crown." But basic revolutions seldom come without warning to those who are watchful. Palace revolutions affecting perhaps only a few personalities at the top may come swiftly and unannounced. But major movements cast their shadows before them and may be anticipated with reasonable attention to the social and economic bases of authority. "Mene mene tekel upharsin" may not always be written on the walls, but the skilled observers of trends and forces may trace the warning hand of revolution. Long neglect or stubbornness and pride may make it too late to save the day for established power.

Potential resistance and potential revolution are among the ways and means of diffusing authority throughout the community. They tend to offset the integration and concentration of power essential to the central core of government, to prevent the hardening of authority into personalism or formalism contrary to the genuine ends of the government or the community.

[10] George S. Pettee, *The Process of Revolution* (1938); Pitirim Sorokin, *The Sociology of Revolution* (1925); Giuseppe Ferrari, *Filosofia della rivoluzione* (rev. ed., 1942); Lyford P. Edwards, *The Natural History of Revolution* (1927); Crane Brinton, *The Anatomy of Revolution* (1938); Leon Trotsky, *History of the Russian Revolution* (1932); my *Political Power*, chapter on "Survival of the Fittest"; see also Part VII on "Resistance and Revolution." For A. J. Toynbee's formula for the disintegration of great states see his *A Study of History*, Vols. V–VI (1939).

Violent revolution is a means of such disorderly character so destructive of many human values that it is invoked only in exceptional circumstances and under very grave provocation. As Locke said, "Those who appeal to Heaven must be sure that Heaven is on their side." Yet no walls of authority can be built strong enough to prevent the entrance of revolution when the hour has struck.

Open revolution is always lurking in the background—the skeleton at the feast of power—a continuing threat to authority not firmly rooted in economic and social realities and in human ideals related to them. Large-scale revolutions have shaken our modern world as never before in equal time in human history. In this century two great revolutions have occurred in Germany and a third is on the way; one revolution in Italy, and then another; revolutions in Spain, China, in South America, and many others. Never were so many people in revolution in so short a period of time as within the last thirty years.

Aristotle found that the basic cause of revolutions is the desire for equality— equals desire absolute equality which they do not possess; or unequals an end of the inequality in which they find themselves.[11] This is true, but we may break this down into further component elements to clarify the problem somewhat. We may consider which ends of the state are drawn in question and what social elements are related to these demands.

It may be observed that many revolutions are precipitated by power-hungry groups, such as the Fascists or the Nazis, whose motif is aggrandizement of personal or group position. This may well be and often is, but the real question is what the motives or interests were to which they successfully addressed themselves in their quest for authority. National security or welfare, or freedom, or order, or justice perhaps? Analyzing in this fashion, we might say that the first German revolution was directed toward freedom and welfare; the next toward national security. The first Russian revolution was concerned with constitutional freedom and order; the second with economic welfare primarily. Mussolini's revolution was concerned with national prestige, and the counter-revolution was also inspired by national security. The Japanese palace revolution was aimed at national security and expansion; the Chinese revolution at security in a democratic framework of order and freedom.

Elsewhere I have indicated the elements of survival which have a bearing upon revolution, and they may be restated here: (1) intimate knowledge of the social composition of authority; (2) accurate distribution of political rewards and punishments; (3) moderation—the golden mean; (4) avoidance of congestion of authority; (5) planning and leadership; and (6) the balance between justice and order.[12]

[11] *Politics*, Book v.

[12] See my *Political Power*, chap. vii: "The Survival of the Fittest."

"Not to know the community and to utilize its experts, not to be able to distribute rewards wisely, not to exercise moderation in government, not to be able to delegate and divide authority, not to have or appear to have plans of responsible leadership for the community, not to be able to maintain a system of order through which the principle of justice permeates; these are the conditions under which rulers often fall. Not that all of these situations must coincide, but a sufficient number of them in an impressive enough combination may precipitate the loss of prestige and power."[13]

The Marxian and later the Nazi theory repudiated the process of peaceful change and concluded that revolution is the only method by which basic social changes may be effected at this time—revolution long enough projected to insure the overthrow of the existing regime. In the straight Marxian doctrine government is the definition of an instrument for the exploitation of the working class, and its disappearance is not merely that of a special group of governors but of the governmental institution itself. The dictatorship of the proletariat might be the interim form of organization, pending the ultimate dissolution of the state.[14] Hitler and Mussolini justified the use of violence and of war as implements in the special form of order sought by them.

Once the revolution is accomplished, however, it is not to be presumed that continuing revolution is the order of the day. Violence may well be invoked as a means of suppressing resistance, but this does not extend to the use of violence against the government. On the contrary, forms of resistance will be rigorously suppressed. Once the favored form of government is established, all forms of counterrevolution are to be promptly and vigorously put down, and all ideas of revolutionary rights suspended or abolished.[15] It is an old saying that the sons of revolutionists are seldom revolutionists.

B. CONSTITUTIONAL CHANGE

The process of peaceful change is symbolized in constitutions, providing bills of rights, a frame of government, and a mode of change. Constitutional government in the period dating from the end of the eighteenth century was itself the recognition of the possibility of conscious social change in the area of government. It was held by Burke and De Maistre that political change can be made only through the processes of history and tradition. It was as boldly proclaimed by Jefferson and others that man may make his government as he goes. Constitutions, themselves established by revolutionary methods, laid the

[13] *Ibid.*, p. 229.

[14] See my *The Role of Politics in Social Change* (1936).

[15] Marx in his earlier phases held that in countries like England and the United States basic change may be made without revolution. These are, it happens, the largest states with the longest experience in self-government.

foundation for peaceful and democratic change, not only in the construction of government but in social and economic processes.

The modern constitution contains formal provisions for its own amendment in a number of different ways in varying political systems. One hundred and fifty years of experience with these several forms is full of significance for the student of government but by no means indicates conclusively the superiority of any one system. That methods of peaceful change are provided is an outstanding consideration.

It is, of course, possible to set up provisions which make change difficult or even impossible. But it would be naïve to expect that such provisions would actually accomplish the end in view. In our own history the Articles of Confederation were made unamendable except by unanimous consent of the states, if no other way could be found. Many of our early constitutions contained no amending clauses. The door was locked and the key was thrown into the well. But ways and means of amendment were readily found.

Extraordinary majorities may be required for basic change or unusual procedures may be rquired in various classes of cases, but custom, statute, and interpretation will not usually be denied if there is insistent need for change.[16] It is important that basic changes should not be lightly made, but, on the other hand, it is vital at times that such changes be made promptly—as a matter of life and death—in emergencies and in war. Lincoln declared that if necessary he would break the Constitution to save the life of the nation. The real guaranty, as Hamilton pointed out, is the "general genius of the government." If this fails, the written documents have little force and are ineffective.

A people like the British, long accustomed to a parliament vested with unlimited sovereignty, with legal power to do anything it may decide upon, may operate such a system without violent or radical change. What could legally happen does not happen, since it breaks against constitutional custom and general opinion. The United States, on the other hand, habituated to a written Constitution with special modes of amendment and of interpretation through the judiciary, has been able to make such adjustments and adaptations as were necessary for the life and growth of the nation from time to time. Each system has been able to bring about both stability and change in periods of notable development. Each nation prefers its own system and would oppose alteration.

A nation adopting a democratic system or other system of government *de novo* would consider the nature of change in relation to its own special background experience and ideals. The equilibrium set up would grow out of the trends and possibilities of the particular social, economic, and political system. The mere adoption of another system successful elsewhere but with widely

---

[16] See Herman Finer, *The Theory and Practice of Modern Government* (rev. ed., 1934), chap. iii; C. V. Laughlin and K. C. Sears, "A Study in Constitutional Rigidity," *University of Chicago Law Review*, X (January, 1943), 142–76; *ibid.*, XI (June, 1944), 374–442.

different *modus operandi* would not of itself accomplish much. It is not impossible that entirely new constructs in the field of orderly change may emerge as a result of new experience and of new reflection on the psychological bases of the problem set. Many of the early ideas as to change were evidently very crude, dating from the days when it was disloyal to think of any change at all and when philosophers defended the changeless state. Superior ways and means of effecting necessary changes and avoiding instability may well be worked out by the new students of government and society, as they focus more sharply on the essential problem.

Many constitutions have had no stabilizing effect, as the record of abortive constitutional efforts in the nineteenth and twentieth centuries shows on many continents. The constitution alone does not complete the stabilizing process and is no automatic guaranty of such a result against military force or economic or other groupings.[17] An effective constitution must have behind it the attitudes, understandings, interests, and ideals of a community in order to serve its avowed purpose.

A constitution, however, is not merely a negative instrument. In the beginning, constitutions, made in the fear of despots, were chiefly concerned with what should not be done, but, as time went on, it appeared clearly that another value of a constitution was that of facilitating necessary change through constitutional channels. From the fear of despotic action, on the one hand, constitution-makers sometimes swung to the fear of hasty popular action—each type of threat requiring systems of elaborate checks and balances.

This is, indeed, the perpetual paradox of politics, that authority must be limited but that in emergencies power must not be restrained. The answer to this problem is not of precise constitutional definition, however useful, but of broad understandings on the part of the community whose good the political system serves, of their sense of tolerance and restraint, of their experience with a series of cases requiring practical judgments.

C. LEGISLATION

Legislation is a standard mode of change of far-reaching significance. Great codes have been built up many times without the invocation of the sword, as the Solonian Code, the Justinian Code, the common law, and much of the old Germanic law.[18]

But social legislation in all Western countries during the last hundred years has wrought sweeping changes in the personal and property relations of millions of people, and that without a blow. In Sweden, England, the United

[17] See my *The Written Constitution and the Unwritten Attitude* (1931).

[18] See James Bryce for comparison of these systems in *Studies in History and Jurisprudence* (1901); Sir Frederick Pollock, *The Genius of the Common Law* (1912); Roscoe Pound, *The Spirit of the Common Law* (1921).

States, and other states, far-reaching systems of social insurance and stabilization have been put into force through the legislative method. Sanitary and housing legislation has been widely enacted. A wide variety of regulatory methods for the control of unfair industrial practices has been enacted. Taxation is a standard method of social change. Land-tenure systems have been modified, banking and credit systems basically changed. Wide-ranging educational systems have been established. Indeed, an enumeration of the breadth and variety of types of legislation would constitute a review of almost every phase of recent social life. So numerous are these changes that Sorel, the arch-apostle of violence, commented on what he calls the "cowardice of capitalism" and its "dangerous" tendency to compromise rather than to enter upon violent ways of settlement. His encouragement of violence was intended fundamentally to offset the compromising tendency of the powers that be, in the fear that the present generation might become too much interested in progress through legislation.[19]

The importance of planning as a stabilizing agency in government as well as in other agencies arises from the fact that it requires a study of historical trends, a look around the present, and a forward-looking inventive projection into the future of a course of action. This attitude helps the citizen to take a long perspective in shaping national or local policies and to produce an evolutionary rather than a revolutionary judgment in the community. Those who have thought of planning as essentially unsettling or disturbing have not directed their attention to the fundamental elements of planning and to its basic balance in the all-round view.

D. TRADITION AND CHANGE

In times of calm the difficulties are greater sometimes and the readjustments more difficult than in periods of stress. The root of this runs deep into human nature. Every personality constructs for himself a synthetic view of life as he goes along. Endowed with a social world by early training, he modifies this as he advances along the way. He is not averse to change—quite the contrary perhaps—but he must know the nature of it and approve the change in general. If he has been accustomed to turning right, it is difficult and seems stupid indeed to turn left, and vice versa. Medical treatment is full of the constantly changing rules of the game which puzzle the learner. But in this field he has learned to conform in the main to the recommendations of the doctor, who may bake or freeze or starve him at will almost. Family or religions or racial tradition cannot long hold out against medicine or engineering, fantastic or "agin' nature" as their management may seem.

Political traditions have this difficulty to overcome: how to retain the precious

---

[19] Georges Sorel, *Reflections on Violence* (1914).

values of social cohesion springing out of the past and how, at the same time and through the same personality, to reach out to the undoubted values of the future? If what is, is sacred, how can it properly be changed? How can the individual build his new world without completely destroying the foundations of belief and habit inherited from the past? Yet vast movements of population and amazing changes in mores are the staple of the world's history, though often accomplished at a huge cost of blood and treasure and with brutality in extreme form.

Yet in other social organizations alongside the state, the emphasis is often on the future: the church has its dreams of the life to come; industry hopes for expansion and development; labor looks to a better day for the worker than the past has given him; science and education strive for finer things in their worlds of activity.

The state has often been handicapped by the necessity of sustaining the past in larger measure than other societies in the community. In a soundly constructed and operating state, however, the past is not merely a reminiscence, a tradition, but a source of inspiration for the future. The spirit, courage, and skill of the great warriors are not dead but live in the present and the future too, providing models for imitation.

Which is of greater value or of greater force—the golden age of the past or the golden age of the future? This is a question which cannot be answered except by an analysis of special situations as they come along. Nor are these two alternatives exclusive in nature, for both may be utilized in the policy of political or other societies. If the treasures of the past are buried or forgotten, we may bring them into the light again, and if the hopes of the future are lost sight of, we may paint them again for inspiration and courage. As Genesis and Revelation have their special values in the religious world, so history and prophecy have their specific values in the world political.

An underlying problem of political intelligence is the shaping of conditions of such a type that the individual may feel at home in his world.[20] If the old is destroyed or abandoned, this does not mean that all the old is bad or that all the new is good. The basic understandings, the basic virtues upon which communities rest, remain the same; but the applications of these principles to new situations vary widely from time to time. Changing application does not bring a new principle but an old one. What is changed is not the rule but the circumstances to which the rule applies as time goes on.

Valuable is the quality commonly called "alertness and adaptability"—more technically the faculty of synthesis—putting together new factors into a new picture. In war there are specific trainings designed to test and train facilities of adaptation to new circumstances—in airplanes, in jungles, in contacts with

[20] Cf. Beardsley Ruml, *Government, Business and Values* (1943).

other peoples with other ways. There are even games of "upset" which children play at times.

How much is new in the new and how much is old in the old? What are the relative proportions of old and new as we move into new situations? How shall we identify them, appraise them, and put them together in our new world? These are often soluble problems in which greater facility would aid in the solution of many perplexing social and political problems. These are, indeed, the identical problems with which men are busy every day in their own affairs, but which they often forget when they enter the field of public affairs, substituting slogans, prejudices, and closed minds for their habitual attitudes in their own undertakings.

Unwillingness to weigh the new and the old is a mark of insecurity in general, or a mark of vested interest and satisfied personality. In general, the institution, political or economic, must be able to justify itself against competitors whether in the industrial market or in the domain of political competition. Yet at all times a wide area of social resources is protected by age, prestige, and monopoly position unassailable under the rules of the day.

The importance of the foregoing lies in the fact that much of the lag in social and political progress is due to the failure to make necessary adaptations to new conditions speedily, in the field either of local government or of world order, of crime and war, of race and class relations.

In these days the ways and means of explaining opportunities for adjustment are far richer than ever before. The radio, the movie, the press, and the mechanism of "advertising" afford opportunity for manifold interpretations of proposed changes or changes actually authorized and about to go into effect. Rationing requirements in war, for example, have been fully explained and ready compliance obtained through general publicity regarding what in fact was a very difficult adjustment for many millions of people to make in many countries. Tax requirements by way of contrast are often poorly explained and the cause of widespread dissatisfaction to many persons. Government may be at all times "your friendly dealer" if sufficient care is taken in adjustment of the old to the new or the new to the old way.

Efforts to bring about what cuts too deeply or unreasonably across the folkways may be thwarted by opposition even under very dictatorial governments, as for illustration the attempt to prevent listening to news broadcasts on the radio, to suppress language or forms of worship, or to enforce, in America, the prohibition of the sale of intoxicating liquors. Where the ground has been ineffectively prepared, the appeal to the old against the unknown has made possible prolonged and tragic opposition to education, sanitation, health, housing, social security, annuities for the aged, accident and unemployment insurance, children's courts, preventive medicine and criminology, railways, airways, highways, and even new modes of fertilizing soil, of mining, of conservation of resources—to mention a few of the many adjustments which advanced at a slow pace for an unnecessarily long time. In many of these cases adherence to custom covered inertia and in various instances special interests. A change denounced as immoral may be only unprofitable or unpleasant for some, although advantageous to others.

The task is basically that of making possible the integration and balance of the personality as he goes along through varying ways of life, making new combinations of views and values as he goes. This is a problem in all types of political association. Those who are concerned with political change may well interest themselves in the unformation of habits as well as with their formation, for one is as vital as the other in the great process of adaptation and adjustment. But precisely here it is seen that habits are modified more readily by persuasion, education, and substitution than by intimidation, violence, and cruelty. There are, to be sure, cataclysms in nature as in human life, but wisdom controls many crises and bends them to the purposes of human satisfaction—all the way from birth to death. The foundation problem is not that of making unceasing change but of preserving the balance between stability and change, of retaining the old values and blending them into the pattern of the new. A fickle and uncertain type of society, political or otherwise, is destructive of the elements of reasonable expectation upon which so much of order, justice, and liberty rests.

VI. CONCLUSIONS

We are unquestionably entering upon a period of far-reaching change, fundamentally affecting many ways of human life, political as well as other. Revolution is already upon us. The technological changes penetrating our daily activities are far more fundamental in their implications for social living than any of the changes suggested by so-called "revolutionaries" of whatever type. These new realities are pressing upon us with tempestuous force. Our problem is to find the best equilibrium among swiftly moving forces which otherwise may find solutions and balances by violence and destruction![21] The test of sound change is found below the surface of the storm. The old is not bad because it is old; nor is the new good because it is new.

But, it may be asked, are there no permanent principles of government upon which we may stand without prospect of continuing change? Is not government a matter of morals rather than of mores? The ends of government as we know them from observation and reflection remain the same—the broad directives—but the situations to which they are applied are as changing as life itself with its myriad processes of proliferation and evolution. We know what order

[21] See my *Civic Education in the United States* (1934); Karl Mannheim, *Man and Society in an Age of Reconstruction* (1940).

is, but under varying conditions the detailed outlines of order alter. We know what justice is, but its particular patterns are differently traced with the growth of social institutions. We know what is the essence of freedom, but its human realization is seen in varying clusters of action widely separated by time and place. We know more and more about the human situations coming within the purview of association, as we learn from reflection and from natural and social science. Thus we learn about preventive medicine, about preventive criminology, about social justice, about education and organization for freedom of the personality, about concert of action for the prevention of war as a means of security and welfare. Biology and psychology and medicine, chemistry and physics, education, and engineering organization indicate points at which application of the ends of government may promote the well-being of emerging personality. Observation and reflection teach us that order, justice, and freedom are for all men and not for the few alone; that all men are equal in their human dignity; that violence and overaggressiveness in persons or in nations may be channeled into better lines; that poverty, pestilence, and famine are not the fate of man; that the weak are not to be abandoned to the mercy of the strong, who have strength without mercy and may contemplate weakness without hope of change. There is every reason to believe that scientific discovery and invention will sweep on in an increasing flood in the period before us and will precipitate changes basically affecting the stability of particular holders of political power. Transportation and communication do not appear to be unconstitutional at any point or unpatriotic, but nonetheless they may be overturning the ancient landmarks as no enemy could possibly do; or they may be modifying the basic controls over human behavior.

One of the greatest needs of our time is the organization of our modern intelligence in terms of understanding of physical inventions in their relation to behavior and social inventions. The wide gap between the understanding of "machines" and of social mechanisms is one of the greatest danger points in our civilization. The farther and the faster one advances without the other, the greater the degree of risk. Furthermore, as danger comes on, the mind trained in machines but not in social mechanisms may recoil in panic and turn against all forms of social change, falling back upon the traditional and unchanging as a port of security, at the very moment when it has been rendered untenable by the new forces of invention and discovery. The next step in this *non sequitur* is to employ violence to repress changes indicated by science. Thus scientific tear gas may be employed to break up freedom of discussion about some point raised by the modern scientific trends, or the radio to spread falsehood, or scientific torture to crush liberty of discussing a problem such as unemployment. When any tensions arise from the failure to assimilate the old to the new, the recourse is likely to be to violence, conspicuously seen in the cases of Germany, Italy, and Russia in recent times. In other nations there is a strong tendency to use violence and repression to prevent even the discussion of the elements of an unpleasant problem or the presentation of alternative modes of procedure. Governmental action or mob violence may be hurled against a new idea; and, if antagonism rises high enough and spreads far enough, the only way out may be violence in one form or another. We are thus far unable to break the dangerous circle of mechanical invention–social distress–need of readjustment–social invention–panicky fear and return to tradition and then violence.

This is partly a problem of general education, partly of special social and civic education and training, but it is chiefly a problem of political maturity and attitudes throughout the entire community. Unfortunately, the personal I.Q. does not always follow the line indicated by political wisdom, because intelligence may be deflected from the common good by considerations of personal or group advantage. The long and dismal array of earlier forebodings and cynicisms regarding many of the basic democratic institutions of our day, as, for example, education, child labor, woman suffrage, the income tax, and social insurance is eloquent in its demand for the very broadest expansion of the zone of sound judgment regarding the common good.

The heaviest burdens rest upon the school, the press, the radio, and the screen, as well as upon the agencies of private as well as of public government. In tension moments the scientist as well as others may inquire, above the clamor of emotion or special interest:

What are the chief points of tension and torsion regarding a change proposed?

What are the strong points in the old system as it has developed and what are its weakest spots?

What are the alternative and the feasible programs of reorganization?

What are the types of change best adapted to this particular phase and form of political development?

What are the ways and means of fitting mechanical and social inventions into the old value system and patterns of action?

All this involves not merely adult education and intelligence but adult discrimination and judgment, adult sense of responsibility, and adult will to action.

Stability and change are not categories to which broad principles can readily be applied, but there are some general considerations of value in facilitating the elusive equilibrium of stability and change. These considerations are discussed in the following paragraphs.

It may be noted in passing that this is not a problem peculiar to the institution of government but runs through many other social structures—business, the church, the school, and otherwhere. Always and everywhere there is the danger of crystallizing a device successful in one situation into a permanent mechanism which is not applicable to other cases. More accurately, the problem is that of distinguishing between the arrangements which are capable of generalization and those which are of temporary and limited significance. This is as true of pedagogy, advertising, and production as it is of the political process. Deadwood, vested interest, and vestigial survivals are the commonplace of institutional development; and wise are the leaders and the groups who can utilize the soundest values for the common good of the particular group and discard the outgrown and outworn. Obsolescence is a continuing problem, involving the highest and best use of the patterns of social change. How can it be detected, what adjustments may be made, and how shall the burdens and benefits of change be most fairly distributed?

1. A climate friendly to new ideas and institutions, a receptive attitude toward social inventiveness, a critical appreciation of new proposals, a recognition and evaluation of new utilities which research and science may bring—but without any presumption that the new may be better than the old. In the broad process of political change there is a heavy burden on the brokers and adjusters of social inventions and on the role of education, conciliation, administration, and flexible statesmanship which will interpret the new to the old and avert the tense moments out of which violence may spring.

2. From time to time it is well to recur to basic principles, to the ends of government, namely, security, order, justice, welfare, and freedom, and to check proposed changes against these high standards. In wartime many important changes are made because they are related to an accepted basic end of government. If a like attitude and policy could be developed in peacetime, with a like will to action, important results might be achieved in the direction of a new drive in government toward general welfare. At the basis of such a result, however, is an underlying unity and political faith permeating political forms and policies. Faith is not the child of violence, but violence often does spring from faith. It is true that faith will co-operate with violence if it sees as the outcome the fulfilment of its dreams and hopes. Germans and Japanese have a form of faith in the end result of their undertakings which imposes upon them vast suffering and sacrifice.[22]

If the application of the ends of government is not changed from time to time, the ends may become the protectors of privilege and drive us in the direct opposite from that of justice, freedom, and welfare. One man's freedom uncurbed may mean another's slavery. Order may be used to protect the justice of the few against the life of many.

From time to time great sacrificial faiths arise. This is not merely faith in a leader, or faith in a law, or faith in a form of government primarily, but faith in some prospect of release or advance to better things. That faith has nothing

[22] Harold J. Laski, *Faith, Reason and Civilization* (1944).

to do with law and order, with decrees and ordinances, with practical judgment and shrewd politics, is one of the oldest illusions of mankind, discovered too late by those who saw their property and their position crumble before the faith of the lowly and the weak.

It may be, and has been, the case that faith inhibits change and struggle against it. But there may be, and has been, faith in the golden future as well as faith in the golden past. It may be said that both change and faith are categories too broad and vague for technical analysis and treatment until we know more about measuring trends, about social inventiveness, and understand more fully the psychology of what we call "faith." Perhaps this is true, but in the meantime revolution is upon us, and we may point out what we see, "in a glass darkly," with whatever value the imperfect vision may have.

3. Significant changes are best made with skilled technical advice, with ample notice to those especially concerned, with full and tolerant discussion. Long-time and fundamental political changes might well be subjected formally to thorough examination by technically and practically competent agencies for their consideration and evaluation, but not for their decision. Conceivably an agency for this purpose—a council of conservation—might be set up in appropriate form with the co-operation of public and private authorities. Such a function can, of course, be exercised by constitutional conventions, by courts, by special commissions of legislative bodies, by planning agencies, or by a wide variety of social research agencies. In American experience such problems of change as those involved in slavery, prohibition, emerging forms of taxation, and race relations are adapted to systematic and formal effort to mark out areas of agreement, disagreement, and neutrality, to determine a level of discourse, to lay a foundation for discussion based on ascertained fact with rational alternative measures well considered.

4. In the making of agreed changes all the available techniques of modern public relations and of superior administration may well be employed to publicize the nature, terms, timing, and rationale of proposed changes, to avoid breaking the continuity of the citizen's cherished world in which his personality is rooted. Changes are best presented and received as opportunities rather than as orders, waiving, of course, emergencies when inaction is worse than some psychological shock.

5. Too great reliance cannot be placed upon automatic machinery either for making or for preventing change. If unanimity or extraordinary majorities are required for constitutional or other change, the veto is placed in the hands of a few who may represent very special interests adversely affected by proposed action; and necessary changes may be prevented or impeded at times when action is urgently required. On the other hand, if all political landmarks are fluid so that vital changes may be made without notice, there is inadequate

protection for general interests against special groups in sudden and temporary authority for the moment.

The real safeguard lies in the moderation and judgment of those in office and in the alertness and wisdom of the political community. Confusion is caused by exclusive reliance upon constitutional or other mechanisms designed to protect the community automatically against danger. Eternal vigilance is a safer guard than an unamendable political document always subject to interpretation and to exception and emergency.

We are on notice that new inventions and contrivances expand the range and scope and speed of human possibilities within a generation, far outstripping any changes we have hitherto known. Physics, biochemistry, psychology, and medicine are bursting with possibilities which sometimes stagger the imagination of the most starry-eyed. The utopians have not been utopian enough to keep pace with the progress of human intelligence in many fields of endeavor.

Our situation leaves room for great improvement in its wisdom and reliability for the high purposes ahead in medicine, education, production, financing. Statesmen struggle with demagogues, charlatans, power-hungry, vested rights and vested wrongs, over what might better be decided in the laboratory or the court by observation, analysis, and reflection committed to the fortunes of battle. Business and government, labor and management, church and state, science and tradition, nation and nation, prevent a unity of action which might prove effective and, in discord, consume vast resources which might be devoted to the welfare of mankind.

Government is the oldest and in some ways the best-tried agency of mankind, and, whatever its temporary aberrations may be—and they are many—there is no reason to conclude that government cannot be kept abreast of the advancing waves of human progress. Its principles and its techniques are capable of dealing with any human problem if they are co-ordinated and inspired by public support and confidence, by faith as well as by force, by intelligence as well as by passion. The correlation between (1) the personalities acquiring power and (2) the needs of the general welfare has often been low; but, with education and attention, the selection of men for official responsibility may relate more closely to the qualities that bring happiness and the higher human values to men.

CHAPTER VIII

THE INTERRELATIONS OF POLITICAL ASSOCIATIONS

I. EARLY TYPES

THE types of historic forms of independent political associations are many, and their interrelations widely varying. Historical evolution, however, has eliminated many types which have appeared from time to time, such as the family and city-state, or the clan and tribe (not wholly), and produced many new combinations of importance, which develop international relations. There are now some fifty-odd independent political associations in the world to which categories of size, ethnic composition, social and economic organization, cultural patterns, broad aims and purposes, and degrees of centralization may be applied aside from variations in forms and organs of government.

It is important to look at the development of various forms of political associations historically in order to put into useful perspective the emerging classifications. The family is an early and simple form of political authority. Here paternal (or maternal) power and political power are united, although custom, religion, and magic brood over the whole scene. Down to this day the familial factor in government is of far-reaching importance in its relation to the political; and in some countries, such as China, family government is still of the very greatest political significance. By means of kinship, a grouping of families into clans or tribes easily bridges over to larger aggregations in ampler form. Anthropology is rich in material bearing upon these primitive types of political association. Much of the world's government has been and is centered in the family.

The city may serve as the unit of political association. Classic cities like Athens and Rome were states as well as urban communities and, with their surrounding area, became majestic centers of authority and of culture. Later the free cities of the medieval period were also impressive focuses of association, political and commercial. It was a long time before Hamburg and Venice, with the rise of nationalism, were absorbed in the larger political association surrounding them. Modern cities with huge populations and resources have found it difficult to find a sound basis even for local self-government.[1]

The feudal state appearing in many widely varying forms rested on inheritance, land, and contract. It was based upon an area not always compact and contiguous, for the lord might have many scattered vassals and himself be the vassal of another lord, and vice versa. These units, essentially restricted in area and numbers, carried on a running struggle with the empire and the

[1] See U. S. National Resources Committee, Research Committee on Urbanism, *Our Cities: Their Role in the National Economy* (June, 1937).

church, with other feudalities, and with the rising nation[2] both in the Occident and in the Orient under varying forms.

"Empire" has always been a loosely used term, intended to cover a wider range of territory and people than the ordinary political society. Egypt, Babylonia, Assyria, the Roman Empire, the Holy Roman Empire, the British Empire, among many others, were larger editions of the smaller states. They were held together by various complex bonds of territory, race, and religion, so widely disparate as to challenge classification.

II. THE NATIONAL STATE

The national state dates from the sixteenth century, emerging as the successor of feudalism, on the one side, and the Holy Roman Empire, on the other. France, Spain, and England took the lead in the establishment of the new political order, with Germany, Japan, and Italy as the most recent arrivals.

The nation is built partly upon ethnic factors and partly upon territory, but it also involves a variety of other elements. Among these are tradition, language, and cultural community, but the exceptions to all these are many and render difficult the sharp delimitation of the national.

Thus new nations developed from seemingly incongruous elements, as in the case of Switzerland and Belgium, while the powerful Scandinavian group produced Sweden, Norway, and Denmark with much in common in cultural origins and interests. From World War I emerged Poland after centuries of eclipse, Yugoslavia, Finland, Czechoslovakia, Latvia, Lithuania, Esthonia, Hungary, and Ireland, along with others. Likewise Japan and China assumed strong national form, with other groups, such as India, struggling in the same direction.

The national state became the central type of political association, large or small in area or population, ethnically homogeneous or heterogeneous, geographically contiguous or not, economically classifiable as capitalistic or collectivist, agricultural, industrial, or otherwise. The nation took over loyalties and patriotisms attached to previous forms of political association such as the city, the ethnic group, the family, and, in wide areas of activity, the ecclesiastical groupings. None of these loyalties was destroyed, but each was embodied in the framework of the national state, which became the most powerful agency in modern social life. The nation took over the love of country in the physical sense of love of soil, the combinations of ethnic-cultural loyalties in great measure, the juristic attributes of sovereignty as the ultimate power of decision in political affairs, and general priority over cultural associations. The ends and tools of government became the ends and tools of the nation.

[2] See account of Japanese feudalism in W. C. MacLeod, *The Origin and History of Politics* (1931).

At the outset the nation's authority rested upon inheritance of political and economic power, through hereditary monarchy and hereditary transmission of the ownership of land. To this was added the doctrine of the divine right of rulers and the special attributes involved in the lawyers' theory of sovereignty. Spain, France, and England consolidated their local political associations and came forward with larger units of authority, firmly intrenched against assaults.

The transition from a landed economy to a predominantly industrial economy was made by the several nations with varying degrees of skill and success. Likewise the transition to a new world, geographically and politically, was a process in which nations such as Spain and Austria were left behind.[3]

Varying forms of nationalism have been distinguished. Hayes, for example, finds humanitarian nationalism, Jacobin nationalism, traditional nationalism, liberal nationalism, and, in the last phase, integral nationalism.[4] The latter form—the integral—is characterized by the militant spirit, a sense of superiority, external and internal. "The nation is the possession in the common of an ancient cemetery," said one enthusiast. Regionalism, religion, language, and, later, monarchism are significant elements in this form of exaggerated nationalism.[5] But the attempt to carry into effect this movement collapsed.

"French nationalism," Hayes says, "is not exclusively or chiefly a product of physical geography or of racial heredity. It is the product of historical human cultural forces. It rests on traditions of politics, religion, language, war, invasion, conquest, economics, and society, which have been fashioned by peculiar and often fortuitous circumstances and which have been preserved and synthesized by great writers and other intellectuals..... And what is most artificial about the whole phenomenon of contemporary French nationalism is the fact that it has been consciously taught to, and thereby imposed upon, the mass of Frenchmen."[6]

"Nationality" and "nation" are used not infrequently in a confusing fashion, and it is not always clear whether the material dealt with is the political unitary group or a cultural group aspiring to political autonomy. Volumes have been

---

[3] For an analysis of this see Oscar Jászi, *The Dissolution of the Habsburg Monarchy* (1929).

[4] C. J. H. Hayes, *Essays on Nationalism* (1926).

[5] See Charles Maurras, *Enquête sur la monarchie* (1925); *La Politique religieuse* (1912).

[6] C. J. H. Hayes, *France: A Nation of Patriots* (1930), p. 16. See J. W. Garner, *Political Science and Government* (1928), chaps. vi–vii; W. A. Dunning, *A History of Political Theories from Rousseau to Spencer* (1920), chap. viii; Friedrich Meinecke, *Weltbürgertum und Nationalstaat* (1911); W. O. E. Mitscherlich, *Nationalismus* (1929). See also G. P. Gooch, *Nationalism* (1920); René Johannet, *Le Principe des nationalités* (1918); J. H. Rose, *Nationality in Modern History* (1916); Hans Kohn, *The Idea of Nationalism* (1944). From another point of view are Robert Michels, *Der Patriotismus* (1929), and W. B. Pillsbury, *The Psychology of Nations* (1919). See also my *The Making of Citizens* (1931) for analysis of various nations; Heinz O. Ziegler, *Die moderne Nation* (1931); Frederick Hertz, *Nationality in History and Politics* (1944).

written on the characteristics of various nations—English, German, French, or otherwise—treatises which in great part are written in anything but an objective manner, and which in the more extreme cases amount to a jingoistic glorification or denunciation of a particular nation.[7]

The right of autonomy enters largely into more recent discussions of nationalism and raises many questions regarding the type of group entitled to self-determination and the nature and limits of the autonomy to be achieved or allowed. What ethnic groups or what particular cultures or combinations of the ethnic and the cultural are justified in demanding political independence is, of course, a topic of controversy, ended sometimes by force of arms, again by political adjustment, or by the process of economic reorganization, but always with an appeal to the common judgment of civilized mankind in the background of rationalization.[8]

Both fascism and naziism emphasized in the extreme the self-sufficiency and adequacy of the state itself without regard to other members of the family of nations. Old-time mercantilism blossomed out into modern autarchy based on military considerations. Both international law and international associations were brushed aside as matters of indifference to vigorous nations knowing their way and their goal. In the name of geopolitics *Lebensraum* was freely interpreted as a pretext for national expansion in the desired directions by the Italian empire or the German Reich, as the case might be. Treaties and agreements were made, it is true, but those who entered into them were fully aware that the binding force of these arrangements was near zero. There was no concealment of the preference of the Duce and the Führer for war as a solution of international difficulties. On the contrary, there was outspoken eulogy of the virtues of war. The "ethnic" impulse became the basis of the nation, primitive urges were the basis of all action, of law, and of justice. "We think with our blood" was placed as a rational view of deliberation and decision. Hence the national urge, as interpreted by the ruler, was the basis of national policy and action.

Several features were added to the idea of nation; one, the mission of the superior race embodied in the special nation of Germany, the master-race (*Herrenvolk*); another, the doctrine of the superiority of the state over the individual, and, finally, the concentration of all political authority in a hier-

---

[7] For a better type see Ernest Barker, *National Character and the Factors in Its Formation* (1927); D. W. Brogan, *The American Character* (1944).

[8] In the Freudian theory the state appears as a substitute for the father as a principle of authority and guidance (Sigmund Freud, *Group Psychology and the Analysis of the Ego* [1922]; cf. H. D. Lasswell, *Psychopathology and Politics* [1930] and *World Politics and Personal Insecurity* [1935], chap. ii). From another point of view the state is an emotional unity, which individuals identify as a unity with themselves. Reservations are expressed by Lasswell and by others. (Cf. Wilhelm Reich, *Massenpsychologie der Faschismus* [1934]).

archy headed by a Führer—totalitarianism. Strictly speaking, the source of legitimacy was not the *Staat* but the *Gemeinschaft*, the socioethnic group back of political forms and authorities, represented by the direct voice of the Führer.

In various forms the national state became the most powerful political agency. It was at once the center of the strongest military powers, the greatest economic resources, unsurpassed as the home of science, technology, culture, and incomparably the most dynamic center of loyalty and patriotism. It adopted and sometimes gave color to (national) religion, to (national) democracy, to (national) capitalism, and to (national) communism. Family, city, science, and religion retained their own priorities, but these, too, were not without the circle of nationalistic influence and direction.

III. COMPETING FORMS OF ASSOCIATION

All was not smooth sailing, however, for the national state. Attacks from many quarters concentrated upon the integrity of the dominant form of political association. Beginning early in the nineteenth century, the anarchists led the way with a series of criticisms of the state, ranging from the ethical to the economic to the biological. Godwin and Proudhon in turn attacked the validity and value of the state as a form of human association and demanded its abolition.

These criticisms, it is true, were not directed solely against the national state as such but against all forms of association political in nature, either because of their inherent character, because of their relation to capitalism, or because they did not reflect the transition from coercion to co-operation in the evolution of mankind. Proudhon early developed a form of "economic federalism," in which producing units might be brought together in a form of union, not political but closely approximating it. "Class" was substituted for nation in the Marxian movement. The old-time nation was held to be the tool of capitalism, and the new association of workers was believed to be on its way, replacing the older forms of political association in an organization which was to be primarily a workers' society. Instead of many units, one was proposed as the union of all the workers of the world. In Russia this idea was given reality and vitality in the development of Old Russia into the U.S.S.R. This system was presented as a goal of general interest and obtained substantial support as against the older national state. But here again Mother Russia reappeared during recent events as a more significant force than the class system, whatever may be the ultimate outcome.

The Hindu poet and philosopher, Tagore, denounced Western industrial-mechanical civilization and nationalism as well. But, in the main, the Eastern groups, including China, Japan, and India, accepted nationalism as a part of their political program and launched out upon struggles to achieve it.

Significant were developments in the bases of association such as the rise of

266

pluralism, which found recruits among the economists, the churches, the jurists, and the critics of statism. The eminent French jurist, Duguit, set alongside the state the values of the groups as rule-makers and lawmakers, following in this respect some of the ideas of Gierke, on the one hand, and the sociologist, Durkheim, on the other. As against excessive nationalism and statism, ecclesiasts defended various forms of pluralistic organization and association and intimated that there were great values in the corporate associations with limited jural purposes within the framework of the nation. Influenced by ecclesiastical litigation, Figgis in his *Churches in the Modern State* sought for a moral basis of social action independent of the authority of the national government. The school of guild socialists advocated the organization of society upon the basis of a modernized form of the medieval guild, as in Cole's *Guild Socialism* and other works of like tenor.

But now vast aggregations of economic power in the shape of international organizations were acquiring wide-ranging political influence and quietly challenging the validity of the national state structure or utilizing it for their purposes. These cartel-like groups indeed preferred to operate through existing state structure, even while they overflowed the banks of the nations, in the widening flood of economic expansion of oil, steel, rubber, dyes, electricity, and the intricacies of patent and credit controls. These economic societies organized the economic world as best they could, with the profit motive as their guiding star, and long since have wielded greater financial and other authority than many of the smaller states. Governments, indeed, have often been at their beck and call—and vice versa. The co-ordination or co-operation of these agencies constitutes a major problem of world organization in the near future. One has only to superimpose an economic map of world economic resources over a political map of nations to discover the variety of adjustments that are required both for peace and for prosperity. Individuals, corporations, cartels, state trading organizations, and combinations of all these forms will bring about many rivalries and clashes, but also open great avenues of opportunity if wiser counsels prevail. But, without some form of higher organization, these forces lead to conflict and war.

Both internal and external structure were challenged by these organized structures in business, labor, and agriculture as well. On the one hand, they lead to the revival of the old "estate-state" of feudal days (*Ständestaat*) which became the basis of the Nazi political organization in modified form, and under the supreme direction of the Führer in a hierarchical system of authority. In quite another framework the corporative organization of self-governing groups was presented by the church. In Italy the corporatives (*corporativi*) became nominally the units of authority under the direction of the Duce.[9]

[9] See James Burnham, *The Managerial Revolution* (1941) and *The Machiavellians* (1943).

This was not the special form advocated by the church but rather a travesty upon it.

The organization of workers likewise advanced with great speed, although more tardily than the large corporations or monopolies and cartels. Labor strength became a formidable element in the social control of the great industrialized states, and at times, as in England, it held a controlling position in the government. The international organization of labor also rapidly developed and became an agency of great influence, especially through the International Labor Organization.

At times there developed a movement in the direction of the industrial self-government, including workers, management, and owners with wide authority over rule-making and rules within their special areas and functions. This might lead to a corporative state not associated with the principle of hierarchy and leadership characteristic of fascism.

The power of these new forces and groups made itself increasingly felt over the world and constituted a challenge of the first order to nationalism, which had been little disturbed since the fall of feudalism. They raised sharply the question as to the optimum size, form, and principle of political association and challenged the politicos to analysis and invention of the first order. They also raised more sharply than ever the problem of the interrelations of these powerful groups, one to another.

IV. FEDERALISM AND REGIONALISM

Types of political association looking toward the aggregation or association of several units in federal forms began to make their appearance very early in Greece and later in Holland. Sometimes these were formed by the union of separate states and sometimes by the decentralization of established nations, as in Brazil and the U.S.S.R. Sometimes these associations were the result of bloody struggles, and again they were established in a peaceful fashion. The number and the variety of these combinations were large, ranging from loose unions to closely knit federal states. The United States, Germany, and Switzerland represented one form of combination.

Various degrees and forms of integration developed and were distinguished as alliances, confederations, and federal states, with many subtle variations among them. Jellinek, for example, enumerated thirty-seven varieties.[10] These associations were usually designed to be more formal and binding than an alliance but less unifying than a national state. The degrees and types of independence and union were, of course, widely different, depending upon the original form of association, upon interpretation, and upon practice. The

[10] See George Jellinek, *Die Lehre von den Staatenverbindungen* (1882). See my *History of the Theory of Sovereignty since Rousseau* (1900), chap. x, on "Federalism and Continental Theory."

United States and Germany, Canada, and Australia, especially, offer many illustrations of the juristic subtleties involved and of the practical problems emerging. The whole range of governmental functions and services inevitably was drawn into consideration, as local and central interests alternately clashed and combined.

The whole broad problem of centralization and decentralization was raised with a series of the legal, structural, administrative, legislative, and ideological questions. Both powers and functions were at issue, with centralization and decentralization running through the problem.

Other large-scale developments of the unit of political association were seen in England and Russia. Out of the British Empire evolved the British Commonwealth of Nations, with dominions of almost completely independent character, as in Canada, Australia, South Africa, and New Zealand. These units found their central unifying point in the British crown, but for most purposes, including war, they were autonomous. Their cohesive power has been demonstrated, however, in two great wars waged as a unit over long periods of time.

The U.S.S.R. in 1944 established sixteen units of the central organization, allocating them powers over external relations and over peace and war, although still within the general range of the Union. In these instances wide stretches of territory and large numbers of people are thus brought within a new form of diffusion of authority, differing from nationalism, on the one hand, and federalism, on the other.[11]

It was confidently predicted by eminent authority that the federal system of the United States could not survive the struggles either of peace or of war, but the prophets were inaccurate, for the United States lived through a desperate civil war and emerged triumphantly from two world wars with strength unsurpassed by any other state. Likewise the British form of commonwealth was freely criticized as impossible of operation. "The thin red line of British power," said the commentator, Homer Lea, "will break at the first rude thrust";[12] yet the Commonwealth of Nations still survives. In both these instances industrial power and cultural advancement have also made notable progress.

Thus it cannot seriously be questioned that far-flung territory, large population, and prosperity are compatible with varying forms of federalism, given democratic controls and an adequate degree of political sagacity and maturity. The three largest and most powerful political associations in the world are of the federalized type, using the term "federal" in its broadest meaning, with many wide possibilities and actualities of variation in practice.

[11] Brazil federalized its form of government but reconsidered later (see W. Y. Elliott, *The New British Empire* [1932]).

[12] *The Day of the Saxon* (1912).

There is ample room for varying types of regional understandings and arrangements either of conventional or of constitutional character in such areas as may be adapted to these structural or functional arrangements. It is significant that physical contiguity is not essential for such association, as the British Commonwealth shows. Functional agreements covering specific types of activities, commercial or otherwise, are also in line of realization without any modification of constitutional structure whatever.[13]

Alliances between two or more states are of types innumerable, as varied as the possible terms and duration of contracts between independent powers. In so-called "personal unions" such as Austria-Hungary and the old-time Sweden-Norway, approach was made to a common government through individuals who were common rulers. Many crowns might be placed upon one head.

The "balance of power" was in a sense an alliance but is more nearly characterized as a part of the grand strategy of one or more states, as the policy of Britain on the continent of Europe aims against the consolidation of overmastering power on the part of any state or combination of states. This involves the shifting of alliances and arrangements from time to time for the purpose of preserving the presumed equilibrium. In our time this doctrine has been expanded in the form of three- or four-power agreements for the stabilization of the world, either within or without the framework of some jural order of the world.[14]

Obviously, there are many embarrassments no matter how the states of the world are parceled out, but these difficulties are no less painful than the experience and contemplation of an unorganized world. In general, it may be said that the balance of power in its traditional form, merely as a method of operation, leaves much to be desired. No merely military balance or economic balance which ignores the position of the smaller states or the goal of a jural order of the world can be more than a temporary expedient. A truly world balance of power, properly implemented, does not differ as much from a jural order of the world as might seem at first thought.

With modern developments of communication and transportation and especially in the area of military technology, the so-called "regions" of the world are in an increasingly parlous status. Smaller states are already in a very difficult position in the face of the emerging airplane and rocket gun, to say nothing of other implements of destruction on their way. Regions are no longer protected from military attack by distance from their neighbors or from the competition of large-scale economic units of trade and commerce. Nor is there any

---

[13] See Walter Lippmann, *U.S. War Aims* (1944).

[14] The most pretentious example of this effort is seen in Lippmann, *op. cit.*, outlining several communities—the Atlantic, the Russian, the Chinese, the Middle East. But see also the following: J. T. Shotwell, *The Great Decision* (1944); Sumner Welles, *The Time for Decision* (1944); W. T. R. Fox, *The Super-powers* (1944).

high degree of precision in marking the geographical or demographic outlines of particular regions in the world into which we move. What are the natural boundaries of Russia, or of China, or of the Anglo-American powers? Where does Africa or India "belong"? It is naïve to suppose that they will settle themselves without reference to the larger area which contains them.

World War I produced the League of Nations, an organization designed to preserve the world from aggression and to establish continually bettering social and political relations among the nations of the earth. Alongside this was set up the International Labor Office. The League, however, proved unequal to the task of stabilizing the nations of the world in the form set up, notwithstanding the high technical excellence of many of its undertakings, notably those in the field of health and of economics. Other nations followed the example of the United States until the League was finally shorn of all its effective authority and prestige.[15] Snapping cords brought a realization that world association was yet to be developed and perfected through more experience.[16]

At the present time the future of international associations remains in doubt, pending the outcome of the war and the form of the resulting peace. Proposals range from military alliances and regional understandings to the formation of a world state, with many forms of intermediate character between these extremes.

The Atlantic Charter and the United Nations with its signatory powers point the way to closer forms of international co-operation, yet undetermined. The guaranties already obtained are far-reaching in their sweep, recognizing self-determination in form of government, access to natural resources, co-operation among nations in living standards and society, and abandonment of aggression. The organization, powers, and activities of the United Nations await the further development of the war and the steps taken to insure the preservation of peace and justice.

In a shrinking world of accelerating transportation and communication, the unit of political aggregation becomes a problem of increasing importance.[17] In the coming world the role of the small state, like Denmark or Belgium, isolated and unprotected, is a difficult one. Such states will look to the protection of some over-all agency willing and able to protect their autonomy. But also for the large states the problem of adequate federation becomes of paramount importance. The alternatives are those of organized interdependency— possibly of a federative character—the development of armed alliances of the larger states, and the organization of an over-all political society.

[15] Mandates under the League of Nations raised many interesting problems regarding the status of the mandated areas (see Quincy Wright, *Mandates under the League of Nations* [1930]).

[16] See, on international attitudes, my *The Making of Citizens*, pp. 310–18.

[17] See Eugene Staley, *This Shrinking World* (1940).

A prime difficulty in undertaking even a preliminary exploration of the possibilities of broader forms of association is that the vocabulary of politics, in its commonly accepted definitions, lags behind political events.[18] The British Empire was blended into the British Commonwealth of Nations by the Statute of Westminster. The symbol of the crown and a common citizenship unite, but do not compel, the peoples of a British federation of nations. There is no adequate terminology with which to label many of the new political phenomena springing up before our eyes. We see, for illustration, that England offered to France, on the eve of her tragic collapse, an absolute union, with common citizenship, common defense, and common currency. If that offer had been made a little sooner, or if the French people had known about it when it was made, or if there had been sufficient political planning to have foreseen such a union, basic liberties long lost in the vast prison camp of France might have been saved. But the concept was so novel and came so suddenly that it was too late.

V. WORLD ORDER

Almost simultaneously with the rise of nations came the appearance of international law.[19] In three centuries or more there has sprung up a vast body of practice and philosophy dealing with basic problems. The history of international practices and agreements, of treaties, of diplomacy, of significant theories of the nature and meaning of international law—these alone fill many ponderous tomes. Spanish, Dutch, German, French, English, and American philosophers of many types have labored hard in the elaboration of international philosophy and practice. Many acute and patient minds have diligently sought to find rules or norms of right or practices and precedents which would possess validity in dealings between states and serve as a basis for the appraisal of international behavior. Is international law based upon convention, upon custom projected, upon reason, upon morality? What sanctions are applicable to violations of such rules of law? Is international law true law, and are there genuine norms of international right demonstrable by human reason? What relations have man-made laws or customs, or divine decrees, or right reason, to the domain of this form of law? And, of course, the eternal question occurs: Who's who in the world of decisionism and interpretation?

Objectives of international law are the amelioration of the atrocities of war,

---

[18] Lasswell, *World Politics and Personal Insecurity.*

[19] Cf. Quincy Wright's classic *A Study of War* (2 vols., 1942) and bibliography there cited; H. C. Koenig (ed.), *Principles for Peace: Selections from Papal Documents* (1943); Guido Gonella, *A World To Reconstruct* (1944); Lyman Bryson *et al.* (eds.), *Approaches to World Peace: Fourth Symposium* (1944); F. E. Johnson (ed.), *Religion and the World Order* (1944); Hans Kelsen, *Allgemeine Staatslehre* (1925); Hornell Hart and Donald L. Taylor, "Was There a Prehistoric Trend from Smaller to Larger Political Units?" *American Journal of Sociology*, XLIX (January, 1944), 289–301.

promotion of the amenities of national relations, development of ways and means of pacific adjustment through structural and procedural devices, reduction of the area of violence in international dealings—all this in the midst of gigantic power struggles and intense rivalry for the possession of profitable or strategic markets, of ethnic and geographic hatreds, and of jealousies of far-reaching proportions.

The most serious problem presented to the builders of international law and relations arises from the difficulty of reconciling a rule governing the jural order of the world with the supreme law governing the many nations of the world, first, as to reasonableness and, second, as to sanctions. The world moves toward world government, in the long run, but in the meantime there are many governments with many minds. How shall these many minds and many interests be adjusted to external norms of right and at the same time provide the necessary sanctions for the enforcement of the rules of law?

This problem is no different from, and no more difficult than, the problem of any nation in reconciling and adjusting the demands of competing pressure groups or individuals within one particular political or nonpolitical association. There are no insuperable barriers against working agreements in principle between nations on a wide range of questions. The practical difficulty is found in the agreement upon and the application of sanctions, to be determined by some agency and administered by some authority. In so far as law rests upon reason or expediency or convention, it is easy to envisage international law, but in so far as force is drawn in question, the issue is on a different level of discourse and practice. After agreement has been reached upon justice, order, welfare, and freedom, there still remain the acute sensitivities of national security, present and anticipated. No matter what is gained by the agreement, there may always be invoked the specter of losing all, through loss of national independence.

IS DEMOCRACY AN OBSTACLE TO INTERNATIONAL ORDER?

Recent objections to the possibility of jural order of the world are the arguments from democracy and from socialism.[20]

International relations was for centuries the tool of monarchs with broad authority—the technique of the diplomats of the court or later of an aristocracy of birth or wealth, trained in the elaborate procedures and practices of international intercourse. It was and still is charged that democracies are either too ignorant or too inflexible to conduct the affairs of large-scale states in effective fashion. The proofs of this postulate are very scanty and inadequate and in the end are found to be substantially the older arguments against democracy itself.

---

[20] See Quincy Wright, "Fundamental Problems of Peacemaking," *Approaches to National Unity: Fifth Symposium of the Conference on Science, Philosophy and Religion in Their Relation to the Democratic Way of Life.*

They rest upon a fundamental distrust of the capacity of democratic societies for the conduct of common affairs on any level—a part of the old and now discredited conclusion that democracies are essentially inefficient and incompetent alike in the management of affairs.

The basis of democracy is confidence in the worth of all men and in their capacity for human association on the highest level. The value of this has been amply demonstrated in economic production, in war, and in scientific and cultural development. To assert the superiority of Japanese, German, and Italian diplomacy in our day carries with it its own refutation. The root difficulty is found in the lingering distrust of the many by the nostalgic few, who remain unreconciled to the growth and dominance of human intelligence on a social scale. Benjamin Franklin in the eighteenth and Eduard Beneš in the twentieth century are striking examples of the ability that may be employed in democratic regimes. The contempt for democratic diplomacy will be found on analysis to signify no more than a general contempt for all forms of democratic policy or administration—the reluctance of the few to admit the values of the many under any scheme of government by the consent of the governed.

The assertion that the people are more ignorant, impetuous, and unstable than the old-time absolutists or the new-time dictators has no basis in reflection or in experience. When war is the sport of kings or of modern Führers, the balance of the world is no more secure than when the ultimate decisions are made by democratic states; on the contrary, the mass is more reliable and more stable. Democracies may organize their affairs in such a way as to preserve the technical values and skills of trained diplomats in the service of the common good.

It is also asserted that democracy is impossible except among a small number of people and in a very restricted area. But although democratic systems of government were originally based on the assumption of a small territory and population, such as Athens or a Swiss canton, while the larger areas and numbers were relegated to nondemocratic states, in recent times all this has changed. It was the liberal-democratic movement that laid the foundations of modern Germany and modern Italy against nondemocratic opposition. The United States of America and Great Britain have presented the case of far-ranging territory developed under democratic rule. The impulse to the formation of the League of Nations and the United Nations is obviously a democratic one. There is nothing incompatible between large-scale units and the democratic form of political association.

There is no reason to conclude that military empire is the best framework in which to unify diverse elements in terms of modern communication and transportation. Military conquest is one way, but the aftereffects of conquest exact a far higher price for necessary or desirable unification than is required.

The areas of autonomy and self-determination which are desirable may more readily be achieved through the methods of persuasion and co-operation with a minimum of violence—itself a low-level form of organization. Fraternalism is more flexible than force as a basis for association, and it further provides elements of tenacity and persistence of the first order.

IS SOCIALISM AN OBSTACLE TO WORLD ORDER?

A more recent objection to the development of a jural order of the world is the charge that socialism or collectivism or national planning will render all international arrangements ineffective. This, too, is fundamentally another phase of fear of popular control as a basis of government. A socialist state has no more reason for opposition in theory or practice to a jural world order than any other type of political society. The formal theory of Marxian socialism, indeed, is founded on the elimination of national boundary lines and the complete annihiliation of the state as an ultimate goal. But socialism in our day tends to be nationalistic, as in the case of Russia, and there remains to be discovered any adequate reason why this system is incompatible with a jural order throughout the world. Commercial and cultural relations may be carried on between socialist states with as little friction as elsewhere between nonsocialistic states. There is no sufficient reason to suppose that the workers of the world will be less ready to unite than members of any other group.[21]

Large-scale economic organizations of the Russian, American, and British types, are on their way throughout the world. Some of these organizations were already more powerful than some of the smaller states before the outbreak of the present conflict. There is no reason to assume that public or private ownership, conduct or control of these associations' many varying forms will obstruct the organization of order throughout the productive world. Capitalism, socialism, and democracy may each be the cause of friction breaking out in armed conflict, but there is no inherent and compelling reason why any one of these systems should find itself unable to operate in a world of law and order. This argument, like the preceding objection, is at bottom the old theory that only an irresponsible élite, political or economic, can operate the mechanisms of human association. Historically and logically this is as out of date as the illusion that democracies could neither make war nor produce ample commodities nor attain a high level of cultural advancement.

We must not fail to recognize, however, that there are those who prefer war to the spread of socialism. They really do not want to accept world peace at the price of tolerating the existence of socialistic states. This is another story and does not bear upon the merits of the socialistic state as adapted to jural order of the world.

[21] Jacob Viner, "The Economic Problem," in *New Perspectives on Peace*, ed. G. B. de Huszar (1944).

Of course, conflicting forms of economic organization, such as the Russian, the British, and the American, may encounter friction and difficulties in the world, just as variations in religion, variations in manners and customs, and variations in culture patterns range from advanced to relatively primitive. Likewise urban and rural, agricultural and industrial, land and seafaring economies, may create difficulties in human relations, whether between nations or between parts of the same nation. These are not insuperable obstacles but invitations to world order—to a system into which the pluralistic differences of man may be fitted with least friction and with the highest degree of diversity in unity.

BASIC CONSIDERATIONS REGARDING INTERNATIONAL ORDER

The process of international association will be facilitated by bearing in mind the following basic considerations underlying the organization of order and peace.

A. ACCEPTANCE OF THE JURAL WORLD ORDER

The acceptance of the jural order of the world as the ultimate point toward which modern civilization moves—an order in which there is justice, order, freedom, and welfare, in which security is guaranteed to all, and in which basic rights may be supplemented and modified by many other authorities, as long as the basic bond is not broken—is the first consideration.

It is not necessary to wait a thousand years, until world jural order is established, before undertaking improvements in the fragmentary order of the present. Quite the contrary, we may move along toward the goal, securing such betterments as are possible at given times and places. This has been, in fact, the course of international law for the last three hundred years. The church, the jurists, the economists, the cultural groupings—all have made their contribution to the final result.

Permanent peace, however, is not merely a negative conception, satisfied with the ending of violence as an instrument of national policy. A world order implies far more. It assumes that there are ideals and interests which are best satisfied by general association; it assumes that justice, order, freedom, and welfare may reach their highest levels when the universal jural association is finally achieved and in successful operation. There are now the ends upon which political societies are based, but the world order offers them in fuller measure—in higher standards of material and spiritual life.

The principles of peace are the fulfilment of the ends of political association—the ends of government itself. They include security, order, justice, welfare, freedom—the basic elements in the essential character of the political. Politics does not aim at the end of struggle. On the contrary, it endeavors to encourage competition, emulation, initiative and enterprise, and resolution and persistence in the growth of personalities, in the adaptation of means to ends. Violence is

276

not the climax of organization but its very lowest form. Peace is not essentially passivity but the highest organization of the highest activities and energies on the highest levels. The virtues of war organization are not lost in peace, but they are developed and perfected on higher levels and for higher ends. Organization, discipline, sacrifice, alertness, resoluteness, toughness of fiber—all these are incorporated in the organism and structure of the higher organization. Peace is not the end of struggle but the finer organization of it.

To speak of a jural order of the world as a superstate is to misunderstand the meaning of government and of state. An organization that makes possible in greatest measure the ends of government is not in opposition to government; it is the fulfilment of the purposes and promises of government. Its design and function are security, order, justice, liberty, welfare—purposes for which the state exists and which, for lack of world order, states have not been able to bring about. If we cannot face these truths, we may prepare for centuries of yet more destructive wars.

War may have been, and at times is still, a necessary element in human life in certain phases of human development. But its trend is to become unnecessary, except as traditional modes of thought and action linger in our lives. This may seem a strange doctrine at this moment of titanic war, but it is based upon the developing knowledge of the possibilities of man's control over nature and over himself in the coming world.

World order is indicated by the inexorable trend in the development of human personality in the light of experience and reflection. World order is no more incompatible with local and personal liberty than are cities, states, nations, or federal associations. Religion, reason, and law are essentially universal in their application to human relations, and human values and interests are best satisfied and realized in the broadest framework of human co-operation and aspiration. There cannot be true security, order, justice, welfare, and freedom short of the sweep and range of world association.

B. RECOGNITION OF EQUALITY

Recognition of equality as the basis of political association—equality of claims and rights, whether of persons or of races or of states—is a difficult doctrine for master-races, master-states, master-individuals, whenever and wherever found. Slavery, serfdom, caste, and privilege are maintained now as ever not by reason or by practical necessity but by ignorance, prejudice, and force. This conclusion has behind it the weight of anthropology, of religion, of philosophers, of law, and of common-sense experience, which mow down one after another the false claims of superiority and special privilege, from the days of Greek and barbarian to the master Aryans, or race supremacy in any form. Slave states and slave personalities alike are creatures in our day of violence and exploitation, however silken the chains. It was Rousseau who said, "If there are slaves by nature, it is because there have been slaves against nature." Given in our day nutrition, medication, education, employment, and access to cultural opportunities, we do not know of any so-called "inferior" races. The tremendous advances of Russia alone show what can be done when opportunity enables men to find the way. When the relation between the stronger and the weaker groups of mankind ceases to become exploitation and arrives at helpful co-operation, another day dawns, not only for the weaker but for the stronger as well. With equality and the dignity of man the guiding stars of intergroup relations, the organization of a jural order of the world becomes not only easier but inevitable, as might and right are blended in a new authority.

C. MUTUAL ADVANTAGE THROUGH CONTRACTUAL RELATIONS

Contracts between individuals, groups, or nations can be based not upon the principle that one loses what the other gains but upon the principle that a fair agreement is mutually beneficial. A contract, indeed, commonly involves "consideration" on both sides; otherwise it is invalid. Likewise contracts between nations may proceed on the theory that mutual benefits are to be derived from the agreement—that both parties are substantial gainers. National agreements in the form of treaties, however, are often based on war or a threat of war, on duress in which the contracting parties are not equal but appear as winner and loser, or as probable winners or losers if the contest is carried further. It is precisely at this point that conflict arises in theory and in symbolism between the *lex talionis* and the law of equal rights of equal parties and that hopeless confusion spreads over the scene. An atmosphere of exploitation, conquest, and war, with servitude and humiliation as the outcome, is one thing; but an atmosphere of co-operation, contract, and mutual gain is quite another. If the contracting parties have definite gains from interrelationship and agreement, the whole character of national relations alters.

It may be said that this is a counsel of perfection, a mere hortatory appeal, which has no immediate or important bearing in the rough world of practical politics. Contract, consent, and mutual advantage are not, however, impractical or idealistic. They are the basis of much of modern life. As democracy with its doctrine of the consent of the governed advances, the significance of contract as an alternative to violence becomes increasingly evident. With the establishment of jural order, contract becomes the symbol of co-operation. It becomes the basis of association for mutual advantage; of interpretation of disputed interpretations of contracts by reason instead of by violence or intimidation, by hope of gain instead of fear of damage, in accordance with recognized principle and procedure and through adjudicating agencies instead of through violence and destruction.

Much unnecessary confusion has been caused by the wrong use of the term "sovereignty." It may be asked: Does not sovereignty stand in the way of a jural order of the world? Are not unlimited sovereignties inconsistent with the reign of world justice and order? Are they not in conflict with the unlimited rights and sovereignties of others? The briefest answer is that there never were unlimited sovereignties in any world of justice and rational order, nor can there ever be. No state can justly demand, for itself or others, omnipotence, but only co-ordination, integration, unity. The truth is that nations never were omnipotent either in fact or in law in their relations with other nations. Whether or not international law is real law, as Kelsen forcefully maintains, justice has actual power among men. That nations have not had full freedom of aggression against their neighbors has never been regarded as a limit upon sovereignty. In a world of order which forbids aggression and outlaws war, nations are not permitted to attack at will. Yet this is not in reality a restriction on the sovereignty of fifty-odd states but a reinforcement of it. Without security against aggression, liberty is not possible for the bulk of mankind. The person who does not consent to some established order becomes an outlaw. He cannot claim a right without conceding the counterright. A nation no more loses its personality within a jural order of the world than does an individual in a democratic society. The nation which will not participate in a world order becomes an outlaw. It cannot claim a right without admitting a rule of law. Neither outlaw individuals nor outlaw nations can complain if the treatment of outlaws is visited upon them.

Nations do not lose by action in concert with other nations in the pursuit of the aims of common humanity. On the contrary, they are gainers. The exchange of piracy for the security of world organization was a good trade. We do not know, of course, how far the Four Freedoms may be taken under general protection or in what manner, but many hope for practical agreement which will bring freedom from fear and want to all men everywhere.

The jural order of the world must have behind it a reserve of economic, social, and cultural advantages and values. A plank in the platform of the United Nations will be the development of the national resources of all peoples and a positive common effort toward the elevation of human standards of living. The authority of the united peoples will not be directed to imperialism, either old fashioned or new, but toward the increasing recognition of the dignity of man and of the right of men everywhere to fair participation in the gains of our civilization—gains the full meaning of which we have hardly begun to realize.

There is nothing in the theory of sovereignty to stand in the way of a jural order of the world, to prevent the co-operation of nations in the larger framework of justice and freedom. Sovereignty is strengthened rather than weakened in any proper sense of the term by association for the broad purposes of human government.

E. REJECTION OF ZENOPHOBIA

What has been called technically "zenophobia," the fear and hatred of strangers, is as old as humanity itself. The unknown, the unfamiliar, or the strange is a signal to put us on guard, to arouse vigilance if not fear, and from fear we may go on to misunderstandings and hate. The stranger becomes the enemy, the object of dislike, distrust, and hate. This in turn colors attitudes toward a wide range of other customs, institutions, practices, and different ways of doing things, political, religious, familial, cultural. Group and national "characters" are built up, with far more emphasis on differences than on identities of belief and practice. The widespread doctrines of racial inequality have deepened and strengthened these fears and hatreds. Indeed, these conclusions are often little more than the rationalization of fears and hates, justifications of prejudices, and more than that, of substantial and selfish interests. Distrust of the unknown has its value, but when projected into a world philosophy, it becomes poison instead of meat.

Religion, philosophy, education, technology, medicine, and trade tend to break down these barriers, but often the progress made is very slow. The new relations in human communication which reduce the area of the unknown and unfamiliar—the telephone, radio, television eventually, the airplane, rapid communication of men, material, and ideas—slowly these diminish the groups who are enemies because they are unknown, unseen, and not understood. The seven seas and the six continents are drawn together in a way that will never be retracted. The same situation which in parts of the United States made the greeting "stranger" a term of friendliness, not of hostility, tends to spread over the earth, until "foreigner" loses identity with "enemy." "Nothing human is foreign to me" was, it is true, a Roman maxim centuries ago, but new meaning is being given to this sound principle of human association as time goes on and developing reason, humanism, and technology are in combination. Fear and distrust of the stranger, the foreigner, may once have been a legitimate generalization from early experience, but it is no longer a valid conclusion in our day.

It is true, however, that mere contact and knowledge are not of themselves adequate to insure friendliness of men, although many differences in culture patterns may melt away under this influence. It may be that differences arising from ignorance, poverty, and low levels of living tend to remain and even to be emphasized. But these, too, disappear with higher regard for the dignity of all men and with improvement of living and working conditions. When there was not enough to go around, perhaps such differentials between the haves and the have-nots were warranted or at least explainable; but, with the modern increase in productivity, the fuller conquest over the forces of nature, and the greater appreciation of the dignity of man, these differences are no longer defensible and tend to disappear.

Human differentials are of profound meaning, since they go to the roots of human psychology. They involve the whole complex process of observing behavior, of classification and interpretation, and of orientation of the observer in the world he sees around him. The "emerging personality" makes his world or has a world made for him as he unfolds, from childhood to maturity. Innumerable ways of behavior and attitudes are taught him by society in the family, the school, the play group, and along the way to the adult status which he finally enters. These precepts and examples contain ways of looking and learning; they contain respect for custom as well as for resourcefulness—ways of adjustment and adaptation of man to nature and of nature to man as he moves ahead in the scale of intelligent operations. Thus the individual personality is molded and matured. In the general framework of the society in which he lives, he pieces together his pattern and picture. The outside world he may know only dimly or know in the contact of life-and-death struggle, in captivity or slavery. Primitive societies found in exogamy a form of interrelationship, and migrations of men have always been a means of diffusion of cultures.

Recent transformations such as the development of the New World, the Old World as among the Russians, the Chinese, and the Japanese, illustrate the rapidity with which changes may be made within a relatively short time and point to other advances in the near future. It is impossible to ignore these possibilities of vast and far-reaching changes in the structure of human association, fundamentally conditioning the course and character of the world into which we move.

The remedies available are complex but not out of reach, for the experience of the world is rich in illustrations of successful and unsuccessful ways and means of improving both personal and group capacity for adjustment. They are extermination, deportation, slavery, exploitation, subjugation, aloofness, and harshness, on the one hand, and toleration, recognition, and economic and cultural encouragement, on the other.

Religion, if it is not tribal in nature; philosophy, if it is cosmopolitan; law, if it is not imprisoned by inflexibility; commerce, where it is not exploitation; education, including both natural and social; and practical technology—all these and others are powerful agents in the process of orientation and adaptation of personalities and of groups of personalities. More powerful than all would be a searchlight of truth showing what we now know about the processes of change, the balance between change and stability, the inner life and unfolding of the human personality, the crowning achievement of creation. If as many billions as war consumes were spent upon education by radio, screen, and press in modern methods of appreciation and adaptation to the known and un-known, the approach to the jural order of the world would be less remote and difficult. [22]

F. CENTER AND CIRCUMFERENCE

A further problem of the interrelations of political societies is found in the satisfactory analysis and demarcation of localism and centralism both as to areas and as to functions. This perennial question of local and central govern-ment may involve city and state or province, state and province in relation to nation, and nations in relation to alliances, confederations, federalisms, unions, and associations of nations in a world order. Often largely a problem of violence, of custom, of tradition, of symbolism, it is also in a deeper sense a problem of the optimum division of governmental labor and functions between the centers and the circumferences. It may well be contended, indeed, that there is no rule of reason governing here and that the supreme arbiter will be sheer force or the projection of ancient custom. The judge may, indeed, prove to be Mars, but there are other tribunals open to human reason.

There are outstanding examples of large-scale organization of authority with wide distribution of functions, as in the United States, in Britain, in Russia; and there are international agreements and arrangements of out-standing significance in recent times. Cities, provinces, and small states have all had to struggle hard to find their proper place in the scheme of things political and otherwise. Urban communities, for example, which now include the major part of the population in several industrial nations have never been given a clear domain of self-government, since the rise of the national state put an end to their political independence. The old-time cities were made subordinate to the nation, and their rights and privileges were almost completely liquidated. This process was perhaps necessary in the formation of the larger political units of our time. Nevertheless, there is an area of local self-government which the urban community with its local interests and its local pride might well be allowed to enjoy. What is properly urban may be difficult to define and ad-minister, but thus far no very serious effort has been made, because of absorp-tion with other and more imperative tasks, notably war and the stabilization of the business cycle. The cultural values of great cities have thus been many times the victim of destructive wars, of terrible industrial crises, of inadequate living and working conditions in times of peace. Cities larger than the smaller nation-states have been held under conditions which would be an occasion for resistance or revolution in many jurisdictions. The doctrine of self-determina-tion was not considered applicable to urban communities, notwithstanding their numbers, wealth, and evident needs of betterment in local conditions, overwhelmed as they were by the priorities of national and class struggle and

[22] See my *The Making of Citizens.*

interest. Yet the cultural values of cities great and small have survived political and class divisions in human history.

Equilibrium between center and circumference remains an unsolved problem not only in government but also in industry and religion. It is particularly urgent in a period of headlong change which shakes the old foundations of time and space. It is, after all, a problem in the diffusion and concentration of functions, of the relations between unity, on the one hand, and diversity, on the other. It may be contended that there are no general principles applicable to such a situation in a changing world. Nevertheless, long political experience warrants setting down here some of the outstanding conclusions drawn from observation and reflection.

1. The various forms of central and local political association are all tools of man and men, existing not for themselves but for the good of those they serve. They are to be judged in the light of the ends of government—security, order, justice, welfare, freedom as far as the political is concerned, regardless for the moment of other values.

2. Both local and central have real values which must be fully considered in any objective analysis of their claims for recognition and acceptance. There is no fundamental presupposition in favor of either of them at the expense of the other. Neither all central is good nor bad, nor is all local good or bad per se.

3. Political values cannot be made too exclusively the canon of priority, for there is a pluralism of values including religious, cultural, economic, and rational, all of which enter into the form of equilibrium.

4. There is no presupposition in favor of large or small areas of organization as protectors of the ends of government, order, justice, welfare, and liberty. There may be oppression, tyranny, arrogance, and arbitrariness in a small unit of government or a large one; in a family, in a tribe, in a city, in a nation, in an occupational or professional group. Freedom, order, and justice may prevail in any of these units. The test is not numbers or area or size but the realization of the valid ends of government, the recognition of the dignity of man and the consent of the governed. The real emphasis belongs on the functions rather than on the structures. Mechanisms are not for themselves but for the ends they serve, the happiness of the human beings who are concerned.

5. Maximum social utility is the canon of distribution of authorities, not the pride of area or of function. The highest utility is found in terms of the common good of those served and as judged by the then canons of appraisal and decision. And this maximum includes potentials as well as current output of advantage.

6. There are undeveloped possibilities of great proportions and meaning in the union of authority by areas, on the one hand, and by functions, on the other hand. One and the same person may be a health officer for the central and the local government, to say nothing of an intermediate agency, or a

school officer, or an officer charged with the administration of regulations regarding industry, agriculture, labor, or other governmental function. Areas, like families, may have "relations" with broad distribution of authorities and functions. Nor can it be forgotten that there is always room for a vast amount of voluntary and unpaid service rendered by thousands of persons whose interest may not be primarily that of any special branch of government, but whose chief concern is the performance of a function for the common good. Most men are not concerned with who has the "power" as much as with what service is actually rendered to them. Much progress has been made since power ceased to be a personal possession, and this notwithstanding the many evasions of modern trusteeship. But there is wide room for further advance in the direction of preventing the perpetuation of vested interests against the common good.

7. Coercion is far less useful than co-operation as a means of establishing and especially of maintaining a desirable equilibrium between areal-functional distributions of authority or between center and circumference.

It is not possible or desirable to eliminate the element of force in dealing with various situations, potential as well as actual force. But many other types of sanctions are available and often more useful. In the end physical violence will be practically eliminated, but this is not the next step.

8. Private as well as public governments constantly deal with the same problem of the balance between center and circumference, of delegation and diffusion of authority as against centralization, of the competing designs of unity and diversity. Business, labor, agricultural groups, churches, schools, clubs, and societies of all description must face the identical problem from time to time in their own operations.

Recently I attended a celebration of the federation of several churches of different denominations. I was interested to see that the formula of agreement was as follows: "In things on which we agree there is unity; in things on which we disagree there is liberty; and in all things good will and the wish to work together."

What is not commonly realized is that, with transportation and communication, we may look to the proliferation of innumerable forms of association, in number and variety such as the world never has seen before, and with powers of control and persuasion never before known on a world scale. In smaller communities these social groupings—the church, the lodge, the sewing circle, the club—have always possessed wide powers of social control, of rule-making and nonpolitical regulation. This same process may appear in the larger world into which we come—or the smaller world perhaps better. Paradoxically, as the world becomes more unified, it may also become more diversified. Political power may lose some of its significance at just the moment when it seems to be increasing. We will need not more, but fewer, policemen. Cultural societies, economic associations, and groupings of every description will girdle the globe and make their influence felt around the world, as they do in smaller localities now. Strategic guidance will be provided by the political, but the role of the nonpolitical will expand in very large measure. There will be room for the International Union of Cities, for the I.L.O., and countless other like agencies.

The greatest obstacle to genuine self-government or autonomy is the lack of world order and social justice. The constant threat of war and the lack of substantial agreement upon the human objectives of government has been more in the way of the devolution and diffusion of political powers than any other single agency. When these obstacles are removed, the autonomy of function or area, local or otherwise, is far more easily established and continued. Once both anarchy and war are eliminated and modes of co-operation for the ends of justice, order, and freedom are founded on the consent of the governed, a new era might dawn for persons and human associations. Then the way might be open to genuine solutions of the problem of the area or unit of political association, in a world of freedom from fear and want.

There is room for and there will be many governments, public and private, in the pluralistic society into which we come. What may be called "governmental government," pursuing the ends of order, justice, welfare, and freedom, needs no more authority than is necessary for these broad purposes. Holders of power are trustees for the community and the common good they serve, in a world dominated by the spirit of co-operation and headed toward the true ends of government. The keynote of government is not centralization and still more centralization. On the contrary, there is more room than ever for genuine decentralization, within nations as well as within a broader government if set up. Continually expanding government defeats itself, except as it can arrange for the devolution of tasks and responsibilities upon a wide variety of other social agencies. There is reason to believe that self-government in the true sense of the term, capacity to perform functions best done by an individual, a special area, or a group, will develop more fully in the future than in the immediate past.

Likewise self-determination in the cultural sense has a wider range of possibilities than ever before in the history of mankind. The rich opportunities of such development have been obscured by the overhanging menace of war and by the survival both of doctrine and of status of inequality as a fixed factor in relations between groups or between individuals.

G. THE ECONOMY OF ABUNDANCE

One of the basic incitements to violence has been that there was not enough of the world's goods to go around among the many claimants, even with the low standards of living accepted as normal in a given time. It is not by accident that pestilence, war, and famine appear in the books of prayer. Hunger was a primitive need that drove men to battle for food, for the domains of others, in varying forms as the food possibilities of man increased from time to time. Want and fear went together, emphasized by the ambitions of the power-hungry. The Malthusian doctrine that population tends to increase more rapidly than the means of subsistence helped later to fortify this ancient idea.

In our day we know that it is not necessary to continue the era of want, either of food or of other basic essentials recognized as parts of our living standards and of our civilization. There are food, shelter, clothing, health, education, and cultural and recreational advantages for every human being if we but reach out and take them. Organization for peaceful development and enjoyment of the available is a prime requisite. There need be no haves and have-nots, no outsiders and insiders, as far as recognized power of productivity is concerned. No human being need suffer because there is not enough to go around. He may suffer because of lack of distribution but not for lack of possible production of goods and services.

The problem confronting us is, therefore, not one of organizing for continuing total war but one of planning our resources for maximum productivity and for fair distribution of the gains of production, not only of goods but of other and higher values than the material.

Specific examples of the possibilities of production are seen in the rapid expansion of Japanese output and in the vast proliferation of the U.S.S.R. The national income of the United States rose from less than forty billion dollars in 1932 to a hundred and fifty billion dollars in 1944. There is every reason to conclude that the national income of all the members of the family of nations could be very largely expanded, even in the states now most highly developed. While in those on a lower level of productivity the expansion might be fantastic.[23] Colonialism and imperialism have done their work, such as it is, in the opening-up of a new world, but immeasurably more remains to be done and can be done in the new New World of opportunity on new social frontiers.

Of course, it is not possible now or ever to satisfy all the desires of all men everywhere, but it would be well within the limits of feasibility to satisfy the basic wants, in terms of minimal standards, of all men everywhere—employment, security, the essential needs of nutrition, health, education, recreation, cultural opportunity now. "We stand at the gates of an age of plenty, key in hand, fumbling at the lock."

Summing up the foregoing considerations, it may be concluded that the jural order of the world may be greatly facilitated by:

A. Recognition of one jural order of the world as a definite and attainable goal of mankind in our time. This involves the end of anarchy and the estab-

[23] See reports of committees of the League of Nations on world needs, clothing, food. Cf. Lewis L. Lorwin, *Postwar Plans of the United Nations* (1943).

lishment of the rule of law; the setting-up of a framework in which security, order, justice, welfare, and freedom may develop on all levels of government, public and private.

B. Recognition of the equality of persons and races.

C. Recognition of the meaning of contract as a formula of mutual advantage in relations of co-operation, whether individual or group, as a development of democracy and the consent of the governed. Contracts between persons or groups of persons are not instruments of death but of development and progress. Faith and good will are as important at this point as law and violence.

D. Recognition of the fact that sovereignty in its modern meaning is not inconsistent with world order and national independence. The genuine attributes of sovereignty are not destroyed but developed by association with other powers concerned with the common good.

E. Organization and education to combat ignorance and misunderstanding regarding other peoples, to offset fear and hate of the stranger.

F. Broader and better-reasoned attitudes toward the equilibrium between center and circumference in political or other association; rejection of size and strength as enemies of mankind.

G. Energetic planning for the expansion of national incomes and the development of resources, human and natural, everywhere—planning that will enlarge production and bring minimum living standards for every man.

VI. EMERGING JURAL ORDER

From the foregoing I pass to a consideration of the immediate problem of the organization of an adequate jural order of the world in our day. This is stated necessarily in the broadest terms, in view of the unsettled outcome of the titanic struggle in which we are engaged. But the features sketched below are applicable to the world situation, no matter what the outcome of World War I or II or, for that matter, III. Complete military victory of either side will settle little unless the sound principles of international or global organization are understood and given practical application.

Observation and reflection indicate clearly that the inevitable unit of political association is mankind. The voice of religion and the trends of history point in the same direction. In a jural order of the world the ends of government may best be served. Security for cultural values, order, justice, welfare, and freedom—these ends may most fully be realized in a world order. The equality and dignity of man, his right to life, liberty, and the pursuit of happiness, the expression and expansion of his personality, and his progressive share in the gains of civilization can best be reached in association with his fellow-men on some world-wide basis. World values and local values, social aims and personal values, are not conflicting if set in the proper frame of association.

For the attainment of such ends there is desirable:

I. A Declaration of the Rights of Man by the United Nations. To this might be added such signatures as may be available from many other associations subscribing.[24] This calls for civil rights and liberties, long recognized in theory, but also it calls for freedom from fear and want, for guaranties of employment, education, health, housing, recreation and cultural advantages, in broadest form a fair share in the growing gains of civilization. A broad statement of these rights is found in the 1944 Declaration of the International Labor Organization.[25]

There is no sound reason why adhesions to such declarations might not be made by private as well as by public governments, by industrial, agricultural, religious, educational, and cultural associations throughout the world from the grass roots up, adding not merely political but also moral force to the declarations of sovereign states. These rights are not merely formally political in the narrower sense of the term, but human and cultural in the broadest sense. They are rights of man pertaining to all those who bear the dignity and the possibilities of human personality.

II. A World Court for the consideration and decision of justiciable questions and for conciliation, arbitration, and like forms of friendly offices.

III. A World Council of the United Nations for such common purposes as may be agreed upon in the interest of the common good, looking to the ends of security, order, justice, welfare, and freedom. I am not discussing here the composition, organization, and powers of such a body. These are of great importance, but of prior importance is an assembly looking at the common good with a view to the common wisdom and judgment, the common will and the common sense of participation in policy.

IV. Investigative and administrative agencies, reasonably integrated, equipped with international civil service, for such objects as may be agreed upon, including health, labor, fiscal arrangements, resources, development and production, and fair distribution of the gains of civilization.

V. An organization of world order capable of using armed force when necessary and appropriate for the jural order of the world. This might be effected in a wide variety of ways, as by a common armed force, by continuing military conversations among leading military powers, by earmarking specific armed forces of nations, available immediately for maintenance of world order.

VI. The reorganization of national state departments dealing with foreign affairs, a new form of "state" department, adapted to modern requirements.[26]

---

[24] Quincy Wright, *Human Rights and the World Order* (1943) and bibliography there cited.

[25] Cf. my *On the Agenda of Democracy* (1941).

[26] See Walter H. C. Laves and Francis O. Wilcox, "Organizing the Government for Participation in World Affairs," *American Political Science Review*, XXXVII (October, 1944), 913–30.

VII. The more extensive use of the principle and procedures of voluntarism, allowing arrangements for specific rights, privileges, differentials, advantages, and immunities, available for those subscribing to them in a global framework, but leaving others outside the area of agreement—sanitary, fiscal, commercial, labor, agricultural, jural, or otherwise. The conventions of the International Labor Organization point the way in this direction. Such arrangements have always been possible by means of treaties, but casting them in the larger framework of a jural order of the world would give them greater strength and promote the habit of co-operation on a broad basis.

VIII. In this connection consideration of various forms of dual citizenship may well find a place. Citizenship is a flexible right which might well function in a dual capacity, as in the United States there is state citizenship and national citizenship with differing rights and duties. It is not impossible that there might be established a limited form of world citizenship, as well as national citizenships, in which legal rights, moral claims, and administrative arrangements might be found co-operating. The "common good" of mankind might find expression in common rights and opportunities and developing means of making them effective.

Many plans for association, making good the common objectives of nations, might be made without formal written constitutional changes. Rather, these plans could be adjustable from time to time and be sufficiently flexible to enable necessary readjustment to be made quickly in accordance with developing needs. Actually, it is this type of co-operation that already is developing in the common defense plans of the United Nations, where the possibilities of united action are impressive.

Machinery for systematically planning the development and utilization of national resources, both physical and human, could be created by joint political action. A number of American and other nations have planning agencies of various types, and almost all are concerned with basic questions of national planning. The higher federalism could be useful to all the peoples of all the nations in their planning, and that without encountering the difficulties in joint administration of operating agencies. This is true because the planning function is not authoritative and coercive but advisory and persuasive in nature. It is relatively easy to interchange ideas and experience about planning of national resources.[27]

SUMMARY

Summarizing, the historic form of political association (omitting form or ends of government) have been based chiefly upon (a) fixed territory, with

[27] The Economic and Social Council of the United Nations would provide an appropriate center for such plans.

exceptions; (*b*) kinship (family and/or race); and (*c*) common culture made up of tradition and expectation, of interests and values.

The basic principle of the association is, of course, the promotion of the common good of the given group and the realization of the ends of the state already discussed here, as variously interpreted by those who make the essential decisions.

Many of the "justifications" for association are spurious in nature, as in the case of alleged special "racial" characteristics or of natural territorial boundaries held to be decreed by nature. The *Blut und Boden* of the Nazis was only transparent propaganda for German imperialism. The combination of various loyalties, values, and interests into a central unity of feeling and action is the heart of the political association. Historic trends, traditions, expectations, a feeling of mutual recognition and identity, adherence to a "way of life," a community of hopes and fears—whether in large or small area—are of the essence of the association. In the nation-state these elements have been combined on an enlarged basis of territory and blood, reinforced commonly by community of language, religion, and culture patterns (with notable exceptions). The national state is the most powerful unit of political association in our time, the point of departure for political prudence and the calculation of statesman-like possibilities. But the national state was modified in the nineteenth century by federalism as in the United States, in the twentieth century by the large-scale regional associations such as Great Britain and Russia, and recently by economic and other occupational groupings. Modern technological and industrial developments profoundly affect present-day political association.

The emerging characteristics of political association are neither territorial nor ethnic but cultural, fraternal, and human in the highest sense of the term. The indications drawn from historical trends, from careful analysis, from reflection and religion alike, point to larger areas of authority and ultimately to a yet larger territorial basis circling the globe, to kinship expanding beyond "race" to the brotherhood of man, and to the recognition of the conclusion of religion and science that "God hath made of one blood all nations of the earth."

There may yet be terrific and devastating wars in which vast areas of the world will be laid waste and periods of anarchy and chaos may follow. But a sounder assumption is that of increasing solidarity, increasing recognition of the universal dignity of man, of increasing concern with the development of co-operation in promoting and perfecting the human personality, of increasing development of closer union between political societies concerned with their own welfare and with the common good of mankind.

CHAPTER IX

THE TRENDS OF GOVERNMENT

THE following paragraphs present a view of the emerging trends of government taken from the principal points of view in this study. It is not my purpose, or within my competence, to write a comprehensive history of government but to outline the outstanding developments in broad form, in order to present a unified picture of the general trends of subordination, superordination, and co-ordination in the political framework. These summarizing paragraphs will further provide a basis for the observations in chapter x on the future of intelligent government.

I. BASES OF GOVERNMENT

We may appraise broadly the elements in the social base of the needs satisfied by political society and their trends even in this difficult stage of development. Geography, natural resources, population, and social organization have played a basic part in government from the earliest times and have found some reflections in classical theory and politics, as in the distinction drawn between Greeks and barbarians and the emphasis on geographical isolation in Plato. In the seventeenth and eighteenth centuries in Bodin and Montesquieu these considerations were more systematically treated by political philosophers and by statesmen. In the nineteenth and twentieth centuries a mass of information and analysis of basic factors in the social composition of states, both natural and human, was collected and analyzed by students and was more intimately interwoven in statecraft than before, alike in the military and in the diplomatic sectors of statesmanship. Three emerging types of conclusions, however, affected the whole movement. These were (1) geopolitics, with emphasis on the determinism of geography and resources, (2) economic and materialistic determinism of the Marxian type, and (3) the doctrines of race differentials and of special race superiority, culminating in the master-people destined to rule the world.

These general conclusions in their extreme and dogmatic form were not generally accepted, but nevertheless they served as a basis of significant political action. But the vital importance of geography, economic and social, of the analysis of human differentials, and of population data as a basis of political society and the formulation of policies was far more fully recognized than ever before. The difficulty was not with the data but with the metaphysics of determinism, on the one hand, and the nationalistic propaganda and imperialism derived from hasty examination of the social bases of the governmental association, on the other.

The importance of comprehensive consideration and analysis of all the resources, natural and human, of a society has been emphasized more sharply than ever before in governmental affairs by the modern planners, from local to national to international. The dogmatisms of Haushofer, Marx, and Hitler are replaced by the technical analyses of land, people, and productive resources of all types in relation to their development by particular political associations. Haphazard and partisan guesses or hopes are thus replaced by technical data and analysis.

There are no recent indications of basic alteration of the biological inheritance of mankind in the near future. The growth of eugenics might ultimately lead to material modifications of the human breeding process, but thus far there is no development in this direction indicative of any substantial change in the immediate future. The natural environment of man has been materially modified by the substitution of secondary environments in defiance of "nature," as in urban centers and colder climates; but, on the whole, the great physical environmental factors in the conditioning of human growth remain much as they were thousands of years ago. The variation in age groupings is marked, but the meaning of the rising number of older persons remains obscure.[1]

In social heritage, however, and in penetration into the knowledge of the processes of nature, there have been and continue to be revolutionary changes which have a direct bearing upon the organization of power situations. And of all these elements the following may be viewed as of greatest significance: science, industrialization, urbanization, leisure time, and education.

The key to the emerging world is found in science and its many by-products, in the rise of intelligence as a factor in human relations, displacing ignorance and tradition as the great facts in human existence. The ultimate implications of this for power patterns have not been clearly observed but are just beginning to dawn upon the advance guard of the new generation. In reality the change about to be wrought in human relations is far more fundamental than has ever occurred even in the most deep-reaching revolutions of the most sanguinary nature in historic times. Control passes from the realm of tradition and force to the realm of constructive intelligence. This is the greatest of all the emerging trends in the organization of authority.

The scientific attitude itself is the most revolutionary of human forces, for it respects neither law nor mores. It involves the substitution for the older traditions of the modern types of adjustment to changing conditions, an open-eyed rather than a blind adaptation. The most striking emerging factor is that of invention, most conspicuous in the field of mechanical contrivance, but also, although less impressive thus far, in the field of social relations. Invention,

---

[1] Warren S. Thompson, *Plenty of People* (1944); National Resources Planning Board, *Human Conservation: The Story of Our Wasted Resources*, prepared by L. K. Frank (1943); Gunnar Myrdal, *Population: A Problem for Democracy* (1940).

mechanical and social, materially modifies the conditions of social living and thereby precipitates power problems of the greatest perplexity in the modern period.

Modern technology and social techniques have overturned many of the ways of life. Famine has been driven back in civilized states, pestilence has been beaten into retreat, and production has advanced to a point where an "economy of plenty" might be set up. Industrialization has thrust agriculture into the background in great sections of the race, while urbanization has transformed the conditions of living for millions of mankind; and with urban industrialism there came new problems of security, equilibrium, leadership. To these facts, catastrophic from the older point of view, the modern world remains largely unadjusted, cherishing many of the attitudes and artifices of periods that have passed forever and celebrating the glories of the old world as it was.

In addition to these factors, there must be taken into consideration, for the purposes of observing whither the trend is carrying us, the major fact of the emerging new leisure of mankind and the new education of mankind, for these will construct a new world from the point of view of power. Education and leisure may bring at first the cruder forms of mass appeal and control, but what will eventually emerge in the form of critical and constructive intelligence when once the new opportunities have been more fully adapted and adjusted?

And what bearing have these situations upon the problem of emerging authority as compared with a world in which most men were uneducated, slaves, serfs, traditional, haunted by magic and superstition, beset by fear of pestilence and famine? These mighty changes, unparalleled both in scope and in speed, have profound and far-reaching effects upon the whole structure and process of power. The family, the church, the industrial organization, the state, the whole political attitude, structure, process, and behavior are fundamentally influenced by these new elements which must be woven into political patterns of a new type.

The social composition of the political changes its form from period to period with varying degrees of complexity and with emphasis on different aspects of human behavior. The relative simplicity of the past century has tended to break up in more recent times, with the rise of organized groups of great importance, until the governmental problem has become externally one of far greater intricacy than heretofore. The pluralism of the Middle Ages may have been more complex than the modern situation, but the pattern of that day has long been forgotten in the power manipulations with which we are familiar.

The main lines of conflict in our day are manifold: between economic "classes," between "races," between "nations," between church and state, and between all of them. Thus the development of the general understandings upon which government rests becomes increasingly complex.

The clash between the competing behavior systems represented by the religious and the political is less severe than in some earlier periods. In recent years the renascence of a social policy in the church and of the stimulation of social activities under the auspices of the ecclesiastical unit, with the entrance of the church into the field of party politics, has enriched the variety of combinations and orientations. In the background, but not far behind, are the conflicts of the competing "race" cultures, which divide the allegiance of the members of the human family and which may stake their claims upon the necessity of political independence or some wide range of autonomy. The industrial class struggle is as bitter as any between other elements, dominant in its claims for consideration and adjustment.

But even in all this confusion guiding lines appear. Economic class lines tend slowly to merge into simpler forms of less antagonistic nature, with one class remaining—near to what we call the middle class but paradoxically without a lower class. The ethnic groupings show signs of breaking up, but only slowly as rapport develops across the difficult ground of cultural and economic relations. What the effect of a jural order of the world and a universal development of high standards of education, health, housing, security, and income might be we can merely conjecture. My forecast, which cannot be more, is that the effect of such developments will be revolutionary in the social relations of mankind and make possible vast proliferations of new intelligence and attitudes favorable to the elimination of so-called racial differentials. It is far too early to attempt to indicate even on the broadest lines the trends of civic cohesion in the future.[2] Ethnic differences may even be intensified for a time with the rise of group spirit in a nationalistic framework; or, on the other hand, they may be minimized with the growth of transportation, communication, elevation of living standards, and the growing regard for the dignity of all men. Patriotism is much the same in small or large units of association or in all types of association.

We are now in the very midst of a confused struggle for which there may come several alternative possibilities, such as the imperialism of a few great powers, or the continuation of aggressive warfare between newly rising cultures and regions, or a brotherhood of equal states in the general framework of a jural order of the world.

What will happen when India and China rise again; when Russia comes to full strength; what might happen when Africa attains consciousness of its strength and, without long political experience of the modern type, undertakes to express itself in an unaccustomed political world of mingled power and finesse? Ethnic and regional differences are not merely intellectual differentials

[2] For some attempts see Oswald Spengler, *The Decline of the West* (1932); A. J. Toynbee, *A Study of History* (1934–39); H. G. Wells, Aldous Huxley, and various other philosophers of history.

but symbolic and emotional overtones which supply a motive for impulsive action long after the other rational differences have disappeared. The reconciliation of value systems and interest will require all the inventiveness of politics and social science, if catastrophe is to be prevented—catastrophe in which our whole civilization might be swept away.

II. ENDS OF GOVERNMENT

Next we may observe the emerging trends of government by noting the course of the several ends of government, the tools utilized by governments, the forms and types of political rule, and other significant factors in political evolution. This is a task of broad generalization in the course of governmental relations for which we are not fully prepared. But some interpretation, however incomplete and tentative, is urgently necessary as a basis for further action. On the basis of such observation, experience, and reflection as is available to me, I offer the following analysis for whatever value it may have or whatever contribution it may make to later and more perfect interpretations.[3]

Observing the ends of government as they evolve, I conclude that external security is diminishing in importance with time, even in full view of the titanic struggle in which we are now engaged. Order and justice are midstream; freedom and welfare are increasing in significance with the course of events. External security may tend to disappear as an important factor in political relations, or, in any case, its importance is certain to be minimized in the present long-time trends to a world jural order.

Justice and order are two abiding functions of government. Order, however, may exist without much justice, and justice may not satisfy the demands of men for more than strictly legal justice in a world of want. It may well be that the burdens of order and justice will fall less heavily upon the political society and more and more upon organizations nonpolitical in character. This might be particularly true of order as discipline and sanctions, and of justice as expressed in primitive institutions. Freedom and welfare are the two ends of the political society which loom largest in the coming forms of the state. Welfare involves increasing productivity of the society and higher standards of living—minimums for all men everywhere, in the domain of internal security.

Order is disturbed from time to time by technical changes which overturn the ancient landmarks of space and time and create new and clashing interests; revolutionary changes in intercommunication and transportation in recent times have created opportunities and difficulties, and at the same time the reorganization of social units has reinforced these difficulties. What is far and what is near, politically, under new conditions? Face-to-face contact, the basis of much association, still stands, but with television, radio, and long-range guns in combination, face-to-face contact may include many persons scattered

[3] See my *Political Power* (1934) and *Prologue to Politics* (1939).

over wide spaces. In like manner rapid transit has overturned the ancient landmarks and compelled the reconsideration of many established units of government—the township, the school district, the county, the nation. What should now be the unit of aggregation for school purposes, for purposes of taxation, for purposes of regulation, for purposes of land and air protection?

How shall the individual be made to feel at home under such conditions? How shall he reorient himself in a new transportation and communication scheme of things? How shall he think his way out of this confusion, in which the meaning of home and locality seems upset? The knots and ties of human intercommunication in a new world of transit now make strange combinations. But large-scale organizations present a like problem of orientation. If the trend toward enlargement of the size of industrial units is checked, that is one thing; but if these trends are not restrained but perhaps enlarged, that is another story. With these technical changes come new social and economic groupings with new demands for balances and understandings between them —whether they are classes, nations, corporate groupings, or other like aggregations of social power, reaching over into political authority. New forms and types of order and organization are consequently springing up on every hand, calling for the application of the general ends of order to specific instances.

Historically a long series of balances has been organized one after another, but probably at no time have there been such rapid changes as in the present and more urgent need for social and political equilibrium. Races, regions, classes, labor and management, business and government, science and tradition, the consent of the governed and the raids of the power-hungry—all these are constantly presenting the problem of adjustment in some new pattern of order. And order, while one of the great ends of government, has often been able to find no other answer than that supplied by war and revolution. The tools of government and of order have also shifted with time, with larger and larger elements of co-operation and persuasion and smaller and smaller elements of violence and custom.

For much the same reasons justice as an end of government has been hard pressed in recent times to put its principles into actual practice. The value systems of the world have been upset, the early systems of recognition, the early forms of participation in the gains of civilization have been modified, millions of men have wakened to political consciousness and interest—men who long were held as slaves or serfs, who "did not belong." Special forms of high, low, and middle justice were cast off. Personal experience and broad philosophies alike have taught slaves, serfs, and other men that wrongs were committed against them and that justice was not being done. Many have lost confidence in the justice of justice under existing conditions and in the agencies of justice which they thought had become the tools of the unjust who were in the seats of power. "To hell with the courts," said a young rioter; "I know what justice is." Sometimes this feeling took the form of anarchism; sometimes of assaults upon the economic order, or capitalism, or democracy, or nationalism and internationalism alike. There can be no true justice except proletarian justice was the cry; or there can be no true justice except Nazi or Fascist justice; or democratic or aristocratic justice. In revolutionary movements the adjudicating agencies often went down along with other instruments of the day; and other laws took their place, still proclaiming justice, however, as an end of government.

Under all these conditions justice was hard pressed to hold its own, between the technical, the economic, the political, and the social revolutions going on. The great unsolved problem was: What is the relation of political justice to social justice, to economic justice, to personal justice in a world of rapid evolution? And the answers were not always ready.

Welfare began as the responsibility of the family or familial unit, a responsibility which still continues throughout the world. Welfare might also become the responsibility of the owner, the master, or the proprietor of lands and estates. Military chiefs have always had the custody of the welfare for fighting purposes of the men under their command and, in general, an eye on the oncoming generation of military possibilities. In other times the caritative functions devolved in large measure upon the church, administering to the weak and helpless. In other cases the local neighborhood, officially or unofficially, concerned itself with the sick and the poor.

With the rise of another economic order, accompanied by increase in production, with frequent lack of stability, with new standards of education and medication, came material changes in the allocation of responsibility for social welfare. The proprietor or owner was no longer held primarily responsible for the welfare of his men, and the burden was increasingly transferred to the government. Education, health, recreation, employment, security from the risks of accident and old age—these functions were in large measure, although by no means completely, made the special responsibility of political authorities, local or central. Lord Keynes declared that the task of production for human material needs is about to be completed with an abundance of goods and services and that the next step is that of adequate social organization to make this productive economic effort fully effective in human life. This places a heavy load upon society, but it does not follow that the administration of so large an undertaking will remain in any central authority, although indicating minimums and general directives.

Freedom is the great aim of the state, and its significance rises with the increasing recognition of the dignity and worth of man and with the increasing possibility of satisfying the demands for the good life, material and otherwise. Freedom is the flowering of human personalities, set forth as the *summum bonum* of social existence—to be sure, in the general framework of the common good—freedom within a civilization in whose gains all participate as time goes on and without too great a lag.

Freedom as the function of government follows a difficult and checkered career of advancement. The Stoic philosophy early celebrated the significance of human liberty and equality, and traces of this were incorporated in the Roman law. The natural law philosophy likewise exalted natural rights and natural liberty, but the task of obtaining political recognition of this principle for more than a few was a difficult one. Only in the modern period was freedom built into the political structure as a part of the function of the state—in fact, as its chief function. Representative institutions, democracy, constitutionalism, all these instruments, were predicated on the protection of the liberty of persons. Often this was more a promise than a fulfilment or perhaps only the recognition of the liberty of a few. But, little by little, natural right went on to civil right, to constitutional right, to political right.

In the early stages liberty was for the relatively few in the community and was chiefly negative in nature: protection against aggression of others or of the government itself. But later governments undertook the guaranty of conditions under which the human person might truly enjoy freedom not only from government but from other economic or social centers of aggression and oppression.

What becomes of individuality, of enterprise, and of liberty in the large-scale organization? It may, indeed, happen that these elements are crushed, down and out, or are seriously diminished in range and importance. In this case size ultimately defeats itself and breaks apart of its own weight; and many would say that this is in the interest of industrial and political liberty alike. It is thinkable, however, that other results may follow. Relationships between management and workers may be adjusted in such fashion as to introduce the factor of participation in the group. Forms of consent of the governed may be established or may grow up informally. The sense of recognition of persons, and their importance, of the existence of personal values, are not of necessity excluded by mere size of organization. The person is not necessarily lost in the size of an organization. He may know his way around and may understand the relationships of various parts of the mechanism of which he is a part, sometimes better than in smaller units of association. Strangeness is a factor not of magnitude altogether but of opportunities for recognition, for friendly social relations.

If industrial operations are highly mechanized and more and more mechanized, it is probable that the hours of labor are more and more shortened, and the individual is released for other activities of a different sort—another life outside the walls opens out in whatever the field of interest may prove to be.

The radio, the telephone, the press, the screen, and, above all, education open many windows to the mind. Freedom of speech, of assembly, of religion, and of motion and occupation is the staple of developing governments in our day. The collective ownership of instruments of production must be viewed in the light of the rise of monopoly and the decline of competition, on the one hand, and of temporary directives as compared with the ultimate outcome in the economic and social world, on the other.

Government may set up strategic controls or broad directives generally agreed upon or demanded, leaving wider freedom than before in a great field of human alternatives and decisions. Inheritance and contract, for example, are creatures of state law and tend to enlarge rather than to diminish the area of individual control over property and action. Their repeal would not be helpful to mankind in general or to persons in particular. Liberty to work is mocked if the unemployed are not given jobs. Their dignity is not advanced by the right to starvation or undernutrition, bad housing or ill-health. On the whole, the quantum of government in the broad sweep of generations remains about the same, relatively. In emergencies, military or industrial, the government will act energetically and comprehensively. In ordinary times the government will reflect the degree and types of social responsibility in the community it serves. Government is the servant of the community, not its master or owner, and only one of a long series of other private governments without whose co-operation political society cannot function.

The question may be asked: Is the trend in the direction of a wider range of governmental functions as time goes on? Analysis is confused by the clash of conflicting interests, with their special hopes and fears coloring the answer. If we look at the family state or the military state, it appears that historically the role of the government was very large. It is frequently declared that in modern times the trend is away from the old-time police state to the new service state. State ownership of the instruments of economic production appears in practice and theory, or socialization of industry is contemplated and practiced at times. That the government is more in evidence now than in the family state or the military state is doubtful. That the government does more in caritative, including educational, activities than in the Middle Ages is clear, and more in industrial regulation than a hundred years ago is also plain. If total war and industrial disequilibrium continue, doubtless the role of government will be large.

From another point of view, however, governmental activity may be measured by the areas of decision, chance, opportunity available to the human personality in the process of self-expression, and expansion in the world around us. Modern civilization opens many closed doors to men, with flying carpets of space and magic, extension of hearing, of vision, taste, smell, rhythm, with destruction of lurking enemies of body and mind, with reconditioning for happiness and enjoyment, and growth of material and higher values. Yet in all this the role of government seems relatively slight. Rules governing medicine are relatively few in any system in comparision with the emancipation from pain and disease. In reality we tread the broad way of the upward path to human freedom, leaving slavery and serfdom behind and below us as we rise.

III. TOOLS OF GOVERNMENT

It is now in order to consider the emerging trends in the instruments of the state. We have classified these as follows: custom, violence, ceremonialism and symbolism, rational consent, including education and persuasion, strategy, and leadership.

Of these various types, which are on the ascendant and which on the decline? Custom and violence are on the decline. Rational consent and education are in the ascendant. The techniques of strategy, early developed with extreme care, seem to remain much the same from time to time, varying with the capacity of the personalities in control for holding in solution vast masses of data essential to decisions. These broad statements require important qualifications and interpretations.

CUSTOM

Custom declines only in the sense that custom is the unreflective basis of institutions. There were times when to reflect upon the origins and meanings of government was treasonable or at least suspect. Enveloped in an atmosphere of superstition, magic, religion, and familial authority, reinforced by violence and by ceremonialism, the reign of custom was challenged with difficulty by a dissident. The policies of the association were largely private affairs rather than public questions, secrets of state, no more to be pried open than military secrets in time of war. Nor should it escape notice that customs might always be changed imperceptibly by those in charge of their declaration and interpretation. Long before there were courts there were authentic persons who might shape the customary to the demands of necessity. The institution of contract was one of the means by which conscious consent entered into public relations, as in the Roman law, the feudal contracts, the common law, the contract of natural law, which finally became the social contract in varying form, the basis of political association.

The massive body of custom, as time-saving habit or routine, continues and will continue as a great "balance wheel" of associations, both public and private and, indeed, of human relations. The custom of the constitution lies at the basis of constitutional government, but this is not custom which may not be challenged, discussed, or altered by accepted procedures. The burning question always is: Who interprets the custom? But the real question is: What made the custom and in what social context?

The year 1945 may seem an unfortunately chosen moment to declare that violence is on the decline—in the midst of the world's greatest sweep of war. But war is likely to be curbed as a result of this titanic struggle. Internal violence is on its way out—as seen at many points. The father's power of life and death over his family, the master's right to brutality over his slaves, the officer's right to kick and beat his subordinates, the institution of the duel, private war and violent feuds, flogging in schools, disfigurements, torture—all tend to disappear as instruments of government or of society. In the broad field of criminology prevention tends to take the place of punishment in many instances.

This does not mean, however, that there will not be an organization of violence for various purposes in future society. But war as an instrument of national policy and violence as the staple of internal order and justice are on the decline in modern civilization and, as far as the eye can see, will continue on their downward way. It is thinkable and possible that there may be yet more dreadful and destructive wars than the world has yet seen, raging over long periods of time and over the whole earth, and such an alternative must always be borne in mind.[4] Yet, in dealing broadly, as here, with the tools of government and their trends, it is clear that we move in the direction of peaceful rather than violent methods of settling disputes between individuals and associations.

SYMBOLISM

Ceremonialism and symbolism no longer possess the overwhelming significance of primitive and early times, when the ceremonial, symbolic, magical-religious pervaded the whole of political and social life. The culture of the group, whatever its size, was embodied in these rituals, and their custodians were in a sense the rulers. Rites and ceremonies were inseparable from law and order, from war and peace, from rewards and punishments of types innumerable. Color, rhythm, sound, demonstrations, celebrations, and structures were woven together in fantastic, beautiful, and terrifying forms. Nature, art, religion, and power were a part of the same garment of social control. It cannot be said that these forms of symbolism ever lost or have now lost their importance as tools of government. But both the external form and the inner spirit have altered in time. The Protestant movement laid less emphasis upon ceremony than the orthodox church, and the democratic development laid less emphasis on ceremony, associated with kings and courts, and more upon "democratic simplicity" of the Jeffersonian type. But governments of the type of Britain retained great superstructures of symbolism surrounding the monarchy, while the democracies began to develop their own forms of ceremony appropriate

[4] See Quincy Wright, *A Study of War* (2 vols., 1942).

to the new regime, notably in France, where art quickly came to the rescue of the nation and the people. Fascism and naziism devised new forms of symbolism typified by the swastika and "Heil Hitler."

On the border line between symbolism and education there developed the instrumentality which came to be called "propaganda," a mass attack of symbolisms and slogans. This is an instrument using the modern techniques of communication in which an appeal to reason and emotion is combined in a manner calculated to move masses of men and women in a given direction of approval or disapproval, action or inaction. Propaganda became a weapon of war alongside armies, navies, and air fleets and likewise an instrument of peace employed for the purposes of obtaining compliance. It is significant under all circumstances, but especially so when freedom of speech, press, and association is suspended. Where counterpropagandas are in action, the force of any special line of appeal is, of course, materially weakened, as one broadcast, so to speak, jams the other.

As distinguished from the early ritual which appealed primarily to ancient unreflecting custom, the modern symbolism takes on a color of appeal to reason and calculated interest, however transparent the fiction may be, as in Japanese broadcasts. It is not suggested that the citizen bow down to idols of color and motion or verbal symbolism but that these reflect an inner soul of reason and ideals old or new. In any case, art still lives in modern times, as vital and vibrant as ever, even though modernism has not yet found its full artistic expression.

CONSENT

On the other hand, rational consent and scientific methods, including education, medicine, and social science, are on the rising curve. In recent years rational consent has been sharply challenged by Nazi and Fascist doctrines and practices and by various forms of determinism. But this challenge has been met and overcome. The dignity of man and his claim to participate in political decisions, in determining the direction of broad public policy, are not likely to be contested again for a long stretch of time. The scope and method of consent may well be the center of discussion and elaborate experiment as time goes on. New and recognized techniques of state, new confidence in the integrity and social responsibility of the holders of authority, may well modify existing forms of consensual arrangements. But the theory of the consent of the governed and the practice of consent continue. Demagogues, power-seekers, and fools and rascals have threatened the integrity of the line of consent but have not succeeded in destroying it except here and there for short periods of time. The steady and unmistakable trend has been in the direction of deeper confidence in the validity of systems of consent. That men do not always act rationally is not a consideration leading to the abandonment of reason as a guiding principle and technique in social relations. This conclusion is itself a nonlogical

302

one, leading only to blind confidence in the strictly logical quality of the élite or hierarchy.

Allied with the rational basis of political association is the development of scientific techniques of government. We must deal with the growth of new types of social controls through the new science of education, preventive medicine, mental hygiene, medical treatment universalized, social work in its new forms, uses of leisure time, eugenics, friendly care, and like methods with their far-reaching implications for the social and political order.

Civic education involves the orientation of the oncoming generation and the determination of its attitudes. Attitudes will be derived from material other than that developed in the formal educational system, but much will be determined there; and it is one of the power centers in a political system. Soviets produce communists; Fascists produce Fascists; and democrats produce democrats. In a sense the power that once was in religion or in the army passes into or is rivaled by the school. Universal education, compulsory education extending over a long series of weeks instead of a short tribal initiation—this produces conditions widely different from those obtaining in earlier periods; and training is now closely related to the center of authority. In earlier times the ruler might be satisfied to have schools of the dominant language or the dominant religion, but now he demands schools producing attitudes upon political and economic affairs.

But this is a heady drink, and in it lurks danger for the power-holder. The indoctrination may be so artificial and wooden that in a changing world it may be dangerous. What has been too rigidly taught may be hard to apply to a new situation unforeseen at the time of the indoctrination. The only safety lies in a liberal education, leaving a wide range of adjustability as time goes on.[5] Further, the authority who attempts to control the school situation may encounter opposition from other members of the family of associations. Chief among them historically are religion and, as a late-comer, the spirit of science itself, with the independence of the professional group of scholars resisting in each case the imposition of a propaganda program by a power group. True education is better adapted to a democratic regime than to one of more limited range, for in a popular system the attitudes developed may be those friendly to associated life rather than in terms of a class or an idol. But it may be and has been applied to the glorification of a class or turned to the personal advantage of a dynasty or a small group of authoritarians.

Organizing power and showmanship are the devices most commonly observed, but deeper down are the more scientific devices in what has been called

---

[5] On this point see my *The Making of Citizens* (1931), in particular the last two chapters, and the other volumes of the "Studies in the Making of Citizens" series, dealing with the problems of several states; also my *Civic Education in the United States* (1934).

"constitutionalism,"[6] the knowledge of the physical-psychological basis of the personality and, on the other hand, the knowledge of symbolism in its relation to individuals and masses. In this instrumentation civic education plays a larger and larger role, along with research and technical intelligence. Constitutionalism and symbolism are two keys to power instrumentation.[7]

Older factors are overshadowed in ultimate significance by the coming evolution of human behavior control in terms which will perhaps destroy the meaning of the present-day politics. Much of the political distress of the present time is based upon personality maladjustments which are preventable in large measure through the employment of the known instrumentalities of science; much of the futility of power struggles is based upon widespread ignorance and ill-trained attitudes to which power-hungry aspirants appeal with success. But these attitudes may be conditioned under the control of science and, with wiser and sounder instruction, may give way to higher standards and levels of intelligence, criticism, appraisal, and appreciation. The shame of power is a reflection of the shame of the community, expressed in the tactics and maneuvers of those who weave their authority from the material they find on the surface of social attitudes and possibilities. The lot of the human race may be basically altered by readjustments in physical-psychic equilibrium and in civic education; and, when these adjustments are once made, the form of the human consent materially alters. The new holders of authority are conditioned in their activities by the new levels of appreciation and agreement.

These developments may seem remote and impractical to those who are not familiar with the recent trends in the field of social science and medical development, but a closer view of what is happening in these directions indicates striking possibilities and probabilities, if we project forward the present trends of science at their present rate and in the present direction. These aids are not based upon utopias but upon scientific developments, and their leitmotif is neither an economic orientation, a religious point of view, nor a political attitude and tendency, but lies in the possibilities of unfolding personality adjustment and institutional developments.

The emerging instrumentation of consent is, then, one of the significant developments of the present and the immediate future and will inevitably affect all the other factors in the power process. It may well be that the new patterns will vary so widely from the long-accepted types called "political" that the experts will find that they are not political at all and discover some other word to use when referring to them.

[6] George Draper, *Human Constitution: A Consideration of Its Relationship to Disease* (1924); see also his *Disease and the Man* (1930); Madison Bentley and E. V. Cowdry, *The Problem of Mental Disorder* (1934); W. H. Sheldon, *The Varieties of Temperament: A Psychology of Constitutional Differences* (1942); Leo Loeb, *The Biological Basis of Individuality* (1945).

[7] See my *New Aspects of Politics* (2d ed., 1931).

Strategy as a tool of government changes its content but not its form. The over-all view, the attempt at integration of various personalities, groups, interests, and ideals, the balance of the external against the internal, the continuing appraisal of men and measures, the regrouping of living forces into new forms and policies—these are as old as political relations. They are well described in the political annals of the Indians, centuries ago, and in scores of other manuals of power from that day to this. Machiavelli's *Prince* is perhaps the classic form, but many other testaments are of almost equal value. Roosevelt, Churchill, Stalin, and Chang Kai-shek display types of strategy developing under widely different conditions, but the technique of one might be transferred to the other, *mutatis mutandis*—in somewhat the same way in which the strategy of leaders of armed forces might transfer their strategic abilities from one social situation to another—and indeed often have. The growth of diplomacy with new techniques of finesse, the development of military strategy in total war, and the higher strategy of industry complicate the problem of the final pattern of governmental strategy.

However, the growth of human intelligence, the subdivision of labor, the rise of science and technology, the accumulation of vast masses of measurable data, and the mature analyses of social considerations have enormously increased the burden of the over-all strategist in our times. Large-scale technical production at all times, total war, revolutionary challenges of basic understandings and institutions—these have enlarged the difficulties as well as the responsibilities of strategists. The range of their information and the demands upon their powers of insight, appraisal, judgment, and action, both instant and long time—such considerations are now the commonplace of those who mold and maintain the basic strategy of the state. Airplanes and submarines, propaganda and revolutions, scientific discovery, new theories and practices of production, new developments in statistics, in history, in administration, in education, in medicine, in engineering, new views of planning, long and short time—these are some of the many factors held in the minds of the rulers who reach a moment when decision is necessary and administration becomes imminent.

It cannot be said that the quality of strategy in governors has improved, but its inner problems are far more complex. It may be that a complex society brings with it a division of labor which more than offsets the complexity. One of the questions we face is the validity of the process by which the decisions are made. Another is the selection and quality of the ultimate judges of strategy in the community.

The trends of leadership as a tool of government vary widely over long periods of time, but outstanding marks are clearly identifiable. Leadership as time goes on is less military in form; it is less surrounded by the aura of the supernatural and the magical. Leadership tends to become less personal and proprietary and more and more a form of trusteeship, more functional and less personal in nature. Vitality, whether physical or intellectual, is still of great importance, but fidelity to the purposes of the group is increasingly demanded. The absolute ruler long since began to call himself the first servant of the state, the supreme interpreter of their interests and welfare.

Of the several traits of leadership already analyzed, social sensitivity, facility in group and personal understandings and contacts, powers of dramatic expression, inventiveness, and high courage are perennially important. Social sensitivity and inventiveness are perhaps more than ever required of the modern political leader. But none of the other qualities can be omitted from his composition. These abilities must be organized and applied on a mass basis, sometimes for many millions; but otherwise they are not so different from the traits found in a leader of a small unit of population. But the significant change resulting from the trends of leadership is that the leader becomes more and more a function of the political society in which he lives and moves and has his being. He becomes an instrument of the group, openly and avowedly, and not merely in a way of speaking. There are, to be sure, many forms of the species demagogue, but these specimens are not new to the taxonomy of politics. The Greek origin of the word dates it back to days when master-demagogues knew how to woo and win the people against their best interest. No more artful tricksters have been developed by later generations.

Modern leaders of the Hitler type have undertaken in vain to upset the trend of political growth and to reverse the movement toward equality and the consent of the governed as a basis of authority. But this effort has not proved a sound foundation for power, even in periods of disunity and difficulty in co-ordination and integration of economico-political issues.

Meanwhile the general diffusion of intelligence and the growth of numerous societies and groups, functional and otherwise, have stimulated the growth of individual leaders and the general understanding of the meaning of leadership among many persons hitherto left out of the world of co-operation and consent. There are many leaders, and many critics of leaders, yet all within the purview of the common good rather than on the old-time feudal basis.

IV. TRENDS IN THE ORGANS OF GOVERNMENT

What is the trend of the growth of organs of government such as the conciliar, the managerial, the adjudicative, the *chef d'état*—looking back over the sweep of experience, or as much of it as the writer can compass.

The organization and powers of the *chef d'état,* already discussed at some length in earlier pages, run the whole gamut of modes of selection, scope, and type of powers. The early head might be father, warrior, priest, proprietor, and sage all in one. Mighty and petty rulers wielded authority over empires or tiny plots. Headship developed special forms in the recent period of democratic development. Democratic tenure of office and wide democratic support affected the manner in which powers might be granted or tolerated by the democracy. The modern chief tends to have a large influence in common affairs. This assumes, however, an operating system of consent of the governed, accepted in principle and implemented sufficiently to provide recurring decisions in practice. The abortive attempt to set up dictatorships under theories of leadership repudiating the doctrines of consent indicates the collapse of the revolt against democratic organization in our times, whatever may be developed in the future.

Along with other governments, public and private, the appearance of leadership in one form or another is inevitable, deriving its strength from below, however, and not from above. Leaders of industry, labor, professions, races, regions, and cults play like parts wherever they are found, with variations, of course, and with authority varying largely with the stress of the time or crisis. The trend is unquestionably in the direction of strong executive leadership, operating under democratic and constitutional surroundings, commanding the consent of the governed freely given and freely taken away if necessary. The American presidency offers the best illustration of such a framework, subject to more careful implementation and general understanding. The modern head is not absolute, irresponsible, or invulnerable, either in theory or in practice. Leadership is subject to periodical appraisal and adjustment by the electors, to review by the judiciary in appropriate instance, and to constant supervision by a conciliar agency of government, which is endowed with perfectly adequate over-all controls which may be exercised when deemed necessary and/or proper. The alternative of the parliamentary system is a defensible alternative, depending upon alternative basic conditions, habits, and tastes in procedure.

The adjudicating functions of government occupy a steady position of significance in all political societies and at most times, but they tend to rise from magic and custom to higher ranges of rational declaration and interpretation of the law. The great codes developed important phases of adjudication. The magnificent structure of the Roman law gave powerful impetus to adjudication everywhere, along with other great legal systems developed by other states. With the rise of democracy and of industrialism, the adjudicating function dealt with widening ranges of personal and property rights, as between individuals and groups and involving the central state itself. The adoption in western Europe of the legal state instead of the power state (*Rechtstaat* and

Machtstaat) was a long step in advance, coinciding with the development of the rule of law instead of the rule of man. These steps went beyond the adjudicative and were intimately intertwined with courts as well as with laws and constitutions. The adjudicators tended to become the custodians of rights in the domain of private and public law alike. At the same time the judges were able to acquire greater independence either from absolutists or from any governmental agency. But, in spite of the immense proliferation of legal decisionism, the tide turned in the direction of legislative law and of administrative adjudication of rights developed in the course of applying the law. In the United States, where the courts exercised the power to declare legislative acts void, large authority was transferred to the adjudicative bodies at the expense of the legislative, but this process was always subject to severe check if it fell behind the public judgment of the equities of the case. It cannot be said that the adjudicative function tended to decline in meaning, but its rapid increase in prestige tended to level down somewhat in a period of very rapid change. The dialectics of adjudication also tended to lag behind the drive of scientific and technical equipment and knowledge in a new period of amazing advancement in invention and management of materials. So well intrenched in political wisdom, however, is the adjudicating technique that even the most violent revolutionary movements did not long disturb its bases, although changing its personnel, scope, and social spirit.

The "law" provides the widest range of development, and it would, of course, be presumptuous to do more than outline here a few salient features. Among these are the transition from customary law to codification, from codification on to constitutional and international law, in which custom and morality again play a larger role, as seen in "constitutional custom" and "international morality." Others are the transition from a government of men to a government of laws; the embodiment of human rights in the structure and function of the law and its application; the gradual recognition of the law as the tool of the common good; its essential conditioning by reason, experience, and the cultural context of the time; and equality of all men before the law. These and many other developments characterized this special tool of government in this field of operations.

The conciliar function emerged early in diverse groups of advisers or consultants, perhaps of the family, the clan, the ruler, whoever he might be, or whatever the source of his authority. Such advisers were useful for counsel, for morale, and for pointing up the unity of the group. Never were they wholly absent, no matter what the name under which they went, whether surrounded with pomp and ceremony or wrapped in secrecy. Some were technicians, some were administrators, some were prophets with a halo. At times the advisers quietly took over the functions of headship in periods of regency or of illness or of weakness of the nominal head of the state.[8]

Such councils were by no means confined to public governments but were found throughout association. The great church councils were eminent and powerful. The College of Cardinals survives as one of the most notable conciliar assemblies. Guilds and their assemblies were famous in their day and still go on, symbolically at least.

Councils from time to time took over formally the functions of leadership and headship, in Spain, in England, and in the Low Provinces. Notably the English Parliament subordinated the crown and became the sovereign body itself, in the name of the nation. Other legislative bodies moved in the same direction, with less conspicuous success, however, in many instances.

The doctrine of the separation of governmental powers in the United States swung away from complete legislative supremacy in the eighteenth century to a combination of legislative and executive authorities as a center of ultimate authority. In revolutionary Russia the Soviets emerged with the legal authority in their hands, but the practical power was soon taken by the party organization.

In recent years the conciliar agencies have experienced difficulty in holding their earlier positions either as irresponsible advisers of others or as responsible over-all authorities. This followed for a variety of reasons already analyzed here, chiefly that of utilizing new technology and management, on the one hand, and, on the other, public rapport under modern conditions.

It has been the lot of the legislative in largest measure to perform the difficult function of intermediating between technical advance and popular understanding and purpose. They have been brokers of the experts to the community and of the community to the experts, never an enviable or easy task, but always fundamentally essential, and especially in democratic societies. While the techniques of the legislative as seen in inquiry, discourse, compromise, and over-all view are old and well tried, the sharper techniques of the adjudicating agencies and the developing managerial devices supply keen competition for the legislative in the race for governmental priorities. Widespread discontent with limping legislative bodies pointed to an overhauling of their organization, methods, and results.

Management came out of the area of magic at a relatively early time, and the managers, particularly in the military field, early demonstrated the value of their services to the state. Later, as administrators of finances and of other affairs of empire, like the Roman and the Saracen, they attained great power and at times in effect controlled the chief decisions of those nominally in

[8] Thomas Mann's *Joseph the Provider* (1944) gives a semihistorical account of a great counselor.

309

authority. With the rise of the great patrimonial estates and later states, such as Prussia and Austria, the managerial personnel became of very great importance in the political society, along with the military administrators. Later, with the division of labor and the high specialization in large industrial enterprises, the managerial group achieved positions of great usefulness and power. The same tendency appeared in public government, where the merit system, career service, and management became the order of the day in well-established governments. With the increasing complexity of functions and especially in a period of rapid change with frequent necessity for readjustment, the administration was called upon more and more for decisions and for application of general policies. Alike in government, in industry, in labor, in agriculture, and in the professions, the managerial elements became of increasing importance. At times they threatened the conciliar agencies with encroachment on their domains, especially if the legislative agencies faltered in the issuance of broad but controlling directives and in the organization of broad but searching forms of supervision over administrative conduct.

Of deep significance was the rise of general staffing in managerial services, military and civilian, and the rise of the higher management in the areas of personnel, planning, budgeting, and other fiscal controls. The furious criticism of bureaucracy assailed the administrators root and branch but often without any fine sense of discrimination and therefore ineffectively. More and more, both in industry and in government, the services of modern science and technology fell into the hands of the servants intrusted with the care of affairs on the side of management rather than of policy.

Meantime the character of organization shifted with the rise of the consent of the governed and with more critical understanding of its methods and purposes. Organization by and large shifted from a personal to a functional basis, from a proprietary office or set of offices to a constitutional system in which the chief emphasis is placed upon functions performed for the general good. Organization tended to become democratic not merely in its authorities but in its social origins, spirit, and aims. With the increasing complexity of modern society, the balance of powers likewise tended to become functional rather than mechanical in character, with the emphasis upon hopeful co-operation for action rather than fearsome blocking against action. This was possible only upon a widely accepted basis of democratic society and confidence in its effective use of its resources.[9]

V. TYPES OF RULE

The broad trend in the general type of government is clearly marked by this time. The government of the one and the government of the few are yielding

[9] See above, chap. iv, for a fuller discussion.

to the government of the bulk of the community. The consent of the governed is becoming the explicit basis for systems of authority as time goes on, and structures, understandings, and procedures in accordance with this principle are being developed and perfected. Democracy, moreover, is not merely a quantitative phenomenon but also a qualitative one. It postulates the dignity of man, his value as a person, and calls for a system of consent as a means of realizing his personality in a framework of the common good, but also makes possible justice, liberty, and equality. Both the ends and the means of democracy are in line with the elements of developing civilization on its technological and its moral side as well.

Absolutism in the scope of authority and inheritance as a basis of continuity are fading away. For the moment older systems of "élites" and of nonconsent are being revived; but, on the whole, they are protests against features of a democratic system which proves in the main dominant. The diagnosis of democracy as essentially sluggish and incompetent is seen to be inaccurate, as evidenced alike in the last two great wars and in the productivity and living standards of the last century during times of peace. The view that democracy is incapable of providing for a fair distribution of the gains of civilization is likewise untenable in the face of developing tendencies in this inevitable direction. The revival of the doctrine of the superiority of the Few in Italy and Germany was only a camouflage for national imperialism in these nations, masking the designs of the military group in Germany and of adventurers in Italy such as D'Annunzio and Mussolini without either military, administrative, or industrial competence. What they really aimed at was a personal state without disturbance by the democratic doctrines and practices of consent. Authority from the top down was the army idea taken over by a group in Italy under the banner of fascism. The Italo-German attacks upon what they termed "plutodemocracy" were never taken seriously by the bulk of mankind. A more popular form was the contrast drawn between the "haves" and the "have-not" nations—again a mask for national imperialism.

The Communist groups, while attacking democracy in general terms and in specific cases of weakness, were aiming at another target. Their efforts were directed primarily against capitalism and only secondarily against democracy and against phases of democratic procedure which seemed to fortify capitalistic positions of intrenched authority. Likewise the revolutionary basis of sovietism rested upon impatience with and lack of faith in the social program of parliamentary democracy. In the Soviet constitution of 1936 recognition was given to fundamental democratic procedures, although not yet carried out in practice. In the meantime the dictatorship of the proletariat was invoked as a means of maintaining a socialistic regime in a period of what was termed "transition." In general, the consent of the governed is the long-time goal of the Soviet system as it develops in the light of experience and in the general trends of world development. Obviously, there is less emphasis on the juristic aspects of democracy and more upon the just distribution of the gains of civilization throughout all the working community. It is significant that Stalin has joined in guaranty of democratic government to Italy through constitutional procedures.

It is probable, then, that the next phase in world development of the political process will see a democratic form of society with variations and mutations in various culture patterns throughout the world. The basic problems are not those of ability to resist and restrain a military group or to provide for a basic national minimum of life but extend to other areas later herein discussed.

Those who conclude that democracy is a body of traditions unchanging and unchangeable, and are always discovering that some new variation in democratic structure and operations is an evidence of weakness, will find that variations may also be looked upon as evidences of strength and vitality. Democracy is not merely a form or a tradition; it is a principle of human behavior and a goal of human ideals—constantly looking forward to higher levels of association and of realization of the finer phases of the human personality. The particular forms which it takes from time to time are important, such as presidential or parliamentary, unicameral or bicameral systems of representation, special modes of voting such as proportional or direct, particular ways of setting up the organs of government and their reciprocal relations. But the essence of popular rule is not its forms but the vital spirit of democracy, the aim of democracy, the extent to which and the ways in which it serves the purpose of promoting the personality of the citizens in the framework of the common good. Traditions and symbols are precious, but only as they serve the present and the future.[10]

Heavily reinforcing the trends toward democratic political society are the double sweep of science and morality. Science, both natural and social, moves in the direction of democracy: (1) by vast increases in productivity which may remove want from the globe, supplying the basic essentials hitherto possessed in limited quantities, and (2) by the development of special techniques of education, medicine, and social adjustment through which the human differentials have far less significance than before. These devices insure a basic minimum of equality for all men. Beyond that there may be wide-ranging inequalities, which do not threaten the basic equality of man and the conditions necessary for full fruition of human personality. Morality, using this as a term to cover the higher values of life, aids the democratic development by its strong emphasis on the dignity and worth of man, and the spiritual importance of furthering the expansion and growth of this personality within the possibilities of the special individual and type. Reversion to caste, slavery, serfdom, and modified forms of peonage is made difficult in the face of such trends, and

[10] For further discussion see my *The New Democracy and the New Despotism* (1939), especially the concluding pages.

efforts to raise the standard of human welfare in this world are fostered. Religion or morality or idealism by whatever name known is not the opium of the people in a developing world of human aspirations.

We may safely conclude, then, that democratic political association, pivoting on the consent of the governed, is on its way in the knowable future. There may well be swings in the political cycle which at times may bring to the top demagogues, special élites, dictators, and men on horseback who will deflect the live stream from its main direction. But the broad indications are that the general movement of democracy will go forward steadily with the growth of intelligence, with improved habits of co-operation, and with a livelier sense of social responsibility and opportunity for personal development.

VI. INFORMAL GOVERNMENT

The shift from formal and informal government is interesting to observe and full of illumination on the course of things political. In early times the informal and customary was really the government, which only slowly was formalized, retaining many familial, tribal ways, magic-sacred—over long stretches of time, and indeed still surviving in our own day. Government in time emerged, and its formalism of structure and process dominated the informal, taking over the mumbo jumbo, the magical, and the sacred as its own attributes. Eventually, jumping centuries now, governments became sovereign, juristically absolute, and fought restrictions and limitations outside the realm of the formal. But now, moving rapidly again, come the revolutionary and the rational, defiant of absolutism and often establishing new customs of their own; above all, establishing the principle of popular sovereignty and the consent of the governed as the basis of authority. Democratic government, however, surrounded itself by various restrictions against arbitrary government and encouraged the growth of widespread suffrage, political parties, free associations of all types, and free expression of opinion about the acts of the governors and of public affairs in general.

Thus we come back again to a range of informal governments, informal associations of innumerable varieties, public and private governments making their contribution to the governance of the locality or of the nation as the case may be—or of the world for that matter. These private associations as in industry assume permanent roles, ranging from old-time guilds to modern corporations and unions. These informal governments continue to proliferate throughout the body politic, irritating or irresponsible as they be at times, but are, on the whole, a great constructive force in bringing critical intelligence to bear upon the nominal rulers of the land. The future of government is conditioned by its insight into the meaning of these groups and ability to assimilate the private and the public in new forms and functions.

In the realm of decision, both public and private, what part will these factors have and how will they play it? In the formation of customary attitudes which underlie all political action, how do they tend to shape the course of affairs? The relative roles of formal and informal government are not easy to appraise with reference to trends. In a democratic society where public opinion plays so large a role, with free press and speech and freedom of organization and association many temporary and provisional organizations are constantly springing up and disappearing after their role is played. This is true of parties, factions, and pressure groups of many types. Other groups are, of course, toughened and stabilized.

The concepts of public and private likewise undergo important changes. There is no longer private property in public government as was long the case[11] when the owner of the land was also the proprietor of the people and of the government. There is no longer hereditary transmission of political power, except in relatively few instances, and these of passing significance. Inheritance of public power as property is thus passing away from human usage. Inheritance in the economic field is still of great importance but is seriously modified by the inheritance taxes which now fall upon transmission.

There are now public profits as well as private profits and public enterprise as well as private enterprise. The whole line between public and private is far less distinct than it once was, although if we go back far enough into the feudal period, the lines are very vague indeed. This should not be taken to mean that there is no dividing-line between the public and the private but that new lines are constantly being drawn, across the old lines in various instances. Areas of privacy may be found in the densest and most complex of populations and social activities, as in a library, a hotel, a retreat, a soundproof seclusion which no one can easily penetrate. There may be fewer hermitages, but there are hermit spots which men may find in the thick of civilization.

VII. RIGHT AND MIGHT

The guaranties of diffusion of authority, or participation in power, of curbs upon aggression and tyranny, are found in the appeal to the higher law and ultimately to revolution. For more than two thousand years natural law in one form or another has been the star of hope in the political system. From the Roman law reflecting Stoic philosophy to the seventeenth-, eighteenth-, and nineteenth-century revolutions against absolutism, reliance upon the supremacy of right over might was an outstanding phenomenon. Flaming bills of rights took constitutional form and were embodied in the structure of public law. In the nineteenth and twentieth centuries came a demand for the broadening of rights to include areas of social and economic significance, lost in the confusion of natural law and rights of man with laissez faire in the economic world.

[11] See my *Public and Private Government* (1944).

314

At the same time came an attack upon the natural law system as a basis of justice and the substitution of an economic system designed for the benefit of the working class. This system rested not upon natural rights but upon practical claims of men, the operation of the economic system by and in the interest of the workers. The philosophical basis remained, however, although shifted from the idealistic to the materialistic by some thinkers.

Revolution continues a constant factor in the political process, nothwithstanding the continuously closer integration of human association. At times the method of ambitious and unscrupulous seekers for power, whether individuals or groups of individuals, revolution also remains the last refuge of the disinherited seeking the common good on higher general levels. In relatively recent times the English revolutions, the American Revolution, countless European revolutions, and, latterly, the Russian revolution have shaken the foundations of established governments and the socioeconomic order. The German and Italian revolutions, while relatively less violent, were illustrative of the unstable equilibrium of all states in times of stress. The South American revolutions further illustrated this situation.

The bases of revolution in modern times are stated increasingly in terms of the common interest and the general good, as interpreted by an ethnic or cultural group, a class, an area, an army, or an adventurer. Significant in the recent history of revolutions are chiefly: (1) the more systematic rationalization of revolutionary movements; (2) the trend to democratic or mass types of revolutionary philosophy; (3) the evolution of new techniques adapted to modern technology and systematized more carefully than in early times (e.g., the organization of propaganda, the seizure of the instruments of communication, of strategic centers of military meaning and of utilities and supplies); and (4) the tendency to revolutions which are fundamental movements but without the use of violence.

Wholly outside the realm of "regular" government, the revolution remains the scourge of the just and the unjust, the last word of outlaws and the disinherited, of men of good will and of adventurers and scoundrels.

If we attempt to characterize the sustaining forces beneath the political surface such as suffrage, parties, pressure groups, and public opinion, we come upon very great difficulties in the way of precise appraisal or logical analysis. The problem of what Dewey called "communication" is vastly important here, but its trends are not easy to discover and define. But not only is communication involved but the organization of relationships arising out of communication. The use of writing, the appearance of printing, the rise of the press, and the invention of telephone, radio, and television are of large and increasing importance in conditioning the intercourse of human beings on levels where they can interchange ideas, emotions, symbols, and judgments that may or may not eventuate in lines of direction and action. Here we come upon a wide range of difference between old-time rumor with its thousand tongues and the modern buzz of radio and press. The secrecy which once enshrouded affairs political now is replaced by all-penetrating publicity—except for military secrets. Voting and political parties have developed into powerful agencies affecting and controlling government. The vote as a technique of choice appeared very early and quickly found a place in the techniques of government. Later it became the tool of men struggling to make good the promises of government by the consent of the governed; still later it become an instrument of selection of officials and an indicator of policies. The trend is unmistakably in the direction of unusual suffrage, eliminating one by one, in a long series of conflicts, the restrictions of property, religion, sex, and race—in area after area.

Parties, at first under the ban as factions, slowly took the shape of political associations and assumed their position as critics or conductors of governmental affairs. The two-party system developed into a multiparty system and back again into a one-party system in recent years in Russia, Italy, and Germany, among others. Powerful pressure existed at all times by the side of the party, at first in the form of religious and racial groups, and later with economic class foundations. At times the pressure groups took the form of parties and again preferred to work through them in various forms. Where special pressure groups were strong enough, new parties tended to appear within the power group, as in industry, labor, agriculture, and ecclesiastical and racial groupings.

Public opinion sprang from humble beginnings, from gossip, murmuring, buzzing dissent, or, on the other hand, approval and applause, coming from a mass of unidentified persons. The popularity of men and of measures was thus subjected to a rude Gallup poll or plebiscite from time immemorial. Unorganized opinion later found more definite channels of expression, and, with the rise of education, however limited, with less economic dependence, with democratic philosophies and programs to rally around, public opinion became more articulate and, in smaller areas, at times dominant. With greater freedom of association, of speech, and of press, this voice became still louder and is more likely to be heeded. Yet later, with the vote, parties, free forums, and communications, the community judgment became increasingly effective in its influence upon officials and policy.

The general trends regarding public opinion may be summarized as follows:

1. The recognition of the existence of public opinion as an operating force in common affairs, long disputed on the ground that public opinion is "unreal," that there is not one but many public opinions, and that mass opinion is, in any event, incompetent and irrelevant.

2. The recognition of public opinion as the basis of modern government under practically all systems of government, including the Nazi system. Hitler

contended that he was a better representative of the community than the so-called representative agencies.

3. The continuing recognition of public opinion as superseding all types of group opinion, running through them and affecting the voice of an over-all community behind them. This is the counter to excessive guildism and separatism of groups in themselves admired as groups but not as the ends of the state. This is, indeed, a phase of the continuing struggle between separatist functionalism and the common or general good as the balance wheel of thought and action in the community.

4. The immense development of ways and means of influencing public opinion, through the agencies of communication and the contrivances of advertising and publicity, as in the power of the triumvirate of press, radio, and screen, outrunning often in vitality and versatility the standard agencies of public authority.

VIII. THE INTERRELATIONS OF POLITICAL ASSOCIATIONS

There are definite trends observable in respect both to the unit of aggregation and to the general form of their relationship. The unit of aggregation tends to be larger in area, although broad cycles of development are observable throughout history. Starting with a very small unit such as a family, a clan, or a tribe, we move on to relatively great empires of the Egyptian, the Indian, and the Persian type; then the small city-state of the Greeks emerges and assumes a powerful position; but the Macedonian and the Roman empires come to the fore with a far wider range of territory. We return to the curious combination of the feudal principality with restricted area, not always contiguous even, and at the same time the Holy Roman Empire with its vast western extent, with the Saracen empire and the Chinese in the Orient. Following this comes the national state, far broader than the feudal and far narrower than the Holy Roman Empire. The national state in turn spreads out into extensive areas such as the British Empire, the United States of America, the Union of Socialist Soviet Republics, and the revival of China. Federalism in various forms enters into the picture with the American Federal Union, the British Commonwealth of Nations, and the Union of Socialist Soviet Republics. Finally, we come to the rise of various forecasts of world organization, such as the League of Nations and the United Nations. From all this it is unmistakable that the trend is in the direction of some form of jural order of the world.

The growth and strength of cities have at times challenged the attention of students of organization, and some have contemplated the rise of city-states again. Auguste Comte proposed a world society with cities as the units—some five hundred of them. The International Union of Cities contains many large and powerful municipalities measured by numbers and population, but it is in no sense a rival of national organizations, nor does this seem likely in any future we may forecast.[12] The national state extends itself in federalized forms, and the federalized forms tend again to associate in various types of world systems of jural order. The urban communities as cities do not fit into this line of development.

Kinship, territory, and race have all been mingled in the modern national state, although ethnic elements have been placed at the fore. This finds its extreme expression in the "pure-race" doctrine of the Nazis but is unable to sustain itself in the modern world. The modern nation and the modern federal orders stretching around the world are mixed in character, including racial and territorial elements, along with many others. Meantime other aggregations have sprung up within the boundaries of the nation and, from the world point of view, are assuming formidable proportions. These are labor, agriculture, and business, in one form and another, developing strength inside the national state and extending far beyond its borders in international form. International cartels of business and the international organizations of labor have become exceedingly important in any realistic view of emerging trends of political association. In the Marxist theory the working class is, indeed, the basis of all political organization, superseding the state and the interstate relations of nations in one universal world proletariat. All these internationals, including also the professional organizations, not omitting the church, are vitally related to the development of national order and of the jural order of the world. Already more than one of these organizations is of larger proportions than some of the smaller nation-states.

The coming pattern of the world order is difficult to forecast but it tends to include the following: military union for prevention of war; judicial organization for various classes of disputes; administrative and technical organization for classes of activities, economic, sanitary, cultural, developmental; and policy-determining agencies developing far more slowly, with advice advancing more firmly than command, with many sanctions other than military or power sanctions. Alternatives are world domination by a single state or a new form of the balance of powers among several nations.

IX. SUMMARY

The preceding pages, incomplete as they are, present a view of the emerging trends of the political process, bringing together the special topics into which the study of government falls. Inadequate as this outline may be, it is presented as reinforcement of what has gone before and a basis for what is to come in the succeeding chapter. From one point of view the history of politics is a dismal and repulsive trail of blood and slime and dirt, of torture, pain, and death, of ill-concealed and insolent ambition, arrogance, intrigue, and treach-

[12] The League of Nations at one time, however, seriously discussed the possibility of cities as rivals of the League itself.

ery, of inhuman slave-drivers and managers of modern type, of adjudicators cleverly twisting the law and fawning upon vested power, of endlessly talking councils.[13]

But we may see also the emergence of law; the rise of order; the organization of justice, of common counsel, of rational discussion, of management, not merely humane, but human. We may see the growth of liberty. We may see the gleam of the wings of human personality emerging from its chrysalis.

In a moment of values often measured by the standards of a pecuniary order, we may see a rising scale of human values richer than riches in a regime of social justice.

We may envisage the stately structure of the new commonwealth, a temple of our common justice, a center of our common interest, a symbol of our common hope.[14]

CHAPTER X

THE FUTURE OF GOVERNMENT

MANY have essayed the projection of what the government might be or ought to be. The future form of the state is not precisely predictable, but the historic trends of human experience are observable, and reflections upon this problem bring a cumulation of probabilities. The uses of imagination and invention in politics are very great. Observation and reflection will be refined with time, assumptions sharpened and subjected to verification, and conclusions purged of obvious errors and moved toward relatively higher levels of plausibility and probability. From time to time we may draw a trial balance, unsatisfactory as it may be from the point of view of the ultimate accounting.

I. UTOPIAS

Many are the utopias that have been constructed by those who peered into the future, but most of them did not penetrate very far beyond the immediate range of their circumstances.[1] From the long and distinguished list of anticipations, I am selecting several different types.[2] It would be superfluous to discuss in detail these well-known analyses of the future state.

[13] See "The Shame of Power" in my *Political Power.*
[14] See my *Prologue to Politics*, pp. 74–75.

[1] See J. O. Hertzler, *The History of Utopian Thought* (1923); Karl Mannheim, *Ideology and Utopia* (1936). American utopias are discussed in my *A History of American Political Theories* (1931), chap. xiv.

[2] More's Utopia, Bacon's New Atlantis, Butler's Erewhon, and Harrington's Oceana are of striking significance. See also H. G. Wells, *The Shape of Things To Come* (1933) and other works; Bernard Shaw, *Everybody's Political What's What?* (1944).

Plato projected an aristocracy pure and simple based upon an especially selected and specially trained body of rulers who became guardians of the law, free from the entanglements of family, property, industry, or other distracting factors. Many of the most beautiful passages in this masterpiece have entranced mankind for two thousand years. Plato's plan applied only to a small group of 5,040.

Plato's pupil, Aristotle, presented an ideal state in the form of a political society which was a mean between numbers and wealth, a society in which power and property were distributed throughout the community in such fashion as to produce a middle-class state. But this state called for a slave class, an industrial class outlawed from the political circle, and for a magnitude of some ten thousand citizens. From the point of view of Plato's aristocracy this was a democratic state, but from the point of view of modern democracy this was an aristocracy, supported by the very best of democratic arguments. The influence of Aristotle's study was fundamentally democratic, however, and his *Politics*, dug up from the ruins after a thousand years of burial, became a medieval bulwark of democratic reflection if not of democratic practice.

Rousseau's *Social Contract* postulated a form of association from which there emerged the general will of which the citizen was an indivisible part and in which he remained as free as before the contract. In this society the general will was sovereign and the government was subject; in meetings en masse of the sovereign people, the problem of continuing both the form of government and the special rulers in charge was submitted to mass determination. The essential in Rousseau's utopia, if thus it may be called, was not the organization of political society, which was notably undeveloped and weak, but the picture of a world in which personal freedom and the general will were reconciled on a basis which was political, but in a way superpolitical, metapolitical. The chains of slavery were broken for all mankind; a positive agency for the common good was set up—an authority—but still the individual was as free as he was before. This was once termed by Kant "carrying the flaming torch into the market place," providing a gospel for the disinherited.

For Anglo-American peoples John Locke's *Two Treatises of Government* was a leading point in the direction of the future. In point of fact a justification of the existing government in England following the revolution of 1688, it laid down general principles which served as a rallying point for several generations. Locke provided a revolutionary basis for government, on the one hand, and, on the other, a formal structure of authority. Dull and unattractive in form, as compared with the *Republic* of Plato or the *Social Contract* of Rousseau, the political philosophy of Locke was far-reaching and penetrating in its influence over wide ranges of mankind. Comparable with this was Montesquieu's *Spirit of Laws*, more attractive in style but less profound in analysis.

A forecast of the future was that presented in the Declaration of Independence. This, with the Preamble to the United States Constitution, contains a statement of the ends of political society toward which practical activity may be directed.

"We hold these truths to be self-evident, that all men are created equal, that they are endowed by their Creator with certain unalienable Rights; that among these are Life, Liberty, and the pursuit of Happiness. That to secure these rights, Governments are instituted among Men, deriving their just powers from the consent of the governed. That whenever any Form of Government becomes destructive of these ends, it is the Right of the People to alter or to abolish it, and to institute new Government."

The Preamble to the Constitution presents a program "to form a more perfect Union, establish justice, insure domestic tranquillity, provide for the common defence, promote the general welfare, and secure the blessings of liberty to ourselves and our posterity."

These are words which point to what government might be.

The Marxian doctrine embodied in the heavy pages of *Das Kapital* and in the flaming language of the *Communist Manifesto* was a political document of far-reaching importance in the evolution of political thought and institutions. On the structural side the effort was barren, since the postulate was the abolition of the state in the long run, assuming that the state is only an instrument of class struggle, ending with the close of the struggle. The reasoning covered more than that, however, since it included (1) a revolutionary basis for a new society and (2) an emerging millennium in which the formula of society would be: "From each according to his ability; to each according to his need." The *modus operandi* was to be the collective ownership of the means of economic production. For the rights of man with procedural guaranties there was substituted material security for all workers in a worker-controlled system of management or government, although government was to disappear eventually.

While the Marxians indignantly repudiated the utopian basis of this society, this is what the plan really was, with a revolutionary basis and a glowing anticipation of the possibilities of the future when the system had been fully and completely established. The widespread influence of this document was unquestionable, challenging as it did the current doctrines of industrio-political society.

Of quite a different type was the ideal state or city depicted in the Book of Revelation. "And God shall wipe away all tears from their eyes; and there shall be no more death, neither sorrow nor crying, neither shall there be any more pain; for the former things are passed away" (21:4). There shall be "no more curse," and there shall be "no night there." Such was "that great city,"

12,000 furlongs square, with all manner of fruit "for the healing of the nations." Many have found solace in the distant scene.[3]

II. THE MODERN PROBLEM

But by now utopias may be woven from a broader basis than ever before, from the discoveries and inventions of reason and experience in the world around us. Our problem is how to utilize our experience and reflection in such a manner as to diminish the possibility of error and increase the chances of correct conclusions. That there is any royal road to such a goal no one can seriously contend, or, if he does, we do not trust him or his panacea. Fundamentally, the gravest of all perils of politics is failure to fill in the gaps among science, religion, economics, and tradition—all in a framework of consent and in a rapidly changing period. Science overturns the landmarks we have long used to guide us and to define our comings and goings. Science has often battled religion, and vice versa, in futile struggles over border lines of behavior. Economics approaches solution, so some of its leaders say, of the problem of production, but we face the problem of distribution and of standards of living appropriate to new standards of production. More precisely, what is happening around us is the modification, and in some instances disintegration, of long-established concepts occupying a central position in the political and economic realms, as well as the social in the broader sense. What is happening to nationalism, collective security, sovereignty, liberty, bills of rights, to individualism, communism, to inheritance, property, profits, personality, power, to sanctions of behavior, in the changing society that is swirling around us?

In many cases it is found that the old clichés and contrasts coming out of an outgrown era have no longer the same application to the emerging future but are modified and combined in widely different forms. Both nationalism and internationalism of the older type are caught up in the whirl of events that leads on to world federation in new and now undefinable types, hitherto impossible without the advent of revolutionary forms of transportation and especially of communication. One voice may reach around the globe, and that may be the voice of reason rather than of force. Nationalism reached the zenith of its power in the nineteenth century and, with the appearance of American federalism, began to yield to broader sweeps of organization. The British Commonwealth of Nations in the nineteenth, and the Soviet Union in the twentieth, point the same way, beyond the country-state, the nation-state, to federations of a different order, including not merely ethnic groups and contiguous territory, but far-flung groups of population held together by looser bonds, and themselves in turn federated in world-wide form. Patriotism, the love of country, remains stronger than ever, but it does not rest upon hatred of the enemy alone.

[3] Compare Augustine's *City of God*.

322

Much of the current speculation regarding government is already out of date. The issues upon which men are most hotly divided or even warring at times are losing their meaning in the rush of social change. For example, the real question is not that of much or little government—individualism or collectivism—but what types of strategic devices are most useful in the given situation and how we can implement them most effectively by governmental or semigovernmental or other agencies. Both capitalism—if by that is meant laissez faire economics—and communism reached their theoretical climax in the nineteenth century and are groping toward ways and means of solving their common problem of production plus distribution under a system of justice. If the problem of sheer production is solved already or on its way, the residual problem is not that of more goods for one and less for another, but of mutual advantage under new formulas of organization and new attitudes of mind. Economics and politics are not really foes; they are members of the same family.

"Freedom from authority" was captured and used as a slogan in the form of "laissez faire" for exploitation by special groups, but it was rescued and turned to the service of the personality of all men and the whole community. Here again the extremes took widely varying and hostile forms at times. Between individualism at one end and collectivism at the other, violent struggle and even revolution, as in Russia, were involved. It cannot be said that this struggle is ended or that it will soon be closed, but it becomes increasingly clearer that neither of these formulas is broad enough to cover the actual situations developing in the modern world. The principle underlying both of them is inadequate to meet the needs of the present problem. Both turn upon an economic interpretation of human affairs and seek an explanation in economic terms, whether we look at Marx or at Mill. Economics, however, is itself a means to an end, and that broader end is obviously more important than the means. That end is the emancipation of the personality for the good life which modern science and organization can produce if permitted the full use of their operative strength.[4]

Full production assured, the political ways and means of establishing rapport are far simpler to set up and are included in the formula of democracy. Government must concern itself as a primary obligation with the just distribution of the gains of civilization and assume responsibility for humane standards of living in the particular stage of production and culture. That the powers of government will constantly expand, relatively to the role of the individual, is partly an illusion. If we look only at the number of governmental acts, the instances of governmental "intervention," as it is termed, it is clear that this number is rapidly increasing; but if we look at the complexity of social rela-

[4] Peter F. Drucker, *The End of Economic Man* (1939); my *The Role of Politics in Social Change* (1936).

323

tionships, at the number of possible "interventions," we may observe that the proportionate number of governmental actions is relatively on the decline. Do new building regulations increase more rapidly than the new dangers from fire, structural collapse, insanitary conditions? Or are they relatively fewer? Are the hospital, the park, and the school roads to serfdom or broad ways to freedom? Strategic controls are the order of the day—controls which facilitate action for human beings.[5] Emancipation and release are in their train.

The war between science and religion was really ended long ago and never had a rational basis; the war between church and state was ended even longer ago and has no present basis in view of the ends of religion or of the government. We do not need the state to play God or the church to play politics. Traditions and ideals may be blended usefully alike in church and in government.

The problem of state-wide balances of power, whether between nations or within nations, is on its way to restatement and reorganization. War is not a solution of relations between political societies. Blocking and balancing alone is not a solution as between organs of government within nations. Rivalry between groups is essential but need not point to futility in action. The ways and means of establishing rapport in this area are now well known, and many models are at hand for use when and as desired.

The struggle between centralization and decentralization is a perennial one, but often it takes the form of an empty struggle between conflicting appetites of politicians or others, seeking for exclusive priorities. We now know that many functions of government are, at one and the same time, central, local, and intermediate, changing as new situations arise in health, education, work, welfare.

Radicalism and conservatism are other hardy perennials but often indicate only differences as to modes and rates of change. "Conservation" and "adaptation" are words with meaning.

All this, or much of it, is obscured by the confusion of the time in which (1) the roles of central and local government are ill defined, (2) the roles of the units in industry are also ill defined, and (3) the grand strategy of society from which, of course, strategic controls emerge is likewise ill defined. In such an atmosphere pleas for liberty may become covers for plunder; and attacks upon bureaucracy, pleas for another bureaucracy of another color—monopoly or cartel, for example. Groups aiming at monopoly may demand liberty—for the purpose of destroying liberty, just as groups clamoring for more authority may contemplate their own personal aggrandizement.

One of the factors which is most disturbing and which makes difficulty in adjusting for all of us is the larger-sized units of operation and the complexity of operations in addition—corporations, unions, internationals, compact minor-

[5] See my *The Role of Politics in Social Change* on strategic controls.

324

ities—and the role of the human personality in these larger and more complex units. We lose sight of the known fact that there may be tyranny in a small group as well as in a large one; that there may be liberty in a large group as well as in a small one, in forty-eight states as well as in thirteen, in a British Commonwealth as well as in a little England. There may be bureaucracy in a little village as well as in a great empire. There may be enterprise and individual initiative in a large unit as well as or sometimes better than in a small one. The larger unit may release individuals through the greater specialization to which they may adapt themselves and find their feet as never before. This does not follow automatically, but it may follow in time slowly or more rapidly by design and plan. Meanwhile, we pass through "growing pains."

The whole problem of the nature and implications of the political order is on the agenda for searching examination, with the use of new techniques, never before available to inquiring students of human nature. Psychology and sociology are lagging behind in this heavy task, but not forever. They will bring with them conclusions of far-reaching importance to mankind. Medicine has already brought forward immense contributions, and mental medicine has still more in store for the benefit of mankind. The master-slave relationship is on its way out of human institutions, and the command-obedience psychology as a basis for governance is also on its way out, beyond any question, however slowly we may seem to move in this desired direction. When education and medicine and economics have done their full work, the human personality will assume new forms of political and social co-operation and control which may make our present constructs seem childish. What these new forms may be I do not know, and I am intelligent enough, I trust, not to try to describe what I do not know about or cannot forecast on the basis of ascertained data and principles.

In the following pages, however, I am setting down the emerging outlines of political development. These considerations are based upon such observation, experience, and reflection as I can command for this occasion.[6]

III. EMERGING POLICIES AND PROGRAMS

A. A JURAL ORDER OF THE WORLD

Most of the classical theory upon this point is not valid now, if it ever was. There cannot be free states unless there is a free world. This does not involve necessarily a world state, but it supposes an end of anarchy between states and the organization of a world order. It presupposes a common understanding of "aggression" and a common method of enforcing the world's ideas of aggression, of basic order, and of basic justice.

---

[6] In other studies I hope to set down in more detail my conclusions on long-time city planning and on the political structure and program of the United States.

There may be many states in the world order, but they will not be states from whose decisions there is no appeal in the hierarchy of justice. There may be sovereigns; but they will not be absolute, unlimited, and unreasonable. There cannot be tiny and isolated states of 5,040 persons as Plato declared, or 10,000, as Aristotle set up, except in a world order. There may be and will be wide areas of autonomy, political and otherwise; but they will not be areas of absolute isolation, unless quarantines are established against them. What Aristotle said of the detached hand—it could exist only if it were a stone hand—will be true of the detached political association in the world order of justice.

The modern drive for world organization is no longer merely the product of ethical hopes alone, or of generalized humanitarianism, but is the fiat of revolutionized transportation and intercommunication, which has reduced the size of the world to its present shrunken dimensions and has necessitated the reorganization of a larger-scale economy. The urge comes from the development of competitive armament; the practical realization of the unpleasant consequences of world anarchy, in which any mad aggressor may disturb the peace of all the others in his world. It takes many to make peace, but one alone may make war; and he may be stopped only by counterwar or force in some equivalent form.

In the coming state the ethnic-territorial basis of association will yield to the broader cosmopolitan emphasis of the unity of mankind. The coming community is not a tribe but mankind. Cultural groups of all types may freely develop in a world order, more freely and fully than ever before in the history of mankind; but the interests of the tribal group will not be the basis of political association. Cultures may exist without crowns of sovereignty, by the tolerance and encouragement of the world in which they are set rather than by the strength of their military armaments. Transportation and communication, airplanes, radio, and television, are moving inexorably forward toward a broader brotherhood of man, toward wider horizons of understanding, of appreciation, and, by the same token, of co-operation.

B. AUTHORITY AS TRUSTEESHIP—CONSENT OF THE GOVERNED—EQUALITY OF MEN AND RACES

There must be recognition of authority as essentially trusteeship rather than ownership. In the religious field, in most of the political fields, and in science this is already recognized; and men are agents, trustees, and servants rather than masters or lords. In the economic field the full implications of this have not been realized, however, as landlords and other lords often think of themselves as independent sovereigns, treating with political and other servants perhaps.

Beyond this comes recognition of the institutionalizing of trusteeship. In the political world responsibility in general was conceded long before responsibility in particular was set up in the form of responsible government. In other areas the general principle is admitted, but the practical application resisted, as when employers resist collective bargaining by their employees or reasonable control by the state itself, asserting the priority of their own interpretation of their interests; or when states resist world order. Industrial autocracy is not consistent with an emerging principle of authority and finds itself swept to one side either by the force of the Communist or by the counterforce of the Fascist or Nazi. The principle of master and man is no longer applicable in the form and with the implications of mastership historically. There will, of course, be leadership and direction, but based upon another principle and in another setting of institutions.

Underlying the trusteeship of the particular governors of the moment lies the consent of the governed as the basis of authority. The consent of the governed rests in turn upon the equality of men, upon the human dignity of all, upon the recognition of this human personality and purpose as the basis of authority and of the structure and functions of government. Equality in the field of right, whether political, politico-ethical, or moral, is the basis of intelligent government in its emerging forms. That there are human differences and differentials does not stand in the way of political equality before the law, or equality in ballotage, or equality in the whole process of the consent of the governed.

Equality applies to races as well as within a particular area or state. This is a hard saying for master-races, so called, master-states, or master-individuals and master-groups wherever found. But the doctrine emerges, however slowly, as a dominant consideration in human government. With whatever hilarity human and racial equality may be scorned by alleged "realists," or by those who accept the idea in principle but kill it in actual practice by cunning evasions, subterfuges, and pretexts, the conclusion has the support of philosophers of law and of religion and the aid of scientists. Slavery, serfdom, caste, and class are now maintained, not by force of reason or practical necessity, but by force of privilege and power usurping the rights of other men by their institutions or their interpretations, adapted to their special interests.

The principle of the consent of the governed and the institutions for its application may well be implemented by increasingly intelligent consideration of problems of government and especially of those problems demanding instant attention of those consenting or opposing. For this purpose communication is as important as participation—communication of experience, reflection, plans, and proposals affecting the community and its members. In the new world into which we come, the press, radio, screen, rapid transportation, and television create new situations in which communication may flourish more freely than before, under favorable conditions. The consideration of the optimum ways and means of uniting the new participation in government with the new modes of communication is one of the paramount problems of the new statesmen. Communication alone will not solve this problem, merely as a mechanical device, but communication in the larger sense makes possible for the first time in history the interchange through modern symbols of those vital human experiences, ideas, interests, and aspirations upon which the unity and harmony of the world depend.

C. RECOGNITION OF REASON, SCIENCE, AND EDUCATION

It is necessary to recognize the role of science and education in the development of any system—of whatever external type, as truly in Japan as in Russia or America. Science is intelligence in human affairs and must enter into any emerging pattern of values and institutions. Traditions may stand in the way of intelligence and often has, and the denial has lost many a battle and ruined empires. But traditions that cannot stand the analysis of science are foredoomed, and their day of departure may be postponed but not prevented in the long run. Beating the tom-toms may arouse the fighting spirit of the group, but the drum itself and the weapons of war are devised by the technicians. Even more, as the study of propaganda develops, may the scientist also be called in to aid in the "making medicine" which is thought essential to preparation for war.

This idea cannot be said to have penetrated through the general attitude toward authority in social affairs, for there still remains a domain into which reason is not welcomed—in dealing with social relations. Science may often be utilized as servant and as tool but not as an equal. Science may be thought useful for industrial chemistry, for example, or for war explosives, but not in shaping the conditions which might make war unnecessary or industrial disturbance less frequent. Moral values may be conjured up against Galileo, or against Darwin, or against dissection of the dead, or against vaccination, or against birth control or sterilization, or against an amendment to a constitution, or against a form of tax which may be found "immoral." Or science itself may, in social affairs, become unscientific through the attitudes and expressions of leaders, such as Alexis Carrel, who at times speak the language of social reaction in the name of science.

In an emerging type of state it will be found indispensable to recognize and foster the enormous values of science in the development of resources and also in the organization of social devices for better utilization of natural—and human—resources. It is important that statesmen and scientists be on speaking terms in peace as well as in war and that they do not forget the philosophers.

In like manner the role of education may well be made a part of emerging forms of association if it is desired to set up a unified system recognizing the elements of which modern civilization is made up. By "education" is meant, however, not merely an official system of propaganda but the systematic training of the human mind and emotions, the development of opportunities for continuing human growth and appreciation. If it be said that all modern systems recognize the values of education and act accordingly, my reply is that educational systems often fall short at precisely the points where they should be opened out—that they restrict education to special sets of values and ignore or prohibit the introduction of others, either directly or by indirection through emphasis and distortion. Many systems are now closed systems, only inadequately dealing with the various forms of values which are essential to the newly emerging type of association appropriate to the newly emerging world.

There can be little doubt that, when education and medicine do their perfect work and produce stabilized personalities of a balanced type, the task of governance will be far lighter than it has been traditionally in the history of mankind. Much of the political sorrow of the world is caused by frustrated personalities, by maladjusted rebels and reactionaries, by those who never grew up or grew up wrong, whose intelligence and emotions were not trained to get along with each other or with other persons. Wide ranges of trouble may be avoided with sounder systems of early training, preventing the growth of the large numbers of twisted and unhappy souls from whom are recruited the armies of crime, low and high, and of disorder and demagoguery, chicanery and chauvinism, low-level susceptibility to appeals of folly and hate.

This may seem more utopian than the old utopias, but I stand by it and am more certain of this point than of any others in this discussion. This was the pet theme of my *Civic Education in the United States*—to which no one paid any attention. I proposed a psychiatrist on the Social Studies Commission but was drowned in inextinguishable laughter.

May there not come a time, it may be asked, when the conclusions of specialists regarding social behavior will be so authentic and indisputable, and so widely sought for and followed, that formalized consent will fade into the background and eventually disappear from the scene entirely? If the wise ones know what to do, why not let them rule?

This is theoretically possible, but it is improbable. Much more will be known about social and political science in the future than now, beyond question; but—

a) There will always be a margin of alternatives—a margin where human values and choices will be important and conclusive. The broadest outlines of political policy will remain subjects for general decision. The alternatives will be more carefully considered, and the elimination of unchecked impossibilities may follow; but the final decision will be generalized rather than specialized.

b) The maintenance of community morale is facilitated by community participation in basic community affairs. Community consciousness of common interest requires common activism in community affairs from time to time. Discipline rests not upon fear but upon common consent.

c) The organization of scientific research and the organization of what is called "planning" will be better organized and articulated with the activities of the government, but they will not take the place of the organization of consent.

But the statesmen—must they survive?

There are those who regard the politicians—the politicos—as having only a nuisance value, and who hence would look forward with keen pleasure to their complete retirement from the ideal community—a world without politicians. In reality, however, the politicos serve a useful and important function in the society and, indeed, are worth more than we pay them now. They are brokers between the isolated technicians and the busy consumers who make up the community. Their weavings-in-and-out, their conversations and orations, their discussions and compromises—these are not all wasted, although some of them are. They are indispensable in the modern society in one form or another—partly as artists, partly as scientists.

It is difficult to maintain that government is more corrupt, incompetent, or unresponsive to social interests than other groupings, judging each group, of course, in the light of its own special and characteristic responsibility. Group defense, order, justice, welfare, and liberty are the ends of government—ends its shares at many points with other groups—and it is in the light of these responsibilities that governmental action or inaction must be appraised.[7]

Government is a cross-section of society, and its composition and conduct are likely to be that of the social forces and attitudes from which it comes. Privilege, exploitation, serfdom, and slavery are not the creatures of government alone; they spring from a society so minded. Likewise crime and unemployment are not the children of government alone. Nor can it be forgotten that the light of publicity in modern times falls far more sharply on the affairs of government than upon private transactions. Political business is in the limelight, while there are no, or relatively few, partisans who specialize in criticism and adverse comment outside government.

It may be maintained that government which has made extensive and notable use of the oral dialectic, historically, through the processes of adjudication and later of conciliar agencies, is not able to adjust itself to the uses of modern forms of inquiry, analysis, and determination. The development of management, however, has opened the way for thorough and expert examination of governmental problems of all types, for their analysis and consideration by courts and by legislative agencies. Expert testimony is now available and is extensively utilized as a basis for oral discussion and determination. The argu-

[7] See my "Government and Intelligence," *Ethics*, LIV (1944), 263–72.

ment may be only the final decision between two conflicting technical views of policy which have been thoroughly considered—the Panama or the Nicaragua Canal for illustration—so that either, alternatively, is technically admissible. It may be a long way from the experts to the final decision, but this is not a situation peculiar to government but one that is common to industry or some other action agency.

The whole broad range of the techniques of modern reason and science is available to government. Great bodies of research in physical and social sciences are built up in many fields by government itself. In the narrower fields of governmental organs and agencies the techniques of psychology, statistics, and the social sciences have been especially drawn upon for intelligent analysis and counsel. The census is a classical example of governmental service in data collection and analysis.

Obviously, many problems are not to be handled by the political society alone but require the co-operation of many other forms of social grouping—the family, the church, the groups of producers, and many other social aggregations with influence and responsibility.

My general conclusions are:

1. Government does not lag behind other competing social groups in the use of current intelligence—in comparison, let us say, with the family, with the church, with producing groups. Sometimes even the professional custodians of learning have been known to fall behind the new truth available. The government has no monopoly upon sluggish, incompetent, or unethical behavior. But there is more pitiless publicity in public than in private affairs.

2. Government often seems to be behind other groups because it is made the scapegoat for social inability to find a solution of a social problem which no one else can solve. Examples are prostitution, gambling, unfair trade practices, strikes, and race relations. All these questions, going deep down into the roots of human relations, the government is expected to solve out of hand; or, if it does not, it is found to lag behind the culture of the time. Perhaps the culture itself is behind what we think it is.

3. The use of heavy penalties by the political society brings down upon it double blame if the action is not wise, or even if it is at times. "No rogue ere felt the halter draw with good opinion of the law"—and much less so if the citizen is not a rogue but an honest man perplexed by some governmental ineptitude.

4. Force, fraud, spoils, and corruption are passing phases of the growth of social and political organization and cannot live in the new day. Their basis is moral and cultural, as well as political, however; and the remedy and prevention are moral, cultural, and political.

5. The prevention of war and unemployment, the greatest scourges of our

time, is well within the known techniques of expert intelligence, if the known ways and means are effectively applied. There is reason to believe that this is in sight.

6. The development of democratic government is a help and not a hindrance to the growth of science and reason in political associations. The combination of scientific possibilities, on the one hand, and the increasing sense of human dignity, on the other, make possible a far more intelligent form of government than ever before in history.

7. We face the almost fantastic advance of science and learning in our day and the prospect of still more rapid progress in the years immediately ahead. On the verge of revolutionary innovations in science and technology, basically affecting the ways of life, we must be able to produce an equally revolutionary advance in facility of adjustment, in sophistication of judgment, in the dynamics of new enterprise. This is the well-known race between "civilization and catastrophe."

But government does not face this crisis alone. The family, the church, industry, agriculture, the human personality itself—all are confronted by the same urgent and overwhelming demand for readjustments of the most of our nature. In time our social and political arrangements may well prove to be as clumsy as those of the primitives at whom we smile. When education, medicine, advance in production, the full implications in the new meaning of time and space—when these factors have been brought to bear upon social living, both government and society will be changed in many ways.

This new order is a challenge not merely to government, not alone to the politicos, but to every form of association and every type of personality in the emerging world.

D. ORGANS OF GOVERNMENT

Adjudicative and consultative agencies of government are among the great triumphs of human intelligence in social relations, and under any and all forms of political or economic structure their function will be pre-eminent. But doubtless human intelligence will refine and perfect their procedures and points of view as time goes on. In the selection of personnel sensitive to scientific and technical change in human relations and on the side of rapport with public opinion there is room for continuing improvement. The adjudicators tend to take a backward look necessarily in a world where precedent plays so significant a part, and the lawmakers tend to look around them, too narrowly often, in their representative capacity. But the forward look of social philosophy is also a part of the governing process, if fossilization and confusion are to be avoided. The emerging analyses of and insights into human personality are likely to produce profound changes, of a character we can now only dimly adumbrate, both in the methods of courts and the ways of lawmakers.

The role of the experts in the court and of press, radio, and screen in the making of law are illustrative of the problems and the possibilities ahead of us. The faltering structure, selection, and role of representative bodies especially is certain to be put in the crucible of analysis and reflection, and what varying forms may emerge, in an era of adjustment both to science and to management, we do not know.[8] But the validity and the value of the skills of adjudicating and consultative bodies are firmly even if clumsily established, as is their ultimate responsibility in a system of the consent of the governed.

Expert management takes its place in the social scheme, alongside the older values of adjudication and common counsel. This is "administration," whether in government, industry, industry-government, or religion. Management was long organized in the church—and that not upon a hereditary basis; it was the basis of modern efficiency in government, developing under the absolutists but improved by the democracies; and in industry management rapidly tends to supersede the other factors in successful operation of an enterprise. Management may become bureaucracy but is, nonetheless, an essential element in association and requires wide recognition of its function in the body politic, economic, cultural. It is the great lubricator of human relations. But management is no longer merely personal patronage or arbitrary judgment; it is based on the dignity of man and on the scientific values of human treatment. It is not merely proprietary or humane; it is scientific and human.

Personnel management under intelligent guidance will greatly increase the quality of public service by throwing light on the perplexed problem of aptitudes for public service (and, incidentally, of all service) by modes of training, selection, adaptation, by methods of operation, by interchange between public, private, and mixed forms of service.

Intelligent fiscal management will be able to utilize modern fiscal devices, controls, and releases, adapted to changing economico-political situations.

Intelligent planning management will be able to analyze trends and possibilities and to aid in the preparation of long-time policies of utilizing resources, human and material, for the benefit of the community and the personalities composing it.[9]

Good administrative management will remove many of our troubles, and so will a higher level of intelligence regarding the role of administration on the part of the community. But there will be no organization of any supreme institute of metaphysics, of faith, or of science that will take the place of the agencies of social morale and intercommunication now labeled as "the statesmen." To all such plans the experts should say, "Get thee behind me, Satan."

[8] This is as true of business and labor as of government (see Beardsley Ruml, *Tomorrow's Business* [1945]).

[9] My "The Possibilities of Planning," *American Journal of Sociology*, XLIX (1944), 397–407.

The role of the headman, leader, or executive has been one of the most perplexing problems from Nero to Hitler. One by one divinity, heredity, age, fighting qualities, and military skill have been cast aside as indices for leadership. The key to evolving leadership is now found in the third of the series of subordination, superordination, and co-ordination. Co-ordination and co-operation are the basis of modern directors, and these are now set in a constitutional and democratic framework of understandings and mechanisms. The whole changing nature of organization tends to emphasize more and more the significance of the leader's function in the affairs of the time and place. Personality is important, but it is secondary in meaning to the function performed and the community served. Understandings of trusteeship and mechanisms of responsibility surround the executive leader with warning signals that mark danger for him or for the community. Within such a framework of understanding and confidence thousands of leaders emerge and serve in thousands of governments, private and public alike. The strength of the leader depends not upon patronage, veto, or showmanship, important as these elements may be, but upon the skill and fidelity with which he operates in a world of community services and community understanding of his responsibilities and trusteeship. In this sense the emerging leader is a projection of types such as Lincoln, Lloyd George, Beneš, Masaryk, Roosevelt, and Churchill.

E. THE PROGRAM OF GOVERNMENT

If the ends of security and order are by way of settlement, a situation not yet assured, intelligent government may direct its attention to justice, welfare, and freedom and their practical implementation. Government cannot escape its share of responsibility for the progressive improvement of human personalities in the framework of the common good but must at all times stand ready to use its friendly offices for the development of a fraternal, equalitarian, libertarian way of life.

This calls for a positive program beyond the role of neutrality or the umpire in the struggle for existence. Intelligent planning involves (1) systematic attention to the growth of the gains of civilization, the mode and range of their distribution, the principles of justice and freedom in their practical application. In addition to the body of civil rights and liberties, this involves (2) a guaranty by the government, as one of the underwriters, of security in employment, minimum standards of health, education, the "social securities," and equal access to the development of creative possibilities in the human personality. The underlying principle of the responsibility of government is more important than the particular policies or mechanisms utilized for the broad purposes in view.

Our coming problems are not adequately described by the current terms "economic collectivism" and "capitalism." They are far broader in scope. They

334

include considerations not merely economic but scientific, technological, engineering, philosophical, ethical, territorial-racial, socio-political. They include ideal as well as material considerations, diverse value systems and ideas, and institutions of many types outside the economic and governmental.

Laissez faire and communism are oversimplifications of problems which are far too complex to be contained by these economic slogans. In one sense all community action is collectivist, but with equal truth it may be said that all communities are made up of human personalities associated for their personal life-advantage as well as for the common good.

Observation, experience, and reflection point to a program in the next stage of development in which government will underwrite, as one of the co-operating underwriters, but fully responsible in the default of others:

The fullest possible development of the productive potential of all our resources, material and human, with assurance of full employment, continuity of income, minimum standards of living, including education, health, housing, the cultural amenities of life, a balance between stability and adventure, and a fair share in the growing gains of civilization.

The fullest possible development of the human personality, in relation to the common good, in a framework of freedoms and rights, of justice, liberty, equality, and the consent of the governed.

The end of world anarchy and the organization of an effective jural order of the world, outlawing aggression and imperialism, old or new fashioned in world relations, encouraging and energizing the fullest development of resources and rights everywhere.

It is vital for the future of ourselves and for the race that we recognize the meaning of government. I make bold to say on the basis of my observation, experience, and reflection ranging over a wide area of opportunity that the capacity of government is the key to the near future. We cannot hope to flout and sneer at government and yet build a sound structure of economic and social life. Government is not the master of men, but men cannot master their problems without it.

The important question is what we propose to do regarding the future development of our resources with reference to specific programs of action directed toward the common good. The development of a dynamic economy will absorb our interests and our energies for some time to come, and this can be achieved without basic changes in our industrial or political economy. That there is an underlying harmony of interests common to groups and individuals and that there are also sharp differences in personal and group advantage goes without saying. But in a dynamic economy, with full employment and full development of national resources, the national income may be so largely increased by superior use of science, by superior forms of organization and management, by superior productivity of goods and services—all well within

335

the bounds of possibility in a free system—that the minor differences of advantage are lost sight of in the larger gains that may accrue to all.

The fear that planning will interfere with the development of free industrial society is groundless. The very purpose of planning is to release human abilities, to broaden the field of opportunity, and to enlarge human liberty. We plan primarily for freedom; the ways and means and instruments are secondary to the main purpose. The right kind of planning—democratic planning —is a guaranty of liberty and the only real assurance in our times that men can be free to make a wide range of choices.

Among the outstanding ways in which human liberty may be expanded by careful planning are:

1. Research, invention, and technological development, which are the bases of our industrial development, would profit by careful planning. Business research, governmental research, academic research—all flourish under a system of freedom, in a climate where their progress is considered one of the mainsprings of human progress and is fostered in every possible way, alike in social and in natural science. Physics, chemistry, biology, engineering, medicine, education, and management are the foundations upon which much of our material and social progress depends, and they flourish best where careful attention is given to their cultivation. In a democratic society these free channels of invention and ingenuity may be kept open to all, without discrimination against race or class.

2. The frontiers of industrial development are wide open. There is every reason to believe that human enterprise and organization are likely in the immediate future to utilize more fully undeveloped resources already known and to go beyond that into the exploration and advancement of entirely new fields of industrial activity. The amazing results following the release of human ingenuity in the present drive for large-scale production show the tremendous possibilities in our present system. Only those whose imagination is dead or dying can fail to recognize the vast peacetime potential of production, once the way is cleared. Obviously, all this is not the task of government alone, but government can keep the channels of enterprise open and can help to plan for continuing growth of essential resources, both material and human.

The 100 per cent attainment of health and education alone would transform national resources in a measure defying precise calculation, but beyond question to a point of incalculable value, even in terms of dollars and cents, to say nothing of human happiness. There is a point at which expenditure for health and education would strike the law of diminishing returns, but we have not yet even come within sight of such a situation.

Free enterprise has far more to fear from lack of planning than from its development and application to national resources. Between fascism, on the one hand, and monopoly and unregulated concentrations of economic power, on the other, the free industrial system and the open free market are hard pressed now. It is not planning that has made difficulties in the smooth working of free competition, that has fostered monopolies, cartels, racketeering, high, low, or medium, but the lack of it.

In the past few years government has brought up to date types of social legislation that were a generation late, such as social security and conservation. We still lag behind at many important points. But the dramatic possibilities of the next period are far more important than either the early planning of our public lands or the later approach to belated social and humanitarian legislation.

We can take the measure of the meaning of both public and private government, and can advance without being frightened either by the word "anarchism" or the word "collectivism" applied to every individual act of the government. We can recognize that government is one of the many agencies necessary to the happiness of mankind, a useful servant of the common good, for purposes willed by the community itself.

Private enterprise and public enterprise and mixed forms of enterprise will take their proper places in the national economy and may dwell together in harmony. There may and will be regional struggles and personal struggles and sectarian struggles and racial rivalries and class struggles, but they will play their proper roles in the broad setting of the common good—not as the lords of creation, but as servants and not as masters of the common good. In a truly free economy—one which is free politically and free economically and free religiously and free culturally—no one element will have a monopoly of decisions affecting the common good.

Many atrocities have been committed in the alleged name of the common man, but usually by special seekers of special privilege taking the name of democracy in vain for their own selfish purposes, with their tongues in their cheeks. But, when men once come really into their own in a fraternal society where the dignity of man and the consent of the governed are actually in force, the vested interests of special groups, political, economic, cultural, racial, or religious, will be relatively insignificant. They may be valued for what they really are.

In that day it will be possible to realize the destiny of modern life more fully than the prophets ever dared to dream. It will be possible to make full use of science and democracy in planning for the expansion of national production, for justice, for the fair distribution of national gains, for far higher standards of living, for liberty, for the recognition of the dignity of man, and for his right to participate fully in the civilization he has helped create.

Such a program is dictated by the growth of human intelligence and its practical application to human needs, by the insistent demands for fraternal recognition and appreciation by fellow-men. It is supported by revolutionary developments of reason, observation, experience, and experiment and made practicable by the discoveries, inventions, and organization of our time which bring vast expansion of man's conscious control over the world around him.

It is no longer utopian to place on the agenda:

The effective outlawry of war

The outlawry of race inequality and personal inequality in an emerging system of resources, rights, and recognitions

The universal organization of the consent of the governed as the basis of political association

The outlawry of social insecurity and want

The outlawry of unfair shares of the gains of civilization

And, finally, the outlawry of governments serving as tools of oppression, exploitation, and privilege, and the recognition of government in theory and practice as an agent of the common good, equipped with modern devices for accomplishing the high purposes of man.

IV. GUIDING PRINCIPLES

A system of guiding considerations in the development of intelligent government includes (*a*) faith in the future; (*b*) incorporation of older value systems in the new system; (*c*) co-operation rather than coercion; and (*d*) emphasis on the creative role of political association.

A. FAITH IN THE FUTURE

It is important to paint a picture of the attainable future in verifiable terms, showing what the gains of civilization are likely to be and holding out definite hope to man. This is the opposite of pessimism, defeatism, drift. The prospects of an emerging civilization can be indicated for the world at large and for individual states by the use of the solid facts of science and technology. The analysis of the world's resources and the possibilities of developing them in the near future, the analysis of the world's income and that of various nations, can be presented roughly but accurately enough to show the dazzling possibilities spread out before mankind. The amazing advance in production in the United States, in Russia, and in Japan in recent years is adequate evidence of the potential if human resources are made available.

These figures show that poverty and want as well as war may be driven from the face of the earth if there is the will to do so, along with pestilence, fire, famine, and flood. These curses are not the acts of God but the results of the inaction of man, whose effort may change the scene into one of opposite color. The immense possibilities in production of material goods may be rivaled by the relief from suffering and pain and the emancipation of the mind from the foul broods that from time to time have settled upon men and desolated their lives.[10]

The advance of the human spirit since the dawning recognition of the dignity of man, his possibilities, and high destiny may be set forth against the prophets of pessimism and disaster, and the future of human ideals and idealisms portrayed in colors as vivid as they are true. For the first time in history utopias need not be woven from fancy and hope but may be constructed from a wealth of science and reason to show indisputable opportunities lying before mankind at this very hour.

B. PLURALISM OF VALUES

There can be an incorporation of older value systems in the new system. It is important to observe the shading of the permanent over into the new and changing, the transitions which distinguish between the old which is outworn and the old which is important in the new. Revolutions that change too much retreat and take up what they abandoned too hastily.

In a revolutionary spirit it is possible to root out religion; it is possible to root out private property; it is possible to root out democracy (or, for that matter, monarchy); it is possible to root out the Jews or other groups disliked, to make a crackling bonfire of the tenderest values and burn them with jubilee of rejoicing. Of course, if necessary change is to be brought about by violence, something must be allowed to the pattern of violence, something of brutality and savagery, since this is the type of change. But far beyond that the hand of violence may reach to attempt the permanent destruction of priceless assets of long-cultivated value systems.

There is nothing in recent social trends to indicate that we are likely to blot out religion, or all privacy of property, or special races, from the earth and set up systems without them. The Jews have wandered long; the church has flourished under persecution—more than in prosperity even; some form of privacy of possession clings even to the most completely communized form of life, in the cell of the monk, in the home of the commissar.

These comments, I may say, are presented as a counsel not of perfection but, on the contrary, of survival in a world of struggling forces and competing values—as a realistic conclusion based upon observation of the difficulties of wholesale destruction of critical and opposing values by builders of authority.

In most wars the enemy survives the peace treaty and remains to be dealt with for a long time—even if his flag never flies again or for a long time. Of course, given sufficient difference in strength, the enemy may be destroyed or permanently disabled, but such a conquest may pull down the conqueror.

[10] Compare the views of Reinhold Niebuhr in *The Children of Light and the Children of Darkness* (1944) and of Harold J. Laski in *Faith, Reason, and Civilization* (1944).

The recurring problem of all power is to remind itself of its own limitations and functions—and this is as true of spiritual authority as of secular. Born in moments of great tension and carrying the weapons of destruction in hand, the tendency of power is to perpetuate the moment of its triumph; to forget the world into which it comes and in which it must live—to forget that the essence of power is creation, not destruction; is trusteeship, not mastery; is leadership, not exploitation. "He that will be first among you, let him become a servant," is a precept of general value in political as well as in ethical affairs. The new value systems, as they emerge from the chaos and defeatism of our day, will include many of the older values developed in experience, among them religious values, chief among the centers of emotional and artistic unification.

Government cannot limit itself to its narrower juristic aspects, important as they have been and will doubtless continue to be. The new government must make a partner of science, a partner of industry, a partner of religion in the best sense of the term. Religion may well abdicate some of its political implications and fraternize more closely with science and with government, as well as with art, in the elaboration of types of human behavior on the idealistic side, while the values of industry may be more closely associated with those of government in the new sense of the term. Industry cannot boycott the state indefinitely.

It is not merely the distribution of the mineral resources of the world, or the horsepower of the world, or the racial differentials of the world, or the title to what is called "property" in the world, or credits or gold, or the territorial boundaries called "states," that prevents the equitable and acceptable reorganization of interests and institutions—important as all these are—but the antagonism of value systems which run down below the obvious surface of the world.

There are possible unifications of value systems, of material interests, so called, of institutions of "steel," "gold," and "the cross," which may be identified running through all these crisscross patterns, if there is the intelligence and the will to weld them into a new form and weave them into a new set of values and symbolisms.

C. CO-OPERATION VERSUS COERCION

In the emerging system of political association, the dominant factor need not be violence and war, although this may be the way to its establishment. It may well be, as Machiavelli suggested, that the prophets who are armed survive those who are not armed, but the instrument of their continuance is co-operation rather than continued force.

Violence is a confession of the lack of power—of weakness rather than strength—in nations as in families. Sparing the rod is no longer considered an evidence of feebleness but of strength—in the family, in the school, in the factory, even in the army itself. The techniques of industry, of the church, of education, and of science—all the principal techniques contributing to the happiness of mankind—are adverse to the use of brutal force; and the trends of modern civilization point irresistibly in this general direction, however loudly the whips may crack at any given moment even now.

The type of the ideal form of political association is not that of an armed camp, of a state, patrolled by unending groups of military or police, with scope and method of obedience fixed by the captain of the troop and enforced by the M.P. The world will be Athens rather than Sparta, it may be safely predicted— or, if unsafely, even so.

Co-operation does not signify the absence of order, hierarchy, discipline, leadership—all of which may flourish in its domain—but signifies relatively light emphasis on brute force and relatively heavy emphasis on the attractive forces of the community—the use of less force and more flowers, of the *miranda* of politics rather than its *horrenda*.

Co-operation involves the closer study of the conditions of human activity and the scientific and human efforts to adapt the conditions of production and consumption to the needs of those who utilize them or are parts of them. It presupposes an educational system pointed up to this purpose and a continuing study of working and living conditions in a world of swift change. To the extent that this is not done or is not possible, violence is employed and break-downs occur.

But precisely here it may be indicated that many of the tension points in our complex modern civilization are to be repaired by medicine and education rather than by violence. If the form of association called "government" insists upon its sword too long or too widely, it will be relegated to the position now occupied by the whip in the school, in the family, and in human toil—and its functions of social mediation and control will be taken over by others better adapted to the needs of the new time. Scientists, priests, physicians, teachers, and managers will be found in greater demand than generals.

Co-operation will not come because men are soft and fearful of war but because they are hard and can face the tough realities of modern existence and are patient enough to seek for solutions in other than angry moods. We will not lack discipline, but discipline will be based upon reasonable understandings and assent and will be directed toward an agreed end. Hate, fear, and force are controllable impulses, not to remain the masters of human fate. I do not proclaim their immediate exit from human affairs but only indicate the inexorable trend toward their controlled existence.

This is a hard saying for some who see in political association only a negative thing—who see only repression, command, and restriction. Is not this the essence of all authority, from the Ten Commandments on down? What else is authority, if not this? Who likes to be commanded, and who loves to be repressed?

Government, however, may well rest upon another basis than this and build upon the creative and productive function of association, political and otherwise. The jurists and the soldiers, and sometimes indeed the priests, have led us far away from a genuine understanding of the true uses of government and social organization.

The true design of authority is not that of destruction but of creation and construction. Theology, itself, in its later forms proclaims God as love rather than as fear, as an attractive force rather than as a point of fear and terror. The king was once the father of his people, not their dictator; creator rather than master. It was only later that kings began to think of themselves as masters, with all the powers of gods but not their responsibilities for rule. Caligula had himself worshiped not as a creator but as a despot. Even the proprietary patrimonial ruler who spoke of "my lands and my people" assumed, in pronouncing the word "my," a form of responsibility, however remote its possibilities of enforcement.

The absolutistic nationalists, however, and later the invisible employers, alike developed the idea of authority as a thing per se—not a godlike responsibility but a personal possession, without responsibility, however, for its care and maintenance. The conception of the police as a repressive power and of the industrial master as not responsible for the welfare of his dependents alike contributed to the widespread dislike of authority and its identification with an alien and unfriendly force, constantly pressing against one's interests.

The industrialist himself was caught often in the same net and came to look upon regulation as essentially negative in nature, as leading always to minus rather than plus. While in the political world he recognized the value of government as a means of maintaining liberty, he did not and does not yet always recognize government as effecting the same result in another domain—his own.

The Marxian economics, it may again be pointed out, went so far astray as to identify all government with repression and to demand its complete abolition, followed in this down to our day by the advocates of communism, vainly protesting that their trend is in the direction of abolishing all political authority.

In another system of values authority may emerge with another connotation, namely, that of creator rather than of repressor. Government may appear—or, authority, however called—as concerned with the release of the individual rather than with his restriction, with production as well as consumption.

Authority is a collective product; yet its purposes are not solely the collectivity as such, but the unfolding of the powers of the members of the community. It may protect privacy as well as the public. It may devote itself to setting up conditions in which personalities may expand in new forms and with richer variety than before.

Quis custodiet ipsos custodes? The answer is, in part, that the custodians themselves will be checked by their own temperament and training. The general understandings of the community itself, rooted in the value system of the time, will operate to "guard the guardians." Deep down in the general understandings of the nature of authority, not merely the nature of its limits but the nature and kind of its possibilities—of its functions as father, as teacher, as physician, as guide, as counselor in a variety of human relations—lies the limitation of power.

If once authority is recognized to be and is an addition to, rather than a subtraction from, life, its status takes on another and quite different form in human thought and feeling. Order and justice become different shapes as their content is recognized to be richer and fuller of human meaning than it has historically been. Authority may be said to acquire a moral and a scientific basis in such a setting and to attach to itself types of allegiance hitherto unrealized. Liberty, justice, and order are not economic primarily, but are social and moral in their implications.

The value systems of a region, a race, or a class, the charm of an engaging personality, the escape from insecurity in some great crisis—all these have been relied upon to support authority; but, once the creative and constructive aspects of authority are recognized, the impulse to support authority is placed upon quite a different basis.

A repressive state cannot very well countenance other repressors alongside it, for they are rivals, perhaps dangerous rivals; and the monopoly of legality is likely to be asserted. But a constructive or creative type of authority will welcome the co-operation of other joint creators engaged in the common task of construction in many different ways of life and may join with them in tolerance and good will as friends rather than as foes.

One of the oldest of human errors in the social field is the confusion of "control" with punitive sanctions, of government with punishment. Indeed, this is true of theology as of politics, since the gods appear as kings; the same idea is symbolized in the master's rod and the boss's whip. Governance may, however, be guidance, leadership, or direction, as well as command, obedience, or punishment.

343

Many groups have modern sanctions as powerful as those of the technical governor, or more so. The doctor has his bromides and even the strait jacket; the teacher has his reprimand and exile; the industrialist has his control over employment and of the wage (in part); the church has its penances here and future penalties in the background. Doctors' orders and bosses' orders are also types of management but without the implications of political authority, yet differing little in last analysis.

To summarize this part of the discussion, the emerging type of state might reach a higher level of purpose and program, embodying higher values and interests, expressed in institutions and understandings. A clearer conception of authority will not settle all the ills that flesh is heir to, but it will aid in the reconciliation of many opposing views, resting upon the fear of what hostile authority might do to their cherished interests and values.

As social and political evolution move along, the quantity of social control need not change much from age to age, but its forms, types, and lines are altered to meet new needs in special periods of tension or relaxation. We now face a period of tension. In these critical moments it is important to look at control and co-operation systems as they actually are, not as we wish they were. Intelligence must follow the problem where it leads, through the complicated labyrinths of human life, through interests, ideas, values, emotions, following the way to such effective forms of co-operation as will promote the happiness and security of mankind, no matter by what name these forms are called. We need not be hypnotized by the labels "political," "economic," "social," or by "anarchism," "laissez faire," "collectivism," but may consider their effects on human life and happiness. Long ago we were warned against putting new wine into old bottles. Out of the ferment of modern reason, science, education, organization, and technology there will emerge new shapes and spirits of co-operation and control, with new institutions and values, serving a new civilization.

We know that we enter an era of creative evolution, and we look forward to adventurous participation in the constructive betterment and transformation of life-conditions.

In the day when this new world to which we come is generally seen and understood—in that day, not only the concepts of power, property, and prestige but also the concept of human differences in capacity enter upon a transformation. Just as government ceases to be chiefly repression, as leadership ceases to be crass domination and exploitation, as property ceases to be largely an economic symbol of exclusive possession, and as work ceases to be chiefly long and grinding toil, the whole nature of authority is being changed from the negative to the positive and is unfolding in its creative aspects. In these oncoming days we realize that not only may men achieve that personal security and community stability which might mean monotony and boredom but they may look forward to adventurous participation in the process of creative evolution—in the constructive transformation and betterment of life-conditions.

The greatest of all revolutions in the whole history of mankind is the acceptance of creative evolution as the proper role of man, for this will eventually transform the spirit and the institutions of education, of industry, and of government, opening a broad way to the realization of the highest and finest values of human life, in a form of association where leaders no longer scream and curse and threaten and where men no longer shuffle, cringe, and fear but stand erect in dignity and liberty and speak with calm voices of what clear eyes may see.

Free men—in free states—in a free world—these the future government may bring.

INDEX

Absolutism, declining role of, 311-12

Adjudication: administrative, 130-32; administrative organization of courts, 125; as ceremony, 129; emerging role of, 332-33; guiding principles of, 125, 128; and interest groups, 128; judicial prestige, 129; judicial review, 131; justiciable cases, 125-26; legal framework in, 126; modern trends in, 307-8; organs of, 123-34; preventive justice, 130; private and public, 124-25; professional, 132; and science, 130; supremacy of law, 132-33; types of law in, 127; *see also* Justice; Law; Legislation

Administration, 130-32, 146, 154, 169-73; bureaucracy as maladministration, 165-67; of courts, 125; emerging role of, 334; military organization, 159-62; modern trends of, 208; prestige of office, 166-67; *see also* Management

Aristocracy, 187-98; aristocratic statesmanship, 194-95; assumptions of, 188; bases of leadership, 190-91; criticism of, 196-98; élite theories of, 188-93; human differentials, 189-90; methods of selecting élite, 193; predicament of aristocratic rule, 195-96

Authority, 138, 174-76, 327; and equality, 327-28; executive (*see* Executive authority); and freedom, 60-62; resistance to (*see* Resistance to authority); as trusteeship, 326-27

Balance of power, 173-77; authority and freedom, 175-76; centralization versus diffusion of authority, 174; personal equation, 176-77; separation of powers, 174-75

Ballot; *see* Voting

Bill of Rights, 219, 222; *see also* Rights of man

Bureaucracy, 165-67; *see also* Administration

Capitalism, 203; *see also* Economic trends

Change, theories of, 242-46; dialectical materialism, 242; social control, 242-43

Change, types of: conditions of peaceful, 250; constitutional, 250-52; intelligence and political adjustments, 254-56; revolution, 248-50, 315; role of ideals, 254; role of tradition, 253-54; social legislation, 252-53

Change, ways and means of, 216-17, 246-56

Church and state, 67-68

City, 262

Civic cohesion (political allegiance), 213-16; early formal codes, 214; irrational basis of, 214-15; as political problem, 215-16; *see also* Consent

Civic freedom; *see* Freedom, civic

Civic loyalty, 82-87, 94-104; *see also* Civic cohesion

Communication, 224; trends in, 315-16

Conciliar organs, 134-49; community and legislature, 147; decision and compromise in policy-formation, 135-36; legislatures in historical perspective, 148-49; limitation of authority, 138; nonpolitical representation, 144; and public opinion, 134-35; and representative government, 138-40; role of legislator, 140-41, 145-46; trends in administrative techniques, 146; trends in government by representation, 144-45; types of legislative function, 141-44; unity in, through discussion, 136-37

Conciliation, 134; modern developments of, 308-9; organized, 137-49

Conflict groups and maintenance of order, 79-81

Consent (social cohesion), 7-19, 230, 231, 253-54; accommodation of groups, 7-8; changing aspects of, 313-14; church (religious vs. secular appeal), 10-12; cultural pattern, 18-19; economic classes, 12-16; emerging problems of, 302-4; family, 8-10; as ideal basis of authority, 327; as means of social control, 93-104; science and government, 17-18; and sovereignty, 39, 40; *see also* Civic cohesion

Conservatism and change, 244-45

Corporative states, 267-68

Crime, control of, 79

Custom, as means of social control, 74-76

Darwinism, 242

Decentralization, 282-85

Democracy: assumptions of, 199-201; and capitalism, 203; changing role of science, 312-13; criticisms of, 201-2, 204-6; definition of, 199; emerging trends of, 312; and freedom, 58-59; modern trends of political organization, 206-11; what it is not, 202-3; and world order, 273-75

Dictatorship, 184-87, 234-35

Diplomacy, as means of social control, 104-7

Disorder: as legal problem, 44-45; as political problem, 42-43; *see also* Order

Economic life, and government, 69-70

Economic organizations, 267, 268

Economic trends, political aspects of, 209-11